Reading Women's Lives

AN INTRODUCTION TO WOMEN'S STUDIES

The Ohio State University Department of Women's Studies

Contributing Editors: Lin Distel, Misty Cummings,
Julia Applegate, and Sharon Ross

SIMON & SCHUSTER CUSTOM PUBLISHING

Cover Art: "The Very Rich Hour: Determining the Astronomical Hour of Past Events," by Joanne Stichweh, 1992.

Cover Design: Sam Pitino

Printed in the United States of America

10 9 8 7 6 5 4 3 2 1

ISBN 0-536-59736-7
BA 96242

SIMON & SCHUSTER CUSTOM PUBLISHING
160 Gould Street/Needham Heights, MA 02194
Simon & Schuster Education Group

Copyright Acknowledgments

Grateful acknowledgment is made to the following sources for permission to reprint material copyrighted or controlled by them:

"The Class Roots of Feminism," by Karen Sacks, reprinted from *Monthly Review*, Vol. 27, No. 9, February 1976, by permission of Monthly Review/MR Press.

"Introduction," by Barbara Smith, reprinted from *Home Girls: A Black Feminist Anthology*, 1983, Kitchen Table: Women of Color Press.

"Oughta be a Woman," by June Jordon and Bernice Johnson Reagon, from *Good News, Chicago*, 1981, Flying Fish Records/ Songtalk Publishing. Reprinted from *Home Girls: A Black Feminist Anthology*, 1983, Kitchen Table: Women of Color Press.

"Womanist," by Alice Walker, reprinted from *In Search of Our Mothers' Gardens: Womanist Prose*, copyright © 1970 by Alice Walker, reprinted by permission of Harcourt Brace & Company.

"Becoming the Third Wave," by Rebecca Walker, reprinted from *Ms. Magazine*, January/February 1992.

"Oppression," by Marilyn Frye, reprinted from *The Politics of Reality: Essays in Feminist Theory*, 1983, by permission of Crossing Press.

"Dyes and Dolls: Multicultural Barbie and the Merchandising of Difference," by Ann du Cille, reprinted by permission from *Differ-*

ences: A Journal of Feminist Cultural Studies, Vol. 6, No. 1, Spring 1994.

"Age, Race, Class and Sex: Women Redefining Difference," by Audre Lorde, reprinted from *Ethics: A Feminist Reader*, edited by Elizabeth Frazer, Jenifer Hornsby , and Sabina Lovibond, 1984, by permission from Crossing Press.

"The Smurfette Principle," by Katha Pollitt, reprinted from *The New York Times*, April 7, 1991. Copyright © 1991 by The New York Times Company. Reprinted by permission.

"Gender Difference and the Question of Sexual Ethics," excerpt from "Defining the Moral Boundaries of Eros: The Feminist Sexuality Debates," reprinted from *Embattled Eros: Sexual Politics and Ethics in Contemporary America*, 1992, by permission of Routledge.

"Homophobia: A Weapon of Sexism," by Suzanne Pharr, 1988, Chardon Press. Distributed by the Women's Project, 2224 Main Street, Little Rock, AR, 72206.

"X: A Fabulous Child's Story," by Lois Gould, reprinted from *Ms. Magazine*, Vol. 1, No. 6, December 1972. Reprinted by permission of the Charlotte Sheedy Literary Agency, Inc. Copyright © 1978 by Lois Gould.

"Can 'He' Mean 'She'? Exploring the Semantics of Political Correctness," by Michele Quinn Cardall, reprinted from *Intercomm*, Vol. 1, No. 1, 1994. Reprinted by permission of the author.

"Sexism in English: A 1990's Update," by Alleen Pace Nilsen.

"The Transformation of Silence into Language and Action," by Audre Lorde, reprinted from *Sister Outsider: Essays and Speeches*, 1984, by permission of Crossing Press.

Excerpt from *The Beauty Myth*, by Naomi Wolf, 1991, William Morrow & Company.

"Arroz Con Pollo vs. Slim Fast," by Linda Delgado, 1992, reprinted from *Women: Images and Realities— A Multicultural Anthology*, edited by Amy Kesselman, Lily D. McNair, and Nancy

Schneidewind, 1995, Mayfield Publishing. Reprinted by permission of the author.

"The Body Politic," by Abra Fortune Chernik, reprinted from *Listen Up: Voices from the Next Feminist Generation*, edited by Barbara Findlen. Copyright © 1995 by Barbara Findlen. Reprinted by permission of Seal Press.

"Homage to My Hips," 1980, and "Homage to My Hair," 1987, by Lucille Clifton, Curtis Brown, Ltd.

"Why I Want a Wife," by Judith Brady writing as Judy Syfers, reprinted from *Radical Feminism*, edited by Anne Koedt and Ellen Levine, 1973, Quadrangle. Reprinted by permission of the author.

"Family and Women's Lives," by Susan Lehrer, 1992, reprinted from *Women: Images and Realities—A Multicultural Anthology*, edited by Amy Kesselman, Lily D. McNair, and Nancy Schneidewind, 1995, Mayfield Publishing. Reprinted by permission of Susan Lehrer, Associate Professor of Sociology, State University of New York, New Paltz.

"The Meaning of Motherhood in Black Culture," by Patricia Hill Collins, 1990, reprinted from Black Feminist Thought, Routledge.

"Eve and Adam: Genesis 2-3 Reread," by Phyllis Trible, reprinted from *Andover Newton Quarterly*, Vol. 13, March 1973, by permission of Andover Newton Theological School.

"What Became of God the Mother? Conflicting Images of God in Early Christianity," by Elaine H. Pagels, reprinted from *Signs*, Vol. 2, No. 2, 1976, by permission of The University of Chicago Press.

"Toward an Ecofeminist Ethic of Shamanism and the Sacred," by Gloria Feman Orenstein, reprinted from *Ecofeminism and the Sacred*, edited by Carol J. Adams, 1993, by permission of Continuum Publishing Group.

"Introduction," by Anne Wilson Schaef, reprinted from *Native Wisdom for White Minds*, 1995, Ballantine Books, a division of Random House, Inc.

Contents

Femininisms and Feminist Movements

Declaration of Sentiments and Resolutions 3
The Seneca Falls Women's Rights Convention of 1848

The Class Roots of Feminism (1976) 9
Karen Sacks

Introduction to Home Girls: A Black Feminist Anthology (1983) 31
Barbara Smith

Womanist *from* In Search of Our Mothers' Gardens (1983) 44
Alice Walker

Becoming the Third Wave (1992) 46
Rebecca Walker

Power, Domination and Differences

Oppression (1983) 53
Marilyn Frye

Dyes and Dolls: Multicultural Barbie and the Merchandising of Difference (1994) 68
Ann duCille

Age, Race, Class and Sex: Women Redefining Difference (1984) 94
Audre Lorde

Socialization: Gender and Sexuality

The Smurfette Principle (1991) 107
Katha Pollitt

from Defining the Moral Boundaries of Eros:
The Feminist Sexuality Debates (1992) 112
Steven Seidman

Homophobia: A Weapon of Sexism (1988) 126
Suzanne Pharr

X: A Fabulous Child's Story (1972) 148
Lois Gould

Language

Can 'He' Mean 'She'? Exploring the Semantics
of Political Correctness (1994) 161
Michele Quinn Cardall

Sexism in English: A 1990s Update (1996) 170
Alleen Pace Nilsen

The Transformation of Silence into Language
and Action (1984) 185
Audre Lorde

Beauty and Images

The Beauty Myth (1991) 193
Naomi Wolf

Arroz Con Pollo vs. Slim Fast (1992) 208
Linda Delgado

The Body Politic (1995) 212
Abra Chernik

Homage to My Hips
Homage to My Hair (1987) 221
Lucille Clifton

Reproduction: Motherhood and the Family

Of Voluntary Motherhood 225
Sarah Grimké

Why I Want a Wife (1973) 230
Judy Syfers

Family and Women's Lives (1992) 234
Susan Lehrer

The Meaning of Motherhood in Black Culture (1992) 243
Patricia Hill Collins

Religion and Spirituality 251

Eve and Adam: Genesis 2–3 Reread (1973) 253
Phyllis Trible

Mrs. Stewart's Farewell Address to Her Friends
in the City of Boston (1833) 264
Maria Stewart

What Became of God the Mother? Conflicting Images
of God in Early Christianity (1976) 274
Elaine H. Pagels

Toward an Ecofeminist Ethic of Shamanism
and the Sacred (1993) 288
Gloria Feman Orenstein

Introduction to Native Wisdom for
White Minds (1995) 313
Anne Wilson Schaef

WOMEN CREATING CULTURE

In Search of Our Mothers' Gardens (1974) 325
Alice Walker

Story of Shakespeare's Sister (1929) 336
Virginia Woolf

Seventeen Syllables (1988) 350
Hisaye Yamamoto

Feminisms and Feminist Movements

Feminism exists in the United States and around the globe as a way of seeing and being in a complex social environment. Feminism is an ethical system; a method of questioning and analysis; and a structured yet fluid perspective for recognizing and untangling the significance of difference in an endlessly varied human community. With the values and principles of feminism, one can explore the dynamics of, not only human behavior in the social environment, but also the obvious and hidden elements which, melded together, form the structure of the social environment.

In this section, we will explore a variety of historical and contemporary feminist orientations. We will examine both the social forces which have given rise to feminisms, and the vision of those forces as perceived through a feminist lens. From the Colonial era in the United States to the late twentieth century, feminisms have enabled and required women to question—themselves, each other, and the social environment. Here, we will begin the consideration of the dynamics of feminisms, and of the movements inspired by those dynamics. As we gaze into history, we will keep an eye on the future and consider the possible impact of feminisms on and in the approaching millennium.

Declaration of Sentiments and Resolutions

The Seneca Falls Women's Rights Convention of 1848

This document, drawn in 1848, was a product of the first meeting on women's rights in the United States. Written in a style mimicking the Declaration of Independence, *this document points out the many injustices women faced at the time. In its Resolutions, the document provides a list of demands for social action on behalf of women in the United States.*

When, in the course of human events, it becomes necessary for one portion of the family of man to assume among the people of the earth a position different from that which they have hitherto occupied, but one to which the laws of nature and of nature's God entitle them, a decent respect to the opinions of mankind requires that they should declare the causes that impel them to such a course.

We hold these truths to be self-evident: that all men and women are created equal; that they are endowed by their Creator with certain inalienable rights; that among these are life, liberty, and the pursuit of happiness; that to secure these rights governments are instituted, deriving their just powers from the consent of the governed. Whenever any form of government becomes destructive of these ends, it is the right of those who suffer from it to refuse allegiance to it, and to insist upon the institution of a new government, laying its foundation on such principles, and organizing its powers in such form, as to them shall seem most likely to effect their safety and happiness. Prudence, indeed, will dictate that governments long established should not be changed for light and transient causes; and accordingly all experience hath shown that mankind are more disposed to suffer, while evils are sufferable, than to right themselves by abolishing the forms to which they were accustomed. But when a long train of abuses and usurpations, pursuing invariably the same object evinces a design to reduce them under absolute despotism, it is their duty to throw off such government, and to provide new guards for their future security. Such has been the patient sufferance of the women under this government, and such is now the necessity which constrains them to demand the equal station to which they are entitled.

The history of mankind is a history of repeated injuries and usurpations on the part of man toward woman, having in direct object the establishment of an absolute tyranny over her. To prove this, let facts be submitted to a candid world.

He has never permitted her to exercise her inalienable right to the elective franchise.

He has compelled her to submit to laws, in the formation of which she had no voice.

He has withheld from her rights which are given to the most ignorant and degraded men—both natives and foreigners.

Having deprived her of this first right of a citizen, the elective franchise, thereby leaving her without representation in the halls of legislation, he has oppressed her on all sides.

He has made her, if married, in the eye of the law, civilly dead.

He has taken from her all right in property, even to the wages she earns.

He has made her, morally, an irresponsible being, as she can commit many crimes with impunity, provided they be done in the presence of her husband. In the covenant of marriage, she is compelled to promise obedience to her husband, he becoming, to all intents and purposes, her master—the law giving him power to deprive her of her liberty, and to administer chastisement.

He has so framed the laws of divorce, as to what shall be the proper causes, and in case of separation, to whom the guardianship of the children shall be given, as to be wholly regardless of the happiness of women—the law, in all cases, going upon a false supposition of the supremacy of man, and giving all power into his hands.

After depriving her of all rights as a married woman, if single, and the owner of property, he has taxed her to support a government which recognizes her only when her property can be made profitable to it.

He has monopolized nearly all the profitable employments, and from those she is permitted to follow, she receives but a scanty remuneration. He closes against her all the avenues to wealth and distinction which he considers most honorable to himself. As a teacher of theology, medicine, or law, she is not known.

He has denied her the facilities for obtaining a thorough education, all colleges being closed against her.

He allows her in Church, as well as State, but a subordinate position, claiming Apostolic authority for her exclusion from the ministry, and, with some exceptions, from any public participation in the affairs of the Church.

He has created a false public sentiment by giving to the world a different code of morals for men and women, by which moral delinquencies which exclude women from society, are not only tolerated, but deemed of little account in man.

He has usurped the prerogative of Jehovah himself, claiming it as his right to assign for her a sphere of action, when that belongs to her conscience and to her God.

He has endeavored, in every way that he could, to destroy her confidence in her own powers, to lessen her self-respect, and to make her willing to lead a dependent and abject life.

Now, in view of this entire disfranchisement of one-half the people of this country, their social and religious degradation—in view of the unjust laws above mentioned, and because women do feel themselves aggrieved, oppressed, and fraudulently deprived of their most sacred rights, we insist that they have immediate admission to all the rights and privileges which belong to them as citizens of the United States.

In entering upon the great work before us, we anticipate no small amount of misconception, misrepresentation, and ridicule; but we shall use every instrumentality within our power to effect our object. We shall employ agents, circulate tracts, petition the State and National legislatures, and endeavor to enlist the pulpit and the press in our behalf. We hope this Convention will be followed by a series of Conventions embracing every part of the country.

Resolutions

WHEREAS, The great precept of nature is conceded to be, that "man shall pursue his own true and substantial happiness." Blackstone in his Commentaries remarks, that this law of Nature being coeval with mankind, and dictated by God himself, is of course superior in obligation to any other. It is binding over all the globe, in all countries and at all times; no human laws are of any validity if contrary to this, and such of them as are valid, derive all their force, and all their validity, and all their authority, mediately and immediately, from this original; therefore,

Resolved, That such laws as conflict, in any way, with the true and substantial happiness of woman, are contrary to the great precept of nature and of no validity, for this is "superior in obligation to any other."

Resolved, That all laws which prevent woman from occupying such a station in society as her conscience shall dictate, or which place her in a position inferior to that of man, are contrary to the great precept of nature, and therefore of no force or authority.

Resolved, That woman is man's equal—was intended to be so by the Creator, and the highest good of the race demands that she should be recognized as such.

Resolved, That the women of this country ought to be enlightened in regard to the laws under which they live, that they may no longer publish their degradation by declaring themselves satisfied with their present position, nor their ignorance, by asserting that they have all the rights they want.

Resolved, That inasmuch as man, while claiming for himself intellectual superiority, does accord to woman moral superiority, it is pre-eminently his duty to encourage her to speak and teach, as she has an opportunity, in all religious assemblies.

Resolved, That the same amount of virtue, delicacy, and refinement of behavior that is required of woman in the social state, should also be required of man, and the same transgressions should be visited with equal severity on both man and woman.

Resolved, That the objection of indelicacy and impropriety, which is so often brought against woman when she addresses a public audience, comes with a very ill-grace from those who encourage, by their attendance, her appearance on the stage, in the concert, or in feats of the circus.

Resolved, That woman has too long rested satisfied in the circumscribed limits which corrupt customs and a perverted application of the Scriptures have marked out for her, and that it is time she should move in the enlarged sphere which her great Creator has assigned her.

Resolved, That it is the duty of the women of this country to secure to themselves their sacred right to the elective franchise.

Resolved, That the equality of human rights results necessarily from the fact of the identity of the race in capabilities and responsibilities.

Resolved, therefore, That, being invested by the Creator with the same capabilities, and the same consciousness of responsibility for their exercise, it is demonstrably the right and duty of woman, equally with man, to promote every righteous cause by every righteous means; and especially in regard to the great subjects of morals and religion, it is self-evidently her right to participate with her brother in teaching them, both in private and in public, by writing and by speaking, by any instrumentalities proper to be used, and in any assemblies proper to be held; and this being a self-evident truth growing out of the divinely implanted principles of human nature, any custom or authority adverse to it, whether modern or wearing the hoary sanction of antiquity, is to be regarded as a self-evident falsehood, and at war with mankind.

[At the last session Lucretia Mott offered and spoke to the following resolution:]

Resolved, That the speedy success of our cause depends upon the zealous and untiring efforts of both men and women, for the overthrow of the monopoly of the pulpit, and for the securing to woman an equal participation with men in the various trades, professions, and commerce.

QUESTIONS

1. Why is it significant that this document is modeled after the *Declaration of Independence?*
2. How do the writers of the document justify their demands?
3. What current feminist issues do not appear in this document?
4. Do you think the document was intended to speak for women of all races, ages, social classes, and ethnicities? Why/why not?

THE CLASS ROOTS OF FEMINISM (1976)

Karen Sacks

Anthropologist and author Karen Sacks traces the economic factors contributing to the development of three distinct movements for the rights of women. Sacks explores the origins of contemporary tensions among these groups of women through her explanation of the differences among each group of women in terms of class and race interests.

This article is a revised version of a paper read at the University of Connecticut Anthropology Department and at the 1973 meetings of the American Anthropological Association. The following people gave various kinds of assistance and very helpful criticism: Mary Clark, Soon Young Yoon, Bill Derman, Bobbye Ortiz, Rayna Reiter, Susan Reverby, the N.Y. Women's Anthropology Conference, and the librarians at the Archives of Labor History and Urban Affairs at Wayne State University. [K. Sacks's note]

During the nineteenth century (say from 1820 to 1920) the women's movement in the United States was not a single movement, but rather three movements which were consciously movements for the rights of women. There was an industrial-working-class women's movement for economic improvement and equality which began with the earliest factories in the United States, the New England textile mills of the 1830s. Second, there was a black women's movement made up of working- and middle-class black women against racism and for both economic improvement and legal equality with whites. This also had its roots in the 1830s, in the black convention movements.* And finally, there was the white middle-class movement for legal equality which had its beginnings in women's attempts to become full legal members of their class, also in the 1830s.

While two well-known histories of the women's movement[1] show clearly that the white middle-class movement did not speak for all women, they do not examine the demands, priorities, and alliances of all three movements from the viewpoint of class roots and class interests. I would like to sketch such an analysis.

Class is the key, in the sense that the material conditions of black and working-class women, as well as the social ideology regarding them, have been very different from the material conditions of white middle-class women and their corresponding social ideologies. In both the colonial period and after independence, the only woman whose place was in the home was the woman of property. Neither slave women nor free propertyless women "belonged" there. Before the growth of industry, the United States had a domestic and agrarian economy in which men and women both could play a productive role "at home," so to speak—provided they owned or leased or otherwise had access to a home with farm (means of production), which most whites and some free blacks did. But those without their own household means of production, both men and women, had to work for someone else. Puritan religion and law in the North and slavery in the South were in agreement that those without property, free or slave, male or female, had an obligation to work for those with property. The terrible stigma attached to idleness by the Puritan religion largely served the interests of employers of labor. Efforts to stimulate a cloth-making industry, dating from the colonial period, emphasize the labor of "our own women and children who are now in a great measure idle."[2] Propertyless people who were not working for a master were a "public nuisance," the "public" in this phrase meaning, of course, people with property (especially manufacturing interests). Several New England states had laws compelling the binding out of children of the poor until the age of marriage. Adult poor, female as well as male, could be punished for "idleness." Thus for free as well as slave women, work outside the home was not looked down upon as unfeminine; rather, it was demanded as the only virtuous activity of propertyless women.

Propertied women, on the other hand, were virtuous and productive mistresses of households—until factories operated by propertyless women began to transform the domestic economy into an industrial one. Then they became ladies ("of leisure" being implicit in the word). The Southern transformation from domestic to industrial economy lay earlier, in the development of plantation slavery, with cotton grown partly by black women and a household run by the labor of black women. Thus, a double standard based on class came into being for women.

The self-consciously feminist movements and groups which developed—chiefly in the North during the nineteenth century—reflect the different circumstances of middle- and working-class women in the pre-Civil War years. Goals and tactics differed by class. Working-class women fought for more wages, equal wages with men, shorter hours, health, safety, and protective legislation. These were clearly class demands, and collective action was used to get them: strikes and unions mainly, but electoral pressure too (even without the vote). But working-class women also formed protective societies which got together for the purpose of self-"improvement" or of coping with various facets of a difficult life, rather than for the purpose of fighting to change social conditions.

The middle-class movement used analogous tactics, but in different proportions. Here, struggles of women to obtain and provide professional education and professional jobs for women, and to speak in public as full members of the anti-slavery movement, were, by and large, waged individually by women, rather than as part of a collective movement. It was the Abolition movement which gave birth to a self-conscious women's movement in the middle class, one which engaged in collective action, largely in the form of legislative petitions.

The pre-Civil War struggles were more social and thus collective among working-class women, and more self-help among middle-class women. This was due largely to the nature of the demands themselves and to the identity of the enemy, or obstacle. Education involved attacking no enemies. Likewise, both black and white women's improvement or protective societies were self-help ventures and did not identify enemies. The economic demands of women factory workers, on the other hand, were pursued solely by collective action directed against both mill owners and legislators.

Along with mill work, teaching school was a widespread women's occupation throughout this period. Not only were teachers and mill girls from the same background (farm families), but some women did both, alternating teaching and mill work. Though mill work paid badly, teaching paid worse. Schools were tiny affairs with few teachers, but factories often had several thousand workers. Despite the relatively better pay, it was the collective situation which allowed women to define "relatively better" as absolutely unsatisfactory by forming their own organization. Teachers, isolated and scattered, seem to have suffered in silence.

In the middle-class movement, collective action focused on those aspects of domestic law which prevented married women from having an independent economic status. Women's right to own inherited property was petitioned for and won without much opposition. But such a law had little relevance to working-class women. The situation in New York, the first state to pass such a law (1848), is illuminating. Its moving force was largely propertied males: "Fathers who had estates to bequeath to their daughters," and "husbands in extensive business operations [who could] see the advantage of allowing the wife the right to hold separate property."[3]

Middle-class women led two other important struggles in the legal realm of household affairs which did have relevance to working-class women: for the right of the woman to her own wages and to custody of children. By 1880 these were won in most states. New York was again the first state in which public sentiment for these changes was organized, beginning in 1854 via a petition campaign throughout the state. Middle-class feminists organized a delegation of working-class women to present this petition to the legislature and argue for it.[4] When it failed to move the legislature, Susan B. Anthony campaigned again throughout the state. Precisely what happened between 1855 and 1860 is not clear. But in 1860 the legislature passed a bill giving women property ownership, the right to collect their own wages, to sue in court, and to inherit the husband's property. It seems, though, that the majority of advances in civil law pertained to property law and thus to the middle and upper classes. While legislatures may have had to be persuaded, there were solid class interests for such reforms among propertied males and females.

As regards working-class women, the middle-class women who gathered at the Rochester women's convention in 1848 seem to have been both conscious of their own class and divided on class vs. sex interests. While all other resolutions passed clearly stated beliefs and principles, this one hedged: Resolved "*that those who* believe the laboring classes of women are oppressed, ought to do all in their power to raise their wages, beginning with their own household servants."[5]

Collective action by textile-mill women preceded that of middle-class women. Textile mills, centered in New England and staffed almost totally by women, were the nuclei of pre-Civil War U.S. industry. The first factory strike took place in 1824, just after the birth of the factories themselves, and involved both men and women. The 1830s saw a large number of strikes and the beginnings of many labor organizations, labor parties and papers, all short-lived. In this context, the record is full of male-female labor cooperation and independent women's actions and organizations. One of these labor parties, the Association of Working People of New Castle, Delaware, demanded the vote for women in 1831.[6]

Women were in the forefront and leadership of trade-union development in the 1840s and the focus was in the textile industry. The mills of the 1830s had been staffed by single women, largely daughters of farmers, who worked for a short time or a specific purpose. In the crisis of 1837 many farms were wiped out, and the workers in the mills during the forties and fifties were, by and large, landless native-born and Irish immigrants who could no longer quit if wages and hours were unsatisfactory. Out of this milieu came a whole host of factory-worker papers and organizations. The New England Female Labor Reform Association (FLRA) under its president, Sarah Bagley, a Lowell factory worker, became the main group for factory women. In addition to organizing in New England, this group stimulated and kept in contact with branches of women textile-worker groups in New York and western Pennsylvania. Though officially an affiliate of the New England Workingmen's Association (NEWA), in reality it was the center of it and provided much of its leadership, particularly in the fight for the ten-hour day. The FLRA argued for a ten-hour law in the Massachusetts legislature and, despite the fact that women could not vote, ran a successful campaign to defeat the re-election of Lowell's state representative, a mill owners' man who opposed the ten-hour bill.

Though women workers were centered in New England, the biggest women's struggle took place in the western Pennsylvania textile mills. Here the workers struck in 1845 for a ten-hour day. After a month, some workers began returning to the mills. But women strikers, aided by a "men's auxiliary," stormed the gates of one factory and threw out the strikebreakers. Despite this militancy, the strikers were told that they would get a ten-hour day only when New England workers did. They then appealed to the NEWA and the FLRA for help. Apparently only the women in New England were ready to call a general strike. In the face of the NEWA's hopelessness, they gave it up. Again in 1848 the Pennsylvania workers went out on strike, and again it looked like defeat. This time, the women, armed with axes, stormed the factory, took on a company of police, captured the strikebreakers, and then closed it down again. The leaders were arrested, but the strike continued. Though they finally won a ten-hour day only by accepting a wage cut, it is not clear whether they soon increased their wages to what they had been for twelve hours' work.[7] In any case, these early textile battles show the militance and leadership women gave to the early labor movement.

Though largely separate, the working-class and middle-class movements had a common ground in the anti-slavery movement. Abolition joined white well-to-do and professional people with free black men and women, and in the 1840s with a growing number of white workers, particularly from the New England textile mills. In Abolition one finds the seeds of class and race conflicts which pitted the women's movements against each other. In the 1830s the anti-slavery movement had split over women's participation, with particularly strong objections coming from the clergy. Middle-class women saw Abolition and women's rights as part of a single movement for extending democracy. In 1832 Lowell factory women formed a Female Anti-Slavery Society, and by 1845 they were fund-raising and circulating anti-slavery petitions, despite hostility on the part of the mill owners.[8] But their reasons for favoring Abolition differed from those of middle-class women. The mill women argued that a labor force in slavery degraded free labor as well as slave labor, and that all labor had a two-faced enemy: "the lord of the loom and the lord of the lash."

Abolition, whether spoken by middle- or working-class people, faced much more organized opposition than women's rights. Mobs in the North were "organized and led by prominent, respected members of the community." And, according to R. B. Nye, the major root of pro-slavery force was economic: fear of displeasing the Southern planter on whom much of New York commerce and rising New England textiles depended.[9] Indeed, H. Josephson has shown how assiduously the New England magnates of the 1840s and 1850s courted the planters and reviled the Abolitionists.[10]

Yet the anti-slavery movement contained much of the racism and class antagonisms which led to three separate and generally antagonistic women's movements after the Civil War. Many white middle-class Abolitionists were violently anti-labor, and most crafts excluded free black workers. While many Abolitionist groups spoke out against job discrimination against black workers in the North, some of their members were at the same time also practicing this same discrimination. In 1852 a number of black men applied for jobs at the businesses of members of the American and Foreign Anti-Slavery Society. Some were rejected outright; others got only menial jobs.[11] The widespread exclusion of black men and women from craft and factory jobs is well known. What has not received adequate treatment is the extent to which employers and workers were responsible for it.

These class and race antagonisms among the Abolitionists (important divisions to be inherited by the women's movement) were deepened by pro-slavery forces. Before the 1830s its defenders rationalized slavery as a necessary evil. To counter anti-slavery forces they developed a whole pseudo-science of white supremacy. Together with nativist corollaries, this became a cornerstone of post-Civil War bourgeois ideology. The war itself gave birth to accelerated industrialization and thus to the development of an industrial working class as well as a more powerful bourgeoisie. The latter took governmental power from the Southern agrarian bourgeoisie. Once in power, the Northern industrialists re-allied themselves with the Southern planters to defeat Reconstruction and entrench their common position against the black and white working class. Economic, political, and legal discrimination against black people was made a virtue through the newly developed national policy of white supremacy; at the same time an anti-foreignism was directed against white working-class immigrants in the North. Racism and nativism were important to the new capitalists because neither black nor white workers passively accepted the conditions of industrial wage slavery. Against this general background, we may better understand the divisions in the developing women's movement.

From the end of the Civil War until 1920, when it collapsed, the white middle-class women's movement defined itself as middle class by excluding black and working-class women. As such women moved from the liberalism of the Reconstruction period to the racist and anti-working-class mainstream of the "progressive era," they took for granted this status quo—a status quo with a sharp division between middle and working classes and with hierarchical divisions within the working class based on race, nationality, and sex. Black men and women were to be confined to agrarian and domestic work; native-born and immigrant white men and women would make up the industrial working class, with skilled crafts largely excluding all save native-born white men.

The Civil War itself led to middle-class women's widespread involvement in a variety of service and professional positions—from nursing and teaching to office work. By and large, the new war opportunities were important for middle-class kinds of jobs, mainly for whites, but some black women also entered, particularly in teaching, through the Freedmen's Bureau. Opportunities were there, but they were not equal. For example, the federal government was delighted to have women replace the male office workers, not least because they worked for half pay. Black women received even less for their work—if they received anything at all. Harriet Tubman had to fight almost until her death before the government would pay her for her very considerable services, both military and civilian, during and after the war. Even then she received a pittance, and that as a pension for her husband. Tubman was nationally famous. It is thus probable that the thousands of less famous black women were treated much worse.

Postwar years, then, saw the growth in numbers of middle-class women as independent earners in largely professional or so-called semi-professional occupations. Materially, they were members of a growing middle class. As such (and like the women factory workers of prewar years) they began developing a stronger class identity. They began to see themselves less as a socially excluded and oppressed segment of humanity and more as second-class members of the white middle class. Black middle-class women were largely prevented from claiming *class* rights by the practice of segregation and white supremacy. As black women they struggled against racial oppression, including the ideological stereotyping of black women as immoral.

The Civil War affected working-class women in some basically different ways than it affected middle-class women, even though there were some superficial similarities. While groups of middle-class women might get together to sew uniforms for the Union army as their patriotic duty, for working-class women taking in sewing of uniforms was wage work for survival in a period of inflation. However, they were often not paid for this work. Apparently the government felt that since middle-class women did not need to be paid, neither did working-class women. The war and postwar years saw working-class women developing their own unions and protective associations, at least in part to combat situations like the above. By and large, these were localized efforts. To some extent, though, they were integrated into the National Labor Union (NLU). Thus, in 1863, women collar workers in Troy, New York, formed a local union and struck successfully for higher wages. Kate Mullaney, their president, became assistant secretary of the NLU. But this women's local disbanded with the demise of the NLU.

To some extent, women's locals were joined with men's local or national organizations in the same industry. The men and women weavers in Fall River exemplify this pattern. In the face of a pay cut in 1875 the men's union voted to acquiesce; the women, knowing the results of the men's meeting, held their own and voted to strike three mills. The men then followed their lead and they won.[12]

Women workers did form one national organization. The Daughters of St. Crispin, begun by women shoe-stitchers in Lynn, Massachusetts, was an organization parallel to the men's Knights of St. Crispin. New England shoe workers, particularly women, had organized before the Civil War. In 1860 they had gone on strike throughout New England in the most extensive pre-Civil War strike.[13] The Daughters of St. Crispin, formed in 1869, had 24 chapters, most of which were in New England—the center of the shoe industry—and in six other states as well. They demanded equal pay for equal work. Though they affiliated with the NLU, they managed to outlast it, staying in existence through much of the 1873 depression, and continuing in New England until 1876. For those days it was a long-lived organization.

The Knights of Labor, the first enduring national labor organization in the United States, saw women and black people as important parts of the working class, and on this basis supported equality within the organization and demanded it of employers. At its first national convention in 1878, they voted for equal pay for equal work, and began from the outset to include women workers in separate locals as well as in male-female locals. The first all-women local, of Philadelphia shoe workers, joined in 1878. By 1886, at the peak of the Knights of Labor, there were about 194 women's locals and about 50,000 women members (8–9 percent of the total). In Massachusetts the proportion was higher: 1 in 7 members were women.[14] The Knights followed the same direction with regard to black workers, organizing them in the South and the North into both black-white and separate black locals. In 1886 there were about 60,000 black Knights out of about 700,000; in 1887 some 90,000 out of about half a million.[15] The Knights did seem to try in practice as well as rhetoric to fight for equal rights for all workers.

By contrast, the newly formed American Federation of Labor, an association of craft unions, supported few working-class women's issues, even though its membership included male-female as well as all-female locals, especially in the United Garment Workers (UGW). But if the UGW is any example of female participation, the AFL did not take the needs of its women members seriously.[16] The AFL did have some unofficial women organizers in the early years. Hannah Morgan organized some 23 women's locals in a variety of jobs; she also built the Illinois Women's Alliance, which led mass campaigns for protective legislation for women and children (and she organized secondarily for suffrage). Also under the AFL, the collar and shirt workers of Troy pulled together again, struck and won in 1891. The leader of the Working Women's Society of New York City unofficially organized women into the AFL, while the society organized support for strikes and for factory legislation.[17]

Meanwhile, the middle-class movement had become mainly a suffrage movement. But it too was divided. The National Women's Suffrage Association (NWSA) Stanton-Anthony wing, though biased in favor of the middle class by its suffrage focus, was willing to join with labor. Anthony and other suffrage leaders organized women's protective societies, supported and helped organize women's unions. For a time Susan Anthony was a member of the Knights of Labor (which favored suffrage). The rival group of suffragists, the American Women's Suffrage Association (AWSA), was anti-labor, narrowly suffragist, and drew its support from professional and leisured middle-class women, mainly through women's clubs.

Until 1890, then, there was a strong organization in the Knights of Labor fighting for equal rights for all labor, as well as a middle-class organization willing to join its main fight for suffrage with the economic demands of working women. Class determined the priorities, but on these issues there was no necessary conflict between them.

But the balance of forces favoring such inter-class cooperation changed in the 1890s. With the demise of the Knights, the AFL faced no competition and freely moved to organize skilled crafts only, largely the province of white, native-born men. Not only by focusing on skilled labor but also by deliberately excluding black and female skilled and semi-skilled workers, the AFL spread racism and sexism during its long-term domination of trade unionism. (It seems to me that modern-day notions about working-class racism and sexism are based heavily on the AFL's practice.) Women continued to form unions, some independent, which had a hard time, and some affiliated with the AFL, which seem to have faced almost equal difficulties.[18] At the same time that the unity of labor was weakened by this organizational practice, the ruling class stepped up its propaganda to cultivate and fix black-white, native-immigrant divisions and conflicts. The suffrage movement, represented by the National American Women's Suffrage Association (NAWSA, the merger of the two suffrage groups), fell solidly into line with them, abandoning even the divided support they had given working-class women in the 1860s.

In 1892, when the Homestead Steel workers struck and were embroiled in a nearly full-scale war to save job and union from Carnegie, the Pinkertons, and federal troops, Lucy Stone wanted to know why the workers didn't start their own businesses if they didn't like their jobs.[19] And Susan Anthony went to labor asking for suffrage support, but refused to do anything about working women's demands until the vote was won. Likewise, she raised her influential voice to argue that NAWSA should do nothing to fight Jim Crow laws barring black people (including black women) from decent railroad seats.

Their arguments for suffrage, as Kraditor has clearly shown,[20] came explicitly to be arguments for enfranchising white, American-born, and educated women as allies with their male counterparts against black and immigrant workers.

> This government is menaced with great danger. . . . That danger lies in the votes possessed by the males in the slums of the cities, and the ignorant foreign vote which was sought to be brought up by each party, to make political success. . . . In the mining districts, the danger has already reached this point—miners are supplied with arms, watching with greedy eyes for the moment when they can get in their deadly work of despoiling the wealth of the country. . . . There is but one way to divert the danger—cut off the vote of the slums and give to woman, who is bound to suffer all, and more than man can, of the evils his legislation has brought upon the nation, the power of protecting herself that man has secured for himself—the ballot.[21]

NAWSA closed ranks against working-class women, not so much by the demand for suffrage itself as by their arguments claiming it should be granted and by their hostility to more pressing needs of women workers and black women of both classes. Thus the 1893 convention of NAWSA passed the following resolution directed against black people in the same way that Catt's speech attacked immigrants and the working class:

> *Resolved*, that without expressing any opinion on the proper qualifications for voting, we call attention to the significant facts that in every State there are more women who can read and write than all negro [*sic*] voters; more American women who can read and write than all foreign voters; so that the enfranchisement of such women would settle the vexed question of rule by illiteracy, whether of home-grown or foreign-born production.[22]

They lashed out at "foreigners" not only for being "ignorant" in general, but for being a major force in opposing women's rights. Kraditor summed up suffrage explanations of why voting in wards with large immigrant populations went against suffrage: "Foreign-born men had been brought up in a culture in which women were inferior [here the suffragists forgot earlier arguments and proudly pointed to the respected position of women in their own society]; . . . the ignorance of the foreign born disqualified them from voting wisely; . . . the new voters generally used alcoholic beverages and feared that woman suffrage would bring prohibition; . . . foreign-born workers in cities voted as dictated by saloonkeepers, rich employers, or party machines."[23] Ironically, when New York finally passed its suffrage referendum in 1917, it was working-class and immigrant New York City which carried it over the opposition from non-worker, native-born upstate! By this time, though, some members of NAWSA had begun to overcome their aversion to the working class, and to campaign in working-class districts. As late as 1916, however, NAWSA had made little effort to communicate across class lines.

While the overt anti-working-class, racist, and nativist arguments remained until the end, there were growing numbers of NAWSA members after the turn of the century who believed it important to speak to the working class. Thus Florence Kelley worked hard to fight the exploitation of workers in the sweatshops and to obtain protective legislation for women workers. She even criticized the anti-foreign mouthings of NAWSA. Yet she too resented being forced to campaign among workers: "[It was] an ignominious way to treat us, to send us to the Chinamen [*sic*] in San Francisco, to the enfranchised Indians of other western states, to the negroes [*sic*], Italians, Hungarians, Poles, Bohemians and innumerable Slavic immigrants in Pennsylvania and other mining States to obtain our rights of suffrage."[24]

Jessie Ashley, treasurer of NAWSA and a socialist, also criticized the association for its anti-worker attitudes, in particular for not addressing its campaigns to the real needs of working-class women—economic needs. But she did accept some very middle-class stereotypes of working-class women. Remarking on the contrast made in another article between the "handsome ladies" at a suffrage parade and the working girls getting onto the subway, Ashley wrote,

> For it is those "handsome ladies," and they alone, who have begun to see that women must stand and think and work together, and they, alas, are not the ones whose need to do so is the greatest. . . . For the most part the handsome ladies are well satisfied with their personal lot, but they want the vote as a matter of justice, while the fluttering, jammed-in subway girls are terribly blind to the whole

> question of class oppression and of sex oppression. Only the women of the working class are really oppressed, but it is not only the working-class women to whom injustice is done. Women of the leisure class need freedom, too.[25]

Considering that this was written less than two years after the massive women's garment strike in New York (where Ashley lived), her talk of working-class women being blind to class oppression flies in the face of reality, as does her notion that only the "handsome ladies" know they must work together. Essentially, Ashley is reflecting the stereotype of the ignorant and docile working girl.

Along with the general racist stereotyping of black people, which NAWSA accepted and propagated, there existed the stigmatizing of black women as "loose" and "immoral." Sometimes this stereotyping was done "sympathetically":

> The negro [*sic*] women of the South are subject to temptations, of which their white sisters of the North have no appreciation, and which come to them from the days of their race enslavement. They are still the victims of the white man under a system tacitly recognized, which deprives them of the sympathy and help of the Southern white women, and to meet such temptations the negro [*sic*] women can only offer the resistance of a low moral standard, an inheritance from the system of slavery, made still lower from a life-long residence in a one-roomed cabin.[26]

But it propagates the same false stereotype of the immoral black woman, adding another kind of fuel to racist propaganda.

Black women, led by black middle-class and professional women, had long before formed their own clubs and expressed a desire to work with the white clubs, which in general the latter refused to do. To combat this racism they formed the National Association of Colored Women. The conditions facing black women differed in many ways from those facing white middle-class women. Black women's clubs organized around providing a particular social service, since public facilities were even less available in black communities than in white working-class communities. They also exposed and organized against lynching and terror campaigns directed against black men and women. At least one club maintained a settlement house and served the poor and working-class neighborhoods through militant action as well as services. Moreover, the membership, if not the leadership, of black women's clubs differed from their white counterparts. While the white clubs were middle class and professional, black club members were often workers, tenant farmers, or poor women. [27]

Even though the suffrage movement somewhat weakened its anti-worker attitude and to some extent its anti-immigrant posture, it never publicly mitigated its racism. This was largely due to the strategy of allying with Southern white middle-class women, who wanted the vote at least as much to maintain white supremacy as to have the vote. As a result of this "Southern strategy," black women were all but kept out of the association.[28] While support for racial equality was ruled out of order as an extraneous issue, the numerous white-supremacy speeches never met any such objection, or any other kind of public objection, for that matter.

What little amelioration there was of NAWSA's anti-worker and anti-immigrant stance came about largely because of the growth of city-wide women's strikes, notably in the garment and textile industries, in 1909 in New York, 1910 in Chicago, and 1912 in Lawrence. Prior to that time a number of white middle-class women—radicals, reformers, and socialists like Jessie Ashley, Ella Reeve Bloor, etc.—had urged concentration on working women's needs. But they were mainly rebuffed by NAWSA.

It was largely through the National Women's Trade Union League (NWTUL), formed in 1903, that the suffrage movement saw possible allies in working-class women. Made up of women trade unionists, but run mainly by middle-class reformers, many of whom were active suffragists, the NWTUL tried to serve two functions. First, in the face of AFL indifference to women workers, it organized women to improve their working conditions through trade unionism. Specifically, it organized women into AFL locals and supported AFL strikes. Its second role was to make trade unionism "respectable" through publicity and by winning middle-class support for strikes. It did succeed in organizing women into the AFL and in making *certain kinds* of unions "respectable." But it did not reform the AFL, which sold out the Chicago clothing strike in 1911. And the following year, despite anger over Chicago, the NWTUL actually helped the AFL break a strike, in Lawrence, Massachusetts.

In this case, the AFL had organized only among skilled (white, male, native-born) workers. But the vast majority were unskilled female, as well as male and immigrant, workers. The IWW [International Workers of the World] represented these workers; and when they walked out, it was the IWW that led this Lawrence strike. Together with the AFL, the Boston TUL set up a relief council which aided only those who pledged to go back to work.[29]

So while they did unionize women and ameliorate some of the anti-worker attitudes in the middle class, their role within the working-class movement was to be in the midst of things, to see that events did not get out of control, and to make sure women workers stayed respectable in bourgeois eyes.

Many women in the Boston TUL were disgusted with the role of their own organization in Lawrence. "Are we, the NWTUL, to ally ourselves inflexibly with the 'stand-patters' of the Labor Movement or are we to hold ourselves ready to aid the 'insurgents,' those who are freely fighting the fight of the exploited, the oppressed, and the weak among the workers?"[30] While this may have been a widespread feeling among NWTUL members, publicly they stood pat with the stand-patters of the AFL. Their official stance appeared in *Life and Labor*, the NWTUL paper:[31] the AFL "refused to take any action during the first fortnight of the strike while it was being led by enemies of organized labor [the IWW], but now that it shows every symptom of collapse they do not propose to allow the misled workers to suffer or lose any opportunity to bring them into recognized trade organizations."[32]

Working-class women, the IWW, the radicals reacted to this suffragist and middle-class bias. One working woman wrote to Leonora O'Reilly of her experience at a New York suffrage conference:

> I feel as if I have butted in where I was not wanted. Miss Hay gave me a badge and was very nice to me but you know they had a school teacher represent the Industrial workers if you ever herd her it was like trying to fill a barrell with water that had no bottom not a word of labor spoken at this convention so far . . . after the hole thing was over some people came to me and said I had a right to speak for labor but they kept away until it was over. . . . I am not goying to wait for sunday meeting I am goying home satturday.[33]

In the New York shirtwaist strike, two upper-class women rented the Hippodrome for a strike-support rally, attended by approximately 8,000 people. Though much has been made of rich women's generosity, Theresa Malkiel, a striker, wrote another side to it in her diary:

> The most of our girls had to walk both ways in order to save their car fare. Many came without dinner, but the collection baskets had more pennies than anything else in them—it was our girls themselves who helped make it up, and yet there were so many rich women present. And I'm sure the speakers made it plain to them how badly the money was needed, then how comes it that out of $300 collected there should be $70 in pennies?[34]

The IWW saw the vote as irrelevant and the suffrage movement as making working women "the tail of a suffrage kite in the hands of women of the very class driving the girls to lives of misery and shame."[35] Yet Elizabeth Gurley Flynn, then an IWW organizer, speaks approvingly of socialists in 1904 organizing working-class women to demand the vote so they can vote on labor issues.[36] Emma Goldman saw suffrage as a "modern fetish" of women who swore loyalty to every institution which oppresses them. "Else how is one to account for the tremendous, truly gigantic effort set in motion by those valiant fighters for a wretched little bill which will benefit a handful of propertied ladies, with absolutely no provision for the vast mass of working women?"[37]

Through the efforts of middle-class NWTUL women, and to some degree those of the militant suffragists' Women's Party, Wage Earners' Suffrage Leagues did come into being and working-class women did march in suffrage demonstrations. But even where working-class women participated in suffrage demands, they did so separately from the middle-class organizations, in a labor-based organization. Suffrage in this context never had a high priority for working-class women as a whole.

The years 1909–1912 marked a huge upsurge in working-class women's activity. The 1909 New York dressmakers' strike, or the "Uprising of 20,000," was the largest women's strike in history. It was followed by many large and small garment and textile strikes and the formation of enduring unions, steps toward the elimination of sweatshops, cutting hours, and increasing pay for women workers. By and large, women won these victories without the ballot.

As a rule, next to nothing is said of black working-class women in these struggles. Though black women were largely excluded from industry before the First World War, and hence from unions, there were black women working in the packinghouses of Chicago, in tobacco warehouses in the South, and as pressers in the garment industry in New York. In 1902 two packinghouse women organized a women's local which included black women. But more significant is a white garment worker and organizer's account of the beginning of the 1909 New York strike. She writes of her anxiety as to whether the women of the shop would walk out at the appointed time. They did, fifteen minutes early, when the fifty-three black women of the pressing department dropped their work and led the whole shop out.[38] Even where black women were employed during and after the First World War, they were largely in the worst jobs, with little or no chance for advancement, and often paid one half or one third what white women received. For example, pressers in the garment industry had the most physically difficult job in that industry. This was the job given to black women.[39]

Whom the women's movements perceived as the enemy illuminates the primacy of class lines over sex. In the working-class movement it was clearly the employer. The suffragists saw their enemies mainly as the liquor interests and, to some extent, big-business interests. Only the Women's Party actually saw the President and much of Congress as real enemies of women. For this breach of class loyalty they got the same treatment as working-class women strikers: jail, police brutality, etc.

The working-class women's movement, rather than dying in 1920, continued in the drives of the 1920s and 1930s to organize in Southern textile and tobacco shops. Here, black and white working-class women not only struggled to overcome racism, but had to take on the AFL[40] directly. Neither before nor since 1920 have women won equal pay for equal work, one of the two long-standing working-class women's demands. However, to the extent that women have won union representation, male-female pay scales have made moves in that direction. The other demand, for unionization itself, also continues. As middle-class women's jobs have become collectivized (teaching, white-collar, health, social work, clerical), middle-class women have also moved into union situations, which at least provide a material basis for middle-class women to join working-class women rather than the ruling class.

ENDNOTES

* I could find very little information on the class composition of black women's organizations, or on the organizations and struggles of working-class black women. Thus there is a data bias of which the reader should be aware. Though there were national black conventions from 1830, the earliest specific mention of women's rights, support for the Seneca Falls Declaration, is in 1848 (R. E. Paulson, *Women's Suffrage and Prohibition* [Glenview: Scott Foresman, 1973], p. 34). The 1848 convention in Cleveland resolved for equality for women with men and for full citizenship, including the vote for black men and women (H. H. Bell, ed., *Minutes and Proceedings of the National Negro Conventions 1830–1864* [New York: Arno Press and the *New York Times, 1969*]).

1. A. Kraditor, *The Ideas of the Woman Suffrage Movement, 1890–1920* (New York: Columbia University Press, 1965); E. Flexner, *Century of Struggle* (New York: Atheneum, 1968).
2. E. Abbott, *Women in Industry* (New York: Appleton and Company, 1913), pp. 21–22.
3. E. C. Stanton, S. B. Anthony, and M. J. Gage, *History of Woman Suffrage*, vol. 1 (Rochester: Chas. Mann), p. 16.
4. A. Henry, *The Trade Union Woman* (New York: Appleton and Company, 1915), p. 254.
5. Stanton, Anthony, and Gage, p. 809. Italics added.
6. On early struggles by women the major source is J. B. Andrews and W. D. P. *Bliss, History of Women in Trade Unions* (vol. 10 of *Report on Conditions of Women and Child Wage Earners in the U.S.*, in 19 vols., U.S. Senate Doc. 645, 61st Cong, 2d Sess.); see also Flexner; Abbott; P. Foner, *History of the Labor Movement in the United States*, vol. 1 (New York: International, 1947); Henry, 1915; and A. Henry, *Women and the Labor Movement* (New York: Doran, 1923). Flexner claims men feared women's competition but gives no specifics. For this early period, only the printers and cigarmakers manifested the conservative stance, though it was later a strong position among conservative skilled trades unions. The instances of early cooperation between men's and women's unions are more impressive: in 1834 the Lady Shoe Binders

of Lynn struck for higher wages and were supported by the men's cordwainers union in the form of money, a pledge not to work for any manufacturer who refused the women's demands, and an attempt to organize a boycott of such (Foner, pp. 108–111). In 1833 the Baltimore seamstresses and tailoresses were supported by the men journeymen tailors (Henry 1923, p. 41). In 1835 the Philadelphia Journeymen Cigarmakers opposed the low wages paid to women and recommended a joint strike. In this city, too, the men cordwainers and Ladies Shoe Binders Society waged a joint strike. In 1831 the New England Farmers, Mechanics and Other Workingmen tried, though without success, to spread unionism from skilled workers to factory women (Foner, pp. 105, 109–111).

7. For differing accounts see Andrews and Bliss, p. 65; Foner, p. 212; Flexner, p. 56.

8. Foner, p. 267.

9. R. B. Nye, *Fettered Freedom: Civil Liberties and the Slave Controversy, 1830–1860* (East Lansing: Michigan State University Press, 1963), p. 194.

10. H. Josephson, *Golden Threads: New England's Mill Girls and Magnates* (New York: Duell, Sloan and Pearce, 1949), pp. 300–303.

11. C. H. Wesley, *Negro Labor in the United States, 1850–1925* (New York: Russell and Russell, 1967), pp. 78–79.

12. In addition to Andrews and Bliss, p. 2, see Abbott, p. 131; and Henry, 1923, p. 48.

13. Foner, p. 241; Henry, 1923, p. 47.

14. Foner, vol. 2, p. 61; Flexner, p. 194.

15. R. Logan, *The Betrayal of the Negro* (New York: Macmillan, 1970), pp. 150–151.

16. M. H. Willett, *The Employment of Women in the Clothing Trade* (New York: AMS Press, 1968).

17. Foner, vol. 2, pp. 189–193.

18. *Ibid.*, pp. 364–366; Foner, vol. 3, pp. 724–727.

19. Kraditor, p. 159.

20. *Ibid.*, chap. 6.

21. Carrie Chapman Catt, in *The Woman's Journal*, 1894; quoted in Flexner, p. 125.

22. *Ibid.*, p. 131.

23. *Ibid.*, p. 128.

24. *Ibid.*, p. 139.

25. *The Woman's Journal*, 1911; quoted in Flexner, P. 157.

26. *Ibid.*, p. 187.

27. G. Lemer, *Black Women in White America* (New York: Pantheon, 1972), pp. 198, 437.

28. Kraditor, pp. 170, 212–214; Logan, pp. 239–241.

29. Foner, vol. 4, pp. 338–339.

30. Letter from Mrs. Clark to Mrs. Robins; quoted in G. Boone, *The Women's Trade Union Leagues in Great Britain and the United States of America* (New York: AMS Press, 1968), p. 106.

31. *Life and Labor*, vol. 2, pp. 73, 77, 196.

32. *Ibid.*, p. 77.

33. Quoted in Kraditor, p. 160.

34. Quoted in R. Jacoby, "Feminism and Class Consciousness in the British and American Women's Trade Union Leagues, 1890–1925." Unpublished ms. (History Dept., University of Michigan, 1973), p. 21.

35. Quoted in Foner, vol. 4, p. 168.

36. E. G. Flynn, *I Speak My Own Piece* (New York: Masses and Mainstream, 1955), p. 46.

37. E. Goldman, *Anarchism and Other Essays* (New York: Mother Earth Publishing Association, 1917), p. 212.

38. A. Hourwich, *I Am a Woman Worker: A Scrapbook of Autobiographies* (New York: Affiliated Schools for Workers, Inc., 1936), p. 110.

39. On pressers' work: J. Laslett, *Labor and the Left* (New York: Basic Books, 1970), p. 103. On discrimination against black women: Henry 1923, pp. 203–206.

40. Supported again by a dying NWTUL. See *Life and Labor Bulletin* (July 1928 and January 1931).

QUESTIONS

1. Identify the three separate movements for women's rights outlined by Sacks in terms of time period, major themes, and "average" participants.
2. How did class shape each of these movements?
3. Compare/contrast the movements in terms of focus and goals.
4. How did race and class come into play in creating divisions among women?

Introduction to Home Girls: A Black Feminist Anthology (1983)

Barbara Smith

A prolific writer, passionate speaker, and powerful activist, Barbara Smith is the co-founder of Kitchen Table: Women of Color Press *(1980) with Audre Lorde. In this essay, Smith explores why many Black and Third World women have not identified with U.S. feminism. Smith also discusses a variety of myths about Black women and feminism, and how those myths have operated strategically to affect the social status of Black women in the United States.*

Black women as a group have never been fools. We couldn't afford to be. Yet in the last two decades many of us have been deterred from identifying with a liberation struggle which might say significant things to women like ourselves, women who believe that we were put here for a purpose in our own right, women who are usually not afraid to struggle.

Although our involvement has increased considerably in recent years, there are countless reasons why Black and other Third World women have not identified with contemporary feminism in large numbers.[1] The racism of white women in the women's movement has certainly been a major factor. The powers-that-be are also aware that a movement of progressive Third World women in this country would alter life as we know it. As a result there has been a concerted effort to keep women of color from organizing autonomously and from organizing with other women around women's political issues. Third World men, desiring to maintain power over "their women" at all costs, have been among the most willing reinforcers of the fears and myths about the women's movement, attempting to scare us away from figuring things out for ourselves.

It is fascinating to look at various kinds of media from the late 1960s and early 1970s, when feminism was making its great initial impact, in order to see what Black men, Native American men, Asian American men, Latino men, and white men were saying about the irrelevance of "women's lib" to women of color. White men and Third World men, ranging from conservatives to radicals, pointed to the seeming lack of participation of women of color in the movement in order to discredit it and to undermine the efforts of the movement as a whole. All kinds of men were running scared because they knew that if the women in their midst were changing, they were going to have to change too. In 1976 I wrote:

> Feminism is potentially the most threatening of movements to Black and other Third World people because it makes it absolutely essential that we examine the way we live, how we treat each other, and what we believe. It calls into question the most basic assumption about our existence and this is the idea that a biological, i.e., sexual identity determines all, that it is the rationale for power relationships as well as for all other levels of human identity and action. An irony is that among Third World people biological determinism is rejected and fought against when it is applied to race, but generally unquestioned when it applies to sex.[2]

In reaction to the "threat" of such change, Black men, with the collaboration of some Black women, developed a set of myths to divert Black women from our own freedom.

Myths

Myth No. 1: The Black woman is already liberated. This myth confuses liberation with the fact that Black women have had to take on responsibilities that our oppression gives us no choice but to handle. That is an insidious, but widespread myth that many Black women have believed themselves. Heading families, working outside the home, not building lives or expectations dependent on males, seldom being sheltered or pampered as women, Black women have known that their lives in some ways incorporated goals that white middle class women were striving for, but race and class privilege, of course, reshaped the meaning of those goals profoundly. As W. E. B. DuBois said so long ago about Black women: ". . . our women in black had freedom contemptuously thrust upon them."[3] Of all the people here, women of color generally have the fewest choices about the circumstances of their lives. An ability to cope under the worst conditions is not liberation, although our spiritual capacities have often made it look like a life. Black men didn't say anything about how poverty, unequal pay, no childcare, violence of every kind including battering, rape, and sterilization abuse, translated into "liberation."

Underlying this myth is the assumption that Black women are towers of strength who neither feel nor need what other human beings do, either emotionally or materially. White male social scientists, particularly Daniel P. Moynihan with his "matriarchy theory," further reinforce distortions concerning Black women's actual status. A song inspired by their mothers and sung by Sweet Honey in the Rock, "Oughta Be A Woman," lyrics by June Jordan and music by Bernice Johnson Reagon, responds succinctly to the insensitivity of the myth that Black women are already liberated and illustrates the home-based concerns of Black feminism:

Oughta Be A Woman

Washing the floors to send you to college
Staying at home so you can feel safe
What do you think is the soul of her knowledge
What do you think that makes her feel safe

Biting her lips and lowering her eyes
To make sure there's food on the table
What do you think would be her surprise
If the world was as willing as she's able

Hugging herself in an old kitchen chair
She listens to your hurt and your rage
What do you think she knows of despair
What is the aching of age

The fathers, the children, the brothers
Turn to her and everybody white turns to her
What about her turning around
Alone in the everyday light

There oughta be a woman can break
Down, sit down, break down, sit down
Like everybody else call it quits on Mondays
Blues on Tuesdays, sleep until Sunday
Down, sit down, break down, sit down

A way outa no way is flesh outa flesh
Courage that cries out at night
A way outa no way is flesh outa flesh
Bravery kept outa sight
A way outa no way is too much to ask
Too much of a task for any one woman[4]

Myth No. 2: Racism is the primary (or only) oppression Black women have to confront. (Once we get that taken care of, then Black women, men, and children will all flourish. Or as Ms. Luisah Teish writes, we can look forward to being "the property of powerful men.")[5]

This myth goes hand in hand with the one that the Black woman is already liberated. The notion that struggling against or eliminating racism will completely alleviate Black women's problems does not take into account the way that sexual oppression cuts across all racial, nationality, age, religious, ethnic, and class groupings. Afro-Americans are no exception.

It also does not take into account how oppression operates. Every generation of Black people, up until now, has had to face the reality that no matter how hard we work we will probably not see the end of racism in our lifetimes. Yet many of us keep faith and try to do all we can to make change now. If we have to wait for racism to be obliterated *before* we can begin to address sexism, we will be waiting for a long time. Denying that sexual oppression exists or requiring that we wait to bring it up until racism, or in some cases capitalism, is toppled, is a bankrupt position. A Black feminist perspective has no use for ranking oppressions, but instead demonstrates the simultaneity of oppressions as they affect Third World women's lives.

Myth No. 3: Feminism is nothing but man-hating. (And men have never done anything that would legitimately inspire hatred.)

It is important to make a distinction between attacking institutionalized, systematic oppression (the goal of any serious progressive movement) and attacking men as individuals. Unfortunately, some of the most widely distributed writing about Black women's issues has not made this distinction sufficiently clear. Our issues have not been concisely defined in these writings, causing much adverse reaction and confusion about what Black feminism really is.[6]

This myth is one of the silliest and at the same time one of the most dangerous. Anti-feminists are incapable of making a distinction between being critically opposed to sexual oppression and simply hating men. Women's desire for fairness and safety in our lives does not necessitate hating men. Trying to educate and inform men about how their feet are planted on our necks doesn't translate into hatred either. Centuries of anti-racist struggle by various people of color are not reduced, except by racists, to our merely hating white people. If anything it seems that the opposite is true. People of color know that white people have abused us unmercifully and it is only sane for us to try to change that treatment by every means possible.

Likewise the bodies of murdered women are strewn across the landscape of this country. Rape is a national pastime, a form of torture visited upon all girls and women, from babies to the aged. One out of three women in the U.S. will be raped during her lifetime. Battering and incest, those home-based crimes, are pandemic. Murder, of course, is men's ultimate violent "solution." And if you're thinking as you read this that I'm exaggerating, please go get today's newspaper and verify the facts. If anything is going down here it's woman-hatred, not man-hatred, a war against women. But wanting to end this war still doesn't equal man-hating. The feminist movement and the anti-racist movement have in common trying to ensure decent human life. Opposition to either movement aligns one with the most reactionary elements in American society.

Myth No. 4: Women's issues are narrow, apolitical concerns. People of color need to deal with the "larger struggle." This myth once again characterizes women's oppression as not particularly serious, and by no means a matter of life and death. I have often wished I could spread the word that a movement committed to fighting sexual, racial, economic, and heterosexist oppression, not to mention one which opposes imperialism, anti-Semitism, the oppressions visited upon the physically disabled, the old and the young, at the same time that it challenges militarism and imminent nuclear destruction is the very opposite of narrow. All segments of the women's movement have not dealt with all of these issues, but neither have all segments of Black people. This myth is plausible when the women's movement is equated only with its most bourgeois and reformist elements. The most progressive sectors of the feminist movement, which includes some radical white women, have taken the above issues, and many more, quite seriously. Third World women have been the most consistent in defining our politics broadly. Why is it that feminism is considered "white-minded" and "narrow" while socialism or Marxism, from verifiably white origins, is legitimately embraced by Third World male politicos, without their having their identity credentials questioned for a minute?

Myth No. 5: Those feminists are nothing but Lesbians. This may be the most pernicious myth of all and it is essential to understand that the distortion lies in the phrase "nothing but" and not in the identification Lesbian. "Nothing but" reduces Lesbians to a category of beings deserving of only the most violent attack, a category totally alien from "decent" Black folks, i.e., not your sisters, mothers, daughters, aunts, and cousins, but bizarre outsiders like no one you know or *ever* knew.

Many of the most committed and outspoken feminists of color have been and are Lesbians. Since many of us are also radicals, our politics, as indicated by the issues merely outlined above, encompass all people. We're also as Black as we ever were. (I always find it fascinating, for example, that many of the Black Lesbian-feminists I know still wear their hair natural, indicating that for us it was more than a "style.") Black feminism and Black Lesbianism are not interchangeable. Feminism is a political movement and many Lesbians are not feminists. Although it is also true that many Black feminists are not Lesbians, this myth has acted as an accusation and a deterrent to keep non-Lesbian Black feminists from manifesting themselves, for fear it will be hurled against them.

Fortunately this is changing. Personally, I have seen increasing evidence that many Black women of whatever sexual preference are more concerned with exploring and ending our oppression than they are committed to being either homophobic or sexually separatist. Direct historical precedent exists for such commitments. In 1957, Black playwright and activist Lorraine Hansberry wrote the following in a letter to *The Ladder*, an early Lesbian periodical:

> I think it is about time that equipped women began to take on some of the ethical questions which a male-dominated culture has produced and dissect and analyze them quite to pieces in a serious fashion. It is time that "half the human race" had something to say about the nature of its existence. Otherwise—without revised basic thinking—the woman intellectual is likely to find herself trying to draw conclusions—moral conclusions—based on acceptance of a social moral superstructure which has never admitted to the equality of women and is therefore immoral itself. As per marriage, as per sexual practices, as per the rearing of children, etc. In this kind of work there may be women to emerge who will be able to formulate a new and possible concept that homosexual persecution and condemnation has at its roots not only social ignorance, but a philosophically active anti-feminist dogma."[7]

I would like a lot more people to be aware that Lorraine Hansberry, one of our most respected artists and thinkers, was asking in a Lesbian context some of the same questions we are asking today, and for which we have been so maligned.

Black heterosexuals' panic about the existence of both Black Lesbians and Black gay men is a problem that they have to deal with themselves. A first step would be for them to better understand their own heterosexuality, which need not be defined by attacking everybody who is not heterosexual.

Home Truths

Above are some of the myths that have plagued Black feminism. The truth is that there is a vital movement of women of color in this country. Despite continual resistance to women of color defining our specific issues and organizing around them, it is safe to say in 1982 that we have a movement of our own. I have been involved in building that movement since 1973. It has been a struggle every step of the way and I feel we are still in just the beginning stages of developing a workable politics and practice. Yet the feminism of women of color, particularly of Afro-American women, has wrought many changes during these years, has had both obvious and unrecognized impact upon the development of other political groupings and upon the lives and hopes of countless women.

The very nature of radical thought and action is that it has exponentially far-reaching results. But because all forms of media ignore Black women, in particular Black feminists, and because we have no widely distributed communication mechanisms of our own, few know the details of what we have accomplished. One of the purposes of *Home Girls* is to get the word out about Black feminism to the people who need it most: Black people in the U.S., the Caribbean, Latin America, Africa—everywhere. It is not possible for a single introduction or a single book to encompass all of what Black feminism is, but there is basic information I want every reader to have about the meaning of Black feminism as I have lived and understood it.

In 1977, a Black feminist organization in Boston of which I was a member from its founding in 1974, the Combahee River Collective, drafted a political statement for our own use and for inclusion in Zillah Eisenstein's anthology *Capitalist Patriarchy and the Case for Socialist Feminism.* In our opening paragraph we wrote:

> The most general statement of our politics at the present time would be that we are actively committed to struggling against racial, sexual, heterosexual, and class oppression and see as our particular task the development of integrated analysis and practice based upon the fact that the major systems of oppression are interlocking. The synthesis of these oppressions creates the conditions of our lives. As Black women we see Black feminism as the logical political movement to combat the manifold and simultaneous oppressions that all women of color face.

The concept of the simultaneity of oppression is still the crux of a Black feminist understanding of political reality and, I believe, one of the most significant ideological contributions of Black feminist thought.

We examined our own lives and found that everything out there was kicking our behinds—race, class, sex, and homophobia. We saw no reason to rank oppressions, or, as many forces in the Black community would have us do, to pretend that sexism, among all the "isms," was not happening to us. Black feminists' efforts to comprehend the complexity of our situation as it was actually occurring, almost immediately began to deflate some of the cherished myths about Black womanhood, for example, that we are "castrating matriarchs" or that we are more economically privileged than Black men. Although we made use of the insights of other political ideologies, such as socialism, we added an element that has often been missing from the theory of others: what oppression is comprised of on a day-to-day, basis, or as Black feminist musician Linda Tillery sings, ". . . what it's really like/ To live this life of triple jeopardy."[8]

This multi-issued approach to politics has probably been most often used by other women of color who face very similar dynamics, at least as far as institutionalized oppression is concerned. It has also altered the women's movement as a whole. As a result of Third World feminist organizing, the women's movement now takes much more seriously the necessity for a multi-issued strategy for challenging women's oppression. The more progressive elements of the left have also begun to recognize that the promotion of sexism and homophobia within their ranks, besides being ethically unconscionable, ultimately undermines their ability to organize. Even a few Third World organizations have begun to include the challenging of women's and gay oppression on their public agendas.

Approaching politics with a comprehension of the simultaneity of oppressions has helped to create a political atmosphere particularly conducive to coalition building. Among all feminists, Third World women have undoubtedly felt most viscerally the need for linking struggles and have also been most capable of forging such coalitions. A commitment to principled coalitions, based not upon expediency, but upon our actual need for each other is a second major contribution of Black feminist struggle. Many contributors to *Home Girls* write out of a sense of our ultimate interdependence. Bernice Johnson Reagon's essay, "Coalition Politics: Turning the Century," should be particularly noted. She writes:

> You don't go into coalition because you just *like* it. The only reason you would consider trying to team up with somebody who could possibly kill you, is because that's the only way you can figure you can stay alive.... Most of the time you feel threatened to the core and if you don't you're not really doing no coalescing.

The necessity for coalitions has pushed many groups to rigorously examine the attitudes and ignorance within themselves which prevent coalitions from succeeding. Most notably, there has been the commitment of some white feminists to make racism a priority issue within the women's movement, to take responsibility for their racism as individuals, and to do antiracist organizing in coalition with other groups. Because I have written and spoken about racism during my entire involvement as a feminist and have also presented workshops on racism for white women's organizations for several years during the 1970s, I have not only seen that there are white women who are fully committed to eradicating racism, but that new understandings of racial politics have evolved from feminism, which other progressive people would do well to comprehend.[9]

Having begun my political life in the Civil Rights movement and having seen the Black liberation movement virtually destroyed by the white power structure, I have been encouraged in recent years that women can be a significant force for bringing about racial change in a way that unites oppressions instead of isolating them. At the same time the percentage of white feminists who are concerned about racism is still a minority of the movement, and even within this minority those who are personally sensitive and completely serious about formulating an *activist* challenge to racism are fewer still. Because I have usually worked with politically radical feminists, I know that there are indeed white women worth building coalitions with, at the same time that there are apolitical, even reactionary, women who take the name of feminism in vain.

One of the greatest gifts of Black feminism to ourselves has been to make it a little easier simply to *be* Black and female. A Black feminist analysis has enabled us to understand that we are not hated and abused because there is something wrong with us, but because our status and treatment is absolutely prescribed by the racist, misogynistic system under which we live. There is not a Black woman in this country who has not, at some time, internalized and been deeply scarred by the hateful propaganda about us. There is not a Black woman in America who has not felt, at least once, like "the mule of the world," to use Zora Neale Hurston's still apt phrase.[10] Until Black feminism, very few people besides Black women actually cared about or took seriously the demoralization of being female *and* colored *and* poor *and* hated.

When I was growing up, despite my family's efforts to explain, or at least describe, attitudes prevalent in the outside world, I often thought that there was something fundamentally wrong with me because it was obvious that me and everybody like me was held in such contempt. The cold eyes of certain white teachers in school, the Black men who yelled from cars as Beverly and I stood waiting for the bus, convinced me that I must have done something horrible. How was I to know that racism and sexism had formed a blueprint for my mistreatment long before I had ever arrived here? As with most Black women, others' hatred of me became self-hatred, which has diminished over the years, but has by no means disappeared. Black feminism has, for me and for so many others, given us the tools to finally comprehend that it is not something we have done that has heaped this psychic violence and material abuse upon us, but the very fact that, because of who we are, we are multiply oppressed. Unlike any other movement, Black feminism provides the theory that clarifies the nature of Black women's experience, makes possible positive support from other Black women, and encourages political action that will change the very system that has put us down.

ENDNOTES

1. The terms Third World women and women of color are used here to designate Native American, Asian American, Latina, and Afro-American women in the U.S. and the indigenous peoples of Third World countries wherever they may live. Both the terms Third World women and women of color apply to Black American women. At times in the introduction Black women are specifically designated as Black or Afro-American and at other times the terms women of color and Third World women are used to refer to women of color as a whole.

2. Smith, Barbara. "Notes for Yet Another Paper on Black Feminism, Or Will the Real Enemy Please Stand Up?" in *Conditions: Five, The Black Women's Issue,* eds. Bethel & Smith. Vol. 2, No. 2 (Autumn, 1979), p. 124.

3. DuBois, W. E. B. *Darkwater, Voices from Within the Veil*, New York: AMS Press, 1969, p. 185.

4. Jordan, June & Bernice Johnson Reagon. "Oughta Be A Woman," *Good News*, Chicago: Flying Fish Records, 1981, Songtalk Publishing Co. Quoted by permission.

5. Teish, Luisah. "Women's Spirituality: A Household Act," in *Home Girls*, ed. Smith. Watertown: Persephone Press, Inc., 1983. All subsequent references to work in *Home Girls* will not be cited.

6. See Linda C. Powell's review of Michele Wallace's *Black Macho and the Myth of the Super Woman* ("Black Macho and Black Feminism") in this volume and my review of Bell Hooks' (Gloria Watkins) *Ain't I A Woman: Black Women and Feminism* in *The New Women's Times Feminist Review*, Vol. 9, no. 24 (November, 1982), pp. 10, 11, 18, 19 & 20 and in *The Black Scholar*, Vol. 14, No. 1 (January/February 1983), pp. 38–45.

7. Quoted from *Gay American History: Lesbians and Gay Men in the U.S.A.*, ed. Jonathan Katz. New York: T. Y. Crowell, 1976, p. 425. Also see Adrienne Rich's "The Problem with Lorraine Hansberry," in "Lorraine Hansberry: Art of Thunder, Vision of light," *Freedomways*, Vol. 19, No. 4, 1979, pp. 247–255 for more material about her woman-identification.

8. Tillery, Linda. "Freedom Time," *Linda Tillery*, Oakland: Olivia Records, 1977, Tuizer Music.

9. Some useful articles on racism by white feminists are Elly Bulkin's "Racism and Writing: Some Implications for White Lesbian Critics." *Sinister Wisdom* 13 (Spring, 1980), pp. 3–22; Minnie Bruce Pratt's "Rebellion." *Feminary*, Vol. 11, Nos. 1 & 2, (1980), pp. 6–20; and Adrienne Rich's "Disloyal to Civilization: Feminism, Racism, Gynephobia." *On Lies, Secrets and Silence: Selected Prose* 1966–1978, New York: W W. Norton, 1979, pp. 275–310.

10. Hurston, Zora Neale. *Their Eyes Were Watching God*. Urbana: University of Illinois, 1937, 1978, p. 29.

QUESTIONS

1. Explain why each of the five myths Smith discusses is a myth.
2. What political purpose do these myths serve? Who benefits from them?
3. What is the concept of the simultaneity of oppression? Why is it a necessary component of Black feminism?

Womanist
from In Search of Our Mothers' Gardens (1983)

Alice Walker

Since the creation of the definition of "womanist" by author/activist Alice Walker, womanism has evolved into an academic, political, and spiritual framework. This broad and playful definition of "womanist" captures the uniqueness and importance of Black feminism in the United States.

Other works by Alice Walker include The Third Life of Grange Copeland *(1970).* In Love and Trouble *(1973),* Meridian *(1976), and* The Color Purple *(1982).*

Womanist 1. From *womanish.* (Opp. of "girlish," i.e., frivolous, irresponsible, not serious.) A black feminist or feminist of color. From the black folk expression of mothers to female children, "You acting womanish," i.e., like a woman. Usually referring to outrageous, audacious, courageous or *willful* behavior. Wanting to know more and in greater depth than is considered "good" for one. Interested in grown-up doings. Acting grown up. Being grown up. Interchangeable with another black folk expression: "You trying to be grown." Responsible. In charge. *Serious.*

2. *Also*: A woman who loves other women, sexually and/or nonsexually. Appreciates and prefers women's culture, women's emotional flexibility (values tears as natural counterbalance of laughter), and women's strength. Sometimes loves individual men, sexually and/or nonsexually. Committed to survival and wholeness of entire people, male *and* female. Not a separatist, except periodically, for health. Traditionally universalist as in: "Mama, why are we brown, pink, and yellow, and our cousins are white, beige, and black?" Ans.: "Well, you know the colored race is just like a flower garden, with every color flower represented." Traditionally capable, as in: "Mama, I'm walking to Canada and I'm taking you and a bunch of other slaves with me." Reply: "It wouldn't be the first time."

3. Loves music. Loves dance. Loves the moon. Loves the Spirit. Loves love and food and roundness. Loves struggle. Loves the Folk. Loves herself. *Regardless.*

4. Womanist is to feminist as purple to lavender.

QUESTIONS

1. How is a womanist different from a feminist?
2. What does Walker's final line, "Womanist is to feminist as purple is to lavender," mean? Why do you think so?
3. What does Walker identify as the cultural source for the "womanist"?

Becoming the Third Wave (1992)

Rebecca Walker

Rebecca Walker, writer and co-founder of the Third Wave Direct Action Corporation (a national non-profit organization promoting young women's leadership and activism), invites us to move our definition of feminism beyond political theory and unvoiced thoughts, and into the realm of "tangible action." If silence is complicity, and anger alienating, then the key to change is a voice that heals. This is Walker's description of "Third Wave" feminism.

I am not one of the people who sat transfixed before the television, watching the Senate hearings. I had classes to go to, papers to write, and frankly, the whole thing was too painful. A black man grilled by a panel of white men about his sexual deviance. A black woman claiming harassment and being discredited by other women. . . . I could not bring myself to watch that sensationalized assault [on] the human spirit.

To me, the hearings were not about determining whether or not Clarence Thomas did in fact harass Anita Hill. They were about checking and redefining the extent of women's credibility and power.

Can a woman's experience undermine a man's career? Can a woman's voice, a woman's sense of self-worth and injustice, challenge a structure predicated upon the subjugation of our gender? Anita Hill's testimony threatened to do that and more. If Thomas had not been confirmed, every man in the United States would be at risk. For how many senators never told a sexist joke? How many men have not used their protected male privilege to thwart in some way the influence or ideas of a woman colleague, friend, or relative?

For those whose sense of power is so obviously connected to the health and vigor of the penis, it would have been a metaphoric castration. Of course, this is too great a threat.

While some may laud the whole spectacle for the consciousness it raised around sexual harassment, its very real outcome is more informative. He was promoted. She was repudiated. Men were assured of the inviolability of their penis/power. Women were admonished to keep their experiences to themselves.

The backlash against U.S. women is real. As the misconception of equality between the sexes becomes more ubiquitous, so does the attempt to restrict the boundaries of women's personal and political power. Thomas's confirmation, the ultimate rally of support for the male paradigm of harassment, sends a clear message to women: "Shut up! Even if you speak, we will not listen."

I will not be silenced.

I acknowledge the fact that we live under siege. I intend to fight back. I have uncovered and unleashed more repressed anger than I thought possible. For the umpteenth time in my 22 years, I have been radicalized, politicized, shaken awake. I have come to voice again, and this time my voice is not conciliatory.

The night after Thomas' confirmation I ask the man I am intimate with what he thinks of the whole mess. His concern is primarily with Thomas' propensity to demolish civil rights and opportunities for people of color. I launch into a tirade. "When will progressive black men prioritize my rights and well-being? When will they stop talking so damn much about 'the race' as if it revolved exclusively around them?" He tells me I wear my emotions on my sleeve. I scream "I need to know, are you with me or are you going to help them try to destroy me?"

A week later I am on a train to New York. A beautiful mother and daughter, both wearing green outfits, sit across the aisle from me. The little girl has tightly plaited braids. Her brown skin is glowing and smooth, her eyes bright as she chatters happily while looking out the window. Two men get on the train and sit directly behind me, shaking my seat as they thud into place. I bury myself in *The Sound and the Fury*. Loudly they begin to talk about women. "Man, I fucked that bitch all night and then I never called her again." "Man, there's lots of girlies over there, you know that ho, live over there by Tyrone? Well, I snatched that shit up."

The mother moves closer to her now quiet daughter. Looking at her small back I can see that she is listening to the men. I am thinking of how I can transform the situation, of all the people in the car whose silence makes us complicit.

Another large man gets on the train. After exchanging loud greetings with the two men, he sits next to me. He tells them he is going to Philadelphia to visit his wife and child. I am suckered into thinking that he is different. Then, "Man, there's a ton of females in Philly, just waitin' for you to give 'em some." I turn my head and allow the fire in my eyes to burn into him. He takes up two seats and has hands with huge swollen knuckles. I imagine the gold rings on his fingers slamming into my face. He senses something, "What's your name, sweetheart?" The other men lean forward over the seat.

A torrent explodes: "I ain't your sweetheart, I ain't your bitch, I ain't your baby. How dare you have the nerve to sit up here and talk about women that way, and then try to speak to me." The woman/mother chimes in to the beat with claps of sisterhood. The men are momentarily stunned. Then the comeback: "Aw, bitch, don't play that woman shit over here 'cause that's bullshit." He slaps the back of one hand against the palm of the other. I refuse to back down. Words fly.

My instinct kicks in, telling me to get out. "Since I see you all are not going to move, I will." I move to the first car. I am so angry that thoughts of murder, of physically retaliating against them, of separatism, engulf me. I am almost out of body, just shy, of being pure force. I am sick of the way women are negated, violated, devalued, ignored. I am livid, unrelenting in my anger at those who invade my space, who wish to take away my rights, who refuse to hear my voice.

As the days pass, I push myself to figure out what it means to be a part of the Third Wave of feminism. I begin to realize that I owe it to myself, to my little sister on the train, to all of the daughters yet to be born, to push beyond my rage and articulate an agenda. After battling with ideas of separatism and militancy, I connect with my own feelings of powerlessness. I realize that I

Name calling-objectification

must undergo a transformation if I am truly committed to women's empowerment. My involvement must reach beyond my own voice in discussion, beyond voting, beyond reading feminist theory. My anger and awareness must translate into tangible action.

I am ready to decide, as my mother decided before me, to devote much of my energy to the history, health, and healing of women. Each of my choices will have to hold to my feminist standard of justice.

To be a feminist is to integrate an ideology of equality and female empowerment into the very fiber of my life. It is to search for personal clarity in the midst of systemic destruction, to join in sisterhood with women when often we are divided, to understand power structures with the intention of challenging them.

While this may sound simple, it is exactly the kind of stand that many of my peers are unwilling to take. So I write this as a plea to all women, especially the women of my generation: Let Thomas' confirmation serve to remind you, as it did me, that the fight is far from over. Let this dismissal of a woman's experience move you to anger. Turn that outrage into political power. Do not vote for them unless they work for us. Do not have sex with them, do not break bread with them, do not nurture them if they do not prioritize our freedom to control our bodies and our lives.

I am not a postfeminism feminist. I am the Third Wave.

Questions

1. Walker's story of her train ride through New York offers an example of sexism in everyday life. How does her story support the concept that words and speech can be as powerful as actions?

2. Consider the little girl on the train . . . the mother . . . the wife of the man sitting next to Walker. How do they illustrate a "domino" (ripple) effect of sexism which is similar to the ripple effect of the Hill/Thomas decision that Walker outlines?

Power, Domination and Differences

"All things being equal" is a common phrase in the English language. And yet, when we turn a feminist lens on the social environment, we often find that all things are *not* equal. Markers of social identity (e.g., race, class, gender) interact with one another within a complex social structure, one which relies on the forces of power and domination to maintain itself. Here in the Western part of the world, much of our thinking is typified by its categorical nature: our tendency to reduce things to mutually exclusive dualisms, or categories, characterized by "either/or." Differences take on profound significance within a social structure which often grants "equality" categorically, based on one's perceived and actual group memberships.

In this section, we will begin to explore the dynamics of power, domination, and differences. We will consider the question, "What difference do differences make in determining the possibilities for one's potential?" We will ask the question macroscopically, from the perspective of the social environment and its effects on individuals. In doing so, we will begin to discover possible explanations for how and why, in twentieth century United States, all things do not seem to be equal.

OPPRESSION (1983)

Marilyn Frye

Philosopher and scholar Marilyn Frye explores the dynamics of oppression in this selection. Through the use of an analogy, Frye attempts to clarify for us the meaning and implications of oppression. Frye's discussion reveals the feminist understanding of oppression, and its insistence on treating people, not as individuals, but as perceived members of socially-defined groups.

It is a fundamental claim of feminism that women are oppressed. The word 'oppression' is a strong word. It repels and attracts. It is dangerous and dangerously fashionable and endangered. It is much misused, and sometimes not innocently.

The statement that women are oppressed is frequently met with the claim that men are oppressed too. We hear that oppressing is oppressive to those who oppress as well as to those they oppress. Some men cite as evidence of their oppression their much-advertised inability to cry. It is tough, we are told, to be masculine. When the stresses and frustrations of being a man are cited as evidence that oppressors are oppressed by their oppressing, the word 'oppression' is being stretched to meaninglessness; it is treated as though its scope includes any and all human experience of limitation or suffering, no matter the cause, degree or consequence. Once such usage has been put over on us, then if ever we deny that any person or group is oppressed, we seem to imply that we think they never suffer and have no feelings. We are accused of insensitivity; even of bigotry. For women, such accusation is particularly intimidating, since sensitivity is one of the few virtues that has been assigned to us. If we are found insensitive, we may fear we have no redeeming traits at all and perhaps are not real women. Thus are we silenced before we begin: the name of our situation drained of meaning and our guilt mechanisms tripped.

But this is nonsense. Human beings can be miserable without being oppressed, and it is perfectly consistent to deny that a person or group is oppressed, without denying that they have feelings or that they suffer.

We need to think clearly about oppression, and there is much that mitigates against this. I do not want to undertake to prove that women are oppressed (or that men are not), but I want to make clear what is being said when we say it. We need this word, this concept, and we need it to be sharp and sure.

I

The root of the word 'oppression' is the element 'press.' *The press of the crowd, pressed into military service; to press a pair of pants, printing press, press the button.* Presses are used to mold things or flatten them or reduce them in bulk, sometimes to reduce them by squeezing out the gasses or liquids in them. Something pressed is something caught between or among forces and barriers which are so related to each other that jointly they restrain, restrict or prevent the thing's motion or mobility. Mold. Immobilize. Reduce.

The mundane experience of the oppressed provides another clue. One of the most characteristic and ubiquitous features of the world as experienced by oppressed people is the double bind—situations in which options are reduced to a very few and all of them expose one to penalty, censure or deprivation. For example, it is often a requirement upon oppressed people that we smile and be cheerful. If we comply, we signal our docility and our acquiescence in our situation. We need not, then, be taken note of. We acquiesce in being made invisible, in our occupying no space. We participate in our own erasure. On the other hand, anything but the sunniest countenance exposes us to being perceived as mean, bitter, angry or dangerous. This means, at the least, that we may be found "difficult" or unpleasant to work with, which is enough to cost one one's livelihood, at worst, being seen as mean, bitter, angry or dangerous has been known to result in rape, arrest, beating and murder. One can only choose to risk one's preferred form and rate of annihilation.

Another example: It is common in the United States that women, especially younger women, are in a bind, where neither sexual activity nor sexual inactivity is all right. If she is heterosexually active, a woman is open to censure and punishment for being loose, unprincipled or a whore. The "punishment" comes in the form of criticism, snide and embarrassing remarks, being treated as an easy lay by men, scorn from her more restrained female friends. She may have to lie and hide her behavior from her parents. She must juggle the risks of unwanted pregnancy and dangerous contraceptives. On the other hand, if she refrains from heterosexual activity, she is fairly constantly harassed by men who try to persuade her into it and pressure her to "relax" and "let her hair down"; she is threatened with labels like "frigid," "uptight," "man-hater," "bitch" and "cocktease." The same parents who would be disapproving of her sexual activity may be worried by her inactivity because it suggests she is not or will not be popular, or is not sexually normal. She may be charged with lesbianism. If a woman is raped, then if she has been heterosexually active she is subject to the presumption that she liked it (since her activity is presumed to show that she likes sex), and if she has not been heterosexually active, she is subject to the presumption that she liked it (since she is supposedly "repressed and frustrated"). Both heterosexual activity and heterosexual nonactivity are likely to be taken as proof that you wanted to be raped, and hence, of course, weren't *really* raped at all. You can't win. You are caught in a bind, caught between systematically related pressures.

Women are caught like this, too, by networks of forces and barriers that expose one to penalty, loss or contempt whether one works outside the home or not, is on welfare or not, bears children or not, raises children or not, marries or not, stays married or not, is heterosexual, lesbian, both or neither. Economic necessity; confinement to racial and/or sexual job ghettos; sexual harassment; sex discrimination; pressures of competing expectations and judgments about *women, wives,* and *mothers* (in the society at large, in racial and ethnic subcultures and in one's own mind); dependence (full or partial) on husbands, parents or the state; commitment to political ideas; loyalties to racial or ethnic or other "minority" groups; the demands of self-respect and responsibilities to others. Each of these factors exists in complex tension with every other, penalizing or prohibiting all of the apparently available options. And nipping at one's heels, always, is the endless pack of little things. If one dresses one way, one is subject to the assumption that one is advertising one's sexual availability; if one dresses another way, one appears to "not care about oneself " or to be "unfeminine." If one uses "strong language," one invites categorization as a whore or slut; if one does not, one invites categorization as a "lady"—one too delicately constituted to cope with robust speech or the realities to which it presumably refers.

The experience of oppressed people is that the living of one's life is confined and shaped by forces and barriers which are not accidental or occasional and hence avoidable, but are systematically related to each other in such a way as to catch one between and among them and restrict or penalize motion in any direction. It is the experience of being caged in: all avenues, in every direction, are blocked or booby trapped.

Cages. Consider a birdcage. If you look very closely at just one wire in the cage, you cannot see the other wires. If your conception of what is before you is determined by this myopic focus, you could look at that one wire, up and down the length of it, and be unable to see why a bird would not just fly around the wire any time it wanted to go somewhere. Furthermore, even if, one day at a time, you myopically inspected each wire, you still could not see why a bird would have trouble going past the wires to get anywhere. There is no physical property of any one wire, *nothing* that the closest scrutiny could discover, that will reveal how a bird could be inhibited or harmed by it except in the most accidental way. It is only when you step back, stop looking at the wires one by one, microscopically, and take a macroscopic view of the whole cage, that you can see why the bird does not go anywhere; and then you will see it in a moment. It will require no great subtlety of mental powers. It is perfectly *obvious* that the bird is surrounded by a network of systematically related barriers, no one of which would be the least hindrance to its flight, but which, by their relations to each other, are as confining as the solid walls of a dungeon.

It is now possible to grasp one of the reasons why oppression can be hard to see and recognize: one can study the elements of an oppressive structure with great care and some good will without seeing the structure as a whole, and hence without seeing or being able to understand that one is looking at a cage and that there are people there who are caged, whose motion and mobility are restricted, whose lives are shaped and reduced.

The arresting of vision at a microscopic level yields such common confusion as that about the male door-opening ritual. This ritual, which is remarkably widespread across classes and races, puzzles many people, some of whom do and some of whom do not find it offensive. Look at the scene of the two people approaching a door. The male steps slightly ahead and opens the door. The male holds the door open while the female glides through. Then the male goes through. The door closes after them. "Now how," one innocently asks, "can those crazy womens-libbers say that is oppressive? The guy *removed* a barrier to the lady's smooth and unruffled progress." But each repetition of his ritual has a place in a pattern, in fact in several patterns. One has to shift the level of one's perception in order to see the whole picture.

The door-opening pretends to be a helpful service, but the helpfulness is false. This can be seen by noting that it will be done whether or not it makes any practical sense. Infirm men and men burdened with packages will open doors for able-bodied women who are free of physical burdens. Men will impose themselves awkwardly and jostle everyone in order to get to the door first. The act is not determined by convenience or grace. Furthermore, these very numerous acts of unneeded or even noisome "help" occur in counterpoint to a pattern of men not being helpful in many practical ways in which women might welcome help. What *women* experience is a world in which gallant princes charming commonly make a fuss about being helpful and providing small services when help and services are of little or no use, but in which there are rarely ingenious and adroit princes at hand when substantial assistance is really wanted either in mundane affairs or in situations of threat, assault or terror. There is no help with the (his) laundry; no help typing a report at 4:00 a.m.; no help in mediating disputes among relatives or children. There is nothing but advice that women should stay indoors after dark, be chaperoned by a man, or when it comes down to it, "lie back and enjoy it."

The gallant gestures have no practical meaning. Their meaning is symbolic. The door-opening and similar services provided are services which really are needed by people who are for one reason or another incapacitated—unwell, burdened with parcels, etc. So the message is that women are incapable. The detachment of the acts from the concrete realities of what women need and do not need is a vehicle for the message that women's actual needs and interests are unimportant or irrelevant. Finally, these gestures imitate the behavior of servants toward masters and thus mock women, who are in most respects the servants and caretakers of men. The message of the false helpfulness of male gallantry is female dependence, the invisibility or insignificance of women, and contempt for women.

One cannot see the meanings of these rituals if one's focus is riveted upon the individual event in all its particularity, including the particularity of the individual man's present conscious intentions and motives and the individual woman's conscious perception of the event in the moment. It seems sometimes that people take a deliberately myopic view and fill their eyes with things seen microscopically in order not to see macroscopically. At any rate, whether it is deliberate or not, people can and do fail to see the oppression of women because they fail to see macroscopically and hence fail to see the various elements of the situation as systematically related in larger schemes.

As the cageness of the birdcage is a macroscopic phenomenon, the oppressiveness of the situations in which women live our various and different lives is a macroscopic phenomenon. Neither can be *seen* from a microscopic perspective. But when you look macroscopically you can see it—a network of forces and barriers which are systematically related and which conspire to the immobilization, reduction and molding of women and the lives we live.

II

The image of the cage helps convey one aspect of the systematic nature of oppression. Another is the selection of occupants of the cages, and analysis of this aspect also helps account for the invisibility of the oppression of women.

It is as a woman (or as a Chicana/o or as a Black or Asian or lesbian) that one is entrapped.

> "Why can't I go to the park; you let Jimmy go!"
>
> "Because it's not safe for girls."
>
> "I want to be a secretary, not a seamstress; I don't want to learn to make dresses."
>
> "There's no work for negroes in that line; learn a skill where you can earn your living."[1]

When you question why you are being blocked, why this barrier is in your path, the answer has not to do with individual talent or merit, handicap or failure; it has to do with your membership in some category understood as a "natural" or "physical" category. The "inhabitant" of the "cage" is not an individual but a group, all those of a certain category. If an individual is oppressed, it is in virtue of being a member of a group or category of people that is systematically reduced, molded, immobilized. Thus, to recognize a person as oppressed, one has to see that individual as belonging to a group of a certain sort.

There are many things which can encourage or inhibit perception of someone's membership in the sort of group or category in question here. In particular, it seems reasonable to suppose that if one of the devices of restriction and definition of the group is that of physical confinement or segregation, the confinement and separation would encourage recognition of the group as a group. This in turn would encourage the macroscopic focus which enables one to recognize oppression and encourages the individuals' identification and solidarity with other individuals of the group or category. But physical confinement and segregation of the group as a group is not common to all oppressive structures, and when an oppressed group is geographically and demographically dispersed the perception of it as a group is inhibited. There may be little or nothing in the situations of the individuals encouraging the macroscopic focus which would reveal the unity of the structure bearing down on all members of that group.[2]

A great many people, female and male and of every race and class, simply do not believe that *woman* is a category of oppressed people, and I think that this is in part because they have been fooled by the dispersal and assimilation of women throughout and into the systems of class and race which organize men. Our simply being dispersed makes it difficult for women to have knowledge of each other and hence difficult to recognize the shape of our common cage. The dispersal and assimilation of women throughout economic classes and races also divides us against each other practically and economically and thus attaches *interest* to the inability to see: for some, jealousy of their benefits, and for some, resentment of the others' advantages.

To get past this, it helps to notice that in fact women of all races and classes *are* together in a ghetto of sorts. There is a women's place, a sector, which is inhabited by women of all classes and races, and it is not defined by geographical boundaries but by function. The function is the service of men and men's interests as men define them, which includes the bearing and rearing of children. The details of the service and the working conditions vary by race and class, for men of different races and classes have different interests, perceive their interests differently, and express their needs and demands in different rhetorics, dialects and languages. But there are also some constants.

Whether in lower, middle or upper-class home or work situations, women's service work always includes personal service (the work of maids, butlers, cooks, personal secretaries),[3] sexual service (including provision for his genital sexual needs and bearing his children, but also including "being nice," "being attractive for him," etc.), and ego service (encouragement, support, praise, attention). Women's service work also is characterized everywhere by the fatal combination of responsibility and powerlessness: we are held responsible and we hold ourselves responsible for good outcomes for men and children in almost every respect though we have in almost no case power adequate to that project. The details of the subjective experience of this servitude are local. They vary with economic class and race and ethnic tradition as well as the personalities of the men in question. So also are the details of the forces which coerce our tolerance of this servitude particular to the different situations in which different women live and work.

All this is not to say that women do not have, assert and manage sometimes to satisfy our own interests, nor to deny that in some cases and in some respects women's independent interests do overlap with men's. But at every race/class level and even across race/class lines men do not serve women as women serve men. "Women's sphere" may be understood as the "service sector," taking the latter expression much more widely and deeply than is usual in discussions of the economy.

III

It seems to be the human condition that in one degree or another we all suffer frustration and limitation, all encounter unwelcome barriers, and all are damaged and hurt in various ways. Since we are a social species, almost all of our behavior and activities are structured by more than individual inclination and the conditions of the planet and its atmosphere. No human is free of social structures, nor (perhaps) would happiness consist in such freedom. Structure consists of boundaries, limits and barriers; in a structured whole, some motions and changes are possible, and others are not. If one is looking for an excuse to dilute the word 'oppression,' one can use the fact of social structure as an excuse and say that everyone is oppressed. But if one would rather get clear about what oppression is not, one needs to sort out the sufferings, harms and limitations and figure out which are elements of oppression and which are not.

From what I have already said here, it is clear that if one wants to determine whether a particular suffering, harm or limitation is part of someone's being oppressed, one has to look at it *in context* in order to tell whether it is an element in an oppressive structure: one has to see if it is part of an enclosing structure of forces and barriers which tends to the immobilization and reduction of a group or category of people. One has to look at how the barrier or force fits with others and to whose benefit or detriment it works. As soon as one looks at examples, it becomes obvious that not everything which frustrates or limits a person is oppressive, and not every harm or damage is due to or contributes to oppression.

If a rich white playboy who lives off income from his investments in South African diamond mines should break a leg in a skiing accident at Aspen and wait in pain in a blizzard for hours before he is rescued, we may assume that in that period he suffers. But the suffering comes to an end; his leg is repaired by the best surgeon money can buy and he is soon recuperating in a lavish suite, sipping Chivas Regal. Nothing in this picture suggests a structure of barriers and forces. He is a member of several oppressor groups and does not suddenly become oppressed because he is injured and in pain. Even if the accident was caused by someone's malicious negligence, and hence someone can be blamed for it and morally faulted, that person still has not been an agent of oppression.

Consider also the restriction of having to drive one's vehicle on a certain side of the road. There is no doubt that this restriction is almost unbearably frustrating at times, when one's lane is not moving and the other lane is clear. There are surely times, even, when abiding by this regulation would have harmful consequences. But the restriction is obviously wholesome for most of us most of the time. The restraint is imposed for our benefit, and does benefit us; its operation tends to encourage our *continued* motion, not to immobilize us. The limits imposed by traffic regulations are limits most of us would cheerfully impose on ourselves given that we knew others would follow them too. They are part of a structure which shapes our behavior, not to our reduction and immobilization, but rather to the protection of our continued ability to move and act as we will.

Another example: The boundaries of a racial ghetto in an American city serve to some extent to keep white people from going in, as well as to keep ghetto dwellers from going out. A particular white citizen may be frustrated or feel deprived because s/he cannot stroll around there and enjoy the "exotic" aura of a "foreign" culture, or shop for bargains in the ghetto swap shops. In fact, the existence of the ghetto, of racial segregation, does deprive the white person of knowledge and harm her/his character by nurturing unwarranted feelings of superiority. But this does not make the white person in this situation a member of an oppressed race or a person oppressed because of her/ his race. One must look at the barrier. It limits the activities and the access of those on both sides of it (though to different degrees). But it is a product of the intention, planning and action of whites for the benefit of whites, to secure and maintain privileges that are available to whites generally, as members of the dominant and privileged group. Though the existence of the barrier has some bad consequences for whites, the barrier does not exist in systematic relationship with other barriers and forces forming a structure oppressive to whites; quite the contrary. It is part of a structure which oppresses the ghetto dwellers and thereby (and by white intention) protects and furthers white interests as dominant white culture understands them. This barrier is not oppressive to whites, even though it is a barrier to whites.

Barriers have different meanings to those on opposite sides of them, even though they are barriers to both. The physical walls of a prison no more dissolve to let an outsider in than to let an insider out, but for the insider they are confining and limiting while to the outsider they may mean protection from what s/he takes to be threats posed by insiders—freedom from harm or anxiety. A set of social and economic barriers and forces separating two groups may be felt, even painfully, by members of both groups and yet may mean confinement to one and liberty and enlargement of opportunity to the other.

The service sector of the wives/mommas/assistants/girls is almost exclusively a woman-only sector; its boundaries not only enclose women but to a very great extent keep men out. Some men sometimes encounter this barrier and experience it as a restriction on their movements, their activities, their control or their choices of "lifestyle." Thinking they might like the simple nurturant life (which they may imagine to be quite free of stress, alienation and hard work), and feeling deprived since it seems closed to them, they thereupon announce the discovery that they are oppressed, too, by "sex roles." But that barrier is erected and maintained by men, for the benefit of men. It consists of cultural and economic forces and pressures in a culture and economy controlled by men in which, at every economic level and in all racial and ethnic subcultures, economy, tradition—and even ideologies of liberation—work to keep at least local culture and economy in male control.[4]

The boundary that sets apart women's sphere is maintained and promoted by men generally for the benefit of men generally, and men generally do benefit from its existence, even the man who bumps into it and complains of the inconvenience. That barrier is protecting his classification and status as a male, as superior, as having a right to sexual access to a female or females. It protects a kind of citizenship which is superior to that of females of his class and race, his access to a wider range of better paying and higher status work, and his right to prefer unemployment to the degradation of doing lower status or "women's" work.

If a person's life or activity is affected by some force or barrier that person encounters, one may not conclude that the person is oppressed simply because the person encounters that barrier or force; nor simply because the encounter is unpleasant, frustrating or painful to that person at that time; nor simply because the existence of the barrier or force, or the processes which maintain or apply it, serve to deprive that person of something of value.

One must look at the barrier or force and answer certain questions about it. Who constructs and maintains it? Whose interests are served by its existence? Is it part of a structure which tends to confine, reduce and immobilize some group? Is the individual a member of the confined group? Various forces, barriers and limitations a person may encounter or live with may be part of an oppressive structure or not, and if they are, that person may be on either the oppressed or the oppressor side of it. One cannot tell which by how loudly or how little the person complains.

IV

Many of the restrictions and limitations we live with are more or less internalized and self-monitored, and are part of our adaptations to the requirements and expectations imposed by the needs and tastes and tyrannies of others. I have in mind such things as women's cramped postures and attenuated strides and men's restraint of emotional self-expression (except for anger). Who gets what out of the practice of those disciplines, and who imposes what penalties for improper relaxations of them? What are the rewards of this self-discipline?

Can men cry? Yes, in the company of women. If a man cannot cry, it is in the company of men that he cannot cry. It is men, not women, who require this restraint; and men not only require it, they reward it. The man who maintains a steely or tough or laid-back demeanor (all are forms which suggest invulnerability) marks himself as a member of the male community and is esteemed by other men. Consequently, the maintenance of that demeanor contributes to the man's self-esteem. It is felt as good, and he can feel good about himself. The way this restriction fits into the structures of men's lives is as one of the socially required behaviors which, if carried off, contribute to their acceptance and respect by significant others and to their own self-esteem. It is to their benefit to practice this discipline.

Consider, by comparison, the discipline of women's cramped physical postures and attenuated stride. This discipline can be relaxed in the company of women; it generally is at its most strenuous in the company of men.[5] Like men's emotional restraint, women's physical restraint is required by men. But unlike the case of men's emotional restraint, women's physical restraint is not rewarded. What do we get for it? Respect and esteem and acceptance? No. They mock us and parody our mincing steps. We look silly, incompetent, weak and generally contemptible. Our exercise of this discipline tends to low esteem and low self-esteem. It does not benefit us. It fits in a network of behaviors through which we constantly announce to others our membership in a lower caste and our unwillingness and/or inability to defend our bodily or moral integrity. It is degrading and part of a pattern of degradation.

Acceptable behavior for both groups, men and women, involves a required restraint that seems in itself silly and perhaps damaging. But the social effect is drastically different. The woman's restraint is part of a structure oppressive to women; the man's restraint is part of a structure oppressive to women.

V

One is marked for application of oppressive pressures by one's membership in some group or category. Much of one's suffering and frustration befalls one partly or largely because one is a member of that category. In the case at hand, it is the category, *woman*. Being a woman is a major factor in my not having a better job than I do; being a woman selects me as a likely victim of sexual assault or harassment; it is my being a woman that reduces the power of my anger to a proof of my insanity. If a woman has little or no economic or political power, or achieves little of what she wants to achieve, a major causal factor in this is that she is a woman. For any woman of any race or economic class, being a woman is significantly attached to whatever disadvantages and deprivations she suffers, be they great or small.

None of this is the case with respect to a person's being a man. Simply being a man is not what stands between him and a better job; whatever assaults and harassments he is subject to, being male is not what selects him for victimization; being male is not a factor which would make his anger impotent—quite the opposite. If a man has little or no material or political power, or achieves little of what he wants to achieve, his being male is no part of the explanation. Being male is something he has going *for* him, even if race or class or age or disability is going against him.

Women are oppressed, *as women*. Members of certain racial and/or economic groups and classes, both the males and the females, are oppressed *as* members of those races and/or classes. But men are not oppressed *as men*.

. . . and isn't it strange that any of us should have been confused and mystified about such a simple thing?

ENDNOTES

1. This example is derived from *Daddy Was A Number Runner*, by Louise Meriwether (Prentice-Hall, Englewood Cliffs, New Jersey, 1970), p. 144.

2. Coerced assimilation is in fact one of the *policies* available to an oppressing group in its effort to reduce and/or annihilate another group. This tactic is used by the U.S. government, for instance, on the American Indians.

3. At higher class levels women may not *do* all these kinds of work, but are generally still responsible for hiring and supervising those who do it. These services are still, in these cases, women's responsibility.

4. Of course this is complicated by race and class. Machismo and "Black manhood" politics seem to help keep Latin or Black men in control of more cash than Latin or Black women control; but these politics seem to me also to ultimately help keep the larger economy in *white* male control.

5. Cf. *Let's Take Back Our Space: "Female" and "Male" Body Language as a Result of Patriarchal Structures*, by Marianne Wex (Frauenliterature-verlag Hermine Fees, West Germany 1979), especially p. 173. This remarkable book presents literally thousands of candid photographs of woman and men, in public, seated, standing and lying down. It vividly demonstrates the very systematic differences in women's and men's postures and gestures.

QUESTIONS

1. Identify Frye's definition of "oppression". What are the crucial elements of the definition?
2. Identify the analogy Frye uses to reveal oppression. How does the analogy help to clarify the meaning of oppression? How does the analogy reinforce Frye's point about using a macroscopic perspective to understand oppression?
3. How does the example of the "rich white playboy" help to clarify Frye's argument about the importance of group membership?

2) Birdcage

Dyes and Dolls: Multicultural Barbie and the Merchandizing of Difference (1994)

Ann duCille

Barbie serves as a powerful symbol of femininity in U.S. culture, one that defines "femininity" as White. Ann DuCille traces the history of multicultural Barbies, and offers the argument that these dolls help to maintain a White standard of beauty. duCille asks us to consider the possibility that images of beauty as White cost the consumer more than money—that, in fact, the cost may include lower self-esteem and a loss of pride in one's body image. Ann duCille is a professor in the Literature Department at the University of California, San Diego.

> *The white missionaries who came to Saint Aug's from New England were darling to us. They gave Bessie and me these beautiful china dolls that probably were very expensive. Those dolls were white, of course. You couldn't get a colored doll like that in those days. Well, I loved mine, just the way it was, but do you know what Bessie did? She took an artist's palette they had also given us and sat down and mixed the paints until she came up with a shade of brown that matched her skin. Then she painted that white doll's face! None of the white missionaries ever said a word about it. Mama and Papa just smiled. (Sarah Delaney)*

> *This is my doll story (because every black journalist who writes about race gets around to it sometime). Back when I started playing with Barbie, there were no Christies (Barbie's black friend, born in 1968) or black Barbies (born in 1980, brown plastic pored into blond Barbie's mold). I had two blonds, which I bought with Christmas money from girls at school.*
>
> *I cut off their hair and dressed them in African-print fabric. They lived together (polygamy, I guess) with a black G. I. Joe bartered from the Shepp boys, my downstairs neighbors. After an "incident" at school (where all of the girls looked like Barbie and none of them looked like me). I galloped down our stairs with one Barbie, her blond head hitting each spoke of the banister, thud, thud, thud. And galloped up the stairs, thud, thud, thud, until her head popped off, lost to the graveyard behind the stairwell. Then I tore off each limb, and sat on the stairs for a long time twirling the torso like a baton. (Lisa Jones)*

Growing up in the 1950s, in the shadow of the second world war, it was natural for children—including little black children like my two brothers and me—to want to play war, to mimic what we heard on the radio, what we watched in black and white on our brand new floor model Motorola. In these war games, everyone wanted to be the Allied troops—the fearless, conquering white male heroes who had made the world safe for democracy, yet again, and saved us all from yellow peril. No one, of course, wanted to play the enemy—who most often was not the Germans or the Italians but the Japanese. So the enemy became or, more rightly, remained invisible, lurking in bushes we shot at with sticks we pretended were rifles and stabbed at with make-believe bayonets. "Take that," we shouted, liberally peppering our verbal assaults with racial epithets. "And that! And that!" It was all in fun—our venom and vigor. All's fair in wars of words. We understood little of what we said and nothing of how much our child's play reflected the sentiments of a nation that even in its finer, prewar moments had not embraced as citizens its Asian immigrants or claimed as countrymen and women their American-born offspring.

However naively imitative, our diatribe was interrupted forever one summer afternoon by the angry voice of our mother, chastising us through the open window. "Stop that," she said. "Stop that this minute. It's not nice. You're talking about the Japanese. *Japanese*, do you understand? And don't let me ever hear you call them anything else." In the lecture that accompanied dinner that evening, we were made to understand not the history of Japanese-Americans, the injustice of internment, or the horror of Hiroshima, but simply that there were real people behind the names we called; that name-calling always hurts somebody, always undermines someone's humanity. Our young minds were led on the short journey from "Jap" to "nigger"; and if we were too young then to understand the origins and fine points of all such pejoratives, we were old enough to know firsthand the pain of one of them.

I cannot claim that this early experience left me free of prejudice, but it did assist me in growing up at once aware of my own status as "different" and conscious of the exclusion of others so labeled. It is important to note, however, that my sense of my own difference was affirmed and confirmed not simply by parental intervention but also by the unrelenting sameness of the tiny, almost exclusively white town in which I was raised. There in the country confines of East Bridgewater, Massachusetts, the adults who surrounded me (except for my parents) were all white, as were the teachers who taught me, the authors who thrilled me (and instilled in me a love of literature), and the neighborhood children who called me nigger one moment and friend the next. And when my brothers and I went our separate ways into properly gendered spheres, the dolls I played with—like almost everything else about my environment—were also white: Betsy Wetsy, Tiny Tears, and Patty Play Pal.

It seems remarkable to me now, as I remember these childish things long since put away, that, for all the daily reminders of my blackness, I did not take note of its absence among the rubber-skin pinkness of Betsy Wetsy, the bald-headed whiteness of Tiny Tears, and the blue-eyed blondness of Patty Play Pal. I was never tempted like Elizabeth Delany to paint the dolls I played with brown like me or to dress them in African-print fabric like Lisa

Jones. (Indeed, I had no notion of such fabrics and little knowledge of the "dark continent" from which they came.) Caught up in fantasy, completely given over to the realm of make-believe, for most of my childhood I neither noticed nor cared that the dolls I played with did not look like me. The make-believe world to which I willingly surrendered more than just my disbelief was thoroughly and profoundly white. That is to say, the "me" I invented, the "I" I imagined, the Self I daydreamed in technicolor fantasies was no more black like me than the dolls I played with. In the fifties and well into the sixties of my childhood the black Other who was my Self, much like the enemy Other who was the foreign body of our war games, could only be imagined as faceless, far away, and utterly unfamiliar.

As suggested by my title, I am going to use the figure of multicultural Barbie to talk about the commodification of race and gender difference. I wanted to back into the present topic, however, into what I have to say about Barbie as a gendered, racialized icon of contemporary commodity culture, by reaching into the past—into the admittedly contested terrain of the personal—to evoke the ideological work of child's play. More than simple instruments of pleasure and amusement, toys and games play crucial roles in helping children determine what is valuable in and around them. Dolls in particular invite children to replicate them, to imagine themselves in their dolls' images. What does it mean, then, when little girls are given dolls to play with that in no way resemble them? What did it mean for me that I was nowhere in the toys I played with?

If the Japan and the Africa of my youth were beyond the grasp (if not the reach) of my imagination, children today are granted instant global gratification in their play—immediate, hands-on access to both Self and Other. Or so we are told by many of the leading fantasy manufacturers—Disney, Hasbro, and Mattel, in particular—whose contributions to multicultural education include such play things as Aladdin (movie, video, and dolls), G.I. Joe (male "action figures" in black and white), and Barbie (now available in a variety of colors and ethnicities). Disneyland's river ride through different nations, like Mattel's Dolls of the World Collection, instructs us that "It's a Small World After All." Those once distant lands of Africa, Asia, Australia, and even the Arctic regions of the North Pole (yes, Virginia, there is an Eskimo Barbie) are now as close to home as the local Toys R Us and F.A.O.

Schwartz. And lo and behold, the inhabitants of these foreign lands—from Disney's Princess Jasmine to Mattel's Jamaican Barbie—are just like us, dye-dipped versions of archetypal white American beauty. It is not only a small world after all, but, as the Grammy award-winning theme from *Aladdin* informs us, "it's a whole new world."

Many of the major toy manufacturers have taken on a global perspective, a kind of nearsightedness that constructs this whole new world as small and cultural difference as consumable. Perhaps nowhere is this universalizing myopia more conspicuous than in the production, marketing, and consumption of Barbie dolls. By Mattel's reckoning, Barbie enjoys 100 percent brand name recognition among girls ages three to ten, ninety-six percent of whom own at least one doll, with most owning an average of eight. Five years ago, as Barbie turned thirty, *Newsweek* noted that nearly 500 million Barbies had been sold, along with 200 million G.I. Joes—"enough for every man, woman, and child in the United States and Europe" (Kantrowitz 59–60). Those figures have increased dramatically in the past five years, bringing the current world-wide Barbie population to 800 million. In 1992 alone, $1 billion worth of Barbies and accessories were sold. Last year, Barbie dolls sold at an average of one million per week, with overall sales exceeding the $1 billion all-time high set the year before. As the *Boston Globe* reported on the occasion of Barbie's thirty-fifth birthday on March 9, 1994, nearly two Barbie dolls are sold every second somewhere in the world; about fifty percent of the dolls sold are purchased here in the United States (Dembner 16).

The current Barbie boom may be in part the result of new, multiculturally oriented developments both in the dolls and in their marketing. In the fall of 1990, Mattel, Inc. announced a new marketing strategy to boost its sales; the corporation would "go ethnic" in its advertising by launching an ad campaign for the black and Hispanic versions of the already popular doll. Despite the existence of black, Asian, and Latina Barbies, prior to the fall of 1990 Mattel's print and TV ads featured only white dolls. In what *Newsweek* described as an attempt to capitalize on ethnic spending power, Mattel began placing ads for Multicultural Barbies in such Afrocentric publications as *Essence* magazine and on such Latin-oriented shows as "Pepe Plata" after market research revealed that most black and Hispanic consumers were unaware of the company's ethnic dolls. This targeted advertising was a smart move, according to the industry analysis cited by *Newsweek*, because "Hispanics buy about $170 billion worth of goods each year, [and] blacks spend even more." Indeed, sales of black Barbie dolls reportedly doubled in the year following this new ethnically-oriented ad campaign.[1] But determined to present itself as politically correct as well as financially savvy, Mattel was quick to point out that ethnic audiences, who are now able to purchase dolls who look like them, also have profited from the corporation's new marketing priorities. Barbie is a role model for all of her owners, according to product manager Deborah Mitchell, herself an African American. "Barbie allows little girls to dream," she asserted—to which the *Newsweek* reporter, added (seemingly without irony): "now, ethnic Barbie lovers will be able to dream in their own image" (Berkwitz 48).

Dream in their own image? The *Newsweek* columnist inadvertently put his finger on precisely what is so troubling to many parents, feminist scholars, and cultural critics about Barbie and dolls like her. Such toys invite, inspire, and even demand a potentially damaging process not simply of imagining but of interpellation. When little girls fantasize themselves into the conspicuous consumption, glamour, perfection, and, some have argued, anorexia of Barbie's world, it is rarely, if ever, "in their own image that they dream."[2] Regardless of what color dyes the dolls are dipped in or what costumes they are adorned with, the image they present is of the same mythically thin, long-legged, luxuriously-haired, buxom beauty. And while Mattel and other toy manufacturers may claim to have the best interests of ethnic audiences in mind in peddling their integrated wares, one does not have to be a cynic to suggest that profit remains the motivating factor behind this merchandising of difference.[3]

Far from simply playing with the sixty or so dolls I have acquired in the past year, then, I take them very seriously. In fact, I regard Barbie and similar dolls as Louis Althusser might have regarded them: as objects that do the dirty work of patriarchy and capitalism in the most insidious way—in the guise of child's play. But, as feminists have protested almost from the moment she hit the market, Barbie is not simply a child's toy or just a teenage fashion doll; she is an icon—perhaps *the* icon—of true white womanhood and femininity, a symbol of the far from innocent ideological stuff of which the (Miss) American dream and other mystiques of race and gender are made.

Invented by Ruth Handler, one of the founders of Mattel, and named after her daughter, Barbie dolls have been a very real force in the toy market since Mattel first introduced them at the American Toy Fair in 1959. In fact, despite the skepticism of toy store buyers—who at the time were primarily men—the first shipment of a half million dolls and a million costumes sold out immediately (Larcen A7). The first Barbies, which were modeled after a sexy German doll and comic strip character named Lilli, were all white, but in 1967 Mattel premiered a black version of the doll called "Colored Francie." "Colored Francie," like white "Francie Fairchild" introduced the year before, was supposed to be Barbie's "MOD'ern" younger cousin. As a white doll modeled and marketed in the image of Hollywood's Gidget, white Francie had been an international sensation, but Colored Francie was not destined to duplicate her prototype's success. Although the "black is beautiful" theme of both the civil rights and black power movements may have suggested a ready market for a beautiful black doll, Colored Francie in fact did not sell well.

Evelyn Burkhalter, owner, operator, and curator of the Barbie Hall of Fame in Palo Alto, California—home to 16,000 Barbie dolls—attributes Colored Francie's commercial failure to the racial climate of the times. Doll purchasing patterns, it seems, reflected the same resistance to integration that was felt elsewhere in the nation. In her implied family ties to white Barbie, Colored Francie suggested more than simple integration. She implied miscegenation: a make-believe mixing of races that may have jeopardized the doll's real market value. Cynthia Roberts, author of *Barbie: Thirty Years of America's Doll* (1989), maintains that Colored Francie flopped because of her straight hair and Caucasian features (44), which seemingly were less acceptable then than now. No doubt Mattel's decision to call its first black Barbie "Colored Francie" also contributed to the doll's demise. The use of the outmoded, even racist term "colored" in the midst of civil rights and black power activism suggested that while Francie might be "MOD'ern," Mattel was still in the dark(y) ages. In any case, neither black nor white audiences bought the idea of Barbie's colored relations, and Mattel promptly took the doll off the market, replacing her with a black doll called Christie in 1968.

While a number of other black dolls appeared throughout the late sixties and seventies—including the Julia doll, modeled after the TV character played by black singer and actress Diahann

Carroll—it was not until 1980 that Mattel introduced black dolls that were called Barbie like their white counterparts. Today, Barbie dolls come in a virtual rainbow coalition of colors, races, ethnicities, and nationalities—most of which look remarkably like the prototypical white Barbie, modified only by a dash of color and a change of costume. It is these would-be multicultural "dolls of the world"—Jamaican Barbie, Nigerian and Kenyan Barbie, Malaysian Barbie, Chinese Barbie, Mexican, Spanish, and Brazilian Barbie, et cetera, et cetera, et cetera—that interest me. For me these dolls are at once a symbol and a symptom of what multiculturalism has become at the hands of the contemporary commodity culture: an easy and immensely profitable way off the hook of Eurocentrism that gives us the face of cultural diversity without the particulars of racial difference.

If I could line up across the page the ninety "different" colors, cultures, and other incarnations in which Barbie currently exists, the fact of her unrelenting sameness (or at least similarity) would become immediately apparent. Even two dolls might do the trick: "My First Barbie" in white and "My First Barbie" in black, for example, or white "Western Fun Barbie" and black "Western Fun Barbie." Except for their dye jobs, the dolls are identical: the same body, size shape, and apparel. Or perhaps I should say *nearly* identical because in some instances—with black and Asian dolls in particular—coloring and other subtle changes (stereotypically slanted eyes in the Asian dolls, thicker lips in the black dolls) suggest differently coded facial features.

In other instances, when Barbie moves across cultural as opposed to racial lines, it is costume rather than color that distinguishes one ethnic group or nation from another. Nigeria and Jamaica, for instance, are represented by the same basic brown body, dolled-up in different native garbs—or Mattel's interpretation thereof.[4] With other costume changes, this generic black body becomes Western Fun Barbie or Marine Barbie or Desert Storm Barbie, and even Presidential Candidate Barbie, who, by the way, comes with a Nancy Reagan-red taking-care-of-business suit as well as a red, white, and blue inaugural ball gown. Much the same is true of the generic Asian doll—sometimes called Kira—who reappears in a variety of different dress-defined ethnicities. In other words, where Barbie is concerned, clothes not only make the woman, they mark the racial and/or cultural difference.

Such difference is marked as well by the cultural history and language lessons that accompany each doll in Mattel's international collection. The back of Jamaican Barbie's box tells us, for example, "*How-you-du* (Hello) from the land of Jamaica, a tropical paradise known for its exotic fruit, sugar cane, breathtaking beaches, and reggae beat!" The box goes on to explain that most Jamaicans have ancestors from Africa. Therefore, "even though our official language is English, we speak patois, a kind of '*Jamaica Talk*,' filled with English and African words." The lesson ends with a brief glossary (eight words) and a few more examples of this "Jamaica Talk," complete with translations: "*A hope yu wi come-a Jamaica!* (I hope you will come to Jamaica!)" and "*Teck care a yusself, mi fren!* (Take care of yourself, my friend!)" A nice idea, I suppose, but for me these quick-and-dirty ethnographies only enhance the extent to which these would-be multicultural dolls treat race and ethnic difference like collectibles, contributing more to commodity culture than to the intercultural awareness they claim to inspire.

Is the current fascination with the black or colored body—especially the female body—a contemporary version of the primitivism of the 1920s? Is multiculturalism to postmodernism what primitivism was to modernism? It was while on my way to a round table discussion on precisely this question that I bought my first black Barbie dolls in March of 1993. As carbon copies of an already problematic original, these colorized Mattel toys seemed to me the perfect tools with which to illustrate the point I wanted to make about the collapse of multiculturalism into an easy pluralism that simply adds what it constructs as the Other without upsetting the fundamental precepts and paradigms of Western culture or, in the case of Mattel, without changing the mold.

Not entirely immune to such critiques, Mattel sought expert advice from black parents and early childhood specialists in the development and marketing of its newest line of black Barbie dolls. Chief among the expert witnesses was clinical psychologist Darlene Powell Hopson, who co-authored with her husband Derek S. Hopson a study of racism and child development entitled *Different and Wonderful: Raising Black Children in a Race-Conscious Society* (1990). As part or their research for the book, the Hopsons repeated a ground-breaking study conducted by black psychologists Kenneth and Mamie Clark in the 1940s.

The Clarks used black and white dolls to demonstrate the negative effects of racism and segregation on black children. When given a choice between a white doll and a black doll, nearly 70 percent of the black children in the study chose the white doll. The Clarks' findings became an important factor in *Brown v. the Board of Education* in 1954. More recently, some scholars have called into question not necessarily the Clarks' findings but their interpretation: the assumption that, in the realm of make-believe, a black child's choosing a white doll necessarily reflects a negative self concept.[5] For the Hopsons, however, the Clarks' research remains compelling. In 1985 they repeated the Clarks' doll test and found that an alarming 65 percent of the black children in their sample chose a white doll over a black one. Moreover, 76 percent of the children interviewed said that the black dolls "looked bad" to them (Hopson xix).

In addition to the clinical uses they make of dolls in their experiments, the Hopsons also give considerable attention to what they call "doll play" in their book, specifically mentioning Barbie. "If your daughter likes 'Barbie' dolls, by all means get her Barbie," they advise black parents. "But also choose Black characters from the Barbie world. *You do not want your child to grow up thinking that only White dolls, and by extension White people, are attractive and nice*" (Hopsons 127, emphasis original). (Note that "Barbie," unmodified in the preceding passage, seems to mean *white* Barbie dolls.) The Hopsons suggest that parents should not only provide their children with black and other ethnic dolls but that they should get involved in their children's doll play. "Help them dress and groom the dolls while you compliment them both," they advise, offering the following suggested routine: "'This is a beautiful doll. It looks just like you. Look at her hair. It's just like yours. Did you know your nose is as pretty as your doll's?'" (119) They also suggest that parents use "complimentary words such as *lovely, pretty, or nice* so that [the] child will learn to associate them with his or her own image" (124).

Certainly it is important to help children feel good about themselves. One might argue, however, that the "just like you" simile and the beautiful doll imagery so central to these suggestions for what the Hopsons call positive play run the risk of transmitting to the child a colorized version of the same old beauty myth. Like Barbie dolls themselves, they make beauty—and by implication worth—a matter of physical characteristics.

In spite of their own good intentions, the Hopsons, in linking play with "beautiful" dolls to positive self-imaging, echoed Mattel's own marketing campaign. It is not surprising, then, that the Hopsons' findings and the interventional strategies they designed for using dolls to instill ethnic pride caught the attention of Mattel. In 1990 Darlene Hopson was asked to consult with the corporation's product manager Deborah Mitchell and designer Kitty Black-Perkins—both African Americans—in the development of a new line of "realistically sculpted" black fashion dolls, Hopson agreed and about a year later Shani and her friends Asha and Nichelle became the newest members of Barbie's ever-expanding family.

Shani means "marvelous" in Swahili, according to the dolls' press kit. But as *Village Voice* columnist Lisa Jones has noted, the name has other meanings as well: "startling, a wonder, a novelty" (36). My own research indicates that while Shani is a Swahili female name meaning marvelous, the Kiswahili word "shani" translates as "an adventure, something unusual" (Stewart 120). So it seems that Mattel's new play thing is not just marvelous, too marvelous for words, but, as her name also suggests, she is difference incarnate—a novelty, a new enterprise or, perhaps, as the black female Other so often is, an exotic. Mattel, it seems to me, both plays up and plays on what it presents as the doll's exotic black-is-beautiful difference. As the back of her package reads:

> Shani means marvelous in the Swahili language . . . and marvelous she is! With her friends Asha and Nichelle, Shani brings to life the special style and beauty of the African American woman.
>
> Each one is beautiful in her own way, with her own lovely skin shade and unique facial features. Each has a different hair color and texture, perfect for braiding, twisting and creating fabulous hair styles! Their clothes, too, reflect the vivid colors and ethnic accents that showcase their *exotic looks* and fashion flair!
>
> Shani, Asha and Nichelle invite you into their glamorous world to share the fun and excitement of being a top model. Imagine appearing on magazine covers, starring in fashion shows, and going to Hollywood parties as you, Shani, Asha and Nichelle live your dreams of beauty and success, loving every marvelous minute! (emphasis added)

While these words attempt to convey a message of black pride—after the fashion of the Hopsons' recommendations for positive play—that message is clearly tied to bountiful hair, lavish and exotic clothes, and other outward and visible signs not of brains but of beauty, wealth, and success. Shani may be a top fashion model, but don't look for her (or, if Mattel's own oft-articulated theory of Barbie as role model holds, yourself or your child) at M.I.T.

Like any other proud, well-to-do parents of a debutante, Mattel gave Shani her own coming out party at the International Toy Fair in February of 1991. This gala event included a tribute to black designers and an appearance by En Vogue singing, the Negro National Anthem, "Lift Every Voice and Sing"—evidently the song of choice of the doll Mattel describes as "tomorrow's African American woman." Also making their debuts were Shani's friends Asha and Nichelle, notable for the different hues in which their black plastic skin comes—an innovation due in part to Darlene Hopson's influence. Shani, the signature doll of the line, is what we call in the culture "brown-skinned"; Asha is honey-colored (some would say "high-yella"); and Nichelle is deep mahogany. Their male friend Jamal, added in 1992, completes the collection.

For the un(make-)believing, the three-to-one ratio of the Shani quartet—three black females to one black male—may be the most realistic thing about these dolls. In the eyes and the advertising of Mattel, however, Shani and her friends are the most authentic black female thing the mainstream toy market has yet produced. "Tomorrow's African American woman" (an appellation which, as Lisa Jones has noted, both riffs and one-ups *Essence*'s "Today's Black Woman") has broader hips, fuller lips, and a broader nose, according to product manager Deborah Mitchell. Principal designer Kitty Black-Perkins, who has dressed black Barbies since their birth in 1980, adds that the Shani dolls are also distinguished by their unique, culturally-specific clothes in "spice tones, [and] ethnic fabrics," rather than "fantasy colors like pink or lavender" (qtd. in Jones 36)—evidently the colors of the faint of skin.

The notion that fuller lips, broader noses, wider hips, and higher derrières somehow make the Shani dolls more realistically African American raises many difficult questions about authenticity, truth, and the ever-problematic categories of the real and the symbolic, the typical and the stereotypical. Just what are we saying when we claim that a doll does or does not "look black"? How does black look? What would it take to make a doll look authentically African American? What preconceived, prescriptive ideals of legitimate blackness are inscribed in such claims of authenticity? How can doll manufacturers or any other image makers—the film industry, for example—attend to cultural, racial, and phenotypical differences without merely engaging the same simplistic big-lips/broad-hips stereotypes that make so many of us—blacks in particular—grit our (pearly white) teeth? What would it take to produce a line of dolls that more fully reflects the wide variety of sizes, stripes, colors, hair styles, occupations, abilities, and disabilities that African Americans—like all people—come in? In other words: what price difference?

If such specificity—such ethnic "authenticity"—were possible to achieve in a doll, its purchase price, I suspect, would be much higher than a profit-driven corporation like Mattel would be willing to pay. Let me again invoke Shani to prove my point. On the one hand, Mattel was concerned enough about producing an ethnically correct black doll to seek the advice of black image specialists such as Darlene Hopson in the development and marketing oh the Shani line. Ultimately, however, the company was not willing to follow the advice of such experts where doing so would cost the corporation more than the price of additional dyes and ethnic fabrics.

For example, Hopson reportedly argued not just for gradations in skin tones in the Shani dolls but also for variations in body type and lengths and styles of hair—for an Afro here or an asymmetrical cut there. But, while Mattel acknowledged both the legitimacy and the ubiquity of such arguments, profit motive mediated against the very realism the corporation set out to achieve in these dolls. "To be truly realistic, one [Shani doll] should have shorter hair," Deborah Mitchell confessed to Lisa Jones. "But little girls of all races love hair play. We added more texture. But we can't change the fact that long, combable hair is still a key seller" (Jones 36).

Mitchell, of course, has a point. It is after all the taste of consumers that is inscribed in Barbie's long, combable hair. In the process of my own archival research—poking around in the dusty aisles of Toys R Us—I encountered a black teenage girl in search, like me, of the latest black Barbie. During the impromptu interview that ensued, my subject confessed to me in gory, graphic details the many Barbie murders and mutilations she had committed over the years. "It's the hair," she said emphatically several times. "The hair, that hair; I want it. I want it." Her words recalled my own torturous childhood struggles with the straightening combs, curling irons, and relaxers that bi-weekly transformed my wooly, "just like a sponge" kinks into what the white kids at school marveled at as my "Cleopatra [read straight] hair." During one of those bi-weekly sessions with my mother and the straightening comb, I was foolish enough to say out loud what I had wished for a long time: that I had straight hair, like the white girls at school. I still remember my mother's hurt, her sense of her daughter's racial heresy. Mitchell and Mattel indeed have a point. The difficult truth may just be that part of Shani's and black Barbie's attraction for little black girls in particular is the escape from their own often shorter, harder-to-comb hair that these dolls' lengthy straight locks represent.

Barbie's svelte figure, like her long combable hair, became Shani's body type as well. And here too marketability seems to have overruled professed attempts to capture the "unique facial features" and the "special style and beauty of the African American people." Even the reported subtle changes that are supposed to signify Shani's black difference—her much-remarked broader hips and elevated buttocks, for example—are little more than optical illusions, according to anthropologists Jacqueline Urla and Alan Swedlund of the University of Massachusetts at Amherst. Urla and Swedlund, who have been studying the anthropometry—the body measurements—of Barbie for some time, argue that, while Shani's hips may appear to be wider, they are actually smaller in both circumference and breadth than those of other Barbie dolls. It is essential, after all, that all the dolls be able to share the same clothes, thus making any dramatic alterations in body type unlikely. The effect of a higher buttocks is achieved, Uria and Swedlund maintain, by changing the angle of the doll's back. In other words, The Shani doll's buttocks may appear stereotypically higher, but she is not really dimensionally different from all the other eleven-and-a-half inch fashion dolls.

Lisa Jones concludes in her *Village Voice* article on Barbie by noting that the women behind Shani—black women like Hopson and Mitchell—want the doll to be more than just a Barbie in blackface. While Hopson, in particular, certainly hoped for—shall I say—*different* difference she nevertheless maintains that the Shani dolls demonstrate "social consciousness on Mattel's part" (Jones 36). British fashion designer and Barbie aficionado extraordinaire BillyBoy made a similar point in praising Mattel for integrating Barbie's family with first Colored Francie and then Christie in the late 1960s (BillyBoy 82). After nearly thirty years, I think we can forgive Mattel its Colored Francie faux pas and perhaps even applaud the attempt. But if Shani (who came out in a new scantily clad Soul Train edition in 1993) stands as Mattel's best effort to "go ethnic,' as it were—to corner the contemporary mainstream market in "realistically sculpted" black dolls that "bring to life" the "special style and beauty of the African-American people"—she stands on shaky ground.

And yet it may not be fair to single out Mattel as an example of what seems to be a national if not international phenomenon. Racial difference, like ethnic Barbie, is a hot commodity, and it isn't only Mattel who is making money. In the words of David Rieff, a contributing editor of *Harper's Magazine*:

> Everything is commodifiable, even Afrocentrism (there is money being made on all Kinte [sic] cloth and Kwanza [sic] paraphernalia that are the rage among certain segments of the black community, and not only the black community), bilingualism (currently the hottest growth market in publishing is Spanish language children's books), and the other "multicultural" tendencies in American society that conservatives fear so desperately.

Rieff goes so far as to call this newly globalized consumer economy multiculturalism's silent partner. I want to be careful in expressing my own concerns about the relationship between multiculturalism and the conspicuous consumption of difference, however, lest my critique appear complicit with that of the conservatives to whom Rieff refers, who fear the possibilities of a truly transformative social, cultural, and economic order, which I in fact would welcome.

All cultural commodities are not created equal. It seems to me that however profitable their production may be for the publishing industry, Spanish-language children's books serve a useful, educational function for their target audiences. On the other hand, even taking into account the argument that black girls need black dolls to play with, I have a difficult time locating the redeeming social value in Mattel's little plastic women, even or perhaps especially—when they are tinted brown and decorated in Kente cloth and Kufi hats, as the new Soul Train Shani dolls are. And while I am certain that hordes of black consumers are grateful for the black haircare products and cosmetics marketed by mainstream corporations such as Clairol, Revlon, and Mary Kay, I am less convinced that J.C. Penney's target audience will really find much cultural enlightenment in the Kente cloth potholders, napkin rings, and dish towels that the store is currently marketing as "expressions of cultural pride."

In *Fashion Influences*, a catalog clearly intended to cater to what it takes to be the tastes of black audiences, J.C. Penney advertises an assortment of housewares, ethnic artifacts, and exclusive designer fashions with "Afrocentric flair." Such specialty items as triple-woven cotton throws, which sell for $50 each, are available in four culturally edifying patterns: 01 Kwanzaa; 02 Kente; 03 Martin Luther King; and 04 Malcolm X. For another $40, customers can complement their Kwanzaa-patterned throw with a Kwanzaa needlepoint pillow. (For the not quite multiculturally literate shopper, Penney's provides a cultural history lesson: "Kwanzaa means 'first fruits of the harvest' in Swahili," the catalogue informs. "Created in 1966, Kwanzaa is a seven-day celebration synthesizing elements from many African harvest festivals.") And just so consumers know precisely how politically correct their Penney's purchases are, many of the catalog descriptions inform shoppers that these Afrocentric items are made in the U.S.A. The Ivory Coast Table Linens, for example, are billed as an "exuberantly colored interpretation of authentic African woven cloth . . . Made in the U.S.A." The Kente-cloth pillows are made in the U.S.A. of fabric imported from Africa, but the MLK and Malcolm X throws are just plain made in the U.S.A. In other words, for not-so-modest prices, culturally and socially-conscious American consumers can look for the union label as they shop for these and other interpretations-of-authentic-African-inspired-made-in-America goods.

Thus it is that from custom-designed bedroom coordinates inspired by mud cloth from Mali in West Africa to an embroidered metallic caftan or "Uwe (pronounced yoo-way, meaning dress)" inspired by "garments worn by the royal court on special occasions," what J.C. Penney is trading in and trading on in this blaxploitation catalog is cultural difference and, if you will, misspent racial pride. Although I doubt that Penney's cares who buys its Kufi hats, black-on-black dishware, and "In Search of Identity" games, it is also clear that the company does not waste such catalogs on just any body. I, for example, have been a loyal Penney's catalog shopper for years; I receive the annual seasonal catalogs, as well as special fliers advertising queen-size fashions. I only happened upon Penney's blaxploitation catalog recently, however, when it was mailed not to me—faithful shopper—nor to my home but to the Center for African American Studies at Wesleyan University. While my shopping history identified me as larger-sized, there was evidently nothing about my purchasing pattern that identified me as black. Penney's marketing division seems to have assumed—quite cleverly, I think—that a Center for African American Studies would be a likely place to find middle-class, culturally-conscious black consumers who might actually be able to afford the high-prized items in its Afrocentric catalog. (What a miscalculation in that last regard.)

I suspect that such catalogs are mailed not only to black studies departments but also to black beauty parlors (indeed I found a similar catalog from Spiegel at the shop where I get my hair cut) and black churches, where there is sure to be a ready-made market for the Sunday-go-to-meetin' hats, high-heel shoes, and church-lady suits "with an Afrocentric flair" that fill their pages. Just to bring this discussion full circle, let me note that six Black Barbie dolls are available through this special catalog—Black Desert Storm Barbie and Ken and Soul Train Shani and her three friends Asha, Nichelle, and Jamal. Army Barbie and Ken are dressed in "authentic desert fatigues with authentic insignias for enlisted personnel," and the Shani dolls are decked out in "cool hip-hop fashions inspired by the hot T.V. dance show." But don't let these patriotic, all-American girls and boys fool you; they are all imported from Malaysia.

The Body Politic(s) of Barbie

Barbie's body is a consumer object itself, a vehicle for the display of clothing and the spectacular trappings of a wealthy teenage fantasy life. Her extraordinary body exists not simply as an example of the fetishized female form typical of those offered up to the male gaze, but as a commodity vehicle itself whose form seduces the beholder and sells accessories, the real source of corporate profit. Like Lay's chips, no one can buy just one outfit for the doll. Barbie is the late capitalist girl incarnate. (McCombie)

In focusing thus far on the merchandising of racial, perhaps more so than gender difference, I do not mean to imply that racial and gender identities are divisible, even in dolls. Nor, in observing that most if not all of Mattel's "dolls of the world" look remarkably like what the company calls the "traditional, blond, blue-eyed Barbie," do I mean to suggest that the seemingly endless recapitulation of the white prototype is the only way in which these dolls are problematic. In fact, the most alarming thing about Barbie may well be the extent to which she functions as what M.G. Lord calls a teaching tool for femininity, whatever her race or ethnicity. Lord, the author of *Forever Barbie: The Unauthorized Biography of a Real Doll*, due out later this year, describes Barbie as a "space-age fertility icon. She looks like a modern woman, but she's a very primitive totem of female power" (qtd. in Dembner 1).

Barbie has long had the eye and ire of feminists, who, for the most part, have reviled her as another manifestation of the damaging myths of female beauty and the feminine body that patriarchy perpetuates through such vehicles as popular and commodity culture. A counter narrative also exists, however, one in which Barbie is not an empty-headed, material girl bimbo, for whom math class is tough, but a feminist heroine, who has been first in war (a soldier who served in the Gulf, she has worn the colors of her country as well as the United Colors of Benetton), first in peace (she held her own summit in 1990 and she's a long-time friend of UNICEF, who "loves all the children of the world"), and always first in the hearts of her country (Americans buy her at the rate of one doll every second). While time does not allow me to reiterate or to assess here all the known critiques and defenses of Barbie, I do want to discuss briefly some of the gender ideals that I think are encoded in and transmitted by this larger-than-life little woman and what Barbie's escalating popularity says about contemporary American culture.

In *Touching Liberty: Abolition, Feminism, and the Politics of the Body* (1993), Karen Sanchez-Eppler argues that all dolls are intended to teach little girls about domesticity (133). If such tutelage is Barbie's not so secret mission, methodology is far more complex and contradictory than that of the Betsy Wetsy and Tiny Tears baby dolls I played with thirty-five years ago. Those dolls invoked and evoked the maternal, as they and the baby bottles and diapers with which they were packaged invited us to nestle, nurse, and nurture. Barbie's curvaceous, big-busted, almost fully female body, on the other hand, summons not the maternal but the sexual, not the nurturant mother but the sensuous woman. As Mel McCombie has argued, rather than rehearsing parenting, as a baby doll does, Barbie's adult body encourages children to dress and redress a fashion doll that yields lessons about sexuality, consumption, and teenage life (3). Put another way, we might say that Barbie is literally and figuratively a titillating toy.

Bodacious as they may be, however, Barbie's firm plastic breasts have no nipples—nothing that might offend, nothing that might suggest her own pleasure. And if her protruding plastic mounds signify a simmering sensuality, what are we to make of her missing genitalia? McCombie suggests that Barbie's genital ambiguity can be read as an "homage to 'good taste'" and as a "reflection of the regnant mores for teenage girls—to be both sexy and adult yet remain virginal" (4). I agree that her body invites such readings, but it also seems to me that there is nothing ambiguous about Barbie's crotch. It's missing in inaction. While male dolls like Ken and Jamal have bumps "down there" and in some instances simulated underwear etched into the plastic, most Barbies come neither with drawers nor with even a hint of anything that needs covering, even as "it" is already covered or erased. As an icon of idealized femininity, then, Barbie is locked into a never-never land in which she must be always already sexual without the possibility of sex. Conspicuously sensual on top but definitively nonsexual below, her plastic body indeed has inscribed within it the very contradictory, whore/madonna messages with which patriarchy taunts and even traumatizes young women in particular.

This kind of speculation about Barbie's breasts has led the doll's creator, Ruth Handler, to chide adults for their nasty minds. "In my opinion people make too much of breasts," Handler has complained. "They are just part of the body" (qtd. in BillyBoy 26). Mrs. Handler has a point (or maybe two). I feel more than just a little ridiculous myself as I sit here contemplating the body parts and sex life of a piece of plastic. What is fascinating, however, what I think is worth studying, what both invites and resists theorizing, is not the lump of molded plastic that is Barbie, but the imaginary life that is not—that is *our* invention. Barbie as a cultural artifact may be able to tell us more about ourselves and our society—more about society's attitudes toward *its* women—than anything we might say about the doll her- or, rather, *itself*.

In the nineteenth century, Alexis de Tocqueville and others argued that you could judge the character, quality, and degree of advancement of a civilization by the status and treatment of its women. What is the status of women in soon to be twenty-first-century America, and can Barbie serve as a barometer for measuring that status? Barbie, it seems to me, is a key player in the process of socialization—of engendering and racialization—that begins in infancy and is furthered by almost everything about our society, including the books children read, the toys they play with, and the cartoons they watch on television.

While changing channels one Saturday morning, I happened upon a cartoon, just a glimpse of which impelled me to watch on. At the point that I tuned in, a big, gray, menacingly male bulldog was barking furiously at a pretty, petite, light-colored cat, who simply batted her long lashes, meowed coquettishly, and rubbed her tiny feline body against his huge canine leg in response. The more the dog barked and growled, the softer the cat meowed, using her slinky feline body and her feminine wiles to win the dog over. Her strategy worked; before my eyes—and, I imagine, the eyes of millions of children, the ferocious beast was transformed into a lovesick puppy dog, who followed the cat everywhere, repeatedly saving her from all manner of evil and danger. Time and time again, the bulldog rescued the helpless, accident-prone pussy from falling girders, on-coming traffic, and other hazards to which she, in her innocent frailty, was entirely oblivious. By the end, the once ferocious bulldog was completely domesticated, as his no longer menacing body became a kind of bed for the cat to nestle in.

There are, of course, a number of ways to read the gender and racial politics of this cartoon. I suppose that the same thought process that theorizes Barbie as a feminist heroine for whom men are mere accessories might claim the kitty cat, too, as a kind of feminist feline, who uses her feminine wiles to get her way. What resonates for me in the cartoon, however, are its beauty and the beast, light/dark, good/evil, female/male, race and gender codes: light, bright, cat-like femininity tames menacing black male bestiality. Make no mistake, however; it is not wit that wins out over barbarism but a mindless, can't-take-care-of-herself femininity.

Interestingly enough, these are the kinds of messages of which fairy tales and children's stories are often made. White knights rescue fair damsels in distress from dark, forbidding evils of one kind or another. As Darlene and Derek Hopson argue: "Some of the most blatant and simplistic representations of white is good and black is evil are found in children's literature," where evil black witches and good white fairies—heroes in white and villains in black—abound (121).

What Barbie dolls, cartoons like the one outlined above, and even the seemingly innocent fairy tales we read to our children seem to me to have in common are the mythologies of race and gender that are encoded in them. Jacqueline Urla and Alan Swedlund maintain that Barbie's body type constructs the bodies of other women as deviant and perpetuates an impossible standard of beauty. Attempting to live up to the Barbie ideal, others argue, fosters eating and shopping disorders in teenage girls—nightmares instead of dreams. BillyBoy, one of Barbie's most ardent supporters, defends his heroine against such charges by insisting that there is nothing abnormal about the proportions of Barbie's body. Rather, he asserts, "she has the ideal that Western culture has insisted upon since the 1920s: long legs, long arms, small waist, high round bosom, and long neck" (22). The irony is that BillyBoy may be right. "Unrealistic" or not, Barbie's weight and measurements (which if proportionate to those of a woman 5′6″ tall would be something like 110 pounds and a top-heavy 39-18-33) are not much different from those of the beauty queens to whom Bert Parks used to sing "Here she is, Miss America. Here she is, our ideal."[6] If Barbie is a monster, she is our monster, our ideal.

"But is Barbie bad?" Someone asked me the other day if a black doll that looks like a white doll isn't better than no black doll at all. I must admit that I have no ready answer for this and a number of other questions posed by my own critique. Although, as I acknowledged in the beginning, the dolls I played with as a child were white, I still remember the first time I saw a black doll. To me, she was the most beautiful thing I had ever seen; I wanted her desperately, and I was never again satisfied with white Betsy Wetsy and blonde, blue-eyed Patty Play Pal. She was something else, something *Other*, like me, and that, I imagine, was the source of her charm and my desire.

If I did not consciously note my own absence in the toys I played with, that absence, I suspect, had a profound effect on me nevertheless. We have only to read Toni Morrison's chilling tale

The Bluest Eye to see the effect of the white beauty myth on the black child. And while they were by no means as dire for me as for Morrison's character Pecola Breedlove, I was not exempt from the consequences of growing up black in a white world that barely acknowledged my existence. I grew up believing I was ugly: my kinky hair, my big hips, the gap between my teeth. I have spent half my life smiling with my hand over my mouth to hide that gap, a habit I only began to get over in graduate school when a couple of Nigerian men told me that in their culture, where my body type is prized much more than Barbie's, such gaps are a sign of great beauty. I wonder what it would have meant for me as a child to see a black doll—or any doll—with big hips and a gap between her two front teeth.

Today, for $24.99, Mattel reaches halfway around the world and gives little girls—black like me—Nigerian Barbies to play with. Through the wonders of plastic, dyes, and mass production, the company brings into the homes of African American children a Nigeria that I as a young child did not even know existed. The problem is that Mattel's Nigeria does not exist either. The would-be ethnic dolls of the world Mattel sells, like their "traditional, blond, blue-eyed" all-American girl prototype, have no gaps, no big ears, no chubby thighs or other "imperfections." For a modest price I can dream myself into Barbie's perfect world, so long as I dream myself in her image. It may be a small world, a whole new world, but there is still no place for me as *me* in it.

This, then, is my final doll story. Groucho Marx said that he wouldn't want to belong to a club that would have him as a member. In that same vein, I am not so sure that most of us would want to buy a doll that "looked like us." Indeed, efforts to produce and market such truer-to-life dolls have not met with commercial success. Cultural critics like me can throw theoretical stones at her all we want, but part of Barbie's infinite appeal is her very perfection, the extent to which she is both product and purveyor of the dominant white Western ideal of beauty.

And what of black beauty? If Colored Francie failed thirty years ago in part because of her Caucasian features, what are we to make of the current popularity and commercial success of Black Barbie and Shani, straight hair and all? Have we progressed to a point where "difference" makes no difference? Or have we regressed to such a degree that "difference" is only conceivable as similarity—as a mediated text that no matter what its dye job ultimately must be readable as white. Listen to our language: we "*tolerate* difference"; we practice "racial tolerance." Through the compound fractures of interpellation and universalization, the Other is reproduced not in her own image but in ours. If we have gotten away from "Us" and "Them," it may be only because Them R Us.

Is Barbie bad? Barbie is just a piece of plastic, but what she says about the economic base of our society—what she suggests about gender and race in our world—ain't good.

I am particularly pleased to be publishing this essay in **differences**, *since its genesis was at a roundtable discussion on multiculturalism and postmodernism, sponsored by the Pembroke Center for Teaching and Research on Women at Brown University, in March of 1993. I wish to thank the many friends and colleagues who have encouraged this project, especially Indira Karamcheti and her four-year-old daughter Gita, who introduced me to the miniature Barbies that come with McDonald's "Happy Meals," and Erness Brody, who, with her daughter Jennifer Brody, is a veteran collector of vintage dolls. I owe a special debt to fellow "Barbiologists" M. G. Lord, Mel McCombie, Jacqueline Urla, and Eric Swedlund, who have so generously shared their research, and to Darlene Powell Hopson for talking with me about her work with Mattel. I wish to acknowledge as well the work of Erica Rand, an art historian at Bates College, who is also working on Barbie.*

ENDNOTES

1. Mattel introduced the Shani doll—a black, Barbie-like doll—in 1991, which also may have contributed to the rise in sales, particularly since the company engaged the services of a PR firm that specializes in targeting ethnic audiences.

2. Of course, the notion of "dreaming in one's own image" is always problematic since dreams, by definition, engage something other than the "real."

3. Olmec Toys, a black-owned company headed by an African American woman named Yla Eason, markets a line of black and Latina Barbie-like dolls called the Imani Collection. Billed on their boxes as "African American Princess" and "Latin American Fantasy," these dolls are also presented as having been designed with the self images of black children in mind. "We've got one thing in mind with all our products," the blurbs on the lmani boxes read: "let's build self-esteem. Our

children gain a sense of self importance through toys. So we make them look like them." Given their obvious resemblance to Barbie dolls—their long, straight hair and pencil-thin plastic bodies—Imani dolls look no more "like them," like "real" black children, than their prototype. Eason, who we are told was devastated by her son's announcement that he couldn't be a super-hero because he wasn't white, may indeed want to give black children toys to play with that 'look like them.' Yet, in order to compete in a market long dominated by Mattel and Hasbro, her company, it seems, has little choice but to conform to the Barbie mold.

4. After many calls to the Jamaican Embassy in Washington, D.C. and to various cultural organizations in Jamaica, I have determined that Jamaican Barbie's costume—a floor-length granny-style dress with apron and headrag—bears some resemblance to what is considered the island's traditional folk costume. I am still left wondering about the decision-making process, however: why the doll representing Jamaica is figured as a maid, while the doll representing Great Britain, for example, is presented as a lady—a blond, blue-eyed Barbie doll dressed in a fancy riding habit with boots and hat.

5. See among others Morris Rosenburg's books *Conceiving the Self* (1979) and *Society and the Adolescent Self-Image* (1980) and William E. Cross's *Shades of Black: Diversity in African American Identity* (1991), all of which challenge the Clarks' findings. Cross argues, for example, that the Clarks confounded or conflated two different issues: attitude toward race in general and attitude toward the self in particular. How one feels about race is not necessarily an index of one's self-esteem.

6. In response to criticism from feminists in particular, the Miss America Pageant has attempted to transform itself from a beauty contest to a talent competition, whose real aim is to give college scholarships to smart, talented women (who just happen to look good in bathing suits and evening gowns). As part of its effort to appear more concerned with a woman's IQ than with her bra size, the pageant did away with its long-standing practice of broadcasting the chest, waist, and hip measurements, as well as the height and weight, of each contestant.

WORKS CITED

Berkwitz, David N. "Finally, Barbie Doll Ads Go Ethnic." *Newsweek*, Aug. 13, 1990, 48.

BillyBoy. *Barbie: Her Life and Times*. New York: Crown, 1987.

Cross, William E., Jr. *Shades of Black: Diversity in African American Identity*. Philadelphia: Temple UP, 1991.

Delany, Sarah, and Delany, A. Elizabeth. *Having Our Say: The Delany Sisters' First 100 Years*. New York: Kodansha, 1993.

Dembner, Alice. "Thirty-five and Still a Doll." *Boston Globe*, March 9, 1994: 1+.

Jones, Lisa. "A Doll Is Born." *Village Voice*, March 26, 1991: 36.

Kantrowitz, Barbara. "Hot Date: Barbie and G.I. Joe." *Newsweek*, February 20, 1989: 59–60.

Hopson, Darlene Powell and Derek S.*Different and Wonderful: Raising Black Children in a Race-Conscious Society*. New York: Simon, 1990.

Larcen, Donna. "Barbie Bond Doesn't Diminish with Age." *Hartford Currant*, Aug. 17, 1993: A6–7.

Lord, M. G. *Forever Barbie: The Unauthorized Biography of a Real Doll*. New York: Morrow, 1994.

McCombie, Mel. "Barbie: Toys Are Us." Unpublished essay.

Morrison, Toni. *The Bluest Eye*. New York: Washington Square, 1970.

Rieff, David. "Multiculturalism's Silent Partner." *Harper's* Aug. 1993: 62–72.

Roberts, Cynthia. *Barbie: Thirty Years of America's Doll*. Chicago: Contemporary, 1989.

Rosenberg, Morris. *Conceiving the Self*. New York: Basic, 1979.

_____. *Society and the Adolescent Self-Image*. Middletown: Wesleyan UP, 1989.

Sanchez-Eppler, Karen. *Touching Liberty: Abolition, Feminism, and the Politics of the Body*. Berkeley: U. of California P., 1993.

Stewart, Julia. *African Names*. New York: Carol, 1993.

Urla, Jacqueline and Alan Swedlund. "The Anthropometry of Barbie: Unsettling Ideals of the Feminine in Popular Culture." *Deviant Bodies*. Ed. Jennifer Terry and Jacqueline Urla. Bloomington: Indiana UP, forthcoming.

QUESTIONS

1. Discuss duCille's unanswered question about whether a Black Barbie is better than no Black doll at all. Where else in popular culture might we direct this question?
2. What does Barbie's (and Shani's, etc.) bodily construction say to the young girls who play with her? Find examples in the article that demonstrate the effect of imagery on young girls.
3. How are the constructions (costumes, boxing, shapes) of multicultural Barbies and their more expensive market value examples of the female body's being a site for politics?

AGE, RACE, CLASS AND SEX: WOMEN REDEFINING DIFFERENCE (1984)

Audre Lorde

Co-founder of Kitchen Table: Women of Color Press *with Barbara Smith, Audre Lorde is a powerful voice in our history. A poet, activist, fiction writer, and essayist, Lorde died in 1993 after a struggle with breast cancer. Here, in her challenge of what she defines as the mythical norm, Lorde asks us to acknowledge difference both within and across categories of age, race, class, and sex. Such an acknowledgment is crucial, Lorde suggests, to understanding the significance of differences in our lives. Lorde reminds us that while building upon commonalities to bridge differences is important, we must not forget the myriad ways those same differences create the unique character and circumstances of women's lives.*

Much of western European history conditions us to see human differences in simplistic opposition to each other: dominant/subordinate, good/bad, up/down, superior/inferior.[1,2] In a society where the good is defined in terms of profit rather than in terms of human need, there must always be some group of people who, through systematized oppression, can be made to feel surplus, to occupy the place of the dehumanized inferior. Within this society, that group is made up of Black and Third World people, working-class people, older people and women.

As a 49-year-old Black lesbian feminist socialist mother of two, including a boy, and a member of an inter-racial couple, I usually find myself a part of some group defined as other, deviant, inferior or just plain wrong. Traditionally, in American society, it is the members of oppressed, objectified groups who are expected to stretch out and bridge the gap between the actualities of our lives and the consciousness of our oppressor. For in order to survive, those of us for whom oppression is as American as apple pie have always had to be watchers, to become familiar with the language and manners of the oppressor, even sometimes adopting them for some illusion of protection. Whenever the need for some pretense of communication arises, those who profit from our oppression call upon us to share our knowledge with them. In other words, it is the responsibility of the oppressed to teach the oppressors their mistakes. I am responsible for educating teachers who dismiss my children's culture in school. Black and Third World people are expected to educate white people as to our humanity. Women are expected to educate men. Lesbians and gay men are expected to educate the heterosexual world. The oppressors maintain their position and evade responsibility for their own actions. There is a constant drain of energy which might be better used in redefining ourselves and devastating realistic scenarios for altering the present and constructing the future.

Institutionalized rejection of difference is an absolute necessity in a profit economy which needs outsiders as surplus people. As members of such an economy, we have *all* been programmed to respond to the human differences between us with fear and loathing and to handle that difference in one of three ways: ignore it, and if that is not possible, copy it if we think it is dominant, or destroy it if we think it is subordinate. But we have no patterns for relating across our human differences as equals. As a result, those differences have been misnamed and misused in the service of separation and confusion.

Certainly there are very real differences between us of race, age, and sex. But it is not those differences between us that are separating us. It is rather our refusal to recognize those differences, and to examine the distortions which result from our misnaming them and their effects upon human behavior and expectation.

Racism, the belief in the inherent superiority of one race over all others and thereby the right to dominance. Sexism, the belief in the inherent superiority of one sex over the other and thereby the right to dominance. Ageism. Heterosexism. Elitism. Classism.

It is a lifetime pursuit for each one of us to extract these distortions from our living at the same time as we recognize, reclaim and define those differences upon which they are imposed. For we have all been raised in a society where those distortions were endemic within our living. Too often, we pour the energy needed for recognizing and exploring difference into pretending those differences are insurmountable barriers, or that they do not exist at all. This results in a voluntary isolation, or false and treacherous connections. Either way, we do not develop tools for using human difference as a springboard for creative change within our lives. We speak not of human difference, but of human deviance.

Somewhere, on the edge of consciousness, there is what I call a *mythical norm,* which each one of us within our hearts knows 'that is not me.' In America, this norm is usually defined as white, thin, male, young, heterosexual, Christian and financially secure. It is with this mythical norm that the trappings of power reside within this society. Those of us who stand outside that power often identify one way in which we are different, and we assume that to be the primary cause of all oppression, forgetting other distortions around difference, some of which we ourselves may be practicing. By and large within the woman's movement today, white women focus upon their oppression as women and ignore differences of race, sexual preference, class and age. There is a pretense to a homogeneity of experience covered by the word *sisterhood* that does not in fact exist.

Unacknowledged class differences rob women of each other's energy and creative insight. Recently a women's magazine collectively made the decision for one issue to print only prose, saying poetry was a less 'rigorous' or 'serious' art form. Yet even the form our creativity takes is often a class issue. Of all the art forms, poetry is the most economical. It is the one which is the most secret, which requires the least physical labor, and the least material, and the one which can be done between shifts, in the hospital pantry, on the subway, and on scraps of surplus paper. Over the last few years, writing a novel on tight finances, I came to appreciate the enormous differences in the material demands between poetry and prose. As we reclaim our literature, poetry has been the major voice of poor, working class and Coloured women. A room of one's own may be a necessity for writing prose, but so are reams of paper, a typewriter and plenty of time. The actual requirements to produce the visual arts also help determine, along class lines, whose art is whose. In this day of inflated prices for material, who are our sculptors, our painters, our photographers? When we speak of a broadly based women's culture, we need to be aware of the effect of class and economic differences on the supplies available for producing art.

As we move toward creating a society within which we can each flourish, ageism is another distortion of relationship which interferes with our vision. By ignoring the past, we are encouraged to repeat its mistakes. The 'generation gap' is an important social tool for any repressive society. If the younger members of a community view the older members as contemptible or suspect or excess, they will never be able to join hands and examine the living memories of the community, nor ask the all important question, 'Why?' This gives rise to a historical amnesia that keeps us working to invent the wheel every time we have to go to the store for bread.

We find ourselves having to repeat and relearn the same old lessons over and over that our mothers did because we do not pass on what we have learned, or because we are unable to listen. For instance, how many times has this all been said before? For another, who would have believed that once again our daughters are allowing their bodies to be hampered and purgatoried by girdles and high heels and hobble skirts?

Ignoring the differences of race between women and the implications of those differences presents the most serious threat to the mobilization of women's joint power.

As white women ignore their built-in privilege of whiteness and define *woman* in terms of their own experience alone, then women of Colour become 'other,' the outsider whose experience and tradition is too 'alien' to comprehend. An example of this is the signal absence of the experience of women of Colour as a resource for women's studies courses. The literature of women of

Colour is seldom included in women's literature courses and almost never in other literature courses, nor in women's studies as a whole. All too often, the excuse given is that the literatures of women of Colour can only be taught by Coloured women, or that they are too difficult to understand, or that classes cannot 'get into' them because they come out of experiences that are 'too different.' I have heard this argument presented by white women of otherwise quite clever intelligence, women who seem to have no trouble at all teaching, and reviewing work that comes out of the vastly different experiences of Shakespeare, Molière, Dostoyefsky and Aristophanes. Surely there must be some other explanation.

This is a very complex question, but I believe one of the reasons white women have such difficulty reading Black women's work is because of their reluctance to see Black women as women and different from themselves. To examine Black women's literature effectively requires that we be seen as whole people in our actual complexities—as individuals, as women, as human—rather than as one of the problematic but familiar stereotypes provided in this society in place of genuine images of Black women. And I believe this holds true for the literatures of other women of Colour who are not Black.

The literatures of all women of Colour recreate the textures of our lives, and many white women are heavily invested in ignoring the real differences. For as long as any difference between us means one of us must be inferior, then the recognition of any difference must be fraught with guilt. To allow women of Colour to step out of stereotypes is too guilt provoking, for it threatens the complacency of those women who view oppression only in terms of sex.

Refusing to recognize difference makes it impossible to see the different problems and pitfalls facing us as women.

Thus, in a patriarchal power system where white skin privilege is a major prop, the entrapments used to neutralize Black women and white women are not the same. For example, it is easy for black women to be used by the power structure against Black men, not because they are men, but because they are Black. Therefore, for Black women, it is necessary at all times to separate the needs of the oppressor from our own legitimate conflicts within our communities. This same problem does not exist for white women. Black women and men have shared racist oppression and still share it, although in different ways. Out of that shared oppression we have developed joint defenses and joint vulnerabilities to each other that are not duplicated in the white community, with the exception of the relationship between Jewish women and Jewish men.

On the other hand, white women face the pitfall of being seduced into joining the oppressor under the pretense of sharing power. This possibility does not exist in the same way for women of Colour. The tokenism that is sometimes extended to us is not an invitation to join power; our racial 'otherness' is a visible reality that makes that quite clear. For white women there is a wider range of pretended choices and rewards for identifying with patriarchal power and its tools.

Today, with the defeat of ERA, the tightening economy and increased conservatism, it is easier once again for white women to believe the dangerous fantasy that if you are good enough, pretty enough, sweet enough, quiet enough, teach the children to behave, hate the right people, marry the right men, then you will be allowed to co-exist with patriarchy in relative peace, at least until a man needs your job or the neighborhood rapist happens along. And true, unless one lives and loves in the trenches it is difficult to remember that the war against dehumanization is ceaseless.

But Black women and our children know the fabric of our lives is stitched with violence and with hatred, that there is no rest. We do not deal with it only on the picket lines, or in the dark midnight alleys, or in the places where we dare to verbalize our resistance. For us, increasingly, violence weaves through the daily tissues of our living—in the supermarket, in the classroom, in the elevator, in the clinic and the schoolyard, from the plumber, the baker, the sales woman, the bus driver, the bank teller, the waitress who does not serve us.

Some problems we share as women, some we do not. You fear your children will grow up to join the patriarchy and testify against you, we fear our children will be dragged from a car and shot down in the street, and you will turn your backs upon the reasons they are dying.

The threat of difference has been no less blinding to people of Colour. Those of us who are Black must see that the reality of our lives and our struggle does not make us immune to the errors of ignoring and misnaming difference. Within Black communities racism is a living reality, differences among us often seem dangerous and suspect. The need for unity is often misnamed as a need for homogeneity, and the Black feminist vision mistaken for betrayal of our common interests as a people. Because of the continuous battle against racial erasure that Black women and Black men share, some Black women still refuse to recognize that we are also oppressed as women, and that sexual hostility against Black women is practiced not only by the white racist society, but implemented within our Black communities as well. It is a disease striking the heart of Black nationhood, and silence will not make it disappear. Exacerbated by racism and the pressures of powerlessness, violence against Black women and children often becomes a standard within our communities, one by which manliness can be measured. But these women-hating acts are rarely discussed as crimes against Black women.

As a group, women of Colour are the lowest-paid wage earners in America. We are primary targets of abortion and sterilization abuse, here and abroad. In certain parts of Africa, small girls are still being sewed shut between their legs to keep them docile and for men's pleasure. This is known as female circumcision, and it is not a cultural affair as the late Jomo Kenyatta insisted, it is a crime against Black women.

Black women's literature is full of the pain of frequent assault, not only by racist patriarchy, but also by Black men. Yet the necessity for and history of shared battle have made us, Black women, particularly vulnerable to the false accusation that anti-sexist is anti-Black. Meanwhile, womanhating as a recourse of the powerless is sapping strength from Black communities, and our very lives. Rape is on the increase, reported and unreported, and rape is not aggressive sexuality, it is sexualized aggression. As Kalamu ya Salaam, a Black male writer, points out. 'As long as male domination exists, rape will exist. Only women revolting and men made conscious of their responsibility to fight sexism can collectively stop rape.'[3]

Differences between ourselves as Black women are also being misnamed and used to separate us from one another. As a Black lesbian feminist comfortable with the many different ingredients of my identity, and a woman committed to racial and sexual freedom from oppression, I find I am constantly being encouraged to pluck out some one aspect of myself and present this as the meaningful whole, eclipsing or denying the other parts of self. But this is a destructive and fragmenting way to live. My fullest concentration of energy is available to me only when I integrate all the parts of who I am, openly, allowing power from particular sources of my living to flow back and forth freely through all my different selves, without the restrictions of externally imposed definition. Only then can I bring myself and my energies as a whole to the service of those struggles which I embrace as part of my living.

A fear of lesbians, or of being accused of being a lesbian, has led many Black women into testifying against themselves. It has led some of us into destructive alliances, and others into despair and isolation. In the white women's communities, heterosexism is sometimes a result of identifying with the white patriarchy, a rejection of that interdependence between women-identified women which allows the self to be, rather than to be used in the service of men. Sometimes it reflects a die-hard belief in the protective colouration of heterosexual relationships, sometimes a self-hate which all women have to fight against, taught us from birth.

Although elements of these attitudes exist for all women, there are particular resonances of heterosexism and homophobia among Black women. Despite the fact that woman-bonding has a long and honourable history in the African and African-American communities, and despite the knowledge and accomplishments of many strong and creative women-identified Black women in the political, social and cultural fields, heterosexual Black women often tend to ignore or discount the existence and work of Black lesbians. Part of this attitude has come from an understandable terror of Black male attack within the close confines of Black society, where the punishment for any female self-assertion is still to be accused of being a lesbian and therefore unworthy of the attention or support of the scarce Black male. But part of this need to misname and ignore Black lesbians comes from a very real fear that openly women-identified Black women who are no longer dependent upon men for their self-definition may well reorder our whole concept of social relationships.

Black women who once insisted that lesbianism was a white women's problem now insist that Black lesbians are a threat to Black nationhood, are consorting with the enemy, are basically un-Black. These accusations, coming from the very women to whom we look for deep and real understanding, have served to keep many Black lesbians in hiding, caught between the racism of white women and the homophobia of their sisters. Often, their work has been ignored, trivialized or misnamed, as with the work of Angelina Grimke, Alice Dunbar-Nelson, Lorraine Hansberry. Yet women-bonded women have always been some part of the power of Black communities, from our unmarried aunts to the amazons of Dahomey.

And it is certainly not Black lesbians who are assaulting women and raping children and grandmothers on the streets of our communities.

Across this country, as in Boston during the spring of 1979 following the unsolved murders of twelve Black women, Black lesbians are spearheading movements against violence against Black women.

What are the particular details within each of our lives that can be scrutinized and altered to help bring about change? How do we redefine difference for all women? It is not our differences which separate women, but our reluctance to recognize those differences and to deal effectively with the distortions which have resulted from the ignoring and misnaming of those differences.

As a tool of social control, women have been encouraged to recognize only one area of human difference as legitimate, those differences which exist between women and men. And we have learned to deal across those differences with the urgency of all oppressed subordinates. All of us have had to learn to live or work or co-exist with men, from our fathers on. We have recognized and negotiated these differences, even when this recognition only continued the old dominant/subordinate mode of human relationship, where the oppressed must recognize the masters' difference in order to survive.

But our future survival is predicated upon our ability to relate within equality. As women, we must root out internalized patterns of oppression within ourselves if we are to move beyond the most superficial aspects of social change. Now we must recognize differences among women who are our equals, neither inferior nor superior, and devise ways to use each other's difference to enrich our visions and our joint struggles.

The future of our earth may depend upon the ability of all women to identify and develop new definitions of power and new patterns of relating across difference. The old definitions have not served us, nor the earth that supports us. The old patterns, no matter how cleverly rearranged to imitate progress, still condemn us to cosmetically altered repetitions of the same old exchanges, the same old guilt, hatred, recrimination, lamentation and suspicion.

For we have, built into all of us, old blueprints of expectation and response, old structures of oppression, and these must be altered at the same time as we alter the living conditions which are a result of those structures. For the master's tools will never dismantle the master's house.

As Paulo Freire shows so well in *The Pedagogy of the Oppressed*,[4] the true focus of revolutionary change is never merely the oppressive situations which we seek to escape, but that piece of the oppressor which is planted deep within each of us, and which knows only the oppressors' tactics, the oppressors' relationships.

Change means growth, and growth can be painful. But we sharpen self-definition by exposing the self in work and struggle together with those whom we define as different from ourselves, although sharing the same goals. For Black and white, old and young, lesbian and heterosexual women alike, this can mean new paths to our survival.

We have chosen each other
and the edge of each others battles
the war is the same
if we lose
someday women's blood will congeal
upon a dead planet
if we win
there is no telling
we seek beyond history
for a new and more possible meeting.[5]

ENDNOTES

1. The editors and publishers gratefully acknowledge permission of Crossing Press © 1984 and Audre Lorde to reproduce 'Age, Race, Class, and Sex: Women Redefining Difference' from *Sister Outsider.*

2. This paper was delivered at the Copeland Colloquium, Amherst College, April 1980.

3. From 'Rape: A Radical Analysis, An African-American Perspective' by Kalamu.

4. Seabury Press: New York, 1970.

5. From 'Outlines', unpublished poem.

QUESTIONS

1. What does Lorde mean by a *mythical norm*? How does the norm work in our society?
2. How do oppositions like dominant/subordinate and good/bad obscure differences?
3. What does Lorde argue is the cultural response to difference in a profit economy? Why?

Socialization: Gender and Sexuality

All of us are socialized in various ways throughout our lifetimes, particularly if we define "socialization" as the process by which we learn the expectations for appropriate and acceptable behavior in a given setting. We are socialized in the workplace, in the classroom, on an athletic team, in a fraternity or sorority—in any environment in which there are identifiable standards for inclusion and expectations for the behavior and attitudes required for continued participation.

In this section, we will consider the dynamics of socialization as a powerful social force in the creation and maintenance of our understandings and demonstrations of both gender and sexuality. We will question the processes and purposes of the socialization of gender in the United States, and we will delve into the relationships between gender and sexuality. We will entertain the possibility that much of what we, as human beings in a social environment, consider to be "natural" may actually be manifestations of the dynamics of socialization.

The Smurfette Principle (1991)

Katha Pollitt

A prolific essayist and contributor of columns to a variety of U.S. print media, Katha Pollitt has written extensively on the subjects of motherhood and family. In this selection, Pollitt turns our attention to pre-school culture. She explores the impact of sexism in pre-school culture on the gender development of children in the United States. Pollitt summarizes her analysis in the concept of the Smurfette Principle, *a reference to the 1970s–80s children's cartoon,* The Smurfs. *Pollitt uses* the Smurfette Principle *to reveal the not-so-subtle evidence of sexism inherent in the process of socialization in the U.S.*

This Christmas, I finally caved in. I gave my 3-year-old daughter, Sophie, her very own cassette of "The Little Mermaid." Now, she, too, can sit transfixed by Ariel, the perky teenager with the curvy tail who trades her voice for a pair of shapely legs and a shot at marriage to a prince. ("On land it's much preferred for ladies not to say a word," sings the cynical sea witch, "and she who holds her tongue will get her man." Since she's the villain, we're not meant to notice that events prove her correct.)

Usually when parents give a child some item they find repellent, they plead helplessness before a juvenile filibuster. But "The

Little Mermaid" was my idea. Ariel may look a lot like Barbie, and her adventure may be limited to romance and over with the wedding bells, but unlike, say, Cinderella or Sleeping Beauty, she's active, brave and determined, the heroine of her own life. She even rescues the prince. And that makes her a rare fish, indeed, in the world of preschool culture.

Take a look at the kids' section of your local video store. You'll find that features starring boys, and usually aimed at them, account for 9 out of 10 offerings. Clicking the television dial one recent week—admittedly not an encyclopedic study—I came across not a single network cartoon or puppet show starring a female. (Nickelodeon, the children's cable channel, has one of each.) Except for the crudity of the animation and the general air of witlessness and hype, I might as well have been back in my own 1960's childhood, nibbling Frosted Flakes in front of Daffy Duck, Bugs Bunny, Porky Pig and the rest of the all-male Warner Brothers lineup.

Contemporary shows are either essentially all-male, like "Garfield," or are organized on what I call the Smurfette principle: a group of male buddies will be accented by a lone female, stereotypically defined. In the worst cartoons—the ones that blend seamlessly into the animated cereal commercials—the female is usually a little-sister type, a bunny in a pink dress and hair ribbons who tags along with the adventurous bears and badgers. But the Smurfette principle rules the more carefully made shows, too. Thus, Kanga, the only female in "Winnie-the-Pooh," is a mother. Piggy, of "Muppet Babies," is a pint-size version of Miss Piggy, the camp glamour queen of the muppet movies. April, of the wildly popular "Teenage Mutant Ninja Turtles," functions as a girl Friday to a quartet of male superheroes. The message is clear. Boys are the norm, girls the variation; boys are central, girls peripheral; boys are individuals, girls types. Boys define the group, its story and its code of values. Girls exist only in relation to boys.

Well, commercial television—what did I expect? The surprise is that public television, for all its superior intelligence, charm and commitment to worthy values, short-changes preschool girls, too. Mister Rogers lives in a neighborhood populated mostly by middle-aged men like himself. "Shining Time Station" features a cartoon in which the male characters are train engines and the female characters are passenger cars. And then there's "Sesame

Street." True, the human characters are neatly divided between the genders (and among the races, too, which is another rarity). The film clips, moreover, are just about the only place on television in which you regularly see girls having fun together, practicing double Dutch, having a sleep-over. But the Muppets are the real stars of "Sesame Street," and the important ones—the ones with real personalities, who sing on the musical videos, whom kids identify with and cherish in dozens of licensed products—are *all* male. I know one little girl who was so outraged and heartbroken when she realized that even Big Bird—her last hope—was a boy that she hasn't watched the show since.

Well, there's always the library. Some of the best children's books ever written have been about girls—Madeline, Frances the badger. It's even possible to find stories with funny, feminist messages, like "The Paperbag Princess." (She rescues the prince from a dragon, but he's so ungrateful that she decides not to marry him, after all.) But books about girls are a subset in a field that includes a much larger subset of books about boys (12 of the 14 storybooks singled out for praise in last year's Christmas roundup in *Newsweek,* for instance) and books in which the sex of the child is theoretically unimportant—in which case it usually "happens to be" male. Dr. Seuss's books are less about individual characters than about language and imaginative freedom—but, somehow or other, only boys get to go on beyond Zebra or see marvels on Mulberry Street. Frog and Toad, Lowly Worm, Lyle the Crocodile, all *could* have been female. But they're not.

Do kids pick up on the sexism in children's culture? You bet. Preschoolers are like medieval philosophers; the text—a book, a movie, a TV show—is more authoritative than the evidence of their own eyes. "Let's play weddings," says my little niece. We grownups roll our eyes, but face it, it's still the one scenario in which the girl is the central figure. "Women are *nurses,*" my friend Arina, a doctor, was informed by her then 4-year-old, Molly. Even my Sophie is beginning to notice the back-seat role played by girls in some of her favorite books. "Who's that?" she asks every time we re-read "The Cat in the Hat." It's Sally, the timid little sister of the resourceful boy narrator. She wants Sally to matter, I think, and since Sally is really just a name and a hair ribbon, we have to say her name again and again.

The sexism in preschool culture deforms both boys and girls. Little girls learn to split their consciousness, filtering their dreams and ambitions through boy characters while admiring the clothes of the princess. The more privileged and daring can dream of becoming exceptional women in a man's world—Smurfettes. The others are being taught to accept the more usual fate, which is to be a passenger car drawn through life by a masculine train engine. Boys, who are rarely confronted with stories in which males play only minor roles, learn a simpler lesson: girls just don't matter much.

How can it be that 25 years of feminist social change have made so little impression on preschool culture? Molly, now 6 and well aware that women can be doctors, has one theory: children's entertainment is mostly made by men. That's true, as it happens, and I'm sure it explains a lot. It's also true that, as a society, we don't seem to care much what goes on with kids, as long as they are reasonably quiet. Marshmallow cereal, junky toys, endless hours in front of the tube—a society that accepts all that is not going to get in a lather about a little gender stereotyping. It's easier to focus on the bright side. I had "Cinderella," Sophie has "The Little Mermaid"—that's progress, isn't it?

"We're working on it," Dulcy Singer, the executive producer of "Sesame Street," told me when I raised the sensitive question of those all-male Muppets. After all, the show has only been on the air for a quarter of a century; these things take time. The trouble is, our preschoolers don't have time. My funny, clever, bold, adventurous daughter is forming her gender ideas right now. I do what I can to counteract the messages she gets from her entertainment, and so does her father—Sophie watches very little television. But I can see we have our work cut out for us. It sure would help if the bunnies took off their hair ribbons, and if half of the monsters were fuzzy, blue—and female.

QUESTIONS

1. Explain *the Smurfette Principle*. Why does Pollitt give the concept the label she does?

2. What types of media does Pollitt argue reflect the Smurfette Principle? What evidence does she provide to substantiate her claims?

3. What does Pollitt argue are the effects of sexism in pre-school culture?

4. Based on Pollitt's discussion of *the Smurfette Principle,* can you formulate a working definition of "sexism"?

FROM Defining the Moral Boundaries of Eros: The Feminist Sexuality Debates (1992)

Steven Seidman

Steven Seidman, Associate Professor of Sociology at SUNY, Albany, is the author of Romantic Longings: Love in America, 1930–1980. *In this selection, Seidman explores the history of feminist debates concerning gender and sexuality. Considering arguments that women are emotionally tied to their sexuality and men are not, Seidman asks us if this stance could be limiting to both women and men. Using cultural research and more scientifically-oriented approaches, Seidman provides differing results about what men and women "want."*

Gender Difference and the Question of Sexual Ethics

The ideology of gender difference has frequently been used to legitimate gender inequality. The notion that women are different has been associated, at least within the middle class since the mid-nineteenth century, with their image as spiritual-moral beings whose proper sphere is the household and whose chief function is to care for men and their productions. Women have been defined in relation to domestic roles which have often left them subordinate to men who were assigned powerful public roles.

The women's movement in the postwar period initially challenged this ideology of difference. Second-wave feminists emphasized the similarities in physical and psychological abilities of men and women as integral to a defense of women's equality. Thus, feminists criticized lingering Victorian images of women as less carnal and less genitally responsive than men, images which reinforced a double standard that denied women their sexual autonomy. They drew upon the research of sexologists (notably Kinsey and Masters and Johnson) that asserted the similar capacities of men and women for sexual arousal and pleasure. By the late 1970s, however, the ideology of difference had reappeared among feminists. To be sure, feminists who stressed gender difference simultaneously insisted upon women's equality. Nevertheless, this feminist discourse of difference carried complicated moral resonances. For example, feminist representations linking women with emotional nurturance, moral guardianship or spiritual healing can easily be accommodated to concepts of women in support and servicing roles. Cultural feminism is perhaps the most prominent ideological expression of this rehabilitated discourse of gender difference among contemporary feminists. To some extent, however, its credibility rests upon a range of feminist-inspired research and theorizing which asserts gender difference. I wish to consider some of this research on gender difference and relate it to the question of feminist sexual ethic.

Feminist social research in the 1970s frequently underscored the persistence of divergent gender patterns. Studies of psychological development contrasted a "feminine personality" whose self is more continuous with others, or relational, to a "masculine personality" characterized by a more rigidly bounded, separate self. Drawing on object-relations psychoanalytic thinking, Nancy Chodorow, for example, concluded that "growing girls come to define and experience themselves as continuous with others; their experience of self contains more flexible or permeable ego boundaries. Boys come to define themselves as more separate and distinct, with a greater sense of rigid ego boundaries and differentiation. The basic feminine sense of self is connected to the world, the basic masculine sense of self is separate." Much research on early childhood development by feminists sought to show that the primary agents of socialization construct identities according to rather conventional concepts of gender difference. Bipolar gender typing was said to begin at birth, extend into adulthood, and encompass every aspect of the self, from the individual's name to his or her dress, toys, play, attitudes towards self, relationships, work, and love. Carol Gilligan's highly influential research featured the gendered character of moral reasoning. Reflecting women's more relational psychic structures and a socialization process that values women's caretaking roles, Gilligan described a so-called feminine morality that emphasizes empathy or being responsive to and taking responsibility for others. This feminine "ethic of care" was contrasted to a "masculine morality" that stresses abstract rights, principles of fairness, and formal procedures and rules. Finally, feminist social researchers claimed to have demonstrated how these basic gender differences are manifested in divergent intimate patterns. In general, they argued that women develop longer-lasting, more emotionally expressive and intimate types of relationships. Their friendships, for example, were said to revolve around intimate personal knowledge, shared feelings and problems, and sustained emotional support. Men's friendships instead cohered around a shared activity or interest; their relationships were said to be characteristically bounded or compartmentalized, so that the sharing of personal feelings and intimate knowledge is quite limited. "Generally," commented Lillian Rubin, "women's friendships with each other rest on shared intimacies, self-revelation, nurturance and emotional support. In contrast, men's relationships are marked by shared activities. Talk usually centers around work, sports, sharing expertise. . . . But, most of the time, their interactions are emotionally contained and controlled. . . ." Similarly, men and women were said to diverge in their approach to love, women adopting a more expressive style emphasizing emotional and verbal intimacy, personal disclosures, and sharing personal problems, while men were said to favor instrumental patterns in which love entails common activities, providing for and protecting a loved one, and practical, financial or technical-mechanical aid.

These psychosocial gender differences were said to extend into the domain of sex in complex ways. A major thesis advanced by feminist researchers was that women approach sex as part of their overall relational involvement. Sex is a way women emotionally invest themselves in a relationship, and presumably experienced by women as meaningless, if not degrading, except as a way to establish, extend, deepen, or confirm a relationship. Because sex has this relational meaning for women, it is said to lack a compulsive, performance-and genital-oriented character. Women's sexuality is described as person-centered, erotically diffuse, nurturing and monogamous.

To the extent that men experience themselves as rigidly bounded, separate individuals who must incessantly produce, achieve, succeed, and control as a condition of masculine self-affirmation, sex is said to become another arena for confirming this separateness and power. Emotional detachment during sex, or its instrumentalization, serves to maintain men's rigid ego boundaries and masculine identity, both of which are threatened by the feelings of dependency and vulnerability evoked during sexual intimacy. Hence, central to male sexuality is a disposition to neutralize the emotional aspects of sex and identify sex as a form of pleasure or play, a mode of control, or a performance through which masculinity is confirmed. Male sexuality is thought to be more compulsive, body and genital-centered, performance-oriented, and promiscuous.

These differences between female and male sexuality are said to be evident in behavior. Consider, for example, adolescent sexual behavior. Studies by feminist researchers of the period claim to show the persistence of traditional gender patterns. Teenage boys are still expected to be the active agents in the sexual exchange; they are expected to initiate sex, and push for sex earlier in relationships and as a condition of the relationship. Boys approach sex as genitally centered and construct it in terms of pleasure, adventure, and masculine performance criteria. They consider sex in various relational contexts, including casual encounters, to be legitimate. Girls are described in this research as less sexually active and motivated. Teenage girls continue to adopt the traditional role of controlling male desire and setting limits. They identify sex as a more diffuse activity and place a high value on hugging, kissing, and touching. Sex is said to be approached by teenage girls as a means to build or sustain a relationship, adolescent girls value sex only if it is coupled to romance and love. In short, feminist researchers believed they had established that gender differences characterize teenage sexual patterns.

This research, which very clearly dovetails with the cultural feminist construction of gender difference, is seriously flawed. Much of this research frames the discussion of female and male sexuality in such abstract and global antithetical terms that it ignores important differences among women and among men as well as important continuities between the two genders. This empirical literature is not innocent of ideological bias.

This feminist empirical construction of contrasting sexual values and orientations promotes stereotyped and reified notions of gender. This bias is at times quite explicit. For example, Angela Hamblin speaks of "our own authentic female sexuality/sensuality . . . which genuinely springs from and expresses our own female nature." Beatrice Faust explains gender difference in biological terms. "Women's need for intimacy in sexual relationships originates in the balance of hormones to which they were exposed in utero. Men's tolerance of impersonal sex derives from a different balance of the same hormones." Statements which generalize to all women at all times betray an essentialist bias. For example, Lillian Rubin remarks that "for a woman, there's no satisfactory sex without an emotional connection." In a more complex matter, arguments for difference that are framed within universal developmental schemes or make transhistorical claims about gender are equally prone to reification. For example, Chodorow's claim that the general condition of mothering by women produces different psychic structures in boys and girls which underpin gender and sexuality differences, *regardless* of sociocultural context and without considering variant configurations of mother-presence and father-absence, runs the risk of universalizing context-specific dynamics.

These feminist discourses reify gender differences in stereotyped ways. Concepts of female and male sexuality appear as uniform, contrasting natural facts. Male sexuality is caricatured by featuring its instrumental aspects. Statements like "for men, the erotic [rather than the emotional] aspect of any relationship remains forever the most compelling" or "[male sexuality] is centered on the genitals and it is closely related to aggression . . . All told, male sexuality is performance oriented," are indicative of this instrumentalist stereotype. These discourses distort by omitting key features of male sexuality and by flattening the concept of male sexuality into a one-dimensional mode.

A nation wide survey of male sexuality done in the late 1970s challenges this feminist stereotype. The men surveyed overwhelmingly favored marriage over an arrangement that allowed for more sexual variety. Half the respondents identified a monogamous marital relationship as their ideal; only 6.3 percent chose "many casual partners" as their preference. Moreover, these men reported that they married primarily for reasons of companionship, home life, children and love—not just for sex or domestic servicing. Their ideal sexual partner was a sexually active woman who initiated sex and was sexually active. Contrary to the image of male sexuality as compulsively genital, 59 percent of the respondents indicated that hugging, kissing, and touching without vaginal intercourse was enjoyable. The survey made it clear, moreover, that by a sexually active and responsive woman these men did not mean a woman who merely serviced their needs. Reciprocity was identified as essential to satisfactory sex. Almost all the men said that it was important for their female partner to have an orgasm, most men saying that they delayed their own until their partner had an orgasmic experience. More than 66 percent of these men report that their partner's satisfaction was the chief criterion for ending sex. Asked what made a good lover, most men answered that it was understanding a woman's sexual needs and making her feel loved. Although most men surveyed felt that love was not necessary for good sex, they insisted that sex was better in a loving relationship. Almost one-half of the respondents indicated that love was the most important thing in their lives. Numerous studies confirmed the point that, though men can and do detach sex from emotions, they also infuse sex with intensely romantic significance. Furthermore, many men of this period did not conceive of these different sexual meanings as contradictory. In other words, sex carried multiple meanings for many postwar men. It was used to affirm their masculinity and to confirm or dramatize their dominance, but also to give and receive pleasure and love. Finally, sex has been experienced by many men in postwar America as a way to explore and show feelings of dependency, vulnerability, and affection that cannot be easily displayed in other spheres. My point is that male sexuality in postwar America is much too complex, diverse, multifaceted, and changing to be reduced to an instrumentalist stereotype.

Women's sexuality is constructed by feminists of the time in an equally one-sided, even if more positive, way. For example,

Ethel Persons' claim that "penile penetration is not essential for women," or her assertion that "whether or not a woman is orgasmic has few implications for [her] personality organization" hardly reflects what women of the time reported in surveys or expressed in a range of public documents. Similarly, Lillian Rubin's flat statement that "for a woman there's no satisfactory sex without an emotional connection" is contradicted by much survey data which documents a trend among both men and women in the postwar period towards accepting hedonistic-expressive sexual constructions. For example, *The Hite Report*, which betrays a clear feminist bias, documents in women's comments the importance of the emotional context of sex. Yet, this survey also discloses a salient genital and orgasmic character to women's sexuality. Women overwhelmingly reported that they liked vaginal intercourse. An orgasmic experience is often described as among their greatest sexual pleasures, and its absence was said to be a great source of personal displeasure. The findings of *The Cosmo Report* further contradict the stereotype that women always imbue sex with deep emotional and romantic significance. Almost 75 percent of the women respondents indicated that good sex is possible without love. Almost 30 percent of the single women said they feel free to have sex outside an ongoing relationship. In fact, one-quarter of the *Cosmo* women acknowledged having between 11–25 sex partners over the course of their lives.

These findings strongly suggest that despite the image of women as person-oriented, monogamous, and romantic, there are many women who approve of and enjoy casual sex. Further evidence that women in postwar America are accepting of pleasure-oriented sex is given in the finding that 73.6 percent of those surveyed said they have participated in an orgy, sex club, or partner-swapping party. Both the *Cosmo Report* and the *Redbook Report* document that many women at times use porn, sex toys (vibrators, feathers, oils, dildos), dress and sex talk to enhance sexual pleasure. The surveys dating from the mid-1970s depict women with sexual values quite similar to men's, at least with respect to being sexually active, accepting a wide spectrum of sex acts and positions, demanding sensual gratification, and being willing to use various techniques and stimuli to enhance pleasure. In general, these women approach sex as having multiple meanings and legitimate social contexts.

The findings of these surveys is supported by research in two unexpected areas: teenage sex and extramarital sex. We have already alluded to research that points to the persistence of traditional sex patterns for adolescent girls. However, researchers are divided over postwar patterns. Some researchers highlight, for example, the decline of the "double standard" which permitted only boys to be sexually active, initiate and direct sex, demand gratification, and be sexually pluralistic. Along several key dimensions (e.g., acceptance of adolescent sex, right to sexual satisfaction, tolerance of sexual pluralism) girls appear to be men's sexual equals, even if some differences and inequalities persist. Furthermore, although girls continue to insist more than boys that sex be tied to romance or love, researchers point out that girls often use the word "love" in a way that lacks its traditional connotation of a long-term relationship involving extended commitments and responsibilities. Frequently, love indicates little more than feelings of attraction or affection with minimal relational involvement. As one researcher put it, "in the absence of notions like commitment and responsibility, horniness can look an awful lot like 'love.'" In other words, some girls have sex for reasons of physical attraction or pleasure but to avoid guilt and disapproval frame sex in the culturally approved language and symbolism of romantic love. This interpretation is further supported when we consider that though teenagers approve of sex as part of a relational commitment, teen romances are notoriously short-lived. In one study, about one-fifth of the boys and one-tenth of the girls said that their most recent sexual affair lasted a week or less; only 14 percent of all teen sexual relationships in this study endured for more than a year. Apparently, the appeal to a relationship as a culturally approved justification for sex is being invoked to allow girls to act on sexual desires for pleasure or adventure they cannot otherwise act upon while remaining a "good girl."

Extramarital sex is another domain in which women's sexuality has been considered to diverge sharply from men's. Yet, some research points towards a convergence in rates of extramarital sex. The studies by Kinsey, Hunt, and Pietropinto and Simenauer suggest a more or less steady rate of extramarital sex by men at about 50 percent. Kinsey reported the rate for women at less than half of that. Hunt found that although there was a dramatic rise in extramarital sex among younger women, the overall rate didn't change much since Kinsey. However, the *Redbook* study reported that by age 30 almost one-third of the wives tried it, by age 40 the figure was 40 percent. The *Cosmo Report* put the figure at 53.7 percent—virtually identical with men. Even more telling is that women, like men, are likely to have extramarital sex *regardless* of whether they are happy in their marriage. Women appear to be involved in extramarital sex for similar reasons as men: sexual freedom, variety, adventure, and the need to feel attractive and desirable. In her study of young adult feminist-oriented women, Lynn Atwater found that extramarital affairs were not traditional romantic involvements; often they were casual and short-termed. Women sought erotic fulfillment, but also an emotionally satisfying relationship where they insisted on being treated as equal partners. Atwater reports that these women typically enjoyed these affairs and benefited by heightened feelings of autonomy. She emphasizes the extent to which these women departed from traditional romantic patterns: "There was virtually no evidence of the traditional model of female sexuality in the descriptions women gave of their extramarital sexual activity. Rather, women demonstrated an evolving script of female sexual expression with a common theme of female-centered sexuality, of enjoyment for oneself, of not living vicariously through one's partner. Women emphasized the gratification that could be obtained through variety in partners. This variety was defined by relations with younger partners (for both physical and expressive reasons), sexual involvement based primarily on erotic attraction to the male body, and, especially, an emphasis on particular sexual activities like cunnilingus, extensive body contact, and kissing." This research suggests, once again, that at least some women conceive of sexual autonomy in terms of expanding erotic options, styles, and relational possibilities in ways typically associated with men.

I do not wish to deny that there are differences in the way contemporary men and women approach sex. Rather, I want to underscore the point that the image of female and male sexuality as contrasting types ignores meaningful continuities between men and women and heterogeneity among them. Stereotyping female and male sexuality in rigid antithetical ways may be an expression of the pessimistic mood of many feminists in the face of what they perceived as an antifeminist backlash. A discourse of gender difference that celebrates the uniqueness of women's sexuality may enhance feminist pride and help to mobilize women to build woman-centered spaces. This discourse will, however, create tensions within the women's movement, because a celebration of women's unique sexuality may stigmatize those women whose sexual longings deviate from that norm. As we have seen, many women do not experience their sexuality as person-centered, diffusely erotic, or necessarily imbued with nurturing, romantic longings. For these women the ideology of gender difference may function to censor or devalue their desire. Moreover, as a flat, one-dimensional concept of female sexuality is elaborated into a feminist sexual ethic, as in the case of cultural feminism, many women will react against it as too restrictive in light of social developments offering expanded possibilities for their sexual autonomy.

The ideology of gender difference, especially as it has been tied to a restrictive sexual ethic, appears somewhat at odds with social trends that promise more gender equality, at least with respect to intimate affairs. To the extent that more women are achieving social positions that enhance their autonomy and equality, they are able to assume *more* control over their sexuality. These women are *less* compelled to approach sex as a domain of danger. Unlike their parents and grandparents, many women reaching maturity in the 1980s are less controlled by their family, men, and by one-dimensional media representations. More women than in the recent past have expanded opportunities for economic independence, political empowerment and lifestyle choice. Women today have relatively easy access to reliable and safe birth control methods. They are socialized into a culture far more sex-positive and with far more heterogeneous sexual images and lifestyle choices than were their predecessors. The 1970s witnessed the appearance of women-centered constructions of female sexuality in women's magazines, in erotica or pornography produced by and for women, in sex manuals that promote a libertarian sexual ethic, in writing and art by women affiliated with the gay culture, and in the cultural productions of major female literary figures and artists. These representations have typically framed femininity as including erotic desire, assertive sexual styles, and intimate lifestyle choice. In these circumstances many women will, and indeed have, repudiated a sexual ideology that stipulates that sex is legitimate only as an expression of love, only as enacted in acts of personal tenderness, and only if confined to long-term relationships.

The persistence of ambivalence among feminists, as is illustrated by the social prominence of cultural feminism, relates, in part, to the fact that sex continues to carry unique dangers for women in a male-dominated society. For example, the risks of unwanted pregnancy and the likelihood of raising a child as a single mother with little or no support from the father makes sex potentially fateful for women in a way it is not for men. The susceptibility of women to sex-related violence, from rape to sexual abuse, gives to sex an edge of peril from which most men feel free. The persistence, even if it is less credible today, of a double standard that renders sexual assertiveness and eroticism self-affirming for men but potentially demeaning, even stigmatizing for women imbues sexual expression that deviates from conventional, romantic, monogamous sexuality with resonances of danger for women. To the extent that some women feel that their socioeconomic insecurity requires them to use their sexuality as a resource to influence men and achieve male social and economic support and protection, these women will perceive a more open, free-wheeling, eroticized sexual ethic as threatening their prospects for a secure, respectable social status. Not only will some women associate certain dangers with sexual expression that men will not, but to the extent that there are elements of a unique women's culture that revolves around the concept of the "good girl" and a culture of romance, some women may feel that only sex that is tied to romance, intimacy, and long-term commitment affirms their feminine self-identity. For these women only sex that sublimates carnal desire into a quest for romance and perhaps maternal longings is experienced as truly self-fulfilling. They may perceive the uncoupling of sex from romantic, intimate and perhaps maternal or domestic longings as both dangerous and alienating.

My point is that the division between sexual romantics and libertarians among feminists reflects, in part, the different ways women are socially positioned to experience the dangers and pleasures of sex. Given women's vulnerability to sexually-related violence, abuse, and harassment; given their continued socially subordinate status; and given aspects of a women's culture that continues to tie femininity to expectations of feminine virtue, some women will accentuate the dangers of sex that is carnal, erotic or casual. Many women will feel pressure to erect rigid controls and place severe restrictions on sex. A sexual romantic ethic will appeal to these women because it builds in protections for women in binding sex to commitment, caring, and respect.

Given social developments that empower more and more women both economically and politically, and given alternative hedonistic-expressive mainstream constructions of female sexuality, many women will feel as much constricted as protected by a romantic sexual ethic. Undoubtedly, the appearance of libertarian sexual ideologies with mass support among women reflects women's changing social condition. At a minimum, it is indicative of the opportunities women perceive today for enhanced sexual autonomy.

Sexual libertarians defend the notion that sex can have multiple meanings and be legitimate in diverse relational contexts. Given an interpersonal context of consent and mutual respect, sex can be legitimate not only as an expression of intimacy or love, but also as a form of play, pleasure, adventure, and communication in relationships as varied as one-time casual encounters and long-term romantic unions. Libertarians do not take issue with the importance of joining sex to romance, love, intimacy, and monogamy. Rather, they object to the position that locates sex only within a unidimensional, moral framework, and to the claim that sex has or should have only one legitimate meaning and proper relational context. Libertarians contend instead that a narrowly conceived feminist sexual orthodoxy, such as cultural feminism, reinforces a patriarchal order that has traditionally limited women's sexual autonomy.

In the early 1980s, a libertarian sexual ideology stepped forward as the major feminist alternative to this sexual romanticism. Its unequivocal defense of sexual tolerance stemming from its minimalist formal ethic appealed to feminists' growing awareness of social and sexual differences among women. Furthermore, the libertarian effort to theorize sex as an analytically autonomous domain irreducible to gender dynamics contributed to freeing sex from the feminist drift into a rigid sexual political orthodoxy. Libertarians force us to approach sex as an order dealing with bodies, desires, pleasures and sexual identities (e.g., gay, lesbian, S/M, leather) that are not collapsible into the terms of gender. Libertarians stand in the way of the hardening of sexual orthodoxies and rigid hierarchies. Yet, in their effort to free sex from a narrow feminist political morality, libertarians have underestimated the extent to which gender remains a pivotal category for analyzing sexual behavior. In particular, they have neglected the persistence of gender differences and the continued dangers of sex for women in a male-privileged society. Similarly, I have argued that a defense of sexual autonomy and pluralism is troublesome when it rests upon a formalistic ethic that cannot further morally discriminate. A sexual ethic that endorses the proliferation of sexualities without considering their qualitative features virtually relinquishes a critical role. Libertarian feminists show an unwillingness to discriminate between sexualities, or endorse restrictions other than on particular acts that are not consensual and reciprocal. This radical retreat from a substantive ethic stems, at least in part, from the fact that the principal proponents of libertarianism among feminists are identified with sexual minority groups, in particular a lesbian or S/M culture. These are groups that are oppressed precisely by a substantive sexual ethic.

By the mid-1980s, cultural feminism lost what ideological hegemony it had achieved through the 1970s. The conference held at Barnard College in 1982, which eventuated in the publication of *Pleasure and Danger*, was a major ideological assault upon cultural feminism. The *Heresies* "Sex Issue," *Powers of Desire* and a series of critiques of the antipornography movement culminating in the book *Women Against Censorship* put C-F on the defensive. Indeed, as we move into the 1990s, cultural feminism is giving way to a postmodern feminism that explodes the category of "women" into a multiplicity of desires, identities and lifestyles that render problematic a concept of sisterhood as anything more than a convenient political fiction.

Yet, women will continue to find C-F, or some variant of sexual romanticism, pertinent, because gender differences persist, in large part because male dominance persists. In this sociocultural and political setting, sex for women will continue to bear an edge of risk and danger. A discourse of sex that focuses on the restrictions and moral limits placed upon it will be perceived by many women to be self-enhancing and empowering. Beyond this continuing relevance to women, the sexual ideology of C-F has broader implications for sexual politics and ethics. Its insistence that a sexual ethic must include a concern with the qualitative dimensions of sex is essential to an analysis and critique of socioerotic behavior. Similarly, this emphasis provides an important standpoint for critical analysis of the contemporary history of sex and current emancipatory ideals. To be more precise, C-F provides a vantage point from which to criticize the identification of sexual liberation with the mere release and increase of sexual desire and behavior. It resists the expectation that sex will satisfy a range of non-sexual needs, and the temptation to burden sex with unrealistic expectations and meanings. Unfortunately, the cultural feminist critique of this narrow ideology of sexual liberation has, all too often, been joined to an equally one-dimensional sexual norm. It needlessly circumscribes the opportunities for sensual and psychic pleasures in sex. It suppresses the possibility that sex can become a basis for the affirmative construction of diverse individual and collective identities. In short, C-F fails to see the progressive openings in recent movements of sexual affirmation and pluralism.

ENDNOTE

Due to editorial error, citations hae been omitted in this selection.

QUESTIONS

1. Do you believe that women are "morally elevated" in their sexuality compared to men? Why/why not? How can labels such as "morally elevated" promote stereotypes about sexual desire?
2. Seidman cites *The Cosmo Report* and *The Hite Report,* and compares their results on women's sexual concerns. How important are such reports in promoting education and awareness about sexuality? Where else might we look for information about stereotypes and misinformation about women's sexual desires/needs?
3. Consider this piece from the perspective of lesbian sexuality. How does a focus on *hetero*sexuality pose ethical issues? Do you think it does? Why/why not?

Homophobia: A Weapon of Sexism (1988)

Suzanne Pharr

Activist and author Suzanne Pharr has given countless workshops and conference presentations on homophobia all over the country. In this selection, Pharr explores and discards popular explanations for the "causes" of homosexuality to conclude that sexuality is "morally neutral." Through her discussion of homophobia and compulsory heterosexuality, Pharr suggests the proposition that negative responses to homosexuality are more concerned with cultural expectations about gender *than about sexuality.*

Homophobia—the irrational fear and hatred of those who love and sexually desire those of the same sex. Though I intimately knew its meaning, the word homophobia was unknown to me until the late 1970s, and when I first heard it, I was struck by how difficult it is to say, what an ugly word it is, equally as ugly as its meaning. Like racism and anti-Semitism, it is a word that calls up images of loss of freedom, verbal and physical violence, death.

In my life I have experienced the effects of homophobia through rejection by friends, threats of loss of employment, and threats upon my life; and I have witnessed far worse things happening to other lesbian and gay people: loss of children, beatings, rape, death. Its power is great enough to keep ten to twenty percent of the population living lives of fear (if their sexual identity is hidden) or lives of danger (if their sexual identity is visible) or both. And its power is great enough to keep the remaining eighty to ninety percent of the population trapped in their own fears.

Long before I had a word to describe the behavior, I was engaged in a search to discover the source of its power, the power to damage and destroy lives. The most common explanations were that to love the same sex was either abnormal (sick) or immoral (sinful).

My exploration of the sickness theory led me to understand that homosexuality is simply a matter of sexual identity, which, along with heterosexual identity, is formed in ways that no one conclusively understands. The American Psychological Association has said that it is no more abnormal to be homosexual than to be left-handed. It is simply that a certain percentage of the population *is*. It is not healthier to be heterosexual or right-handed. What is unhealthy—and sometimes a source of stress and sickness so great it can lead to suicide—is homophobia, that societal disease that places such negative messages, condemnation, and violence on gay men and lesbians that we have to struggle throughout our lives for self-esteem.

The sin theory is a particularly curious one because it is expressed so often and with such hateful emotion both from the pulpit and from lay people who rely heavily upon the Bible for evidence. However, there is significant evidence that the approximately eight references to homosexuality in the Bible are frequently read incorrectly, according to Dr. Virginia Ramey Mollenkott in an essay in *Christianity and Crisis*:

> Much of the discrimination against homosexual persons is justified by a common misreading of the Bible. Many English translations of the Bible contain the word homosexual in extremely negative contexts. But the fact is that the word *homosexual* does not occur anywhere in the Bible. No extant text, no manuscript, neither Hebrew nor Greek, Syriac, nor Aramaic, contains the word. The terms *homosexual* and *heterosexual* were not developed in any language until the 1890's, when for the first time the awareness developed that there are people with a lifelong, constitutional orientation toward their own sex. Therefore the use of the word *homosexuality* by certain English Bible translators is an

> example of the extreme bias that endangers the human and civil rights of homosexual persons. (*pp. 383–4, Nov. 9, 1987*)

Dr. Mollenkott goes on to add that two words in I Corinthians 6:9 and one word in Timothy 1:10 have been used as evidence to damn homosexuals but that well into the 20th century the first of these was understood by everyone to mean masturbation, and the second was known to refer to male prostitutes who were available for hire by either women or men. There are six other Biblical references that are thought by some to refer to homosexuals but each of these is disputed by contemporary scholars. For instance, the sin in the Sodom and Gommorah passage (Genesis 19:1–10) is less about homosexuality than it is about inhospitality and gang rape. The law of hospitality was universally accepted and Lot was struggling to uphold it against what we assume are heterosexual townsmen threatening gang rape to the two male angels in Lot's home. While people dwell on this passage as a condemnation of homosexuality, they bypass what I believe is the central issue or, if you will, *sin*; Lot's offering his two virgin daughters up to the men to be used as they desired for gang rape. Here is a perfectly clear example of devaluing and dehumanizing and violently brutalizing women.

The eight Biblical references (and not a single one by Jesus) to alleged homosexuality are very small indeed when compared to the several hundred references (and many by Jesus) to money and the necessity for justly distributing wealth. Yet few people go on a rampage about the issue of a just economic system, using the Bible as a base.

Finally, I came to understand that homosexuality, heterosexuality, bisexuality are *morally neutral*. A particular sexual identity is not an indication of either good or evil. What is important is not the gender of the two people in relationship with each other but the content of that relationship. Does that relationship contain violence, control of one person by the other? Is the relationship a growthful place for the people involved? It is clear that we must hold all relationships, whether opposite sex or same sex, to these standards.

The first workshops that I conducted were an effort to address these two issues, and I assumed that if consciousness could be raised about the invalidity of these two issues then people would stop feeling homophobic and would understand homophobia as a civil rights issue and work against it. The workshops took a high moral road, invoking participants' compassion, understanding, and outrage at injustice.

The eight-hour workshops raised consciousness and increased participants' commitment to work against homophobia as one more oppression in a growing list of recognized oppressions, but I still felt something was missing. I felt there was still too much unaccounted for power in homophobia even after we looked at the sick and sinful theories, at how it feels to be a lesbian in a homophobic world, at why lesbians choose invisibility, at how lesbian existence threatens male dominance. All of the pieces seemed available but we couldn't sew them together into a quilt.

As I conducted more workshops over the years I noticed several important themes that led to the final piecing together:

1. Women began to recognize that economics was a central issue connecting various oppressions;
2. Battered women began talking about how they had been called lesbians by their batterers;
3. Both heterosexual and lesbian women said they valued the workshops because in them they were given the rare opportunity to talk about their own sexuality and also about sexism in general.

Around the same time (1985–86), the National Coalition Against Domestic Violence (NCADV) entered into a traumatic relationship with the U.S. Department of Justice (DOJ), requesting a large two-year grant to provide domestic violence training and information nationally. At the time the grant was to be announced, NCADV was attacked by conservative groups such as the Heritage Foundation as a "pro-lesbian, pro-feminist, anti-family" organization. In response to these attacks, the DOJ decided not to award a grant; instead they formulated a "cooperative agreement" that allowed them to monitor and approve all work, and they assured conservative organizations that the work would not be pro-lesbian and anti-family. The major issue between NCADV and the DOJ became whether NCADV would let an outside agency define and control its work, and finally, during never-ending concern from the DOJ about "radical" and "lesbian" issues, the agreement was terminated by NCADV at the end of the first year. Throughout that year, there were endless statements and innuendoes from the DOJ and some members of NCADV's membership about NCADV's lesbian leadership and its alleged concern for only lesbian issues. Many women were damaged by the crossfire, NCADV's work was stopped for a year, and the organization was split from within. It was lesbian baiting at its worst.

As one of NCADV's lesbian leadership during that onslaught of homophobic attacks, I was still giving homophobia workshops around the country, now able to give even more personal witness to the virulence of the hatred and fear of lesbians and gay men within both institutions and individuals. It was a time of pain and often anger for those of us committed to creating a world free of violence, and it was a time of deep distress for those of us under personal attack. However, my mother, like many mothers, had always said, "All things work for the good," and sure enough, it was out of the accumulation of these experiences that the pieces began coming together to make a quilt of our understanding.

On the day that I stopped reacting to attacks and gave my time instead to visioning, this simple germinal question came forth for the workshops: "What will the world be like without homophobia in it—for everyone, female and male, whatever sexual identity?" Simple though the question is, it was at first shocking because those of us who work in the anti-violence movement spend most of our time working with the damaging, negative results of violence and have little time to vision. It is sometimes difficult to create a vision of a world we have never experienced, but without such a vision, we cannot know clearly what we are working toward in our social change work. From this question, answer led to answer until a whole appeared of our collective making, from one workshop to another.

Here are some of the answers women have given:

- Kids won't be called tomboys or sissies; they'll just be who they are, able to do what they wish.

- People will be able to love anyone, no matter what sex; the issue will simply be whether or not she/he is a good human being, compatible, and loving.

- Affection will be opened up between women and men, women and women, men and men, and it won't be centered on sex; people won't fear being called names if they show affection to someone who isn't a mate or potential mate.

- If affection is opened up, then isolation will be broken down for all of us, especially for those who generally experience little physical affection, such as unmarried old people.
- Women will be able to work whatever jobs we want without being labeled masculine.
- There will be less violence if men do not feel they have to prove and assert their manhood. Their desire to dominate and control will not spill over from the personal to the level of national and international politics and the use of bigger and better weapons to control other countries.
- People will wear whatever clothes they wish, with the priority being comfort rather than the display of femininity or masculinity.
- There will be no gender roles.

It is at this point in the workshops—having imagined a world without homophobia—that the participants see the analysis begin to fall into place. Someone notes that all the things we have been talking about relate to sexual gender roles. It's rather like the beginning of a course in Sexism 101. The next question is "Imagine the world with no sex roles—sexual identity, which may be in flux, but no sexual gender roles." Further: imagine a world in which opportunity is not determined by gender or race. Just the imagining makes women alive with excitement because it is a vision of freedom, often just glimpsed but always known deep down as truth. Pure joy.

We talk about what it would be like to be born in a world in which there were no expectations or treatment based on gender but instead only the expectation that each child, no matter what race or sex, would be given as many options and possibilities as society could muster. Then we discuss what girls and boys would be like at puberty and beyond if sex role expectations didn't come crashing down on them with girls' achievement levels beginning to decline thereafter; what it would be for women to have the training and options for economic equity with men; what would happen to issues of power and control, and therefore violence, if there were real equality. To have no prescribed sex roles would open the possibility of equality. It is a discussion women find difficult to leave. Freedom calls.

Patriarchy—an enforced belief in male dominance and control—is the ideology and sexism the system that holds it in place. The catechism goes like this: Who do gender roles serve? Men and the women who seek power from them. Who suffers from gender roles? Women most completely and men in part. How are gender roles maintained? By the weapons of sexism: economics, violence, homophobia.

Why then don't we ardently pursue ways to eliminate gender roles and therefore sexism? It is my profound belief that all people have a spark in them that yearns for freedom, and the history of the world's atrocities—from the Nazi concentration camps to white dominance in South Africa to the battering of women—is the story of attempts to snuff out that spark. When that spark doesn't move forward to full flame, it is because the weapons designed to control and destroy have wrought such intense damage over time that the spark has been all but extinguished.

Sexism, that system by which women are kept subordinate to men, is kept in place by three powerful weapons designed to cause or threaten women with pain and loss. As stated before, the three are economics, violence, and homophobia. The stories of women battered by men, victims of sexism at its worst, show these three forces converging again and again. When battered women tell why they stayed with a batterer or why they returned to a batterer, over and over they say it was because they could not support themselves and their children financially, they had no skills for jobs, they could not get housing, transportation, medical care for their children. And how were they kept controlled? Through violence and threats of violence, both physical and verbal, so that they feared for their lives and the lives of their children and doubted their own abilities and self-worth. And why were they beaten? Because they were not good enough, were not "real women," were dykes, or because they stood up to him as no "real woman" would. And the male batterer, with societal backing, felt justified, often righteous, in his behavior—for his part in keeping women in their place.

Economics must be looked at first because many feminists consider it to be the root cause of sexism. Certainly the United Nations study released at the final conference of the International Decade on Women, held in Nairobi, Kenya, in 1985, supports that belief: of the world's population, women do 75% of the work, receive 10% of the pay and own 1% of the property. In the United States it is also supported by the opposition of the government to the idea of comparable worth and pay equity, as expressed by Ronald Reagan who referred to pay equity as "a joke." Obviously, it is considered a dangerous idea. Men profit not only from women's unpaid work in the home but from our underpaid work within horizontal female segregation such as clerical workers or upwardly mobile tokenism in the workplace where a few affirmative action promotions are expected to take care of all women's economic equality needs. Moreover, they profit from women's bodies through pornography, prostitution, and international female sexual slavery. And white men profit from both the labor of women and of men of color. Forced economic dependency puts women under male control and severely limits women's options for self-determination and self-sufficiency.

This truth is borne out by the fact that according to the National Commission on Working Women, on average, women of all races working year round earn only 64 cents to every one dollar a man makes. Also, the U.S. Census Bureau reports that only 9 percent of working women make over $25,000 a year. There is fierce opposition to women gaining employment in the nontraditional job market, that is, those jobs that traditionally employ less than 25 percent women. After a woman has gained one of these higher paying jobs, she is often faced with sexual harassment, lesbian baiting, and violence. It is clear that in the workplace there is an all-out effort to keep women in traditional roles so that the only jobs we are "qualified" for are the low-paid ones.

Actually, we have to look at economics not only as the root cause of sexism but also as the underlying, driving force that keeps all the oppressions in place. In the United States, our economic system is shaped like a pyramid, with a few people at the top, primarily white males, being supported by large numbers of unpaid or low-paid workers at the bottom. When we look at this pyramid, we begin to understand the major connection between sexism and racism because those groups at the bottom of the pyramid are women and people of color. We then begin to understand why there is such a fervent effort to keep those oppressive systems (racism and sexism and all the ways they are manifested) in place to maintain the unpaid and low-paid labor.

Susan DeMarco and Jim Hightower, writing for *Mother Jones* report that *Forbes* magazine indicated that "the 400 richest families in America last year had an average net worth of $550 million each. These and less than a million other families—roughly one percent of our population—are at the prosperous tip of our society. . . . In 1976, the wealthiest 1 percent of America's families owned 19.2 percent of the nation's total wealth. (This sum of wealth counts all of America's cash, real estate, stocks, bonds, factories, art, personal property, and anything else of financial value.) By 1983, those at this 1 percent of our economy owned 34.3 percent of our wealth. . . . *Today the top 1 percent of Americans possesses more net wealth than the bottom 90 percent.*" (My italics.) (*May, 1988, pp. 32–33*)

In order for this top-heavy system of economic inequity to maintain itself, the 90 percent on the bottom must keep supplying cheap labor. A very complex, intricate system of institutionalized oppressions is necessary to maintain the status quo so that the vast majority will not demand its fair share of wealth and resources and bring the system down. Every institution—schools, banks, churches, government, courts, media, etc., as well as individuals must be enlisted in the campaign to maintain such a system of gross inequity.

What would happen if women gained the earning opportunities and power that men have? What would happen if these opportunities were distributed equitably, no matter what sex one was, no matter what race one was born into, and no matter where one lived? What if educational and training opportunities were equal? Would women spend most of our youth preparing for marriage? Would marriage be based on economic survival for women? What would happen to issues of power and control? Would women stay with our batterers? If a woman had economic independence in a society where women had equal opportunities, would she still be thought of as owned by her father or husband?

Economics is the great controller in both sexism and racism. If a person can't acquire food, shelter, and clothing and provide them for children, then that person can be forced to do many things in order to survive. The major tactic, worldwide, is to provide unrecompensed or inadequately recompensed labor for the benefit of those who control wealth. Hence, we see women performing unpaid labor in the home or filling low-paid jobs, and we see people of color in the lowest-paid jobs available.

The method is complex: limit educational and training opportunities for women and for people of color and then withhold adequate paying jobs with the excuse that people of color and women are incapable of filling them. Blame the economic victim and keep the victim's self-esteem low through invisibility and distortion within the media and education. Allow a few people of color and women to succeed among the profit-makers so that blaming those who don't "make it" can be intensified. Encourage those few who succeed in gaining power now to turn against those who remain behind rather than to use their resources to make change for all. Maintain the myth of scarcity—that there are not enough jobs, resources, etc., to go around—among the middle class so that they will not unite with laborers, immigrants, and the unemployed. The method keeps in place a system of control and profit by a few and a constant source of cheap labor to maintain it.

If anyone steps out of line, take her/his job away. Let homelessness and hunger do their work. The economic weapon works. And we end up saying, "I would do this or that—be openly who I am, speak out against injustice, work for civil rights, join a labor union, go to a political march, etc.—if I didn't have this job. I can't afford to lose it." We stay in an abusive situation because we see no other way to survive.

In the battered women's movement abusive relationships are said to be about power and control and the way out of them is through looking at the ways power and control work in our lives, developing support, improving self-esteem, and achieving control over our decisions and lives. We have yet to apply these methods successfully to our economic lives. Though requiring massive change, the way there also lies open for equality and wholeness. But the effort will require at least as much individual courage and risk and group support as it does for a battered woman to leave her batterer, and that requirement is very large indeed. Yet battered women find the courage to leave their batterers every day. They walk right into the unknown. To break away from economic domination and control will require a movement made up of individuals who possess this courage and ability to take risks.

Violence is the second means of keeping women in line, in a narrowly defined place and role. First there is the physical violence of battering, rape, and incest. Often when battered women come to shelters and talk about their lives, they tell stories of being not only physically beaten but also raped and their children subjected to incest. Work in the women's anti-violence movement during almost two decades has provided significant evidence that each of these acts, including rape and incest, is an attempt to seek power over and control of another person. In each case, the victim is viewed as an object and is used to meet the abuser's needs. The violence is used to wreak punishment and to demand compliance or obedience.

Violence against women is directly related to the condition of women in a society that refuses us equal pay, equal access to resources, and equal status with males. From this condition comes men's confirmation of their sense of ownership of women, power over women, and assumed right to control women for their own means. Men physically and emotionally abuse women because they *can*, because they live in a world that gives them permission. Male violence is fed by their sense of their *right* to dominate and control, and their sense of superiority over a group of people who, because of gender, they consider inferior to them.

It is not just the violence but the threat of violence that controls our lives. Because the burden of responsibility has been placed so often on the potential victim, as women we have curtailed our freedom in order to protect ourselves from violence. Because of the threat of rapists, we stay on alert, being careful not to walk in isolated places, being careful where we park our cars, adding incredible security measures to our homes—massive locks, lights, alarms, if we can afford them—and we avoid places where we will appear vulnerable or unprotected while the abuser walks with freedom. Fear, often now so commonplace that it is unacknowledged, shapes our lives, reducing our freedom.

As Bernice Reagan of the musical group Sweet Honey in the Rock said at the 1982 National Coalition Against Domestic Violence conference, women seem to carry a genetic memory that women were once burned as witches when we stepped out of line. To this day, mothers pass on to their daughters word of the dangers they face and teach them the ways they must limit their lives in order to survive.

Part of the way sexism stays in place is the societal promise of survival, false and unfulfilled as it is, that women will not suffer violence if we attach ourselves to a man to protect us. A woman without a man is told she is vulnerable to external violence and, worse, that there is something wrong with her. When the male abuser calls a woman a lesbian, he is not so much labeling her a woman who loves women as he is warning her that by resisting him, she is choosing to be outside society's protection from male institutions and therefore from wide-ranging, unspecified, ever-present violence. When she seeks assistance from woman friends or a battered women's shelter, he recognizes the power in woman bonding and fears loss of her servitude and loyalty: the potential loss of his control. The concern is not affectional/sexual identity: the concern is disloyalty and the threat is violence.

The threat of violence against women who step out of line or who are disloyal is made all the more powerful by the fact that women do not have to do anything—they may be paragons of virtue and subservience—to receive violence against our lives: the violence still comes. It comes because of the woman-hating that exists throughout society. Chance plays a larger part than virtue in keeping women safe. Hence, with violence always a threat to us, women can never feel completely secure and confident. Our sense of safety is always fragile and tenuous.

Many women say that verbal violence causes more harm than physical violence because it damages self-esteem so deeply. Women have not wanted to hear battered women say that the verbal abuse was as hurtful as the physical abuse: to acknowledge that truth would be tantamount to acknowledging that *virtually every woman is a battered woman.* It is difficult to keep strong against accusations of being a bitch, stupid, inferior, etc., etc. It is especially difficult when these individual assaults are backed up by a society that shows women in textbooks, advertising, TV programs, movies, etc., as debased, silly, inferior, and sexually objectified, and a society that gives tacit approval to pornography. When we internalize these messages, we call the result "low self-esteem," a therapeutic individualized term. It seems to me we should use the more political expression: when we internalize these messages, we experience *internalized sexism,* and we experience it in common with all women living in a sexist world. The violence against us is supported by a society in which woman-hating is deeply imbedded.

In "Eyes on the Prize," a 1987 Public Television documentary about the Civil Rights Movement, an older white woman says about her youth in the South that it was difficult to be anything different from what was around her when there was no vision for another way to be. Our society presents images of women that say it is appropriate to commit violence against us. Violence is committed against women because we are seen as inferior in status and in worth. It has been the work of the women's movement to present a vision of another way to be.

Every time a woman gains the strength to resist and leave her abuser, we are given a model of the importance of stepping out of line, of moving toward freedom. And we all gain strength when she says to violence, "Never again!" Thousands of women in the last fifteen years have resisted their abusers to come to this country's 1100 battered women's shelters. There they have sat down with other women to share their stories, to discover that their stories again and again are the same, to develop an analysis that shows that violence is a statement about power and control, and to understand how sexism creates the climate for male violence. Those brave women are now a part of a movement that gives hope for another way to live in equality and peace.

Homophobia works effectively as a weapon of sexism because it is joined with a powerful arm, heterosexism. Heterosexism creates the climate for homophobia with its assumption that the world is and must be heterosexual and its display of power and privilege as the norm. Heterosexism is the systemic display of homophobia in the institutions of society. Heterosexism and homophobia work together to enforce compulsory heterosexuality and that bastion of patriarchal power, the nuclear family. The central focus of the right-wing attack against women's liberation is that women's equality, women's self-determination, women's control of our own bodies and lives will damage what they see as the crucial societal institution, the nuclear family. The attack has been led by fundamentalist ministers across the country. The two areas they have focused on most consistently are abortion and homosexuality, and their passion has led them to bomb women's clinics and to recommend deprogramming for homosexuals and establishing camps to quarantine people with AIDS. To resist marriage and/or heterosexuality is to risk severe punishment and loss.

It is not by chance that when children approach puberty and increased sexual awareness they begin to taunt each other by calling these names: "queer," "faggot," "pervert." It is at puberty that the full force of society's pressure to conform to heterosexuality and prepare for marriage is brought to bear. Children know what we have taught them, and we have given clear messages that those who deviate from standard expectations are to be made to get back in line. The best controlling tactic at puberty is to be treated as an outsider, to be ostracized at a time when it feels most vital to be accepted. Those who are different must be made to suffer loss. It is also at puberty that misogyny begins to be more apparent, and girls are pressured to conform to societal norms that do not permit them to realize their full potential. It is at this time that their academic achievements begin to decrease as they are coerced into compulsory heterosexuality and trained for dependency upon a man, that is, for economic survival.

There was a time when the two most condemning accusations against a woman meant to ostracize and disempower her were "whore" and "lesbian." The sexual revolution and changing attitudes about heterosexual behavior may have led to some lessening of the power of the word *whore,* though it still has strength as a threat to sexual property and prostitutes are stigmatized and abused. However, the word *lesbian* is still fully charged and carries with it the full threat of loss of power and privilege, the threat of being cut asunder, abandoned, and left outside society's protection.

To be a lesbian is to be *perceived* as someone who has stepped out of line, who has moved out of sexual/economic dependence on a male, who is woman-identified. A lesbian is perceived as someone who can live without a man, and who is therefore (however illogically) against men. A lesbian is perceived as being outside the acceptable, routinized order of things. She is seen as someone who has no societal institutions to protect her and who is not privileged to the protection of individual males. Many heterosexual women see her as someone who stands in contradiction to the sacrifices they have made to conform to compulsory heterosexuality. A lesbian is perceived as a threat to the nuclear family, to male dominance and control, to the very heart of sexism.

Gay men are perceived also as a threat to male dominance and control, and the homophobia expressed against them has the same roots in sexism as does homophobia against lesbians. Visible gay men are the objects of extreme hatred and fear by heterosexual men because their breaking ranks with male heterosexual solidarity is seen as a damaging rent in the very fabric of sexism. They are seen as betrayers, as traitors who must be punished and eliminated. In the beating and killing of gay men we see clear evidence of this hatred. When we see the fierce homophobia expressed toward gay men, we can begin to understand the ways sexism also affects males through imposing rigid, dehumanizing gender roles on them. The two circumstances in which it is legitimate for men to be openly physically affectionate with one another are in competitive sports and in the crisis of war. For many men, these two experiences are the highlights of their lives, and they think of them again and again with nostalgia. War and sports offer a cover of all-male safety and dominance to keep away the notion of affectionate openness being identified with homosexuality. When gay men break ranks with male roles through bonding and affection outside the arenas of war and sports, they are perceived as not being "real men," that is, as being identified with women, the weaker sex that must be dominated and that over the centuries has been the object of male hatred and abuse. Misogyny gets transferred to gay men with a vengeance and is increased by the fear that their sexual identity and behavior will bring down the entire system of male dominance and compulsory heterosexuality.

If lesbians are established as threats to the status quo, as outcasts who must be punished, homophobia can wield its power over all women through lesbian baiting. Lesbian baiting is an attempt to control women by labeling us as lesbians because our behavior is not acceptable, that is, when we are being independent, going our own way, living whole lives, fighting for our rights, demanding equal pay, saying no to violence, being self-assertive, bonding with and loving the company of women, assuming the right to our bodies, insisting upon our own authority, making changes that include us in society's decision-making; lesbian baiting occurs when women are called lesbians because we resist male dominance and control. And it has little or nothing to do with one's sexual identity.

To be named as lesbian threatens all women, not just lesbians, with great loss. And any woman who steps out of role risks being called a lesbian. To understand how this is a threat to all women, one must understand that any woman can be called a lesbian and there is no real way she can defend herself: there is no way to credential one's sexuality. ("The Children's Hour," a Lillian

Hellman play, makes this point when a student asserts two teachers are lesbians and they have no way to disprove it.) She may be married or divorced, have children, dress in the most feminine manner, have sex with men, be celibate—but there are lesbians who do all those things. *Lesbians look like all women and all women look like lesbians.* There is no guaranteed method of identification, and as we all know, sexual identity can be kept hidden. (The same is true for men. There is no way to prove their sexual identity, though many go to extremes to prove heterosexuality.) Also, women are not necessarily born lesbian. Some seem to be, but others become lesbians later in life after having lived heterosexual lives. Lesbian baiting of heterosexual women would not work if there were a definitive way to identify lesbians (or heterosexuals).

We have yet to understand clearly how sexual identity develops. And this is disturbing to some people, especially those who are determined to discover how lesbian and gay identity is formed so that they will know where to start in eliminating it. (Isn't it odd that there is so little concern about discovering the causes of heterosexuality?) There are many theories: genetic makeup, hormones, socialization, environment, etc. But there is no conclusive evidence that indicates that heterosexuality comes from one process and homosexuality from another.

We do know, however, that sexual identity can be in flux, and we know that sexual identity means more than just the gender of people one is attracted to and has sex with. To be a lesbian has as many ramifications as for a woman to be heterosexual. It is more than sex, more than just the bedroom issue many would like to make it: it is a woman-centered life with all the social interconnections that entails. Some lesbians are in long-term relationships, some in short-term ones, some date, some are celibate, some are married to men, some remain as separate as possible from men, some have children by men, some by alternative insemination, some seem "feminine" by societal standards, some "masculine," some are doctors, lawyers and ministers, some laborers, housewives and writers: what all share in common is a sexual/affectional identity that focuses on women in its attractions and social relationships.

If lesbians are simply women with particular sexual identity who look and act like all women, then the major difference in living out a lesbian sexual identity as opposed to a heterosexual identity is that as lesbians we live in a homophobic world that threatens and imposes damaging loss on us for being *who we are*, for choosing to live whole lives. Homophobic people often assert that homosexuals have the choice of not being homosexual; that is, we don't have to act out our sexual identity. In that case, I want to hear heterosexuals talk about their willingness not to act out their sexual identity, including not just sexual activity but heterosexual social interconnections and heterosexual privilege. It is a question of wholeness. It is very difficult for one to be denied the life of a sexual being, whether expressed in sex or in physical affection, and to feel complete, whole. For our loving relationships with humans feed the life of the spirit and enable us to overcome our basic isolation and to be interconnected with humankind.

If, then, any woman can be named a lesbian and be threatened with terrible losses, what is it she fears? Are these fears real? Being vulnerable to a homophobic world can lead to these losses:

- *Employment*. The loss of job leads us right back to the economic connection to sexism. This fear of job loss exists for almost every lesbian except perhaps those who are self-employed or in a business that does not require societal approval. Consider how many businesses or organizations you know that will hire and protect people who are openly gay or lesbian.
- *Family*. Their approval, acceptance, love.
- *Children*. Many lesbians and gay men have children, but very, very few gain custody in court challenges, even if the other parent is a known abuser. Other children may be kept away from us as though gays and lesbians are abusers. There are written and unwritten laws prohibiting lesbians and gays from being foster parents or from adopting children. There is an irrational fear that children in contact with lesbians and gays will become homosexual through influence or that they will be sexually abused. Despite our knowing that 95 percent of those who sexually abuse children are heterosexual men, there are no policies keeping heterosexual men from teaching or working with children, yet in almost every school system in America, visible gay men and lesbians are not hired through either written or unwritten law.

- *Heterosexual privilege and protection.* No institutions, other than those created by lesbians and gays—such as the Metropolitan Community Church, some counseling centers, political organizations such as the National Gay and Lesbian Task Force, the National Coalition of Black Lesbians and Gays, the Lambda Legal Defense and Education Fund, etc.—affirm homosexuality and offer protection. Affirmation and protection cannot be gained from the criminal justice system, mainline churches, educational institutions, the government.

- *Safety.* There is nowhere to turn for safety from physical and verbal attacks because the norm presently in this country is that it is acceptable to be overtly homophobic. Gay men are beaten on the streets; lesbians are kidnapped and "deprogrammed." The National Gay and Lesbian Task Force, in an extended study, has documented violence against lesbians and gay men and noted the inadequate response of the criminal justice system. One of the major differences between homophobia/heterosexism and racism and sexism is that because of the Civil Rights Movement and the women's movement racism and sexism are expressed more covertly (though with great harm); because there has not been a major, visible lesbian and gay movement, it is permissible to be overtly homophobic in any institution or public forum. Churches spew forth homophobia in the same way they did racism prior to the Civil Rights Movement. Few laws are in place to protect lesbians and gay men, and the criminal justice system is wracked with homophobia.

- *Mental health.* An overtly homophobic world in which there is full permission to treat lesbians and gay men with cruelty makes it difficult for lesbians and gay men to maintain a strong sense of well-being and self-esteem. Many lesbians and gay men are beaten, raped, killed, subjected to aversion therapy, or put in mental institutions. The impact of such hatred and negativity can lead one to depression and, in some cases, to suicide. The toll on the gay and lesbian community is devastating.

- *Community.* There is rejection by those who live in homophobic fear, those who are afraid of association with lesbians and gay men. For many in the gay and lesbian community, there is a loss of public acceptance, a loss of allies, a loss of place and belonging.
- *Credibility.* This fear is large for many people: the fear that they will no longer be respected, listened to, honored, believed. They fear they will be social outcasts.

The list goes on and on. But any one of these essential components of a full life is large enough to make one deeply fear its loss. A black woman once said to me in a workshop, "When I fought for Civil Rights, I always had my family and community to fall back on even when they didn't fully understand or accept what I was doing. I don't know if I could have borne losing them. And you people don't have either with you. It takes my breath away."

What does a woman have to do to get called a lesbian? Almost anything, sometimes nothing at all, but certainly anything that threatens the status quo, anything that steps out of role, anything that asserts the rights of women, anything that doesn't indicate submission and subordination. Assertiveness, standing up for oneself, asking for more pay, better working conditions, training for and accepting a non-traditional (you mean a man's?) job, enjoying the company of women, being financially independent, being in control of one's life, depending first and foremost upon oneself, thinking that one can do whatever needs to be done, but above all, working for the rights and equality of women.

In the backlash to the gains of the women's liberation movement, there has been an increased effort to keep definitions man-centered. Therefore, to work on behalf of women must mean to work against men. To love women must mean that one hates men. A very effective attack has been made against the word *feminist* to make it a derogatory word. In current backlash usage, *feminist* equals *man-hater* which equals *lesbian.* This formula is created in the hope that women will be frightened away from their work on behalf of women. Consequently, we now have women who believe in the rights of women and work for those rights while from fear deny that they are feminists, or refuse to use the word because it is so "abrasive."

So what does one do in an effort to keep from being called a lesbian? She steps back into line, into the role that is demanded of her, tries to behave in such a way that doesn't threaten the status of men, and if she works for women's rights, she begins modifying that work. When women's organizations begin doing significant social change work, they inevitably are lesbian-baited; that is, funders or institutions or community members tell us that they can't work with us because of our "man-hating attitudes" or the presence of lesbians. We are called too strident, told we are making enemies, not doing good.

The battered women's movement has seen this kind of attack: the pressure has been to provide services only, without analysis of the causes of violence against women and strategies for ending it. To provide only services without political analysis or direct action is to be in an approved "helping" role; to analyze the causes of violence against women is to begin the work toward changing an entire system of power and control. It is when we do the latter that we are threatened with the label of man-hater or lesbian. For my politics, if a women's social change organization has not been labeled lesbian or communist, it is probably not doing significant work; it is only "making nice."

Women in many of these organizations, out of fear of all the losses we are threatened with, begin to modify our work to make it more acceptable and less threatening to the male-dominated society which we originally set out to change. The work can no longer be radical (going to the root cause of the problem) but instead must be reforming, working only on the symptoms and not the cause. Real change for women becomes thwarted and stopped. The word *lesbian* is instilled with the power to halt our work and control our lives. And we give it its power with our fear.

In my view, homophobia has been one of the major causes of the failure of the women's liberation movement to make deep and lasting change. (The other major block has been racism.) We were fierce when we set out but when threatened with the loss of heterosexual privilege, we began putting on brakes. Our best-known nationally distributed women's magazine was reluctant to print articles about lesbians, began putting a man on the cover several times a year, and writing articles about women who succeeded in a man's world. We worried about our image, our being all right, our being "real women" despite our work. Instead of talking about the elimination of sexual gender roles, we stepped back and talked about "sex role stereotyping" as the issue. Change around the edges for middle class white women began to be talked about as successes. We accepted tokenism and integration, forgetting that equality for all women, for all people—and not just equality of white middle class women with white men—was the goal that we could never put behind us.

But despite backlash and retreats, change is growing from within. The women's liberation movement is beginning to gain strength again because there are women who are talking about liberation for all women. We are examining sexism, racism, homophobia, classism, anti-Semitism, ageism, ableism, and imperialism, and we see everything as connected. This change in point of view represents the third wave of the women's liberation movement, a new direction that does not get mass media coverage and recognition. It has been initiated by women of color and lesbians who were marginalized or rendered invisible by the white heterosexual leaders of earlier efforts. The first wave was the 19th and early 20th century campaign for the vote; the second, beginning in the 1960s, focused on the Equal Rights Amendment and abortion rights. Consisting of predominantly white middle class women, both failed in recognizing issues of equality and empowerment for all women. The third wave of the movement, multi-racial and multi-issued, seeks the transformation of the world for us all. We know that we won't get there until everyone gets there; that we must move forward in a great strong line, hand in hand, not just a few at a time.

We know that the arguments about homophobia originating from mental health and Biblical/religious attitudes can be settled when we look at the sexism that permeates religious and psychiatric history. The women of the third wave of the women's liberation movement know that *without the existence of sexism there would be no homophobia.*

Finally, we know that as long as the word lesbian can strike fear in any woman's heart, then work on behalf of women can be stopped; the only successful work against sexism must include work against homophobia.

QUESTIONS

1. Identify and summarize the various explanations for homosexuality presented in the article. How does Pharr use this research to make her claim that sexuality is "morally neutral"?

2. What does Pharr identify as the system which holds patriarchal ideology in place? What are the three weapons of this system? How do they work to reinforce expectations about *gender*?

3. Explain Pharr's concept of *compulsory heterosexuality*. What does "compulsory" mean? Do you agree with Pharr's argument about the relationship between homophobia and the creation of heterosexuality? Why/why not?

X: A Fabulous Child's Story (1972)

Lois Gould

Lisa Gould is a writer and journalist, whose novels include Such Good Friends *(1970),* Necessary Objects *(1972), and* La Presidenta *(1981). In this short story, Lois Gould points out our culture's obsession with gender. Through the story of X, Gould explores the constraints created by gender expectations, as well as their pervasive nature. In the life of X, Gould presents the possibilities for the development of unique human potential in a social environment which does not emphasize gender.*

Once upon a time, a baby named X was born. This baby was named X so that nobody could tell whether it was a boy or a girl. Its parents could tell, of course, but they couldn't tell anybody else. They couldn't even tell Baby X, at first.

You see, it was all part of a very important Secret Scientific Xperiment, known officially as Project Baby X. The smartest scientists had set up this Xperiment at a cost of Xactly 23 billion dollars and 72 cents, which might seem like a lot for just one baby, even a very important Xperimental baby. But when you remember the prices of things like strained carrots and stuffed bunnies, and popcorn for the movies and booster shots for camp, let alone 28 shiny quarters from the tooth fairy, you begin to see how it adds up.

Also, long before Baby X was born, all those scientists had to be paid to work out the details of the Xperiment, and to write the *Official Instruction Manual* for Baby X's parents and, most important of all, to find the right set of parents to bring up Baby X. These parents had to be selected very carefully. Thousands of volunteers had to take thousands of tests and answer thousands of tricky questions. Almost everybody failed because, it turned out, almost everybody really wanted either a baby boy or a baby girl, and not Baby X at all. Also, almost everybody was afraid that a Baby X would be a lot more trouble than a boy or a girl. (They were probably right, the scientists admitted, but Baby X needed parents who wouldn't *mind* the Xtra trouble.)

There were families with grandparents named Milton and Agatha, who didn't see why the baby couldn't be named Milton or Agatha instead of X, even if it *was* an X. There were families with aunts who insisted on knitting tiny dresses and uncles who insisted on sending tiny baseball mitts. Worst of all, there were families that already had other children who couldn't be trusted to keep the secret. Certainly not if they knew the secret was worth 23 billion dollars and 72 cents—and all you had to do was take one little peek at Baby X in the bathtub to know if it was a boy or a girl.

But, finally, the scientists found the Joneses, who really wanted to raise an X more than any other kind of baby—no matter how much trouble it would be. Ms. and Mr. Jones had to promise they would take equal turns caring for X, and feeding it, and singing it lullabies. And they had to promise never to hire any baby-sitters. The government scientists knew perfectly well that a baby-sitter would probably peek at X in the bathtub, too.

The day the Joneses brought their baby home, lots of friends and relatives came over to see it. None of them knew about the secret Xperiment, though. So the first thing they asked was what kind of a baby X was. When the Joneses smiled and said, 'It's an X!" nobody knew what to say. They couldn't say, "Look at her cute little dimples!" And they couldn't say, "Look at his husky little biceps!" And they couldn't even say just plain "kitchy-coo." In fact, they all thought the Joneses were playing some kind of rude joke.

But, of course, the Joneses were not joking. "It's an X" was absolutely all they would say. And that made the friends and relatives very angry. The relatives all felt embarrassed about having an X in the family. "People will think there's something wrong with it!" some of them whispered. "There is something wrong with it!" others whispered back.

"Nonsense!' the Joneses told them all cheerfully. "What could possibly be wrong with this perfectly adorable X?"

Nobody could answer that, except Baby X, who had just finished its bottle. Baby X's answer was a loud, satisfied burp.

Clearly, nothing at all was wrong. Nevertheless, none of the relatives felt comfortable about buying a present for a Baby X. The cousins who sent the baby a tiny football helmet would not come and visit any more. And the neighbors who sent a pink-flowered romper suit pulled their shades down when the Joneses passed their house.

The *Official Instruction Manual* had warned the new parents that this would happen, so they didn't fret about it. Besides, they were too busy with Baby X and the hundreds of different Xercises for treating it properly.

Ms. and Mr. Jones had to be Xtra careful about how they played with little X. They knew if they kept bouncing it up in the air and saying how *strong* and *active* it was, they'd be treating it more like a boy than an X. But if all they did was cuddle it and kiss it and tell it how *sweet* and *dainty* it was, they'd be treating it more like a girl than an X.

On page 1,654 of the *Official Instruction Manual,* the scientists prescribed: "plenty of bouncing and plenty of cuddling, *both.* X ought to be strong and sweet and active. Forget about *dainty* altogether."

Meanwhile, the Joneses were worrying about other problems. Toys, for instance. And clothes. On his first shopping trip, Mr. Jones told the store clerk, "I need some clothes and toys for my new baby." The clerk smiled and said, "Well, now, is it a boy or a girl?" "It's an X," Mr. Jones said, smiling back. But the clerk got all red in the face and said huffily, "In *that* case, I'm afraid I can't help you, sir." So Mr. Jones wandered helplessly up and down the aisles trying to find what X needed. But everything in the store was piled up in sections marked "Boys" or "Girls." There were "Boys' Pajamas" and "Girls' Underwear" and "Boys' Fire Engines" and "Girls' Housekeeping Sets." Mr. Jones went home without buying anything for X. That night he and Ms. Jones consulted page 2,326 of the *Official Instruction Manual.* "Buy plenty of everything!" it said firmly.

So they bought plenty of sturdy blue pajamas in the Boys' Department and cheerful flowered underwear in the Girls' Department. And they bought all kinds of toys. A boy doll that made pee-pee and cried, "Pa-pa." And a girl doll that talked in three languages and said, "I am the Pres-i-dent of Gen-er-al Mo-tors." They also bought a storybook about a brave princess who rescued a handsome prince from his ivory tower, and another one about a sister and brother who grew up to be a baseball star and a ballet star, and you had to guess which was which.

The head scientists of Project Baby X checked all their purchases and told them to keep up the good work. They also reminded the Joneses to see page 4,629 of the *Manual*, where it said, "Never make Baby X feel *embarrassed* or *ashamed* about what it wants to play with. And if X gets dirty climbing rocks, never say 'Nice little Xes don't get dirty climbing rocks.'"

Likewise, it said, "If X falls down and cries, never say 'Brave little Xes don't cry.' Because, of course, nice little Xes do get dirty, and brave little Xes do cry. No matter how dirty X gets, or how hard it cries, don't worry. It's all part of the Xperiment."

Whenever the Joneses pushed Baby X's stroller in the park, smiling strangers would come over and coo: "Is that a boy or a girl?" The Joneses would smile back and say, "It's an X." The strangers would stop smiling then, and often snarl something nasty—as if the Joneses had snarled at *them*.

By the time X grew big enough to play with other children, the Joneses' troubles had grown bigger, too. Once a little girl grabbed X's shovel in the sandbox, and zonked X on the head with it. "Now, now, Tracy," the little girl's mother began to scold, "little girls mustn't hit little . . . " and she turned to ask X, "Are you a little boy or a little girl, dear?"

Mr. Jones who was sitting near the sandbox, held his breath and crossed his fingers.

X smiled politely at the lady, even though X's head had never been zonked so hard in its life. "I'm a little X," X replied.

"You're a *what*?" the lady exclaimed angrily. "You're a little b-r-a-t, you mean!"

"But little girls mustn't hit little Xes, either!" said X, retrieving the shovel with another polite smile. "What good does hitting do, anyway?"

X's father, who was still holding his breath, finally let it out, uncrossed his fingers, and grinned back at X.

And at their next secret Project Baby X meeting, the scientists grinned, too. Baby X was doing fine.

But then it was time for X to start school. The Joneses were really worried about this, because school was even more full of rules for boys and girls, and there were no rules for Xes. The teacher would tell boys to form one line, and girls to form another line. There would be boys' games and girls' games, and boys' secrets and girls' secrets. The school library would have a list of recommended books for girls, and a different list of recommended books for boys. There would even be a bathroom marked BOYS and another one marked GIRLS. Pretty soon boys and girls would hardly talk to each other. What would happen to poor little X?

The Joneses spent weeks consulting their *Instruction Manual* (there were $249^1/_2$ pages of advice under "First Day of School"), and attending urgent special conferences with the smart scientists of Project Baby X.

The scientists had to make sure that X's mother had taught X how to throw and catch a ball properly, and that X's father had been sure to teach X what to serve at a doll's tea party. X had to know how to shoot marbles and how to jump rope and, most of all, what to say when the Other Children asked whether X was a Boy or a Girl.

Finally, X was ready. The Joneses helped X button on a nice new pair of red-and-white checked overalls, and sharpened six pencils for X's nice new pencil box, and marked X's name clearly on all the books in its nice new book bag. X brushed its teeth and combed its hair, which just about covered its ears, and remembered to put a napkin in its lunchbox.

The Joneses had asked X's teacher if the class could line up alphabetically, instead of forming separate lines for boys and girls. And they had asked if X could use the principal's bathroom, because it wasn't marked anything except BATHROOM. X's teacher promised to take care of all those problems. But nobody could help X with the biggest problem of all—Other Children.

Nobody in X's class had ever known an X before. What would they think? How would X make friends?

You couldn't tell what X was by studying its clothes—overalls don't even button right-to-left, like girls' clothes, or left-to-right, like boys' clothes. And you couldn't guess whether X had a girl's short haircut or a boy's long haircut. And it was very hard to tell by the games X liked to play. Either X played ball very well for a girl, or else X played house very well for a boy.

Some of the children tried to find out by asking X tricky questions, like "Who's your favorite sports star?" That was easy. X had two favorite sports stars: a girl jockey named Robyn Smith and a boy archery champion named Robin Hood. Then they asked, "What's your favorite TV program?" And that was even easier. X's favorite TV program was "Lassie," which stars a girl dog played by a boy dog.

When X said that its favorite toy was a doll, everyone decided that X must be a girl. But then X said that the doll was really a robot, and that X had computerized it, and that it was programmed to bake fudge brownies and then clean up the kitchen. After X told them that, the other children gave up guessing what X was. All they knew was they'd sure like to see X's doll.

After school, X wanted to play with the other children. "How about shooting some baskets in the gym?" X asked the girls. But all they did was make faces and giggle behind X's back.

"How about weaving some baskets in the arts and crafts room?" X asked the boys. But they all made faces and giggled behind X's back too.

That night, Ms. and Mr. Jones asked X how things had gone at school. X told them sadly that the lessons were okay, but otherwise school was a terrible place for an X. It seemed as if Other Children would never want an X for a friend.

Once more, the Joneses reached for their *Instruction Manual.* Under "Other Children," they found the following message: "What did you Xpect? *Other Children* have to obey all the silly boy-girl rules, because their parents taught them to. Lucky X—you don't have to stick to the rules at all! All you have to do is be yourself. P.S. We're not saying it'll be easy."

X liked being itself. But X cried a lot that night, partly because it felt afraid. So X's father held X tight, and cuddled it, and couldn't help crying a little, too. And X's mother cheered them both up by reading an Xciting story about an enchanted prince called Sleeping Handsome, who woke up when Princess Charming kissed him.

The next morning, they all felt much better, and little X went back to school with a brave smile and a clean pair of red-and-white checked overalls.

There was a seven-letter-word spelling bee in class that day. And a seven-lap boys' relay race in the gym. And a seven-layer-cake baking contest in the girls' kitchen corner. X won the spelling bee. X also won the relay race. And X almost won the baking contest, except it forgot to light the oven. Which only proves that nobody's perfect.

One of the Other Children noticed something else, too. He said: "Winning or losing doesn't seem to count to X. X seems to have fun being good at boys' skills *and* girls' skills."

"Come to think of it," said another one of the Other Children, "maybe X is having twice as much fun as we are!"

So after school that day, the girl who beat X at the baking contest gave X a big slice of her prize-winning cake. And the boy X beat in the relay race asked X to race him home.

From then on, some really funny things began to happen. Susie, who sat next to X in class, suddenly refused to wear pink dresses to school any more. She insisted on wearing red-and-white checked overalls—just like X's. Overalls, she told her parents, were much better for climbing monkey bars.

Then Jim, the class football nut, started wheeling his little sister's doll carriage around the football field. He'd put on his entire football uniform, except for the helmet. Then he'd put the helmet *in* the carriage, lovingly tucked under an old set of shoulder pads. Then he'd start jogging around the field, pushing the carriage and singing "Rock-a-bye Baby" to his football helmet. He told his family that X did the same thing, so it must be okay. After all X was now the team's star quarterback.

Susie's parents were horrified by her behavior, and Jim's parents were worried sick about his. But the worst came when the twins, Joe and Peggy, decided to share everything with each other. Peggy used Joe's hockey skates, and his microscope, and took half his newspaper route. Joe used Peggy's needlepoint kit, and her cookbooks, and took two of her three baby-sitting jobs. Peggy started running the lawn mower, and Joe started running the vacuum cleaner.

Their parents weren't one bit pleased with Peggy's wonderful biology experiments, or with Joe's terrific needlepoint pillows. They didn't care that Peggy mowed the lawn better, and that Joe vacuumed the carpet better. In fact, they were furious. It's all that little X's fault, they agreed. Just because X doesn't know what it is, or what it's supposed to be, it wants to get everybody else mixed up, too!

Peggy and Joe were forbidden to play with X any more. So was Susie, and then Jim, and then *all* the Other Children. But it was too late; the Other Children stayed mixed up and happy and free, and refused to go back to the way they'd been before X.

Finally, Joe and Peggy's parents decided to call an emergency meeting of the school's Parents' Association, to discuss "The X Problem." They sent a report to the principal stating that X was a "disruptive influence." They demanded immediate action. The Joneses, they said, should be *forced* to tell whether X was a boy or a girl. And then X should be *forced* to behave like whichever it was. If the Joneses refused to tell, the Parents' Association said, then X must take an Xamination. The school psychiatrist must Xamine it physically and mentally, and issue a full report. If X's test showed it was a boy, it would have to obey all the boys' rules. If it proved to be a girl, X would have to obey all the girls' rules.

And if X turned out to be some kind of mixed-up misfit, then X should be Xpelled from the school. Immediately!

The principal was very upset. Disruptive influence? Mixed-up misfit? But X was an Xcellent student. All the teachers said it was a delight to have X in their classes. X was president of the student council. X had won first prize in the talent show, and second prize in the art show, and honorable mention in the science fair, and six athletic events on field day, including the potato race.

Nevertheless, insisted the Parents' Association, X is a Problem Child. X is the Biggest Problem Child we have ever seen!

So the principal reluctantly notified X's parents that numerous complaints about X's behavior had come to the school's attention. And that after the psychiatrist's Xamination, the school would decide what to do about X.

The Joneses reported this at once to the scientists, who referred them to page 85,759 of the *Instruction Manual*. "Sooner or later," it said, "X will have to be Xamined by a psychiatrist. This may be the only way any of us will know for sure whether X is mixed up—or whether everyone else is."

The night before X was to be Xamined, the Joneses tried not to let X see how worried they were. "What if . . . ?" Mr. Jones would say. And Ms. Jones would reply, "No use worrying." Then a few minutes later, Ms. Jones would say, "What if . . . ?" and Mr. Jones would reply, "No use worrying."

X just smiled at them both, and hugged them hard and didn't say much of anything. X was thinking. What if . . . ? And then X thought: No use worrying.

At Xactly 9 o'clock the next day, X reported to the school psychiatrist's office. The principal, along with a committee from the Parents' Association, X's teacher, X's classmates, and Ms. and Mr. Jones, waited in the hall outside. Nobody knew the details of the tests X was to be given, but everybody knew they'd be very hard, and that they'd reveal Xactly what everyone wanted to know about X, but were afraid to ask.

It was terribly quiet in the hall. Almost spooky. Once in a while, they would hear a strange noise inside the room. There were buzzes. And a beep or two. And several bells. An occasional light would flash under the door. The Joneses thought it was a white light, but the principal thought it was blue. Two or three children swore it was either yellow or green. And the Parents' Committee missed it completely.

Through it all, you could hear the psychiatrist's low voice, asking hundreds of questions, and X's higher voice, answering hundreds of answers.

The whole thing took so long that everyone knew it must be the most complete Xamination anyone had ever had to take. Poor X, the Joneses thought. Serves X right, the Parents' Committee thought. I wouldn't like to be in X's overalls right now, the children thought.

At last, the door opened. Everyone crowded around to hear the results. X didn't look any different; in fact, X was smiling. But the psychiatrist looked terrible. He look as if he was crying! "What happened?" everyone began shouting. Had X done something disgraceful? "I wouldn't be a bit surprised!" muttered Peggy and Joe's parents. "Did X flunk the *whole* test?" cried Susie's parents. "Or just the most important part?" yelled Jim's parents.

"Oh, dear," sighed Mr. Jones.

"Oh, dear," sighed Ms. Jones.

"*Sssh,*" ssshed the principal. "The psychiatrist is trying to speak."

Wiping, his eyes and clearing his throat, the psychiatrist began, in a hoarse whisper. "In my opinion," he whispered—you could tell he must be very upset—"in my opinion, young X here . . ."

"Yes? Yes?" shouted a parent impatiently.

"*Sssh!*" ssshed the principal.

"Young *Sssh* here, I mean young X," said the doctor, frowning, "is just about . . . "

"Just about *what*? Let's have it!" shouted another parent.

" . . . just about the *least* mixed-up child I've ever Xamined!" said the psychiatrist.

"Yay for X!" yelled one of the children. And then the others began yelling, too. Clapping and cheering and jumping up and down.

"SSSH!" SSShed the principal, but nobody did.

The Parents' Committee was angry and bewildered. How *could* X have passed the whole Xamination? Didn't X have an *identity* problem? Wasn't X mixed up at *all*? Wasn't X *any* kind of a misfit? How could it *not* be, when it didn't even *know* what it was? And why was the psychiatrist crying?

Actually, he had stopped crying and was smiling politely through his tears. "Don't you see?" he said. "I'm crying because it's wonderful! X has absolutely no identity problem! X isn't one bit mixed up! As for being a misfit—ridiculous! X knows perfectly well what it is! Don't you, X?" The doctor winked, X winked back.

"But what *is* X?" shrieked Peggy and Joe's parents. "We still want to know what it is!"

"Ah, yes," said the doctor, winking again. "Well, don't worry. You'll all know one of these days. And you won't need me to tell you.'

"What? What does he mean?" some of the parents grumbled suspiciously.

Susie and Peggy and Joe all answered at once. "He means that by the time X's sex matters, it won't be a secret any more!"

With that, the doctor began to push through the crowd toward X's parents. "How do you do," he said, somewhat stiffly. And then he reached out to hug them both. "If I ever have an X of my own," he whispered, "I sure hope you'll lend me your instruction manual."

Needless to say, the Joneses were very happy. The Project Baby X scientists were rather pleased, too. So were Susie, Jim, Peggy, Joe, and all the Other Children. The Parents' Association wasn't, but they had promised to accept the psychiatrist's report, and not make any more trouble. They even invited Ms. and Mr. Jones to become honorary members, which they did.

Later that day, all X's friends put on their red-and-white checked overalls and went over to see X. They found X in the back yard, playing with a very tiny baby that none of them had ever seen before. The baby was wearing very tiny red-and-white checked overalls.

"How do you like our new baby?" X asked the Other Children proudly.

"It's got cute dimples," said Jim.

"It's got husky biceps, too," said Susie.

"What kind of baby is it?' asked Joe and Peggy.

X frowned at them. "Can't you tell?" Then X broke into a big, mischievous grin. *"It's a Y!'*

QUESTIONS

1. Why do many of the story's characters react negatively to X and X's parents?
2. Why do you think it is important to so many of the characters that they know what X's gender is?
3. What advantages might X have over the other children in the story because X is raised as both a boy and a girl?
4. Why do "we" feel the need to categorize people by their gender?

2. We need to place everything - Curiosity

3. Advantages - gets to experience many different things
more options
Best of both worlds

Language

Some theorists suggest that language simultaneously provides for us the possibility of, and the limitations in, our abilities to communicate and to understand the complexities of both the natural and the social environments. In many ways, the language which is available to us determines what can be spoken, as well as reveals what has been suppressed, or made invisible, within a social structure. A consideration of language—how we use words, the implicit (hidden) significance of various terms and constructions—is also a consideration of how multiple systems comprise the whole of the social environment.

In this section, we turn our feminist attention to the dynamics of language. We will consider language as both a tool of oppression, and as a key to liberation and freedom. We will ask whether our language has been, and continues to be, a thread in the fabrics of colonialism and discrimination in the United States. And we will think about whether and how language—and its companion, silence—can be reconstructed to enable the full development of human potential in all of its varied forms.

CAN 'HE' MEAN 'SHE'? EXPLORING THE SEMANTICS OF POLITICAL CORRECTNESS (1994)

Michelle Quinn Cardall

The English language includes the use of generic terms, terms which theoretically do not imply gender and can be used to identify either males or females, or both. In this selection, Michelle Quinn Cardall explores the debate over generic terms. Through her discussion of the "sides" of the debate, Cardall raises the issue of whether the focus *of the debate is misdirected. She then suggests an alternative for how we might evaluate the cultural use of the generic 'he.'*

Michelle Quinn Cardall received both her B.A. and M.A. from Brigham Young University, where she has taught writing courses.

The Debate

For the past two decades, a debate has raged about the use of "he" as a gender-neutral pronoun. Contradictory experiments abound. For example, in one such experiment, three researchers asked college students to write a fictional story based on the following theme: "In a large coeducational institution the average student will feel isolated in ____ introductory courses" (Moulton, Robinson, & Elias, 1978, p. 1034). In the blank, the researches inserted either "his," "his or her," or "their." The researchers then studied whether the gender of the main character in the stories created by the students varied according to the pronoun used in the suggested topic. The results of the experiment suggested that "using male terms in their 'gender-neutral' sense induces people to think of males in contexts that are explicitly gender-neutral" (p. 1034). In other words, they claimed that their experiment showed that the pronoun "he" and its possessive forms always carried male connotations, even when they were meant to apply to males and females equally.

In a study published six years later, however, a group of researchers challenged the results of this experiment and several similar ones. They claimed that all these experiments had been too obvious in their approaches and therefore might have led the students to merely copy the "language forms used in the" suggested situation (Cole, Hill, & Dayley, 1983, p. 745). This group imitated the previous experiment but, unlike those who first conducted the experiment, did not evaluate the connotations of the pronouns based on the use of pronouns in the story. Instead the new experiment focused on a questionnaire given the participants, which asked them to rate the main character in their stories based on certain established gender particular bipolar adjectives. For example, the character could be rated small or large, weak or strong, or very active or very passive (p. 740). The results of this second experiment suggested that "he" could be used without male connotations in a gender-neutral context.

Semantics

This argument continues across the nation, and a complete victory for either side seems unlikely. One side argues that "he" cannot really be used to refer to both males and females, but always carries a male connotation which discriminates against the other half of the race. In other words, this side's argument is that even when the informative connotation of "he" includes both men and women, the affective connotation of "he" includes just men. The other side states just as adamantly that "he" has always been the gender-neutral pronoun in English, and that it always will be.

This side does not believe that "he" always evokes male imagery and thus excludes women, and it sees the suggested alternatives to the gender-neutral "he" as awkward, ungrammatical, and inaccurate. The study of semantics shows that the debate can never be decided either way because the connection between the word and its meaning exists only in the mind of the user. There is no real connection between the word and the object it symbolizes. This means that communication is only possible because society has agreed that particular symbols will be used to designate particular objects. When symbols are used in ways other than those commonly accepted by a particular society, communication within that society breaks down. This is exactly what has happened with the simple pronoun "he," which to some people is either the third-person, singular, male pronoun or the third-person, singular, gender-neutral pronoun and to some people is only a male-signifying pronoun.

Grammar

The arguments used by traditional grammarians are simple but weighty. Calvert Watkins, the Chairman of the Department of Linguistics at Harvard, once stated that the use of "he" as a "gender-neutral or unspecified term" was "simply a matter of grammar," that was not worth any "anxiety" from those concerned with matters of gender relations (quoted in Hill, 1986, p. 50). His remarks are typical of many such arguments which simply state, this is how it is, and this is how it always will be. He goes on to further solidify his position by drawing upon history as evidence. "This reflects the ancient pattern of the Indo-European languages," he says (p. 51). This approach to the question basically assumes that because tradition stipulates that people should recognize "he" as a neuter pronoun, people do recognize "he" as a neuter pronoun.

Without even taking on Watkins's assumption that people do think the way they should think, however, some have argued with Watkins's ideas. Alette Olin Hill (1986) argues that "an ancient Indo-European language pattern seldom has a bearing on English usage today" (p. 51), and Ann Bodine (1975) points out that throughout history "they" has been used as a singular, neuter, third-person pronoun just as much as "he" has (p. 129). She quotes many sentences in which the use of "they" as a singular, gender-neutral pronoun is common among educated people: "Anyone can do it if they try hard enough," and "Who dropped their ticket?" are examples (p. 131). She and many others argue that it is just as appropriate to use "they" as a singular, neuter, third-person pronoun as it is to use "he." Furthermore, she states that "they" is preferable because a reader is less likely to become confused about the pronoun's number than the pronoun's gender. The grammarian's case for the use of "he" as a gender-neutral pronoun is thus far from air-tight. Not only can the grammarian not prove that people do think the way they should think, but he or she cannot prove that people actually should think that "he" should be used as a singular, gender-neutral pronoun.

Other Factors

The truth is, communicators must always be careful to avoid ambiguities in pronoun references. A sentence using "they" in place of "he" can easily be ambiguous if the sentence has both a singular and a plural noun to which "they" could refer. An example of this is: "If a poet is careless in the use of metaphors, they will confuse the reader." Here it is unclear whether the metaphors or the poet is doing the confusing. We have all read or heard sentences where careless pronoun usage has led to vagueness and perhaps even humor, for example: "When the doctor gave the baby a shot, he cried."

The movement to prove that "he" is not a gender-neutral pronoun has arguments which do more than just try to disprove the arguments of traditionalists like Dr. Watkins. For instance, Wendy Martyna, one advocate of the abolition of "he" as a gender-neutral referent, explains that there are three problems with its use: ambiguity, exclusiveness, and inequity. *Ambiguity*, she explains, stems from the difficulty distinguishing between the gender-neutral "he" and the male "he." *Exclusiveness* is the injustice of those instances in which a supposed generic "he" clearly excludes a female interpretation. As an example of exclusiveness, she quotes the following sentence: "Man's vital necessities include food, water, and access to females." Here the sentence begins with an apparently gender-neutral "man," similar to the gender-neutral "he" but completely excludes females from the informative connotation with the end of the sentence (Martyna, 1978, pp. 131–132).

Inequity, the third problem with the use of the supposedly gender-neutral "he" is "the nonparallelism between the male and female pronoun" which exists because "she" is never used gender-neutrally. Martyna asserts that this objection would remain even if "he" created no confusion in its generic usage. "It is the assumed equivalence of maleness with humanness that is at issue" (p. 132). Along these same lines, Moulton, et al. (1978), the researchers who first conducted the experiment asking students to write the story, compared the gender-neutral "he" to the use of Kleenex to refer to all tissue, pointing out that this is to the economic benefit of Kleenex and the "economic detriment of brands ignored by this terminology" (p. 1035).

The issue that receives the most attention, however, is the ambiguity. Many people have spent a great deal of energy trying to prove that often people read "he" as a male referent when gender is not specified in a sentence. For example, in the sentence "If a person wants to go to college, he must work hard in high school," "he" might just as easily refer to males only as to males and females. One researcher explains that,

> Not only do some students comprehend it as specifically male, and other students as a human referent, but the same students render contradictory judgements, deciding in one instance that "he" includes "she," and in another, that it does not. (quoted in Hill, 1986, p. 58)

The same researcher points out that in "educational materials, the sex-specific 'he' appears five to ten times for every generic 'he'" (p. 59). This, she explains, makes students less likely to think of "he" as gender-neutral even when it is meant that way. Through experimentation, this researcher found that many students had a difficult time using "he" to refer to a possible female referent even when they realized that "he" was not being used in a gender-specific way (p. 59).

There has been a great deal of experimentation, like that done by this researcher, by other researchers who hope to show that people do not think of "he" as a gender-neutral pronoun when gender is not specified by the context. This is exactly what the experiment which asked students to write stories about a college student hoped to prove. Other researchers, however, have found it difficult to prove what connections between the symbol and the referent actually exist in the minds of the users. As mentioned,

Cole, et al. (1983), in their experiments on the subject, showed that much prior research had been flawed because it was obvious to the subject of the experiment what the researcher was looking for (p. 745).

Although Cole, et al. hoped their own experimentation would provide evidence that supported arguments against the use of "he" as a neuter pronoun, in their experimentation they found "no empirical evidence to support the claim that, in and of itself, the generic pronoun gives rise to thoughts of men" (p. 747). They also found that substituting "he/she" for the generic "he" did not make people any more likely to picture a woman (p. 747). Their research did show, however, that when the gender-neutral "he" was used in the same sentence with the gender-neutral "man," a more masculine image was generally pictured by readers than if the pronoun "they" was used instead of "he." They now wonder if the problem behind the interpretation of the gender-neutral "he" as a male "he" stems more from context than from individual words (p. 749).

The arguments are just as inconclusive about other aspects of the debate as this one is about ambiguity. For example, both Martyna (1978) and Moulton et al. (1978) asserted that since the supposedly gender-neutral "he" is never used to refer to a definitely female referent, it cannot be truly gender-neutral. Moulton et. al asserted: "It would be a rare person who could . . . say of a female, 'He's the best.'" "If 'he' and 'man' are genuinely gender-neutral, then they ought to be applicable to any person regardless of gender," she continued (p. 1033).

Proof or Disproof?

Ironically, the very people on the watch for inequality in language proved that by this argument "he" genuinely is gender-neutral. For example, in its "Guidelines for Nonsexist Use of Language" an American Psychological Association task force showed that the use of "he" in reference to obviously female referents is common enough to warrant attention. The report in the June 1975 issue of *American Psychologist* only mentions seven specific guidelines, and the first one mentioned is the directive that the pronoun "'he" should not be used in reference to women. The guidelines contain an example of a sentence which contains this mistake: "The individual's freedom to bear children should not be defined by his education, income, or race" (p. 682). If this mistake were uncommon, it is doubtful that the task force would have found it necessary to comment on it. Therefore, since these guidelines show that "he" is commonly used to refer to women, by Moulton et al. (1978) and Martyna's (1978) own arguments, "he" must really be a gender-neutral pronoun.

Interestingly, in *Understanding Poetry* by Brooks and Warren (1945), it is explained that in a certain poem, "the poet is not merely interested in telling the story in as clear a way as possible; he has, in fact, a real intention quite different than that of telling a story" (p. 140). The poet referred to here is Amy Lowell, obviously a woman. This is an example of sexist usage. It shows that women really were unequally represented and excluded by the prevalent use of the pronoun "he."

Obviously, those who claimed that "he" was never used to refer to women were wrong. The pronoun "he," in fact, seems to be in a no-win situation. According to some, if it is not used to refer to women then it cannot possibly be truly gender-neutral, but according to others, if it is used to refer to women then it is obviously sexist and offensive. Maybe the argument that Moulton et al. and Martyna should have been making is not that "he" is never used to refer to women but that because it is offensive to refer to women as "he," "he" cannot be a gender-neutral pronoun. In any case, after reading the seemingly endless arguments on both sides of the issue, a parable created by psychologist Virginia Valian and linguist Jerrold Katz seemed increasingly wise. I would like to repeat it here.

> In culture R the language is such that the pronouns are different according to the color of the people involved, rather than their sex . . . the unmarked pronoun just happens to be the one used for white people. In addition, the colored people just happen to constitute an oppressed group. Now imagine that this oppressed group begins complaining about the use of the "white" pronoun to refer to all people. Our linguists presumably then say, "now, now, there is really no cause for anxiety or pronoun-envy." It isn't a question of linguistics, but of how the people involved feel. (quoted in Martyna, 1980, p. 482).

Conclusion

After reading these arguments I realized that no amount of reasoning matters as much as a simple understanding of how those involved feel.

The debate about the pronoun "he" has existed since "nearly a century ago, [when] a lawyer named Charles Crozat Converse proposed that we do away with the generic 'he' and substitute a word of his own invention: 'thon'" (Martyna, 1978, p. 131). Although they have had a hundred years, those on both sides of the issue have failed to prove that most of society connects the symbol "he" with its referent in one particular way. Unable to resolve this argument, the two groups have gone on to fight about possible substitutions for "he" as a gender-neutral pronoun. Similar problems have arisen in discussions about using the pronoun "they" as a gender-neutral, singular pronoun. The arguments seem likely to continue indefinitely.

Ironically, in one way both sides are correct. For traditional grammarians, "he" does mean both "he" and "she" in certain contexts just as much as it only means "he" in other contexts. The reference or connection they create in their own minds makes "he" mean both of these things. For other people, however, the reference existing in their minds connects "he" only with a male referent. Because the only connection between the word and the referent is through the mind of the user, both of these connections must be correct.

It seems unlikely that either side of the argument will completely change their way of thinking to allow agreement in the near future. Only when both sides stop theorizing about what "he" should mean and instead think about how people feel, can a compromise be reached.

REFERENCES

APA task force on issues of sexual bias in graduate education: Guidelines for nonsexist use of language. (1975, June). *American Psychologist*, 30, 682–684.

Bodine, A. (1975). Androcentrism in prescriptive grammar: Singular "they," sex indefinite "he," and "he or she." *Language in Society*, 4, 129–146.

Brooks, C., Jr., & Warren, R. P. (1945). *Understanding poetry: An anthology for college students*. New York: Holt & Company.

Cole, M. C., Hill, F. A., & Dayley, L. J. (1983). Do masculine pronouns used generically lead to thought of men? *Sex Roles*, 9 (6), 737–750.

Hill, A. O. (1986). *Mother tongue, father tongue: A decade of linguistic revolt*. Indianapolis: Indiana University Press.

Martyna, W. (1980). Beyond the "he/man" approach: The case for nonsexist language. *Signs*, 5, 482–493.

Martyna, W. (1978). What does "He" mean? *Journal of Communication*. 28 (1), 131–138.

Moulton, J., Robinson, G. M., & Elias, C. (1978). Sex bias in language use: "Gender-neutral" pronouns that aren't. *American Psychologist*, 33, 1032–1036.

QUESTIONS

1. What is "the debate" which serves as the starting point for Cardall's argument? Explain what each of the "two sides" is arguing in the debate.
2. How does a consideration of semantic principles reconfigure the debate?
3. Explain the grammarian's argument in favor of the generic nature of 'he'. Do all grammarians subscribe to this argument? Why/why not?
4. Explain the arguments which advocate the abolishment of the generic 'he'. Identify the reasons given for why 'he' should *not* be used generically.
5. How does Cardall suggest we might "resolve" the debate?

"Sexism in English: A 1990s Update" (1996)

Alleen Pace Nilsen

What assumptions about gender are embedded in the language we use? In this selection, Alleen Pace Nilsen examines various parts of speech to reveal the underlying "gender messages" in them. In her attempt to identify and understand sexism in the English language, Nilsen offers the reader a challenge. Nilsen suggests that, as a first step toward removing the sexism inherent in the English language, we consider changing our ways of thinking about masculinity and femininity.

Alleen Pace Nilsen has co-edited Sexism and Language *(1977), and coauthored two other books on language with her husband, Don Nilsen. She received her Ph.D. from the University of Iowa, and is now a professor and administrator at Arizona State University.*

Twenty years ago I embarked on a study of the sexism inherent in American English. I had just returned to Ann Arbor, Michigan, after living for two years (1967–69) in Kabul, Afghanistan, where I had begun to look critically at the roles society assigned to women. The Afghan version of the *chaderi* prescribed for Moslem women was particularly confining. Few women attended the American-built Kabul University where my husband was teaching linguistics because there were no women's dormitories, which meant that the only females who could attend were those whose families happened to live in the capital city. Afghan jokes and folklore were blatantly sexist, for example this proverb, "If you see an old man, sit down and take a lesson; if you see an old woman, throw a stone."

But it wasn't only the native culture that made me question women's roles; it was also the American community. Nearly six hundred Americans lived in Kabul, mostly supported by U. S. taxpayers. The single women were career secretaries, school teachers, or nurses. The three women who had jobs comparable to the American men's jobs were textbook editors with the assignment of developing reading books in Dari (Afghan Persian) for young children. They worked at the Ministry of Education, a large building in the center of the city. There were no women's restrooms, so during their two-year assignment whenever they needed to go to the bathroom they had to walk across the street and down the block to the Kabul Hotel.

The rest of the American women were like myself—wives and mothers whose husbands were either career diplomats, employees of USAID, or college professors who had been recruited to work on various contract teams including an education team from Teachers College, Columbia University and an agricultural team from the University of Wyoming. These were the women who were most influential in changing my way of thinking. We were suddenly bereft of our traditional roles; some of us became alcoholics; others got very good at bridge, while others searched desperately for ways to contribute either to our families or to the Afghans. The local economy provided few jobs for women and certainly none for foreigners; we were isolated from former friends and the social goals we had grown up with. Most of us had three servants (they worked for $1.00 a day) because the cook refused to wash dishes and the dishwasher refused to water the lawn or sweep the sidewalks—it was their form of unionization. Occasionally, someone would try to get along without servants, but it was impossible because the houses were huge and we didn't have the mechanical aids we had at home. Drinking water had to be brought from the deep well at the American Embassy, and the kerosene and wood stoves had to be stocked and lit. The servants were all males, the highest-paid one being the cook who could usually speak some English. Our days revolved around supervising these servants. One woman's husband got so tired of hearing her complain about such annoyances as the *bacha* (the housekeeper) stealing kerosene and needles and batteries, and about the cook putting chili powder instead of paprika on the deviled eggs, and about the gardener subcontracting his work and expecting her to pay all his friends that he scheduled an hour a week for listening to complaints. The rest of the time he wanted to keep his mind clear to focus on his important work with his Afghan counterparts and with the president of the university and the Minister of Education. What he was doing in this country was going to make a difference! In the great eternal scheme of things, of what possible importance could be his wife's trivial troubles with the servants?

These were the thought in my mind when we finished our contract and returned in the fall of 1969 to the University of Michigan in Ann Arbor. I was surprised to find that many other women were also questioning the expectations that they had grown up with. In the spring of 1970, a women's conference was announced. I hired a babysitter and attended, but I returned home more troubled than ever. Now that I knew housework was worth only a dollar a day, I couldn't take it seriously, but I wasn't angry in the same way these women were. Their militancy frightened me. Since I wasn't ready for a revolution, I decided I would have my own feminist movement. I would study the English language and see what it could tell me about sexism. I started reading a desk dictionary and making notecards on every entry that seemed to tell something about male and female. I soon had a dog-eared dictionary, along with a collection of notecards filling two shoe boxes.

Ironically, I started reading the dictionary because I wanted to avoid getting involved in social issues, but what happened was that my notecards brought me right back to looking at society. Language and society are as intertwined as a chicken and an egg. The language that a culture uses is telltale evidence of the values and beliefs of that culture. And because there is a lag in how fast a language changes—new words can easily be introduced, but it takes a long time for old words and usages to disappear—a careful look at English will reveal the attitudes that our ancestors held and that we as a culture are therefore predisposed to hold. My notecards revealed three main points. Friends have offered the opinion that I didn't need to read the dictionary to learn such obvious facts. Nevertheless, it was interesting to have linguistic evidence of sociological observations.

Women Are Sexy; Men Are Successful

First, in American culture a woman is valued for the attractiveness and sexiness of her body, while a man is valued for his physical strength and accomplishments. A woman is sexy. A man is successful.

A persuasive piece of evidence supporting this view are the eponyms—words that have come from someone's name—found in English. I had a two-and-a-half-inch stack of cards taken from men's names, but less than a half-inch stack from women's names, and most of those came from Greek mythology. In the words that came into American English since we separated from Britain, there are many eponyms based on the names of famous American men: bartlett pear, boysenberry, diesel engine, franklin stove, ferris wheel, gattling gun, mason jar, sideburns, sousaphone, schick test, and Winchester rifle. The only common eponyms taken from American women's names are *Alice blue* (after Alice Roosevelt Longworth), *bloomers* (after Amelia Jenks Bloomer), and *Mae West jacket* (after the buxom actress). Two out of the three feminine eponyms relate closely to a woman's physical anatomy, while the masculine eponyms (except for *sideburns* after General Burnsides) have nothing to do with the namesake's body, but instead honor the man for an accomplishment of some kind.

Although in Greek mythology women played a bigger role than they did in the biblical stories of the Judeo-Christian cultures and so the names of goddesses are accepted parts of the language in such place names as Pomona from the goddess of fruit and Athens from Athena and in such common words as *cereal* from *Ceres, psychology* from Psyche, and *arachnoid* from Arachne, the same tendency to think of women in relation to sexuality is seen in the eponyms *aphrodisiac* from Aphrodite, the Greek name for the goddess of love and beauty, and *venereal disease,* from Venus, the Roman name for Aphrodite.

Another interesting word from Greek mythology is *Amazon.* According to Greek folk etymology, the *a* means "without" as in *atypical*, or *amoral* while *mazon* comes from *mazos*, meaning *breast* as still seen in *mastectomy*. In the Greek legend, Amazon women cut off their right breasts so that they could better shoot their bows. Apparently, the storytellers had a feeling that for women to play the active, "masculine" role that the Amazons adopted for themselves, they had to trade in part of their femininity.

This preoccupation with women's breasts is not limited to ancient stories. As a volunteer for the University of Wisconsin's *Dictionary of American Regional English (DARE)*, I read a western trapper's diary from the 1830s. I was to make notes of any unusual usages or language patterns. My most interesting finding was that he referred to a range of mountains as *The Teats*, a metaphor based on the similarity between the shapes of the mountains and women's breasts. Because today we use the French wording, *The Grand Tetons*, the metaphor isn't as obvious, but I wrote to the mapmakers and found the following listings: *Nippletop* and *Little Nipple Top* near Mt. Marcy in the Adirondacks, *Nipple Mountain* in Archuleta County, Colorado, *Nipple Peak* in Coke County, Texas, *Nipple Butte* in Pennington, South Dakota, *Squaw Peak* in Placer County, California (any many other locations), *Maiden's Peak* and *Squaw Tit* (they're the same mountain) in the Cascade Range in Oregon, *Mary's Nipple* near Salt Lake City, Utah, and *Jane Russell Peaks* near Stark, New Hampshire.

Except for the movie star Jane Russell, the women being referred to are anonymous—it's only a sexual part of their body that is mentioned. When topographical features are named after men, it's probably not going to be to draw attention to a sexual part of their bodies but instead to honor individuals for an accomplishment. For example, no one thinks of a part of the male body when hearing a reference to Pike's Peak, Colorado, or Jackson Hole, Wyoming.

Going back to what I learned from my dictionary cards, I was surprised to realize how many pairs of words we have in which the feminine word has acquired sexual connotations while the masculine word retains a serious businesslike aura. For example, a *callboy* is a person who calls actors when it is time for them to go on stage, but a *callgirl* is a prostitute. Compare *sir* and *madam*. *Sir* is a term of respect while *madam* has acquired the specialized meaning of a brothel manager. Something similar has happened to *master* and *mistress*. Would you rather have a painting by *an old master* or *an old mistress*?

It's because the word *woman* had sexual connotations, as in "She's his woman," that people began avoiding its use, hence such terminology as *ladies' room, lady of the house,* and *girls' school* or *school for young ladies*. Feminists, who ask that people use the word woman rather than *girl* or *lady,* are rejecting the idea that *woman* is primarily a sexual term. They have been at least partially successful in that today *woman* is commonly used to communicate gender without intending implications about sexuality.

I found two hundred pairs of words with masculine and feminine forms, e.g., *heir-heiress, hero-heroine, steward-stewardess, usher-usherette,* etc. In nearly all such pairs, the masculine word is considered the base with some kind of a feminine suffix being added. The masculine form is the one from which compounds are made, e.g., from *king-queen* comes *kingdom* but not queendom, from *sportsman-sportslady* comes *sportsmanship*. There is one—and only one—semantic area in which the masculine word is not the base or more powerful word. This is in the area dealing with sex and marriage. When someone refers to a *virgin,* a listener will probably think of a female unless the speaker specifies *male* or uses a masculine pronoun. The same is true for *prostitute.*

In relation to marriage, there is much linguistic evidence showing that weddings are more important to women than to men. A woman cherishes the wedding and is considered a bride for a whole year, but a man is referred to as a groom only on the day of the wedding. The word *bride* appears in *bridal attendant, bridal gown, bridesmaid, bridal shower,* and even *bridegroom. Groom* comes from the Middle English *grom,* meaning "man," and in this sense is seldom used outside of a wedding. With most pairs of male/female words, people habitually put the masculine word first—Mr. and Mrs., *his and hers, boys and girls, men and women, kings and queens, brothers and sisters, guys and dolls, and host and hostess*—but it is the bride and groom who are talked about, not the *groom and bride.*

The importance of marriage to a woman is also shown by the fact that when a marriage ends in death, the woman gets the title of *widow*. A man gets the derived title of *widower*. This term is not used in other phrases or contexts, but *widow* is seen in *widowhood, widow's peak,* and *widow's walk*. A widow in a card game is an extra hand of cards, while in typesetting it is an extra line of type.

How changing cultural ideas bring changes to language is clearly visible in this semantic area. The feminist movement has caused the differences between the sexes to be downplayed, and since I did my dictionary work two decades ago, the word *singles* has largely replaced such sex-specific and value-laden terms as *bachelor, old maid, spinster, divorcee, widow,* and *widower.* And in 1970 I wrote that when a man is called a *professional* he is thought to be a doctor or a lawyer, but when people hear a woman referred to as a *professional,* they are likely to think of a prostitute. That's not as true today because so many women have become doctors and lawyers that it's no longer incongruous to think of women in those professional roles.

Another change that has taken place is in wedding announcements. They used to be sent out from the bride's parents and did not even give the name of the groom's parents. Today, most couples choose to list either all or none of the parent's names. Also it is now much more likely that both the bride and groom's picture will be in the newspaper, while a decade ago only the bride's picture was published on the "Women's" or "Society" page. Even the traditional wording of the wedding ceremony is being changed. Many officials now pronounce the couple "husband and wife" instead of the old "man and wife," and they ask the bride if she promises "to love, honor, and cherish," instead of "to love, honor, and obey."

Women Are Passive; Men Are Active

The wording of the wedding ceremony also relates to the second point that my cards showed, which is that women are expected to play a passive or weak role while men play an active or strong role. In the traditional ceremony, the official asks, "Who gives the bride away?" and the father answers, "I do." Some fathers answer, "Her mother and I do," but that doesn't solve the problem inherent in the question. The idea that a bride is something to be handed over from one man to another bothers people because it goes back to the days when a man's servants, his children and his wife were all considered to be his property. They were known by his name because they belonged to him and he was responsible for their actions and their debts.

The grammar used in talking or writing about weddings as well as other sexual relationships shows the expectation of men playing the active role. Men *wed* women while women *become* brides of men. A man *possesses* a woman; he *deflowers* her; he *performs;* he *scores;* he *takes away* her virginity. Although a woman can *seduce* a man, she cannot offer him her virginity. When talking about virginity, the only way to make the woman the actor in the sentence is to say that "She lost her virginity," but people lose things by accident rather than by purposeful actions, and so she's only the grammatical, not the real-life, actor.

The reason that women tried to bring the term *Ms.* into the language to replace *Miss* and *Mrs.* relates to this point. Married women resented being identified only under their husband's names. For example, when Susan Glascoe did something newsworthy, she would be identified in the newspaper only as Mrs. John Glascoe. The dictionary cards showed what appeared to be an attitude on the part of editors that it was almost indecent to let a respectable woman's name march unaccompanied across the pages of a dictionary. Women were listed with male names whether or not the male contributed to the woman's reason for being in the dictionary or in his own right was as famous as the woman. For example, Charlotte Bronte was identified as Mrs. Arthur B. Nicholls, Amelia Earhart as Mrs. George Palmer Putnam, Helen Hayes as Mrs. Charles MacArthur, Jenny Lind as Mme. Otto Goldschmit, Cornelia Otis Skinner as the daughter of Otis Skinner, Harriet Beecher Stowe as the sister of Henry Ward Beecher, and Edith Sitwell as the sister of Osbert and Sacheverell. A very small number of women got into the dictionary without the benefit of masculine escort. They were rebels and crusaders: temperance leaders Frances Elizabeth Caroline Willard and Carry Nation, women's rights leaders Carrie Chapman Catt and Elizabeth Cady Stanton, birth control educator Margaret Sanger, religious leader Mary Baker Eddy, and slaves Harriet Tubman and Phyllis Wheatley.

Etiquette books used to teach that if a woman had *Mrs.* in front of her name then the husband's name should follow because *Mrs.* is an abbreviated form of *Mistress* and a woman couldn't be a mistress of herself. As with many arguments about "correct" language usage, this isn't very logical because *Miss* is also an abbreviation of *Mistress.* Feminists hoped to simplify matters by introducing *Ms.* as an alternative to both *Mrs.* and *Miss,* but what happened is that *Ms.* largely replaced *Miss* to become a catch-all business title for women. Many married women still prefer the title *Mrs.,* and some resent being addressed with the term *Ms.* As one frustrated newspaper reporter complained, "Before I can write about a woman, I have to know not only her marital status but also her political philosophy." The result of such complications may contribute to the demise of titles which are already being ignored by many computer programmers who find it more efficient to simply use names; for example in a business letter: "Dear Joan Garcia," instead of "Dear Mrs. Joan Garcia," "Dear Ms. Garcia," or "Dear Mrs. Louis Garcia."

The titles given to royalty provide an example of how males can be disadvantaged by the assumption that they are always to play the more powerful role. In British royalty, when a male holds a title, his wife is automatically given the feminine equivalent. But the reverse is not true. For example, a *count* is a high political officer with a *countess* being his wife. The same is true for a *duke* and a *duchess* and a *king* and a *queen*. But when a female holds the royal title, the man she marries does not automatically acquire the matching title. For example, Queen Elizabeth's husband has the title of *prince* rather than *king*, but if Prince Charles should become king while he is still married to Lady or Princess Diana, she will be known as the queen. The reasoning appears to be that since masculine words are stronger, they are reserved for true heirs and withheld from males coming into the royal family by marriage. If Prince Phillip were called *King Phillip*, it would be much easier for British subjects to forget where the true power lies.

The names that people give their children show the hopes and dreams they have for them, and when we look at the differences between male and female names in a culture we can see the cumulative expectations of that culture. In our culture girls often have names taken from small, aesthetically pleasing items, e.g., *Ruby*, *Jewel*, and *Pearl*. *Esther* and *Stella* mean "star." *Ada* means "ornament," and *Vanessa* means "butterfly." Boys are more likely to be given names with meanings of power and strength, e.g., *Neil* means "champion," *Martin* is from Mars, the god of war, *Raymond* means "wise protection," *Harold* means "chief of the army," *Ira* means "vigilant," *Rex* means "king," and *Richmond* means "strong king."

We see similar differences in food metaphors. Food is a passive substance just sitting there waiting to be eaten. Many people have recognized this and so no longer feel comfortable describing women as "delectable morsels." However, when I was a teenager, it was considered a compliment to refer to a girl (we didn't call anyone a woman until she was middle-aged) as *a cute tomato, a peach, a dish, a cookie, honey, sugar,* or *sweetie-pie.* When being affectionate, women will occasionally call a man *honey* or *sweetie,* but in general, food metaphors are used much less often with men than with women. If a man is called *a fruit,* his masculinity is being questioned. But it's perfectly acceptable to use a food metaphor if the food is heavier and more substantive than that used for women. For example, pinup pictures of women have long been known as *cheesecake,* but when Burt Reynolds posed for a nude centerfold, the picture was immediately dubbed *beefcake,* cf. *a hunk of meat.* That such sexual references to men have come into the general language is another reflection on how society is beginning to lessen the differences between their attitudes toward men and women.

Something similar to the *fruit* metaphor happens with references to plants. We insult a man by calling him a *pansy,* but it wasn't considered particularly insulting to talk about a girl being *a wallflower, a clinging vine,* or *a shrinking violet,* or to give girls such names as *Ivy, Rose, Lily, Iris, Daisy, Camellia, Heather,* and *Flora.* A plant metaphor can be used with a man if the plant is big and strong, for example Andrew Jackson's nickname of *Old Hickory.* Also, the phrases *blooming idiots* and *budding geniuses* can be used with either sex, but notice how they are based on the most active thing a plant can do, which is to bloom or bud.

Animal metaphors also illustrate the different expectations for males and females. Men are referred to as *studs, bucks,* and *wolves* while women are referred to with such metaphors as *kitten, bunny, beaver, bird, chick,* and *lamb.* In the 1950s we said that boys went *tomcatting,* but today it's just *catting around* and both boys and girls do it. When the term *foxy,* meaning that someone was sexy, first become popular, it was used only for girls, but now someone of either sex can be described as a *fox.* Some animal metaphors that are used predominantly with men have negative connotations based on the size and/or strength of the animals, e.g., *beast, bullheaded, jackass, rat, loanshark,* and *vulture.* Negative metaphors used with women are based on small animals, e.g., *social butterfly, mousy, catty,* and *vixen.* The feminine terms connote action, but not the same kind of large-scale action as with the masculine terms.

Women Are Connected with Negative Connotations, Men with Positive Connotations

The final point that my notecards illustrated was how many positive connotations are associated with the concept of masculine, while there are either trivial or negative connotations connected with the corresponding feminine concept. An example from the animal metaphors makes a good illustration. The word *shrew* taken from the name of a small but especially vicious animal was defined in my dictionary as "an ill-tempered scolding woman," but the word *shrewd* taken from the same root was defined as "marked by clever, discerning awareness" and was illustrated with the phrase "a shrewd businessman."

Early in life, children are conditioned to the superiority of the masculine role. As child psychologists point out, little girls have much more freedom to experiment with sex roles than do little boys. If a little girl acts like a *tomboy*, most parents have mixed feelings, being at least partially proud. But if their little boy acts like a *sissy* (derived from *sister*), they call a psychologist. It's perfectly acceptable for a little girl to sleep in the crib that was purchased for her brother, to wear his hand-me-down jeans and shirts, and to ride the bicycle that he has outgrown. But few parents would put a boy baby in a white and gold crib decorated with frills and lace, and virtually no parents would have their little boy wear his sister's hand-me-down dresses, nor would they have their son ride a girl's pink bicycle with a flower-be-decked basket. The proper names given to girls and boys show this same attitude. Girls can have "boy" names—*Cris, Craig, Jo, Kelly, Shawn, Teri, Toni,* and *Sam*—but it doesn't work the other way around. A couple of generations ago, *Beverly, Frances, Hazel, Marion,* and *Shirley* were common boys' names. As parents gave these names to more and more girls, they fell into disuse for males, and some older men who have these names prefer to go by their initials or by such abbreviated forms as *Haze* or *Shirl*.

When a little girl is told to *be a lady*, she is being told to sit with her knees together and to be quiet and dainty. But when a little boy is told to *be a man*, he is being told to be noble, strong, and virtuous—to have all the qualities that the speaker looks on as desirable. The concept of manliness has such positive connotations that it used to be a compliment to call someone a *he-man*, to say that he was doubly a man. Today many people are ambivalent about this term and respond to it much as they do to the word *macho*. But calling someone a *manly man* or *a virile man* is nearly always meant as a compliment. *Virile* comes from the Indo-European *vir* meaning "man," which is also the basis of *virtuous*. Contrast the positive connotations of both *virile* and *virtuous* with the negative connotations of *hysterical*. The Greeks took this latter word from their name for *uterus* (as still seen in *hysterectomy*). They thought that women were the only ones who experienced uncontrolled emotional outbursts and so the condition must have something to do with a part of the body that only women have.

Differences between positive male and negative female connotations can be seen in several pairs of words which differ denotatively only in the matter of sex. *Bachelor* as compared to *spinster* or *old maid* has such positive connotations that women try to adopt them by using the term *bachelor-girl* or *bachelorette*. *Old maid* is so negative that it's the basis for metaphors: pretentious and fussy old men are called *old maids*, as are the leftover kernels of unpopped popcorn and the last card in a popular children's game.

Patron and *matron* (Middle English for *father* and *mother*) have such different levels of prestige that women try to borrow the more positive masculine connotations with the word *patroness*, literally "female father." Such a peculiar term came about because of the high prestige attached to a *patron* in such phrases as *a patron of the arts* or *a patron saint*. *Matron* is more apt to be used in talking about a woman in charge of a jail or a public restroom.

When men are doing jobs that women often do, we apparently try to pay the men extra by giving them fancy titles; for example, a male cook is more likely to be called a *chef*, while a male seamstress will get the title of *tailor*. The armed forces have a special problem in that they recruit under such slogans as "The Marine Corps Builds Men!" and "Join the Army! Become a Man." Once the recruits are enlisted, they find themselves doing much of the work that has been traditionally thought of as "woman's work." The solution to getting the work done and not insulting anyone's masculinity was to change the titles as shown below:

waitress	—>	orderly
nurse	—>	medic or corpsman
secretary	—>	clerk-typist
assistant	—>	adjutant
dishwasher	—>	KP (kitchen police) or kitchen helper

Compare *brave* and *squaw*. Early settlers in America truly admired Indian men and hence named them with a word that carried connotations of youth, vigor, and courage. But they used the Algonquin's name for "woman," and over the years it developed almost opposite connotations to those of *brave*. *Wizard* and *witch* contrast almost as much. The masculine *wizard* implies skill and wisdom combined with magic, while the feminine *witch* implies evil intentions combined with magic. Part of the unattractiveness of both *witch* and *squaw* is that they have been used so often to refer to old women, something with which our culture is particularly uncomfortable, just as the Afghans were. Imagine my surprise when I ran across the phrases *grandfatherly advice* and *old wives' tales* and realized that the underlying implication is the same as the Afghan proverb about old men being worth listening to while old women talk only foolishness.

Other terms which show how negatively we view old women as compared to young women are *old nag* as compared to *filly*, *old crow* or *old bat* as compared to *bird*, and being *catty* as compared to being *kittenish*. There is no matching set of metaphors for men. The chicken metaphor tells the whole story of a woman's life. In her youth she is a *chick*. Then she marries and begins *feathering her nest*. Soon she begins feeling *cooped up*, so she goes to *hen parties* where she *cackles* with her friends. Then she has her *brood*, begins to *henpeck* her husband, and finally turns into *an old biddy*.

I embarked on my study of the dictionary not with the intention of prescribing language change but simply to see what the language would tell me about sexism. Nevertheless I have been both surprised and pleased as I've watched the changes that have occurred over the past two decades. I'm one of those linguists who believe that new language customs will cause a new generation of speakers to grow up with different expectations. This is why I'm happy about people's efforts to use inclusive language, to say *he* or *she* or *they* when speaking about individuals whose names they do not know. I'm glad that leading publishers have developed guidelines to help writers use language that is fair to both sexes, and I'm glad that most newspapers and magazines list women by their own names instead of only by their husbands' names and that educated and thoughtful people no longer begin their business letters with "Dear Sir" or "Gentlemen," but instead use a memo form or begin with such salutations as "Dear Colleagues," "Dear Reader," or "Dear Committee Members." I'm also glad that such words as *poetess, authoress, conductress,* and *aviatrix* now sound quaint and old fashioned and that *chairman* is giving way to *chair* or *head, mailman* to *mail carrier, clergy*man to *clergy,* and *stewardess* to *flight attendant.* I was also pleased when the National Oceanic and Atmospheric Administration bowed to feminist complaints and in the late '70s began to alternate men's and women's names for hurricanes. However, I wasn't so pleased to discover that the change did not immediately erase sexist thoughts from everyone's mind as shown by a headline about Hurricane David in a 1979 New York tabloid, "David Rapes Virgin." More recently a similar metaphor appeared in a headline in the *Arizona Republic* about Hurricane Charlie: "Charlie Quits Carolinas, Flirts with Virginia."

What these incidents show is that sexism is not something existing independently in American English or in the particular dictionary that I happened to read. Rather, it exists in people's minds. Language is like an x-ray in providing visible evidence of invisible thoughts. The best thing about people being interested in and discussing sexist language is that as they make conscious decisions about what pronouns they will use, what jokes they will tell or laugh at, how they will write their names, or how they will begin their letters, they are forced to think about the underlying issue of sexism. This is good, because as a problem that begins in people's assumptions and expectations, it's a problem that will be solved only when a great many people have given it a great deal of thought.

QUESTIONS

1. Why does Nilsen begin her consideration of sexism in the English language? What does she argue is the relationship between language and culture?

2. What is an eponym? What does a study of eponyms suggest about cultural views of women and men?

3. What are "paired terms"? What does a study of paired terms suggest abut cultural views of women and men?

4. What does an analysis of marriage-related terms and the culture of weddings reveal about cultural perceptions of men and women? What does an analysis of the culture of weddings suggest about the relationship between language and culture? How does the same analysis reveal changes in the degree of sexism in the English language?

5. What does Nilsen suggest an analysis of language reveals about the gender socialization process and about the cultural valuation of the masculine and the feminine? What definition of "sexism" can you develop from Nilsen's argument?

The Transformation of Silence into Language and Action (1984)

Audre Lorde

An African-American lesbian scholar, Audre Lorde uses provocative language to challenge us to hear the enormous strain of silence on the possibilities for social change. Lorde passionately urges those of us who are silent, and who have been silenced, to find our voices and reclaim the power of language. She reminds us of both the dangers of silence and incredible rewards of speech. Audre Lorde's directive offers its practitioner freedom from the bonds of silence, and empowerment in the expression of one's voice.

I have come to believe over and over again that what is most important to me must be spoken, made verbal and shared, even at the risk of having it bruised or misunderstood. That the speaking profits me, beyond any other effect. I am standing here as a Black lesbian poet, and the meaning of all that waits upon the fact that I am still alive, and might not have been. Less than two months ago I was told by two doctors, one female and one male, that I would have to have breast surgery, and that there was a 60 to 80 percent chance that the tumor was malignant. Between that telling and the actual surgery, there was a three-week period of the agony of an involuntary reorganization of my entire life. The surgery was completed, and the growth was benign.

But within those three weeks, I was forced to look upon myself and my living with a harsh and urgent clarity that has left me still shaken but much stronger. This is a situation faced by many women, by some of you here today. Some of what I experienced during that time has helped elucidate for me much of what I feel concerning the transformation of silence into language and action.

In becoming forcibly and essentially aware of my mortality, and of what I wished and wanted for my life, however short it might be, priorities and omissions became strongly etched in a merciless light, and what I most regretted were my silences. Of what had I *ever* been afraid? To question or to speak as I believed could have meant pain, or death. But we all hurt in so many different ways, all the time, and pain will either change or end. Death, on the other hand, is the final silence. And that might be coming quickly, now, without regard for whether I had ever spoken what needed to be said, or had only betrayed myself into small silences, while I planned someday to speak, or waited for someone else's words. And I began to recognize a source of power within myself that comes from the knowledge that while it is most desirable not to be afraid, learning to put fear into a perspective gave me strength.

I was going to die, if not sooner then later, whether or not I had ever spoken myself. My silences had not protected me. Your silence will not protect you. But for every real word spoken, for every attempt I had ever made to speak those truths for which I am still seeking, I had made contact with other women while we examined the words to fit a world in which we all believed, bridging our differences. And it was the concern and caring of all those women which gave me strength and enabled me to scrutinize the essentials of my living.

The women who sustained me through that period were Black and white, old and young, lesbian, bisexual, and heterosexual, and we all shared a war against the tyrannies of silence. They all gave me a strength and concern without which I could not have survived intact. Within those weeks of acute fear came the knowledge—within the war we are all waging with the forces of death, subtle and otherwise, conscious or not—I am not only a casualty, I am also a warrior.

What are the words you do not yet have? What do you need to say? What are the tyrannies you swallow day by day and attempt to make your own, until you will sicken and die of them, still in silence? Perhaps for some of you here today, I am the face of one of your fears. Because I am woman, because I am Black, because I am lesbian, because I am myself—a Black woman warrior poet doing my work—come to ask you, are you doing yours?

And of course I am afraid, because the transformation of silence into language and action is an act of self-revelation, and that always seems fraught with danger. But my daughter, when I told her of our topic and my difficulty with it, said, "Tell them about how you're never really a whole person if you remain silent, because there's always that one little piece inside you that wants to be spoken out, and if you keep ignoring it, it gets madder and madder and hotter and hotter, and if you don't speak it out one day it will just up and punch you in the mouth from the inside."

In the cause of silence, each of us draws the face of her own fear—fear of contempt, of censure, or some judgment, or recognition, of challenge, of annihilation. But most of all, I think, we fear the visibility without which we cannot truly live. Within this country where racial difference creates a constant, if unspoken, distortion of vision, Black women have on one hand always been highly visible, and so, on the other hand, have been rendered invisible through the depersonalization of racism. Even within the women's movement, we have had to fight, and still do, for that very visibility which also renders us most vulnerable, our Blackness. For to survive in the mouth of this dragon we call america, we have had to learn this first and most vital lesson—that we were never meant to survive. Not as human beings. And neither were most of you here today, Black or not. And that visibility which makes us most vulnerable is that which also is the source of our greatest strength. Because the machine will try to grind you into dust anyway, whether or not we speak. We can sit in our corners mute forever while our sisters and our selves are wasted, while our children are distorted and destroyed, while our earth is poisoned; we can sit in our safe corners mute as bottles, and we will still be no less afraid.

In my house this year we are celebrating the feast of Kwanza, the African-american festival of harvest which begins the day after Christmas and lasts for seven days. There are seven principles of Kwanza, one for each day. The first principle is Umoja, which means unity, the decision to strive for and maintain unity in self and community. The principle for yesterday, the second day, was Kujichagulia—self-determination—the decision to define ourselves, name ourselves, and speak for ourselves, instead of being defined and spoken for by others. Today is the third day of Kwanza, and the principle for today is Ujima—collective work and responsibility—the decision to build and maintain ourselves and our communities together and to recognize and solve our problems together.

Each of us is here now because in one way or another we share a commitment to language and to the power of language, and to the reclaiming of that language which has been made to work against us. In the transformation of silence into language and action, it is vitally necessary for each one of us to establish or examine her function in that transformation and to recognize her role as vital within that transformation.

For those of us who write, it is necessary to scrutinize not only the truth of what we speak, but the truth of that language by which we speak it. For others, it is to share and spread also those words that are meaningful to us. But primarily for us all, it is necessary to teach by living and speaking those truths which we believe and know beyond understanding. Because in this way alone we can survive, by taking part in a process of life that is creative and continuing, that is growth.

And it is never without fear—of visibility, of the harsh light of scrutiny and perhaps judgment, of pain, of death. But we have lived through all of those already, in silence, except death. And I remind myself all the time now that if I were to have been born mute, or had maintained an oath of silence my whole life long for safety, I would still have suffered, and I would still die. It is very good for establishing perspective.

And where the words of women are crying to be heard, we must each of us recognize our responsibility to seek those words out, to read them and share them and examine them in their pertinence to our lives. That we not hide behind the mockeries of separations that have been imposed upon us and which so often we accept as our own. For instance, "I can't possibly teach Black women's writing—their experience is so different from mine." Yet how many years have you spend teaching Plato and Shakespeare and Proust? Or another, "She's a white woman and what could she possibly have to say to me?" Or, "She's a lesbian, what would my husband say, or my chairman?" Or again, "This woman writes of her sons and I have no children." And all the other endless ways in which we rob ourselves of ourselves and each other.

We can learn to work and speak when we are afraid in the same way we have learned to work and speak when we are tired. For we have been socialized to respect fear more than our own needs for language and definition, and while we wait in silence for that final luxury of fearlessness, the weight of that silence will choke us.

The fact that we are here and that I speak these words is an attempt to break silence and bridge some of those differences between us, for it is not difference which immobilizes us, but silence. And there are so many silences to be broken.

QUESTIONS

1. What does Lorde suggest are the consequences of remaining silent? What is her concept of *the tyrannies of silence*?
2. How do you see speech and language functioning as actions?
3. In what ways does fear work to silence human speech? How have you encountered fear as a silencer in your life?

Beauty and Images

Beauty: what is it? How do we decide what it is and who/what possesses it? What does it mean to possess it? What are the implications of being perceived as *not* possessing beauty? Can the ideology of beauty, reinforced by an extensive and deeply embedded array of popularly-presented images, be one of the social forces which conspires to create the reality of women's and men's lives?

In this section, we ask these questions and others about the dynamics of beauty and images of representation in historical and contemporary social life in the United States. We will explore beauty ideology and the politics of the physical body. We will ask whether the fact that much of our first impressions of, and reactions to, one another is shaped by evaluation of the physical body and affects both our personal lives and our lives as beings in a social environment. We will consider beauty as a force of power and domination, particularly as beauty is defined in dominant social representations. We will wonder whether an image of "beauty" depicts far more than the image itself; we will ask what's *behind* the image, as well as explore the significance of what social representations of beauty render invisible.

THE BEAUTY MYTH (1991)

Naomi Wolf

Many feminist theorists suggest that, for females, the awareness of and attention toward physical appearance is socially defined as a crucial element in female identity formation. Essayist and public speaker Naomi Wolf has published in a wide range of the popular press, from Esquire *to the* Wall Street Journal. *In this selection, Naomi Wolf explores beauty ideology in today's society by examining its historical roots and its contemporary effects. Wolf suggests that our culture's beauty ideology is based on a mythical perception of "beauty". And yet, she suggests that the power to influence the lives and status of women in society remains firmly entrenched in what Wolf calls "social fictions".*

At last, after a long silence, women took to the streets. In the two decades of radical action that followed the rebirth of feminism in the early 1970s, Western women gained legal and reproductive rights, pursued higher education, entered the trades and the professions, and overturned ancient and revered beliefs about their social role. A generation on, do women feel free?

The affluent, educated, liberated women of the First World, who can enjoy freedoms unavailable to any women ever before, do not feel as free as they want to. And they can no longer restrict to the subconscious their sense that this lack of freedom has something to do with—with apparently frivolous issues, things that really should not matter. Many are ashamed to admit that such trivial concerns—to do with physical appearance, bodies, faces, hair, clothes—matter so much. But in spite of shame, guilt, and denial, more and more women are wondering if it isn't that they are entirely neurotic and alone but rather that something important is indeed at stake that has to do with the relationship between female liberation and female beauty.

The more legal and material hindrances women have broken through, the more strictly and heavily and cruelly images of female beauty have come to weigh upon us. Many women sense that women's collective progress has stalled; compared with the heady momentum of earlier days, there is a dispiriting climate of confusion, division, cynicism, and above all, exhaustion. After years of much struggle and little recognition, many older women feel burned out; after years of taking its light for granted, many younger women show little interest in touching new fire to the torch.

During the past decade, women breached the power structure; meanwhile, eating disorders rose exponentially and cosmetic surgery became the fastest-growing medical specialty. During the past five years, consumer spending doubled, pornography became the main media category, ahead of legitimate films and records combined, and thirty-three thousand American women told researchers that they would rather lose ten to fifteen pounds than achieve any other goal. More women have more money and power and scope and legal recognition than we have ever had before; but in terms of how we feel about ourselves *physically*, we may actually be worse off than our unliberated grandmothers. Recent research consistently shows that inside the majority of the West's controlled, attractive, successful working women, there is a secret "underlife" poisoning our freedom; infused with notions of beauty, it is a dark vein of self-hatred, physical obsessions, terror of aging, and dread of lost control.

It is no accident that so many potentially powerful women feel this way. We are in the midst of a violent backlash against feminism that uses images of female beauty as a political weapon against women's advancement: the beauty myth. It is the modern version of a social reflex that has been in force since the Industrial Revolution. As women released themselves from the feminine mystique of domesticity, the beauty myth took over its lost ground, expanding as it waned to carry on its work of social control.

The contemporary backlash is so violent because the ideology of beauty is the last one remaining of the old feminine ideologies that still has the power to control those women whom second wave feminism would have otherwise made relatively uncontrollable: It has grown stronger to take over the work of social coercion that myths about motherhood, domesticity, chastity, and passivity, no longer can manage. It is seeking right now to undo psychologically and covertly all the good things that feminism did for women materially and overtly.

This counterforce is operating to checkmate the inheritance of feminism on every level in the lives of Western women. Feminism gave us laws against job discrimination based on gender; immediately case law evolved in Britain and the United States that institutionalized job discrimination based on women's appearances. Patriarchal religion declined; new religious dogma, using some of the mind-altering techniques of older cults and sects, arose around age and weight to functionally supplant traditional ritual. Feminists, inspired by Friedan, broke the strangle-hold on the women's popular press of advertisers for household products, who were promoting the feminine mystique; at once, the diet and skin care industries became the new cultural censors of women's intellectual space, and because of their pressure, the gaunt, youthful model supplanted the happy housewife as the arbiter of successful womanhood. The sexual revolution promoted the discovery of female sexuality; "beauty pornography"—which for the first time in women's history artificially links a commodified "beauty" directly and explicitly to sexuality—invaded the mainstream to undermine women's new and vulnerable sense of sexual self-worth. Reproductive rights gave Western women control over our own bodies; the weight of fashion models plummeted to 23 percent below that of ordinary women, eating disorders rose exponentially, and a mass neurosis was promoted that used food and weight to strip women of that sense of control. Women insisted on politicizing health; new technologies of invasive, potentially deadly "cosmetic" surgeries developed apace to re-exert old forms of medical control of women.

Every generation since about 1830 has had to fight its version of the beauty myth. "It is very little of me," said the suffragist Lucy Stone in 1855, "to have the right to vote, to own property, etcetera, if I may not keep my body, and its uses, in my absolute right." Eighty years later, after women had won the vote, and the first wave of the organized women's movement had subsided, Virginia Woolf wrote that it would still be decades before women could tell the truth about their bodies. In 1962, Betty Friedan quoted a young woman trapped in the Feminine Mystique: "Lately, I look in the mirror, and I'm so afraid I'm going to look like my mother." Eight years after that, heralding the cataclysmic second wave of feminism, Germaine Greer described "the Stereotype": "To her belongs all that is beautiful, even the very word beauty itself . . . she is a doll . . . I'm sick of the masquerade." In spite of the great revolution of the second wave, we are not exempt. Now we can look out over ruined barricades: A revolution has come upon us and changed everything in its path, enough time has passed since then for babies to have grown into women, but there still remains a final right not fully claimed.

The beauty myth tells a story: The quality called "beauty" objectively and universally exists. Women must want to embody it and men must want to possess women who embody it. This embodiment is an imperative for women and not for men, which situation is necessary and natural because it is biological, sexual, and evolutionary: Strong men battle for beautiful women, and beautiful women are more reproductively successful. Women's beauty must correlate to their fertility, and since this system is based on sexual selection, it is inevitable and changeless.

None of this is true. "Beauty" is a currency system like the gold standard. Like any economy, it is determined by politics, and in the modern age in the West it is the last, best belief system that keeps male dominance intact. In assigning value to women in a vertical hierarchy according to a culturally imposed physical standard, it is an expression of power relations in which women must unnaturally compete for resources that men have appropriated for themselves.

"Beauty" is not universal or changeless, though the West pretends that all ideals of female beauty stem from one Platonic Ideal Woman; the Maori admire a fat vulva, and the Padung, droopy breasts. Nor is "beauty" a function of evolution: Its ideals change at a pace far more rapid than that of the evolution of species, and Charles Darwin was himself unconvinced by his own explanation that "beauty" resulted from a "sexual selection" that deviated from the rule of natural selection; for women to compete with women through "beauty" is a reversal of the way in which natural selection affects all other mammals. Anthropology has overturned the notion that females must be "beautiful" to be selected to mate: Evelyn Reed, Elaine Morgan, and others have dismissed sociobiological assertions of innate male polygamy and female monogamy. Female higher primates are the sexual initiators; not only do they seek out and enjoy sex with many partners, but "every nonpregnant female takes her turn at being the most desirable of all her troop. And that cycle keeps turning as long as she lives." The inflamed pink sexual organs of primates are often cited by male sociobiologists as analogous to human arrangements relating to female "beauty," when in fact that is a universal, nonhierarchical female primate characteristic.

Nor has the beauty myth always been this way. Though the pairing of the older rich men with young, "beautiful" women is taken to be somehow inevitable, in the matriarchal Goddess religions that dominated the Mediterranean from about 25,000 B.C.E. to about 700 B.C.E., the situation was reversed: "In every culture, the Goddess has many lovers. . . . The clear pattern is of an older woman with a beautiful but expendable youth—Ishtar and Tammuz, Venus and Adonis, Cybele and Attis, Isis and Osiris . . . their only function the service of the divine 'womb.'" Nor is it something only women do and only men watch: Among the Nigerian Wodaabes, the women hold economic power and the tribe is obsessed with male beauty; Wodaabe men spend hours together in elaborate makeup sessions, and compete—provocatively painted and dressed, with swaying hips and seductive expressions—in beauty contests judged by women. There is no legitimate historical or biological justification for the beauty myth; what it is doing to women today is a result of nothing more exalted than the need of today's power structure, economy, and culture to mount a counteroffensive against women.

If the beauty myth is not based on evolution, sex, gender, aesthetics, or God, on what is it based? It claims to be about intimacy and sex and life, a celebration of women. It is actually composed of emotional distance, politics, finance, and sexual repression. The beauty myth is not about women at all. It is about men's institutions and institutional power.

The qualities that a given period calls beautiful in women are merely symbols of the female behaviour that that period considers desirable: *The beauty myth is always actually prescribing behavior and not appearance.* Competition between women has been made part of the myth so that women will be divided from one another. Youth and (until recently) virginity have been "beautiful" in women since they stand for experiential and sexual ignorance. Aging in women is "unbeautiful" since women grow more powerful with time, and since the links between generations of women must always be newly broken: Older women fear young ones, young women fear old, and the beauty myth truncates for all the female life span. Most urgently, women's identity must be premised upon our "beauty" so that we will remain vulnerable to outside approval, carrying the vital sensitive organ of self-esteem exposed to the air.

Though there has, of course, been a beauty myth in some form for as long as there has been patriarchy, the beauty myth in its modern form is a fairly recent invention. The myth flourishes when material constraints on women are dangerously loosened. Before the Industrial Revolution, the average woman could not have had the same feelings about "beauty" that modern women do who experience the myth as continual comparison to a mass-disseminated physical ideal. Before the development of technologies of mass production—daguerreotypes, photographs, etc.—an ordinary woman was exposed to few such images outside the Church. Since the family was a productive unit and women's work complemented men's, the value of women who were not aristocrats or prostitutes lay in their work skills, economic shrewdness, physical strength, and fertility. Physical attraction, obviously, played its part; but "beauty" as we understand it was not, for ordinary women, a serious issue in the marriage marketplace. The beauty myth in its modern form gained ground after the upheavals of industrialization, as the work unit of the family was destroyed, and urbanization and the emerging factory system demanded what social engineers of the time termed the "separate sphere" of domesticity, which supported the new labor category of the "breadwinner" who left home for the workplace during the day. The middle class expanded, the standards of living and of literacy rose, the size of families shrank; a new class of literate, idle women developed, on whose submission to enforced domesticity the evolving system of industrial capitalism depended. Most of our assumptions about the way women have always thought about "beauty" date from no earlier than the 1830s, when the cult of domesticity was first consolidated and the beauty index invented.

For the first time new technologies could reproduce—in fashion plates, daguerreotypes, tintypes, and rotogravures—images of how women should look. In the 1840s the first nude photographs of prostitutes were taken; advertisements using images of "beautiful" women first appeared in mid-century. Copies of classical artworks, postcards of society beauties and royal mistresses, Currier and Ives prints, and porcelain figurines flooded the separate sphere to which middle-class women were confined.

Since the Industrial Revolution, middle-class Western women have been controlled by ideals and stereotypes as much as by material constraints. This situation, unique to this group, means that analyses that trace "cultural conspiracies" are uniquely plausible in relation to them. The rise of the beauty myth was just one of several emerging social fictions that masqueraded as natural components of the feminine sphere, the better to enclose those women inside it. Other such fictions arose contemporaneously: a version of childhood that required continual maternal supervision; a concept of female biology that required middle-class women to act out the roles of hysterics and hypochondriacs; a conviction that respectable women were sexually anesthetic; and a definition of women's work that occupied them with repetitive, time-consuming, and painstaking tasks such as needlepoint and lacemaking. All such Victorian inventions as these served a double function—that is, though they were encouraged as a means to expend female energy and intelligence in harmless ways, women often used them to express genuine creativity and passion.

But in spite of middle-class women's creativity with fashion and embroidery and child rearing, and, a century later, with the role of the suburban housewife that devolved from these social fictions, the fictions' main purpose was served: During a century and a half of unprecedented feminist agitation, they effectively counteracted middle-class women's dangerous new leisure, literacy, and relative freedom from material constraints.

Though these time- and mind-consuming fictions about women's natural role adapted themselves to resurface in the post-war Feminine Mystique, when the second wave of the women's movement took apart what women's magazines had portrayed as the "romance," "science," and "adventure" of homemaking and suburban family life, they temporarily failed. The cloying domestic fiction of "togetherness" lost its meaning and middle-class women walked out of their front doors in masses.

So the fictions simply transformed themselves once more: Since the women's movement had successfully taken apart most other necessary fictions of femininity, all the work of social control once spread out over the whole network of these fictions had to be reassigned to the only strand left intact, which action consequently strengthened it a hundredfold. This reimposed onto liberated women's faces and bodies all the limitations, taboos, and punishments of the repressive laws, religious injunctions and reproductive enslavement that no longer carried sufficient force. Inexhaustible but ephemeral beauty work took over from inexhaustible but ephemeral housework. As the economy, law, religion, sexual mores, education, and culture were forcibly opened up to include women more fairly, a private reality colonized female consciousness. By using ideas about "beauty," it reconstructed an alternative female world with its own laws, economy, religion, sexuality, education, and culture, each element as repressive as any that had gone before.

Since middle-class Western women can best be weakened psychologically now that we are stronger materially, the beauty myth, as it has resurfaced in the last generation, has had to draw on more technological sophistication and reactionary fervor than ever before. The modern arsenal of the myth is a dissemination of millions of images of the current ideal; although this barrage is generally seen as a collective sexual fantasy, there is in fact little that is sexual about it. It is summoned out of political fear on the part of male-dominated institutions threatened by women's freedom, and it exploits female guilt and apprehension about our own liberation—latent fears that we might be going too far. This frantic aggregation of imagery is a collective reactionary hallucination willed into being by both men and women stunned and disoriented by the rapidity with which gender relations have been transformed: a bulwark of reassurance against the flood of change. The mass depiction of the modern woman as a "beauty" is a contradiction: Where modern women are growing, moving, and expressing their individuality, as the myth has it, "beauty" is by definition inert, timeless, and generic. That this hallucination is necessary and deliberate is evident in the way "beauty" so directly contradicts women's real situation.

And the unconscious hallucination grows ever more influential and pervasive because of what is now conscious market manipulation: powerful industries—the $33-billion-a-year diet industry, the $20-billion cosmetics industry, the $300-million cosmetic surgery industry, and the $7-billion pornography industry—have arisen from the capital made out of unconscious anxieties, and are in turn able, through their influence on mass culture, to use, stimulate, and reinforce the hallucination in a rising economic spiral.

This is not a conspiracy theory; it doesn't have to be. Societies tell themselves necessary fictions in the same way that individuals and families do. Henrik Ibsen called them "vital lies," and psychologist Daniel Goleman describes them working the same way on the social level that they do within families: "The collusion is maintained by directing attention away from the fearsome fact, or by repackaging its meaning in an acceptable format." The costs of these social blind spots, he writes, are destructive communal illusions. Possibilities for women have become so open-ended that they threaten to destabilize the institutions on which a male-dominated culture has depended, and a collective panic reaction on the part of both sexes has forced a demand for counterimages.

The resulting hallucination materializes, for women, as something all too real. No longer just an idea, it becomes three-dimensional, incorporating within itself how women live and how they do not live: It becomes the Iron Maiden. The original Iron Maiden was a medieval German instrument of torture, a body-shaped casket painted with the limbs and features of a lovely, smiling young woman. The unlucky victim was slowly enclosed inside her; the lid fell shut to immobilize the victim, who died either of starvation or, less cruelly, of the metal spikes embedded in her interior. The modern hallucination in which women are trapped or trap themselves is similarly rigid, cruel, and euphemistically painted. Contemporary culture directs attention to imagery of the Iron Maiden, while censoring real women's faces and bodies.

Why does the social order feel the need to defend itself by evading the fact of real women, our faces and voices and bodies, and reducing the meaning of women to these formulaic and endlessly reproduced "beautiful" images? Though unconscious personal anxieties can be a powerful force in the creation of a vital lie, economic necessity practically guarantees it. An economy that depends on slavery needs to promote images of slaves that "justify" the institution of slavery. Western economies are absolutely dependent now on the continued underpayment of women. An ideology that makes women feel "worth less" was urgently needed to counteract the way feminism had begun to make us feel worth more. This does not require a conspiracy; merely an atmosphere. The contemporary economy depends right now on the representation of women within the beauty myth. Economist John Kenneth Galbraith offers an economic explanation for "the persistence of the view of homemaking as a 'higher calling'"; the concept of women as naturally trapped within the Feminine Mystique, he feels, "has been forced on us by popular sociology, by magazines, and by fiction to disguise the fact that woman in her role of consumer has been essential to the development of our industrial society. . . . Behavior that is essential for economic reasons is transformed into a social virtue." As soon as a woman's primary social value could no longer be defined as the attainment of virtuous domesticity, the beauty myth redefined it as the attainment of virtuous beauty. It did so to substitute both a new consumer imperative and a new justification for economic unfairness in the workplace where the old ones had lost their hold over newly liberated women.

Another hallucination arose to accompany that of the Iron Maiden: The caricature of the Ugly Feminist was resurrected to dog the steps of the women's movement. The caricature is unoriginal; it was coined to ridicule the feminists of the nineteenth century. Lucy Stone herself, whom supporters saw as "a prototype of womanly grace . . . fresh and fair as the morning," was derided by detractors with "the usual report" about Victorian feminists: "a big masculine woman, wearing boots, smoking a cigar, swearing like a trooper." As Betty Friedan put it presciently in 1960, even before the savage revamping of that old caricature: "The unpleasant image of feminists today resembles less the feminists themselves than the image fostered by the interests who so bitterly opposed the vote for women in state after state." Thirty years on, her conclusion is more true than ever: That resurrected caricature, which sought to punish women for their public acts by going after their private sense of self, became the paradigm for new limits placed on aspiring women everywhere. After the success of the women's movement's second wave, the beauty myth was perfected to checkmate power at every level in individual women's lives. The modern neuroses of life in the female body spread to woman after woman at epidemic rates. The myth is undermining—slowly, imperceptibly, without our being aware of the real forces or erosion—the ground women have gained through long, hard, honorable struggle.

The beauty myth of the present is more insidious than any mystique of femininity yet: A century ago, Nora slammed the door of the doll's house; a generation ago, women turned their backs on the consumer heaven of the isolated multiapplianced home; but where women are trapped today, there is no door to slam. The contemporary ravages of the beauty backlash are destroying women physically and depleting us psychologically. If we are to free ourselves from the dead weight that has once again been made out of femaleness, it is not ballots or lobbyists or placards that women will need first; it is a new way to see.

QUESTIONS

1. Why does Wolf argue that consideration of "the beauty myth" is an important element in an understanding of the status of women in contemporary society?

2. What does Wolf identify as "the beauty myth"? Why does she identify it *as* a myth? How does the myth affect the lives of women today?

3. What is Wolf's conceptualization of "beauty"? What evidence does she offer to support her conceptualization?

4. What does Wolf suggest is the historical origin of today's beauty ideology? Identify the social fictions Wolf argues helped to create beauty ideology. What is a social fiction?

ENDNOTES

Cosmetic surgery: *Standard and Poor's Industry Surveys* (New York: Standard and Poor's Corp., 1988).

Pornography main media category: See "Crackdown on Pornography: A No-Win Battle," *U. S. News and World Report,* June 4, 1984. The Association of Fashion and Image Consultants tripled its membership between 1984 and 1989 alone (Annetta Miller and Dody Tsiantar, *Newsweek,* May 22, 1989). During the five or six years prior to 1986, consumer spending rose from $300 billion to $600 billion.

Thirty-three thousand American women, University of Cincinnati College of Medicine, 1984: Wooley, S. C., and O. W. Wooley, "Obesity and Women: A Closer Look at the Facts," *Women's Studies International Quarterly,* vol. 2 (1979), pp. 69–79. Data reprinted in "33,000 Women Tell How They Really Feel About Their Bodies," *Glamour,* February 1984.

Recent research shows: See Dr. Thomas Cash, Diane Cash, and Jonathan Butters, "Mirror-Mirror on the Wall: Contrast Effects and Self-Evaluation of Physical Attractiveness," *Personality and Social Psychology Bulletin,* September 1983, vol. 9, no. 3. Dr. Cash's research shows very little connection between "how attractive women are" and "how attractive they feel themselves to be." All the women he treated were, in his terms, "extremely attractive," but his patients compare themselves only to models, not to other women.

Very little to me: Lucy Stone, 1855, quoted in Andrea Dworkin, *Pornography: Men Possessing Women* (New York: Putnam, 1981), p. 11.

A doll: Germaine Greer, *The Female Eunuch* (London: Paladin Grafton Books, 1970), pp. 55, 60.

Myth: See also Roland Barthes's definition: "It [myth] transforms history into nature. . . . Myth has the task of giving an historical intention a natural justification, and making contingency appear eternal." Roland Barthes, "Myth Today," *Mythologies* (New York: Hill and Wang, 1972), p. 129.

Anthropologist Bronislaw Malinowski's definition of "a myth of origin" is relevant to the beauty myth: A myth of origin, writes Ann Oakley, "tends to be worked hardest in times of social strain, when the state of affairs portrayed in the myth are called into question." Ann Oakley, *Housewife: High Value/Low Cost* (London: Penguine Books, 1987), p. 163.

Platonic: See Plato's discussion of Beauty in *Symposium*. For varying standards of beauty, see Ted Polhemus, *Body-Styles* (Luton, England: Lennard Publishing, 1988).

Sexual selection; Darwin . . . was unconvinced: See Cynthia Eagle Russett, "Hairy Men and Beautiful Women," *Sexual Science: The Victorian Construction of Womanhood* (Cambridge, Mass.: Harvard University Press, 1989), pp. 78–103.

On page 84 Russett quotes Darwin: "Man is more powerful in body and mind than woman, and in the savage state he keeps her in a much more abject state of bondage, than does the male of any other animal; therefore it is not surprising that he should have gained the power of selection. . . . As women have long been selected for beauty, it is not surprising that some of their successive variations should have been transmitted exclusively to the same sex; consequently that they should have transmitted beauty in a somewhat higher degree to their female than to their male offspring, and thus have become more beautiful, according to general opinion, than men." Darwin himself noticed the evolutionary inconsistency of this idea that, as Russett puts it, "a funny thing happened on the way up the ladder: among humans, the female no longer chose but was chosen." This theory "implied an awkward break in evolutionary continuity," she observes: "In Darwin's own terms it marked a rather startling reversal in the trend of evolution."

See also Natalie Angier, "Hard-to-Please Females May Be Neglected Evolutionary Force," *The New York Times*, May 8, 1990, and Natalie Angier, "Mating for Life? It's Not for the Birds or the Bees," *The New York Times*, August 21, 1990.

Evolution: See Evelyn Reed, *Woman's Evolution: From Matriarchal Clan to Patriarchal Family* (New York: Pathfinder Press, 1986); and Elaine Morgan, *The Descent of Woman* (New York: Bantam Books, 1979). See especially "the upper primate," p. 91.

Goddess: Rosalind Miles, *The Women's History of the World* (London: Paladin Grafton Books, 1988), p. 43. See also Merlin Stone, *When God Was a Woman* (San Diego: Harvest Books, 1976).

Wodaabe tribe: Leslie Woodhead, "Desert Dandies," *The Guardian*, July 1988.

In the West African Fulani tribe young women choose their husbands on the basis of their beauty: "The contestants . . . take part in the yaake, a line-up in which they sing and dance, stand on tip-toe and make faces, rolling and crossing their eyes and grimacing to show off their teeth to the judges. They keep this up for hours, aided by the consumption of stimulating drugs beforehand. Throughout all this, old ladies in the crowd hurl criticisms at those who do not live up to the Fulani idea of beauty." [Polhemus, op. cit., p. 21]

See also Carol Beckwith and Marion van Offelen, *Nomads of Niger* (London: William Collins Sons & Co. Ltd., 1984), cited in Carol Beckwith, "Niger's Wodaabe: People of the Taboo," *National Geographic*, vol. 164, no. 4, October 1983, pp. 483–509.

Paleolithic excavations suggest that it has been human males rather than females to whom adornment was assigned in prehistoric societies; in modern tribal communities men generally adorn at least as much as women, and often hold "a virtual monopoly" over adornment. The Sudanese Nuba, the Australian Waligigi, and the Mount Hagen men of New Guinea also spend hours painting themselves and perfecting their hairstyles to attract the women, whose toilette takes only minutes. See Polhemus, op. cit., pp. 54–55.

Technologies: See, for example, Beaumont Newhall, *The History of Photography from 1839 to the Present* (London: Secker & Warburg, 1986), p. 31. Photograph *Academie*, c. 1845, photographer unknown.

Powerful industries: Diet items are a $74-billion-a-year industry in the United States, totaling one-third the nation's annual food bill. See David Brand, "A Nation of Healthy Worrywarts?," *Time*, July 25, 1988.

$33-billion-a-year diet industry: Molly O"Neill, "Congress Looking into the Diet Business," *The New York Times*, March 28, 1990.

$300-million-a-year cosmetic surgery industry: *Standard and Poor's Industry Surveys*, op. cit. 1988.

$7 billion pornography industry, "Crackdown on Pornography," op. cit.

Vital lies: Daniel Goleman, *Vital Lies, Simple Truths: The Psychology of Self-Deception* (New York: Simon and Schuster, 1983), pp. 16–17, quoting Henrik Ibsen's phrase: "The vital lie continues unrevealed, sheltered by the family's silence, alibis, stark denial."

A higher calling: John Kenneth Galbraith, quoted in Michael H. Minton with Jean Libman Block, *What Is a Wife Worth?* (New York: McGraw-Hill, 1984), pp. 134–135.

Ugly Feminist: Marcia Cohen, *The Sisterhood: The Inside Story of the Women's Movement and the Leaders Who Made It Happen* (New York: Ballantine Books, 1988), pp. 205, 206, 287, 290, 322, 332.

Swearing like a trooper: Betty Friedan, *The Feminine Mystique* (London: Penguin Books, 1982), p. 79, quoting Elinor Rice Hays, *Morning Star: A Biography of Lucy Stone* (New York: Harcourt, 1961), p. 83.

Unpleasant image: Friedan, op. cit., p. 87.

Arroz Con Pollo vs. Slim Fast (1992)

Linda Delgado

Latina women, sandwiched between Latino culture and mainstream U. S. culture, encounter mixed messages about beauty and body size. In this essay, Linda Delgado addresses how these multiple and mixed messages create confusion for young Latina women in the United States. Through her discussion, Delgado raises for us the question of beauty norms and their impact on women's ability to develop their unique potential.

To many white American women, thinness and tallness are essential parts of beauty. Yet in Spanish, the words *delgada* and *flaca* have a different connotation. Both words mean thin. *Delgada* connotes thin and weak, while *flaca* connotes thin as in skinny. Neither is very flattering. In fact, the question that usually follows after someone notices you are looking rather *delgada* is whether you have been ill.

Weight problems, aside from their health implications, are not seen as important in Latino culture as they are in mainstream American culture. There is a ceremonial importance to food and many rituals assigned to the sharing of food with others. Recently during a warm-up exercise in a new class, students were asked to introduce themselves by identifying with a particular food. A young Dominican woman said she was like *arroz con pollo* (rice with chicken). Her reason for picking this dish was that rice with chicken symbolized warmth, love, and acceptance. It is a dish made for new neighbors, new in-laws, and new friends to celebrate important events. It means welcome and good luck.

The breaking of bread with family, friends, and strangers is part of Latino hospitality. "*Mi casa, su casa*" is an unaltered tradition. When you visit my aunt's house, for example, go there hungry! The variety and amounts of food are quite extraordinary. I get full just looking at the table! Not only must you partake of everything there, you must also keep in mind that there are at least three or four desserts to follow. On special occasions, such as Easter, Christmas, and Mother's Day, everyone has a signature dish, and part of the celebration is sharing these delicacies. Failure to eat the right amount will cause personal distress to the hostess. What did she do wrong? At my aunt's house, usually my grandmother will ask if you have been sick or if your children have been giving you a hard time. There must be some explanation why you have not eaten your share of food. By "your share of food" they mean enough to feed a small army! The word "diet" or "calories" is never mentioned. For the current generations, these messages can be confusing.

Putting weight on your bones, as my grandmother explains it, is necessary for many reasons. First of all, how else can you carry the burdens of being a woman? You have to eat in order to have the strength to deal with a husband and/or children (regardless of the fact that, at present, you may be 11 years old). You have to eat to have the strength to deal with *lo que Dios te mande,* whatever God sends you because *uno nunca sabe lo de mañana, so uno tierne que aprobechar lo de hoy*, we never know what tomorrow may bring, so we have to enjoy what we have today. Living in New York, you also have to eat in order to deal with the cold, wintry weather. There is always a good reason for a second or third helping of food. In the film *Acting Our Age,* an African-American woman about the age of 65 expresses her concern for the next generation of young women. She says, "Now that black women are being used as models and thought of as beautiful, they will pick up the same false notions about beauty as white women." I think this is also true for Latinas in the United States.

One of my childhood memories was an episode involving my grandmother when I was in the fifth grade. She picked me up at school and told my mother we were going shopping. Well, we did, but first she had someplace to take me. For as long as I could remember, I was a tall and very skinny child. That day, my grandmother and I took a bus ride into Manhattan to a nutrition clinic. She swore I was undernourished and that something was wrong. The doctor said I was healthy and of a good weight. My grandmother was quite surprised and, in fact, didn't believe him.

Having a "good set of hips" means not only that you can carry a child well but also that you can manage whatever your husband has in store for you. "You have to eat in order to have strength." So, from the time you are an infant, chubbiness is applauded as healthy. As you grow older, mental and physical well-being are assessed by your outer appearance. Thin is not sexy. It is unhealthy, unappealing, and sad. My grandmother told me that I didn't look strong enough to carry my bookbag and asked how was I going to carry whatever God sent my way. I learned early in life to expect to bear something! That was part of the gender-role experience.

Interestingly, flabbiness is not acceptable, either. Flabbiness is a sign of laziness and overindulgence. Formal exercise is not part of the Latino culture for women, while men often play softball, handball, or paddle ball. It is generally accepted that women who are flabby and out of shape must not be taking care of their homes, themselves, or their children. They must be watching *novelas*. Women's exercise happens in the course of cleaning, cooking, and caring for children.

In the dating game, life gets really confusing for young Latinas. If women look too much like the models, they will be considered the kind of women men play with but don't necessarily marry. A man brings a woman who is a size 10 or 12 home to mother and a family dinner, but a woman who is size 5 or 6, you have to keep away from your brother! A 16-year-old Puerto Rican student recently told me that her boyfriend wanted her to put on some weight before the summer. She said that he was not pleased at the fact that other men were watching her on the beach last summer. The other side of the problem was that her mother had taught her that if she gained weight, she would not have any boyfriends. When I heard this story, it reminded me of the African-American woman in the film and her description of "false notions about beauty."

Some of my fondest memories are wrapped in the warmth of mealtimes. Special foods are part of special holidays. Watching generations of women cook and exchange recipes, taking in all the wonderful aromas and feeling their sense of pride and accomplishment as they fulfilled their understood role, was positive for me. Although their place of power was in the kitchen, I learned how that power worked. Being in the kitchen did not mean being passive or subservient. It meant doing your share of the business of parenting and partnering, since the kitchen is the center of family activity. It is a place of importance in the Latino household. Feeding those whom you care about is nurturing the entire unit, and eating all of your *arroz con pollo* means you are loved for your efforts in return.

There are many mixed messages to negotiate in a cross-cultural environment. Immigrants, like everyone else, want to belong. They find themselves trapped somewhere between the cultural values of their home and their host country. Although some can negotiate the conflict better than others, it nevertheless distorts views of the self. Reconciliation of different cultural repertoires is quite a challenge, especially for young Latinas who are trying to "fit in."

QUESTIONS

1. What is the ideal body size for women within Latino culture? How is this ideal different from the dominant U. S. cultural definition of beauty?
2. What does Delgado imply about the frequently assumed "naturalness" and rigidity of beauty norms?
3. What similarities/differences do you see in Delgado's discussion of beauty ideals and Wolf's discussion of the beauty myth?

The Body Politic
(1995)

Abra Chernik

Abra Chernik, a screenwriter and activist/public speaker on eating disorders, shares her own experience with eating disorders in this selection. Chernik explains that eating disorders have their roots in U. S. culture, and suggests that our society rewards *women who have anorexia and bulimia. Chernik demonstrates how her recovery was politically motivated by the realization that she was losing more than weight—and that these losses are encouraged by aspects of everyday life.*

My body possesses solidness and curve, like the ocean. My weight mingles with Earth's pull, drawing me onto the sand. I have not always sent waves into the world. I flew off once, for five years, and swirled madly like a cracking brown leaf in the salty autumn wind. I wafted, dried out, apathetic.

I had no weight in the world during my years of anorexia. Curled up inside my thinness, a refugee in a cocoon of hunger, I lost the capacity to care about myself or others. I starved my body and twitched in place as those around me danced in the energy of shared existence and progressed in their lives. When I graduated from college crowned with academic honors, professors praised my potential. I wanted only to vanish.

It took three months of hospitalization and two years of outpatient psychotherapy for me to learn to nourish myself and to live in a body that expresses strength and honesty in its shape. I accepted my right and my obligation to take up room with my figure, voice and spirit. I remembered how to tumble forward and touch the world that holds me. I chose the ocean as my guide.

Who disputes the ocean's fullness?

Growing up in New York City, I did not care about the feminist movement. Although I attended an all-girls high school, we read mostly male authors and studied the history of men. Embracing mainstream culture without question, I learned about womanhood from fashion magazines, Madison Avenue and Hollywood. I dismissed feminist alternatives as foreign and offensive, swathed as they were in stereotypes that threatened my adolescent need for conformity.

Puberty hit late; I did not complain. I enjoyed living in the lanky body of a tall child and insisted on the title of "girl." If anyone referred to me as a "young woman," I would cry out, horrified, "Do not call me the W word!" But at sixteen years old, I could no longer deny my fate. My stomach and breasts rounded. Curly black hair sprouted in the most embarrassing places. Hips swelled from a once-flat plane. Interpreting maturation as an unacceptable lapse into fleshiness, I resolved to eradicate the physical symptoms of my impending womanhood.

Magazine articles, television commercials, lunchroom conversation, gymnastics coaches and write-ups on models had saturated me with diet savvy. Once I decided to lose weight, I quickly turned expert. I dropped hot chocolate from my regular breakfast order at the Skyline Diner. I replaced lunches of peanut butter and Marshmallow Fluff sandwiches with small platters of cottage cheese and cantaloupe. I eliminated dinner altogether and blunted my appetite with Tab, Camel Lights, and Carefree bubble gum. When furious craving overwhelmed my resolve and I swallowed an extra something, I would flee to the nearest bathroom to purge my mistake.

Within three months, I had returned my body to its preadolescent proportions and had manipulated my monthly period into drying up. Over the next five years, I devoted my life to losing my weight. I came to resent the body in which I lived, the body that threatened to develop, the body whose hunger I despised but could not extinguish. If I neglected a workout or added a pound or ate a bite too many, I would stare in the mirror and drown myself in a tidal wave of criticism. Hatred of my body generalized to hatred of myself as a person, and self-referential labels such as "pig," "failure" and "glutton" allowed me to believe that I deserved punishment. My self-hatred became fuel for the self-mutilating behaviors of the eating disorder.

As my body shrank, so did my world. I starved away my power and vision, my energy and inclinations. Obsessed with dieting, I allowed relationships, passions and identity to wither. I pulled back from the world, off of the beach, out of the sand. The waves of my existence ceased to roll beyond the inside of my skin.

And society applauded my shrinking. Pound after pound the applause continued, like the pounding ocean outside the door of my beach house.

The word "anorexia" literally means "loss of appetite." But as an anorexic, I felt hunger thrashing inside my body. I denied my appetite, ignored it, but never lost it. Sometimes the pangs twisted so sharply, I feared they would consume the meat of my heart. On desperate nights I rose in a flannel nightgown and allowed myself to eat an unplanned something.

No matter how much I ate, I could not soothe the pangs. Standing in the kitchen at midnight, spotlighted by the blue-white light of the open refrigerator, I would frantically feed my neglected appetite: the Chinese food I had not touched at dinner; ice cream and whipped cream; microwaved bread; cereal and chocolate milk; doughnuts and bananas. Then, solid sadness inside my gut, swelling agitation, a too-big meal I would not digest. In the bathroom I would rip off my shirt, tie up my hair, and prepare to execute the desperate ritual, again. I would ram the back of my throat with a toothbrush handle, crying, impatient, until the food rushed up. I would vomit until the toilet filled and I emptied, until I forgave myself, until I felt ready to try my life again. Standing up from my position over the toilet, wiping my mouth, I would believe that I was safe. Looking in the mirror through puffy eyes in a tumescent face, I would promise to take care of myself. Kept awake by the fast, confused beating of my heart and the ache in my chest, I would swear I did not miss the world outside. Lost within myself, I almost died.

By the time I entered the hospital, a mess of protruding bones defined my body, and the bones of my emaciated life rattled me crazy. I carried a pillow around because it hurt to sit down, and I shivered with cold in sultry July. Clumps of brittle hair clogged the drain when I showered, and blackened eyes appeared to sink into my head. My vision of reality wrinkled and my disposition turned mercurial as I slipped into starvation psychosis, a condition associated with severe malnutrition. People told me that I resembled a concentration camp prisoner, a chemotherapy patient, a famine victim or a fashion model.

In the hospital, I examined my eating disorder under the lenses of various therapies. I dissected my childhood, my family structure, my intimate relationships, my belief systems. I participated in experiential therapies of movement, art and psychodrama. I learned to use words instead of eating patterns to communicate my feelings. And still I refused to gain more than a minimal amount of weight.

I felt powerful as an anorexic. Controlling my body yielded an illusion of control over my life; I received incessant praise for my figure despite my sickly mien, and my frailty manipulated family and friends into protecting me from conflict. I had reduced my world to a plate of steamed carrots, and over this tiny kingdom I proudly crowned myself queen.

I sat cross-legged on my hospital bed for nearly two months before I earned an afternoon pass to go to the mall with my mother. The privilege came just in time; I felt unbearably large and desperately wanted a new outfit under which to hide gained weight. At the mall, I searched for two hours before finally discovering, in the maternity section at Macy's, a shirt large enough to cover what I perceived as my enormous body.

With an hour left on my pass, I spotted a sign on a shop window: "Body Fat Testing, $3.00." I suggested to my mother that we split up for ten minutes; she headed to Barnes & Noble, and I snuck into the fitness store.

I sat down in front of a machine hooked up to a computer, and a burly young body builder fired questions at me:

"Age?"

"Twenty-one."

"Height?"

"Five nine."

"Weight?"

"Ninety-nine."

The young man punched my statistics into his keyboard and pinched my arm with clippers wired to the testing machine. In a moment, the computer spit out my results. "Only ten percent body fat! Unbelievably healthy. The average for a woman your age is twenty-five percent. Fantastic! You're this week's blue ribbon winner."

I stared at him in disbelief. *Winner? Healthy? Fantastic?* I glanced around at the other customers in the store, some of whom had congregated to watch my testing, and I felt embarrassed by his praise. And then I felt furious. Furious at this man and at the society that programmed him for their ignorant approbation of my illness and my suffering.

"I am dying of anorexia," I whispered. "Don't congratulate me."

I spent my remaining month in the hospital supplementing psychotherapy with an independent examination of eating disorders from a social and political point of view. I needed to understand why society would reward my starvation and encourage my vanishing. In the bathroom, a mirror on the open door behind me reflected my backside in a mirror over the sink. Vertebrae poked at my skin, ribs hung like wings over chiseled hip bones, the two sides of my buttocks did not touch. I had not seen this view of myself before.

In writing, I recorded instances in which my eating disorder had tangled the progress of my life and thwarted my relationships. I filled three and a half Mead marble notebooks. Five years' worth of: *I wouldn't sit with Daddy when he was alone in the hospital because I needed to go jogging; I told Derek not to visit me because I couldn't throw up when he was there; I almost failed my comprehensive exams because I was so hungry; I spent my year at Oxford with my head in the toilet bowl; I wouldn't eat the dinner my friends cooked me for my nineteenth birthday because I knew they had used oil in the recipe; I told my family not to come to my college graduation because I didn't want to miss a day at the gym or have to eat a restaurant meal.* And on and on for hundreds of pages.

This honest account of my life dissolved the illusion of anorexic power. I saw myself naked in the truth of my pain, my loneliness, my obsessions, my craziness, my selfishness, my defeat. I also recognized the social and political implications of consuming myself with the trivialities of calories and weight. At college, I had watched as classmates involved themselves in extracurricular clubs, volunteer work, politics and applications for jobs and graduate schools. Obsessed with exercising and exhausted by starvation, I did not even consider joining in such pursuits. Despite my love of writing and painting and literature, despite ranking at the top of my class, I wanted only to teach aerobics. Despite my adolescent days as a loud-mouthed, rambunctious class leader, I had grown into a silent, hungry young woman.

And society preferred me this way: hungry, fragile, crazy. *Winner! Healthy! Fantastic!* I began reading feminist literature to further understand the disempowerment of women in our culture. I digested the connection between a nation of starving, self-obsessed women and the continued success of the patriarchy. I also cultivated an awareness of alternative models of womanhood. In the stillness of the hospital library, new voices in my life rose from printed pages to echo my rage and provide the conception of my feminist consciousness.

I had been willing to accept self-sabotage, but now I refused to sacrifice myself to a society that profited from my pain. I finally understood that my eating disorder symbolized more than "personal psychodynamic trauma." Gazing in the mirror at my emaciated body, I observed a woman held up by her culture as the physical ideal because she was starving, self-obsessed and powerless, a woman called beautiful because she threatened no one except herself. Despite my intelligence, my education, and my supposed Manhattan sophistication, I had believed all the lies; I had almost given my life in order to achieve the sickly impotence that this culture aggressively links with female happiness, love and success. And everything I had to offer to the world, every tumbling wave, every thought and every passion, nearly died inside me.

As long as society resists female power, fashion will call healthy women physically flawed. As long as society accepts the physical, sexual and economic abuse of women, popular culture will prefer women who resemble little girls. Sitting in the hospital the summer after my college graduation, I grasped the absurdity of a nation of adult women dying to grow small.

Armed with this insight, I loosened the grip of the starvation disease on my body. I determined to recreate myself based on an image of a woman warrior. I remembered my ocean, and I took my first bite.

Gaining weight and getting my head out of the toilet bowl was the most political act I have ever committed.

I left the hospital and returned home to Fire Island. Living at the shore in those wintry days of my new life, I wrapped myself in feminism as I hunted sea shells and role models. I wanted to feel proud of my womanhood. I longed to accept and honor my body's fullness.

During the process of my healing, I had hoped that I would be able to skip the memory of anorexia like a cold pebble into the dark winter sea. I had dreamed that in relinquishing my obsessive chase after a smaller body, I would be able to come home to rejoin those whom I had left in order to starve, rejoin them to live together as healthy, powerful women. But as my body has grown full, I have sensed a hollowness in the lives of women all around me that I had not noticed when I myself stood hollow. I have made it home only to find myself alone.

Out in the world again, I hear the furious thumping dance of body hatred echoing every place I go. Friends who once appeared wonderfully carefree in ordering late-night french fries turn out not to eat breakfast or lunch. Smart, talented, creative women talk about dieting and overeating and hating the beach because they look terrible in bathing suits. Famous women give interviews insulting their bodies and bragging about bicycling twenty-four miles the day they gave birth.

I had looked forward to rejoining society after my years of anorexic exile. Ironically, in order to preserve my health, my recovery has included the development of a consciousness that actively challenges the images and ideas that define this culture. Walking down Madison Avenue and passing emaciated women, I say to myself, *those women are sick.* When smacked with a diet commercial, I remind myself, *I don't do that anymore.* I decline invitations to movies that feature anorexic actors, I will not participate in discussions about dieting, and I refuse to shop in stores that cater to women with eating-disordered figures.

Though I am critical of diet culture, I find it nearly impossible to escape. Eating disorders have woven their way into the fabric of my society. On television, in print, on food packaging, in casual conversation and in windows of clothing stores populated by ridiculously gaunt mannequins, messages to lose my weight and control my appetite challenge my recovered fullness. Finally at home in my body, I recognize myself as an island in a sea of eating disorders, a sea populated predominantly by young women.

A perversion of nature by society has resulted in a phenomenon whereby women feel safer when starving than when eating. Losing our weight boosts self-esteem, while nourishing our bodies evokes feelings of self-doubt and self-loathing.

When our bodies take up more space than a size eight (as most of our bodies do), we say, *too big*. When our appetites demand more than a Lean Cuisine, we say, *too much*. When we want a piece of a friend's birthday cake, we say, *too bad*. Don't eat too much, don't talk too loudly, don't take up too much space, don't take from the world. Be pleasant or crazy, but don't seem hungry. Remember, a new study shows that men prefer women who eat salad for dinner over women who eat burgers and fries.

So we keep on shrinking, starving away our wildness, our power, our truth.

Hiding our curves under long T-shirts at the beach, sitting silently and fidgeting while others eat dessert, sneaking back into the kitchen late at night to binge and hating ourselves the next day, skipping breakfast, existing on diet soda and cigarettes, adding up calories and subtracting everything else. We accept what is horribly wrong in our lives and fight what is beautiful and right.

Over the past three years, feminism has taught me to honor the fullness of my womanhood and the solidness of the body that hosts my life. In feminist circles I have found mentors, strong women who live with power, passion and purpose. And yet, even in groups of feminists, my love and acceptance of my body remains unusual.

Eating disorders affect us all on both a personal and a political level. The majority of my peers—including my feminist peers—still measure their beauty against anorexic ideals. Even among feminists, body hatred and chronic dieting continue to consume lives. Friends of anorexics beg them to please start eating; then these friends go home and continue their own diets. Who can deny that the millions of young women caught in the net of disordered eating will frustrate the potential of the next wave of feminism?

Sometimes my empathy dissolves into frustration and rage at our situation. For the first time in history, young women have the opportunity to create a world in our image. But many of us concentrate instead on recreating the shape of our thighs.

As young feminists, we must place unconditional acceptance of our bodies at the top of our political agenda. We must claim our bodies as our own to love and honor in their infinite shapes and sizes. Fat, thin, soft, hard, puckered, smooth, our bodies are our homes. By nourishing our bodies, we care for and love ourselves on the most basic level. When we deny ourselves physical food, we go hungry emotionally, psychologically, spiritually and politically. We must challenge ourselves to eat and digest, and allow society to call us too big. We will understand their message to mean too powerful.

Time goes by quickly. One day we will blink and open our eyes as old women. If we spend all our energy keeping our bodies small, what will we have to show of our lives when we reach the end? I hope we have more than a group of fashionably skinny figures.

QUESTIONS

1. Why does Chernik say that pulling her head out of the toilet bowl was the most political move she had ever made? What other seemingly body-related decisions in her article are actually actions with political effect?

2. What are some of the examples Chernik gives of how our culture supports and rewards eating disorders? Where can we intervene in this process, and encourage young females to claim their right "to take up room"?

Homage to My Hips
Homage to My Hair
(1987)

Lucille Clifton

In each of these two poems, Lucille Clifton challenges Euro-American traditional standards of beauty. In the tapestries of her writing, Clifton celebrates that which is culturally defined as falling outside of beauty norms—big hips and nappy hair.

Lucille Clifton, born in 1936, currently lives in Maryland and California, where she teaches at the University of Santa Cruz. She is the author of several books of poetry and has also written a number of children's books.

Homage to My Hips

these hips are big hips
they need space to
move around in.
they don't fit into little
petty places. these hips
are free hips.
they don't like to be held back.
these hips have never been enslaved,
they go where they want to go
they do what they want to do.
these hips are mighty hips.
these hips are magic hips.
I have known them
to put a spell on a man and
spin him like a top!

Homage to My Hair

when i feel her jump up and dance
i hear the music! my God
i'm talking about my nappy hair!
she is a challenge to your hand
black man,
she is as tasty on your tongue as good greens
black man,
she can touch your mind
with her electric fingers and
the grayer she do get, good God,
the blacker she do be!

QUESTIONS

1. What do the poems indicate about specific problems Black women face in their confrontation with beauty norms?
2. In what ways are U.S. beauty norms racist? Think of some examples of how this racism is reflected in our culture.
3. Why do you think Clifton celebrates her hips and hair in these poems?

Reproduction: Motherhood and the Family

It is possible to broadly summarize the necessary activities of social life as "production, consumption, and reproduction." We construct, we make use of what has been created, and we re-create ourselves. And yet, feminism asks the question, "How is reproduction different from production, both in activity and in the social consideration and valuing of the activity?" Historically, women's primary roles have been defined as "wife" and "mother," and women today still are expected to bear the primary responsibility for childcare and family maintenance. Although family structures and methods of both production and reproduction have changed through time, it is possible to pinpoint the ways reproduction may help to structure the social environment.

In this section, we will be concerned with the dynamics of reproduction: reproduction as childbearing; reproduction of the family and its attendant roles; reproduction as production; reproduction as creation; and reproduction as a possible avenue for social forces of power and domination to replicate themselves. We will explore historical and contemporary themes of motherhood, particularly as they have shaped the boundaries of women's participation in the social environment. We will consider the impact of various markers of social identity (e.g., race, class, gender) on our understanding of the reproduction of motherhood and the family.

Of Voluntary Motherhood

Sarah Grimké

In a time in our history when a married woman's reproductive history was often characterized by more miscarriages and abortions than live births, Sarah Grimké's voice articulates a feminist call for the reconstruction of reproduction within the context of marriage. Within her conceptualization of "voluntary motherhood," Grimké presents a perspective which was relatively well-formed at the time—that the excessive burdens of uncontrolled childbearing had profound effects on both the health and status of women, on children's health and development, and on the crucial institution of marriage.

Sarah Grimké (1792–1873), one of fourteen children, never married, but helped care for the three children of her younger sister Angelina Grimké Weld. Her sister suffered poor health through most of her married life due to a prolapsed uterus caused by childbirth difficulties.

Among nineteenth-century reformers, notions about the "natural laws" of sexual abstinence (based on observations of animal mating behavior) laid the foundations of the future birth-control movement. Emphasizing a woman's right to determine whether or not she should become pregnant, and her right to resist a man's "ungoverned passion," even in marriage, this essay by Sarah Grimké expressed ideas that were widespread at the time. Women's rights advocates perceived "voluntary motherhood" through abstinence a necessity for personal freedom, not a restriction (as twentieth-century women would later claim). Prominent doctors wrote textbooks and warned their patients that marital intercourse should not occur more than once or twice a month in order to preserve male as well as female health. "Sexual excess," even within marriage, was considered contrary to the laws of nature.

Sarah Grimké (1792–1873), one of fourteen children, never married. Instead, she devoted herself to caring for the three children of her sister, Angelina Grimké Weld. Angelina (1805–79) suffered poor health most of her married life, apparently from a prolapsed uterus caused by childbirth difficulties. Thus Sarah's ideas on marriage also had a pragmatic basis.

From Sarah Grimké, "Marriage," 1855, Weld-Grimké Papers, William L. Clements Library, University of Michigan, Ann Arbor, pp. 4–9, 18–19, 21.

An eminent physician of Boston once remarked that if in the economy of nature, the sexes alternated in giving birth to children no family would ever have more than three, the husband bearing one & the wife two. But the *right* to decide this matter has been almost wholly denied to woman. How often is she forced into an untimely motherhood which compels her to wean her babe, thus depriving it of that nutriment provided by nature as the most bland & fitting, during the period of dentition. Thousands of deaths from this cause, in infancy, are attributed by superstition & ignorance to the dispensations of Divine Providence. How many thousand, too, of miscarriages are forced upon woman by the fact that man lives down that law of his being which would protect her from such terrible consequences just as animal instinct protects the female among brutes. To save woman from legalized licentiousness is then one of the reasons why we plead for *equality of rights*.

No one can fail to see that this condition of things results from several causes:

1. Ignorance of those physical laws which every man & woman *ought* to know before marriage, the knowledge of which has been withheld from the young, under a false & fatal idea of

delicacy. Many a man ruins his own health & that of his wife & his children too, thro' ignorance. A diffusion of knowledge respecting these laws would greatly defuse existing evils.

2. A false conception in man & woman of *his* nature & necessities. The great truth that the most concentrated fluid of the body has an office to perform in the product of *great tho'ts & original ideas,* as well as in the reproduction of the species is known to few & too little appreciated by all. The prodigal waste of this by legalized licentiousness has dwarfed the intellect of man. . . .

3. The fact that many legal marriages are not love marriages. In a pure, true relation between the sexes, no difficulties can ever arise, but a willing recognition of each other's right & mutual wants, naturally & spontaneously resulting in voluntary motherhood, a joyful appreciation of the blessedness of parentage, the birth of healthy, comely children & a beautiful home.

But it may be asked, what is to be done in cases of uncongenial marriages. Are not such men & women to follow their attractions outside of the legal relation. I unhesitatingly answer No! Where two persons have established a false marriage relation, *they are bound to abide by the consequences* of the mistake they have made. Perhaps they did love each other, but a nearer intimacy has frozen this love or changed it into disgust. Or, theirs may have been a marriage of *convenience,* or one for the sake of obtaining a house, a fortune, a position in life: or it may have been a mere act of obedience to parents, or of gratitude, or a means of canceling a monied obligation. Multiform are the *unworthy* motives which seduce men & women into this sacred relation. In all these cases, let them abide the consequences of their own perversion of marriage, in exchanging personal chastity for the pride of life, vanity in dress, position or a house to live in, without that *love* which alone can make that house a *home.*

In some cases, it may be duty for the parties to separate, but let both keep themselves pure, so long as both are living. Let them accept the discipline thus afforded, & spiritual strength & growth will be their reward.

The Doctrine that human beings are to follow their attractions, which lies at the base of that miscalled "free love" system, is fraught with infinite danger. We are too low down to listen for one moment to its syren voice. . . .

Let me then exculpate "the woman's rights movement," from the charge of "tending directly and rapidly to the Free Love system, & nullifying the very idea of Marriage as anything more than a partnership at will." On the contrary our great desire is to purify & exalt the marriage relation & destroy *all* licentiousness. . . .

. . . Man seems to feel that Marriage gives him the control of Woman's person just as the Law gives him the control of her property. Thus are her most sacred rights destroyed by that very act, which, under the laws of Nature should enlarge, establish & protect them. In marriage is the origin of Life—in it woman finds herself endowed with a creative energy she never possessed before. In it new aspirations take possession of her, an indescribable longing after motherhood as the felt climax of her being. She joyfully gives herself away, that she may receive the germ of a new being, & true to nature, would fain retire within herself & absorb & expend all her energies in the development of this precious germ. But alas! How few are permitted, unmolested to pursue that end, which for the time being, has become the great object of life. How often is she compelled by various considerations to yield to the *unnatural* embraces of her husband, & thus to endanger the very existence of her embryo babe. How often is it sacrificed to the ungoverned passion of its own father, & the health of the mother serious impaired. Every unnatural process is deleterious, hence abortions are destructive to the constitution & many women are broken down in the prime of life by them alone, & their haggard countenances too plainly reveal their secret sorrows. A lady once said to me I have but one child, but I have has 12 miscarriages—another had 4 children & 15 abortions. And why I would ask this untimely casting of her fruit? Do the beasts of the field miscarry? Why not? *They* are governed by instinct. Are the *brutes* safe during the period of gestation whilst *Woman* is not! . . .

. . . Again—look at the burdens imposed upon her by the care of many children following in quick succession. How can any mother do her duty to her family, if in 8 years she have 6 children. Look at the unnatural tug upon her constitution, her night watches, her sore vexations & trials & causes nameless & numberless, that wear away her life. If men had to alternate with their wives, the duties of the nursery, fewer & further between would be its inmates.

QUESTIONS

1. What is Grimké's conceptualization of "voluntary motherhood"? Why does she advocate voluntary motherhood within marriage?
2. What reasons does Grimké offer to support her argument for voluntary motherhood? What consequences does she suggest result in marriages which do not confine reproduction within the boundaries of voluntary motherhood?
3. How does voluntary motherhood affect the marriage relationship? How does the nature of a particular marriage relationship affect the likelihood of voluntary motherhood within the relationship?
4. Do you think Grimké's argument, penned over one-hundred years ago, has validity in contemporary U.S. society? Why/why not? Restate Grimké's reasons for voluntary motherhood in your own words.

Why I Want a Wife (1973)

Judy Syfers

In this selection, Judy Syfers points out the many ways in which being a wife limits women to the advantage of men. Although a tone of irony is woven through Syfers' essay, the seriousness of her topic is quite real. In today's society, the traditional assignment of domestic labor as a female responsibility persists in spite of changes in the configuration of the "typical" U.S. family. Syfers' essay implies some of the ways these traditional assignments break down in our current culture.

I belong to that classification of people known as wives. I am a wife. And, not altogether incidentally, I am a mother.

Not too long ago a male friend of mine appeared on the scene fresh from a recent divorce. He had one child, who is, of course, with his ex-wife. He is looking for another wife. As I thought about him while I was ironing one evening, it suddenly occurred to me that I, too, would like to have a wife. Why do I want a wife?

I would like to go back to school so that I can become economically independent, support myself, and, if need be, support those dependent upon me. I want a wife who will work and send me to school. And while I am going to school I want a wife to take care of my children. I want a wife to keep track of the children's doctor and dentist appointments. And to keep track of mine, too. I want a wife to make sure my children eat properly and are kept clean. I want a wife who will wash the children's clothes and keep them mended. I want a wife who is a good nurturant attendant to my children, who arranges for their schooling, makes sure that they have an adequate social life with their peers, takes them to the park, the zoo, etc. I want a wife who takes care of the children when they are sick, a wife who arranges to be around when the children need special care, because, of course, I cannot miss classes at school. My wife must arrange to lose time at work and not lose the job. It may mean a small cut in my wife's income from time to time, but I guess I can tolerate that. Needless to say, my wife will arrange and pay for the care of the children while my wife is working.

I want a wife who will take care of *my* physical needs. I want a wife who will keep my house clean. A wife who will pick up after my children, a wife who will pick up after me. I want a wife who will keep my clothes clean, ironed, mended, replaced when need be, and who will see to it that my personal things are kept in their proper place so that I can find what I need the minute I need it. I want a wife who cooks the meals, a wife who is a *good* cook. I want a wife who will plan the menus, do the necessary grocery shopping, prepare the meals, serve them pleasantly, and then do the cleaning up while I do my studying. I want a wife who will care for me when I am sick and sympathize with my pain and loss of time from school. I want a wife to go along when our family takes a vacation so that someone can continue to care for me and my children when I need a rest and change of scene.

I want a wife who will not bother me with rambling complaints about a wife's duties. But I want a wife who will listen to me when I feel the need to explain a rather difficult point I have come across in my course of studies. And I want a wife who will type my papers for me when I have written them.

I want a wife who will take care of the details of my social life. When my wife and I are invited out by my friends, I want a wife who will take care of the babysitting arrangements. When I meet people at school that I like and want to entertain, I want a wife who will have the house clean, will prepare a special meal, serve it to me and my friends and not interrupt when I talk about things that interest me and my friends. I want a wife who will have arranged that the children are fed and ready for bed before my guests arrive so that the children do not bother us. I want a wife who takes care of the needs of my guests so that they feel comfortable, who makes sure that they have an ashtray, that they are passed the hors d'oeuvres, that they are offered a second helping of the food, that their wine glasses are replenished when necessary, that their coffee is served to them as they like it. And I want a wife who knows that sometimes I need a night out by myself.

I want a wife who is sensitive to my sexual needs, a wife who makes love passionately and eagerly when I feel like it, a wife who makes sure that I am satisfied. And, of course, I want a wife who will not demand sexual attention when I am not in the mood for it. I want a wife who assumes the complete responsibility for birth control, because I do not want more children. I want a wife who will remain sexually faithful to me so that I do not have to clutter up my intellectual life with jealousies. And I want a wife who understands that *my* sexual needs may entail more than strict adherence to monogamy. I must, after all, be able to relate to people as fully as possible.

If, by chance, I find another person more suitable as a wife than the wife I already have, I want the liberty to replace my present wife with another one. Naturally, I will expect a fresh, new life; my wife will take the children and be solely responsible for them so that I am left free.

When I am through with school and have a job, I want my wife to quit working and remain at home so that my wife can more fully and completely take care of a wife's duties.

My God, who *wouldn't* want a wife?

QUESTIONS

1. Are there any benefits to having a husband? Why/why not? If there are benefits, how do they compare to the benefits of having a wife?

2. Syfers suggests that the major benefits to having a wife are the enhancement of one's being able to get an education and the ability to pursue a career. Given that many married women today have a

career, what "new" kinds of limitations do you understand the role of "wife" to have on a woman?

3. Given Syfers' argument, why wouldn't she write an article entitled, "Why I Want a Husband?

husbands are taken care of

FAMILY AND WOMEN'S LIVES (1992)

Susan Lehrer

In this selection, Susan Lehrer discusses the historical, social and economic factors that have shaped traditional understandings of family. *Lehrer draws connections among these sociocultural definitions of* family *and the role of women in the family. Such connections make it possible to understand women's position in the family as a function of the nuclear family structure. Lehrer suggests it is this nuclear family structure which ignores the social reality of alternative family arrangements, and advocates an expanded definition of "family".*

We tend to think about the family as a natural, biological unit. After all, everyone knows it takes two to make a baby. What is meant by family is more than biological relations, of course. In current debates, one specific form of family is referred to as "traditional:" the nuclear family—mother, father, and their children, living together, with the father the main breadwinner and the mother responsible for the home. It is maintained and reinforced by law and the state, and forms the basis for social policy toward women and children. Yet only about 25% of American households are married couples and their children; the "traditional" version, in which the father is the sole family breadwinner, accounts for only 8.2% of American households and certainly does not reflect the realities of most of us (U.S. Bureau of the Census, 1991, p. 145).

Overwhelmingly, women's family life includes responsibility for children and the home (called "women's work"), but women also work outside the home in the paid labor force—including over half of women with children under one year of age. Using the outdated, inaccurate picture of "family," however, prevents the needs of women and real-life families from being recognized. This essay explores some of the broad historical changes that have changed the family, and the way in which family structure defines the opportunities, economic situation, and social position of women.

Historical Overview

Before industrialization, the family was a working, productive unit, with women producing goods for family consumption, as well as maintaining the family's health and material well-being. For example, in *Little House on the Prairie*, Laura Ingalls Wilder describes her childhood frontier family in which Ma's contribution was clear and valued, and Pa's work took place within the family setting as well. This continued into the late nineteenth and early twentieth centuries in rural areas.

With the beginnings of industrialization, a major shift occurred, as "work" became something done outside the home, for pay, by men. "Women's work" within the home (called housework) was not paid labor and hence not seen as "real work." Thus, the roles of breadwinner and homemaker that are often taken for granted as "natural" are the result of specific historical changes like industrialization, and are, as Jesse Bernard (1981) put it, specific to a very short period in human history. The household itself changed from a unit of production to one primarily of consumption.

Although men were the main workers (for pay), right from the beginning of industrialization, women also worked outside their homes. For example, in making cloth (which was one of the first industries affected by the Industrial Revolution), young women were the main source for factory workers, because men's labor was needed in agricultural production and therefore scarce. Women received wages that were one-quarter to one-half those of men. From the beginning of wage labor and capitalist production for profit, the wage structure itself has been different (and lower) for female workers than for male workers. Although male workers were not well paid, their wages were expected to support a family; women were not expected to be self-supporting, let alone able to support anyone else. This meant women were dependent upon men for support, even when they did work outside the home.

The "power of the purse" reinforced the husband's control over his family. Under English common law, which our legal system is based on, when a woman married, she lost her own legal identity and her legal right to contract. For instance, her husband had control over all money and property of the family, including her wages. Marriage represented a legal contract in which women's status was subordinate to her husband's. Women's current subordination in marriage is rooted in legal tradition as well as in economic arrangements.

As commercial and industrial development expanded and a national economy emerged in the later 1800s, women's world was still supposed to be centered within the household—she was the "angel of the hearth," available to provide material and emotional comfort for the man, who braved the world of commercial competition. This idealized version of family was never quite accurate even in the nineteenth century. For middle-class women, it meant complete economic dependence on the goodwill of their husbands and fathers. Less well-off women worked in factories and sweatshops as young women or whenever they were not supported by a man's income. Women also added to the household income by taking in boarders or doing washing—usually ignored by official counts of family income and employment (Bose, 1987 :113).

Enslaved African-American women were expected to perform similar tasks as men, and in the United States, unlike other countries, even slave marriage was not recognized by white law. African-American women worked in the fields as well as in the slave master's household. Nonetheless, studies indicate that many enslaved families sought to maintain strong ties (which amounted to an act of subversion under slavery), and after emancipation, large-scale relocations of African Americans were often an attempt to reunite families broken apart by slavery (Gutman, 1983). After slavery, whites still expected African-American wives to work for them; they were considered lazy if they presumed to stay home and act like ladies (Jones, 1985 : 59). Thus we see that the "traditional" family was only expected to apply to certain groups and not others—white, middle-class families primarily.

From this brief historical background, it is clear that the family is not a natural, unchanging entity, but it changes along with social and economic shifts in the larger social world. We are again in a time when these larger social forces are visibly changing the way families function. Although the number of women working outside the home has been slowly increasing since the early 1900s, the increase in the past two decades has been astounding. The vast majority of women now combine outside work and family life, and in addition, the proportion of women who are heads of households, never married, and working has also increased dramatically.

The Nuclear Family: It's a Different Place for Women Than Men

The idealized image of family relationships is that they are warm, loving, and occasionally quarrelsome but, in the long run, supportive. As the saying goes, family is where, when you go there, they have to take you in. The image of the nuclear family—with the father the main money-maker and responsible for making the important decisions in the family—continues to be a very strong influence on family lifestyles. Choices made within the family setting that appear to be simply logical or natural are, in fact, the consequence of the nuclear family structure. For instance, since the man's job is considered the mainstay of the family, his occupational shifts take first place over other family concerns. Because his earnings are likely to be greater than his wife's if she works, her job is considered the logically expendable one. If they have children, the wife is the one who is going to quit work and "stay home with the baby." If his career plans favor relocation to a different city, hers are likely to suffer. This, in turn, reinforces the disparity in their earnings, making it seem natural that his job is the one that is really important, while hers is secondary. Many women's reluctance to plan a career (as distinguished from a job to earn money) reflects the reality that they are expected to fit it in around everything else in the family. Many men agree that their wife's education, job, and career plans are worthwhile, as long as dinner is still on the table, the house in order, and the kids taken care of when he walks in the door. Some men still talk about taking responsibility for their own child as "baby-sitting."

The reality is that different family members experience the "same" family very differently. Where money is short, it is women who "bridge the gap between what a household's resources really are and what a family's position is supposed to be" (Rapp, 1982: 175). They stretch the available food, clothing, and resources to make ends meet. Where a family consistently comes up short at the end of the paycheck, it is the woman who eats less and does without, in order that the kids and husband can have enough. To talk about a family's standard of living as if all family members shared the same level of well-being or poverty is misleading. Yet social scientists typically use the husband's occupation in defining social class and just assume that the rest of the family is included. And defining a family's class by the husband's occupation does not provide a basis for understanding the very different life chances that men and women face within the "same" family, given the realities of divorce and single parenthood.

Families: A Multitude of Possibilities

Probably the most talked-about change in American families in recent years has been the increase in family households headed by women. Women heading families face a series of obstacles that reflect the unwillingness of policy makers to recognize and address their condition. In order to work and support their families, women must have child care; then they must earn enough to provide for their families. Women's earnings are still less than 70% of men's. The good news is that this is a greater proportion than it has been in the recent past; the bad news is that this is because of the relative *decline* in men's earnings rather than an increase in women's overall income. This means that women heading households are more likely to be poor, not only because there is only one earner in the family but because that earner is a woman. It also means that the lack of affordable child care hits women who are heads of family especially hard. Yet American social policy has not recognized that child care is just as much a social necessity as educating children. The United States is far behind most European countries, which train child-care specialists and provide care for children from the youngest ages.

For many women, the descent to poverty occurs as a result of divorce. This is more likely to happen for white women than for black women, partly because of the overall lower earnings of black men relative to white men. Despite all the jokes about men paying their life fortune in alimony to ex-wives, the reality is that men's standard of living goes *up* following divorce, while women's drops precipitously. One study found that a year after divorce, men's standard of living improved 42%, while women's *dropped* by 73% (Weitzman, 1985).

The transition from Mrs. to ex-Mrs. is especially difficult for older, long-married women, who often do not have marketable skills to support themselves. The tragic irony is that it is precisely those women who acceded to cultural expectations to stay at home and be good wives and mothers who suffer the most both economically and emotionally. Women whose whole sense of identity centers around being a wife and mother must cope with profound loss of meaning as well as the economic shock of divorce. These older women are the ones more likely to get alimony (as distinguished from child support). Younger women from shorter-term marriages are unlikely to be awarded alimony and often are unable to even collect child support. In 1990, there were 10 million women living with children whose fathers were not in the home; only half were awarded child support at all, and only half of those received the full amount (U.S. Bureau of the Census, Feb. 1992, p. 2). Responsibility for children following divorce still rests overwhelmingly with the mother, despite all the movies depicting the hilarious, heart-warming adventures of men raising children.

The reasons for the increase in families headed by women are complex and cannot be reduced to a simple explanation. Young women are more likely to have worked. Shotgun weddings are less common now than in the past (judging by the fact that many fewer pregnant women marry before their first child is born (U.S. Bureau of the Census, 1992, p. 2). The options of abortion, and refusing to marry someone you don't like, are more acceptable now. Other explanations look at economic factors affecting couples' financial prospects as they consider marriage. There is extensive urban unemployment and poverty among young people, for whom education is less likely to lead to jobs that pay enough to support a family. The reality is, almost 25% of families with children were headed by women in 1990, compared with less than 12% in 1970. Single-parent families are 28% of families with children under 18; less than 14% of them are headed by the father. Many African-American families are headed by women—56%, compared with 19% for white families and 29% for Hispanic-American families. And remember, not all families involve children—they also include elders or other relatives in the household (U.S. Bureau of the Census, 1992, p. 7).

Married couples with children still depend upon the wife to do the "second shift"—the housework. The time women spent on housework remained about the same whether they worked or not. This may be beginning to change—partly because women have simply stopped doing so much of it, but also because couples believe in sharing household work (Schor, 1991: 103).

Despite the variety of social arrangements in which people live their lives, social policy and law penalize those who do not live in nuclear family settings. One of the ways this happens is by excluding non-legally married family members from health insurance plans—without which Americans cannot afford to be sick. The high cost of medical coverage has now reached crisis proportions nationally. The United States is the only major industrial nation (besides South Africa) that does not have national health coverage for everybody. Hospitals frequently restrict visits for very ill people to "immediate family," meaning legal spouses, and also deny information and decision making to non-legally married couples of any sort. This exclusion especially affects gay couples (Thompson and Andrzejewski, 1988). The increasing numbers of people affected by these exclusions are being encouraged to declare so-called "living wills" and powers of attorney so that the person they designate will be accorded the rights and responsibilities that a legal spouse would be without question.

Mom and Apple Pie?

The conservatives who attack the women's movement for being anti-family have a specific form of the family in mind—one that certainly does not correspond to what real families are like. These fundamentalist doctrines of the political far right rigidly interpret the Bible to justify the patriarchal family, attack women's rights, and use the power of the laws to support their views. It is interesting that in times of social change—like the mid-1800s in the throes of industrialization, and our own time—ideologies advocating a return to an earlier, past "golden age" surface.

Now, even the basic, biological fact that it takes two to make a baby seems to be blurring at the edges with the advances of reproductive technologies. A woman may be pregnant and give birth to a child to whom she is not genetically related, from an ovum that was fertilized in vitro (outside the woman's body). The child then may potentially have two completely different sets of parents. What is the legal status of the woman who was pregnant with the child? What "rights," if any, has she to be considered the "mother"? Is a "contract" to give up the child after birth enforceable if she changes her mind? These are unresolved questions. Typically, the couple wishing to become parents is wealthy enough to pay large medical and legal fees, while the woman having the child has much lower income and less to spend on lawyers. Our thinking about women, pregnancy, parenting, and family will need to take these issues into account.

Another possibility is that a woman who wants to become pregnant but is having difficulties can opt for series of fertility treatments or implanting of fertilized eggs—procedures that are experimental and extremely expensive, uncomfortable, and uncertain. Others want to be parents but not within a male-female household, either gay/lesbian couples or single persons. All of these can also become families with parents who raise children, wipe sniffly noses, and clap at school plays. The challenge is to creatively respond to changed conditions, and to help shape that change in ways that will enhance rather than stifle peoples' lives.

REFERENCES

Bernard, Jessie. "The Good Provider Role: Its Rise and Fall," *American Psychologist* vol. 36, No. 1, Jan. 1981, pp. 1–12.

Bose, Christine, "Devaluing Women's Work: The Undercount of Women's Employment in 1900 and 1980," in Christine Bose, Roslyn Feldberg, and Natalie Sokoloff, eds. *Hidden Aspects of Womens' Work,* New York: Praeger, 1987, pp. 95–115.

Gutman, Herbert, "Persistent Myths About the Afro-American Family," in Michael Gordon, ed. *The American Family in Social-Historical Perspective,* 3rd ed. New York: St. Martins Press, 1983, pp. 459 -481.

Jones, Jacqueline. *Labor of Love, Labor of Sorrow: Black Women, Work and the Family from Slavery to the Present.* New York: Vintage, 1985.

Rapp, Rayna. "Family and Class in Contemporary America: Notes Toward an Understanding of Ideology," in Barrie Thorne and Marilyn Yalom, eds. *Rethinking the Family: Some Feminist Questions.* New York: Longman, 1982.

Schor, Juliet. *The Overworked American: The Unexpected Decline of Leisure.* New York: Basic Books, 1991.

Thompson, Karen, and Andrzejewski, Julie. *Why Can't Sharon Kowalski Come Home*? San Francisco: Spinster/Aunt Lute Book Company, 1988.

U.S. Bureau of the Census, U.S. Department of Commerce, "Household and Family Characteristics: March 1990 and 1989," *Current Population Reports*, Population Characteristics, Series P -20, No. 447, 1991.

U.S. Bureau of the Census, U.S. Department of Commerce, "How We're Changing, Demographic State of the Nation:

QUESTIONS

1. How might you define "family" after reading this essay? How does your definition allow for alternative family arrangements?
2. In what ways does divorce affect women differently than men, according to Lehrer? Can you think of other effects the author does not identify?
3. How does Lehrer suggest that family structure influences the definition of a woman's role within a family?

The Meaning of Motherhood in Black Culture (1992)

Patricia Hill Collins

Patricia Hill Collins, Professor of Sociology and Black Studies at the University of Cincinnati, is a leading scholar in black feminist thought. In this essay, excerpted from her influential book, Black Feminist Thought, *Collins examines the unique approach to motherhood and childcare which typifies the African-American community in the United States. Collins explains both the nature of motherhood within the African-American community and the impact of motherhood on the lives of Black women. This community-based approach to motherhood often stimulates political activism, and creates both an 'ethic of caring' and 'personal accountability' as essential elements of motherhood. Collins suggests that motherhood exists as a symbol of personal and political power in the African-American community.*

Bloodmothers, Othermothers, and Women-Centered Networks

In African-American communities, the boundaries distinguishing biological mothers of children from other women who care for children are often fluid and changing. Biological mothers or bloodmothers are expected to care for their children. But African and African-American communities have also recognized that vesting one person with full responsibility for mothering a child may not be wise or possible. As a result, "othermothers," women who assist bloodmothers by sharing mothering responsibilities, traditionally have been central to the institution of Black motherhood.[1]

The centrality of women in African-American extended families is well known.[2] Organized, resilient, women-centered networks of bloodmothers and othermothers are key in understanding this centrality: Grandmothers, sisters, aunts, or cousins acted as othermothers by taking on childcare responsibilities for each other's children. When needed, temporary childcare arrangements turned into long-term care or informal adoption.[3]

In African-American communities, these women-centered networks of community-based childcare often extend beyond the boundaries of biologically related extended families to support "fictive kin."[4] Civil rights activist Ella Baker describes how informal adoption by othermothers functioned in the Southern, rural community of her childhood:

> My aunt who had thirteen children of her own raised three more. She had become a midwife, and a child was born who was covered with sores. Nobody was particularly wanting the child, so she took the child and raised him . . . and another mother decided she didn't want to be bothered with two children. So my aunt took one and raised him . . . they were part of the family.[5]

Even when relationships were not between kin or fictive kin, African-American community norms were such that neighbors cared for each other's children. In the following passage, Sara Brooks, a Southern domestic worker, describes the importance of the community-based childcare that a neighbor offered her daughter. In doing so, she also shows how the African-American cultural value placed on cooperative childcare found institutional support in the adverse conditions under which so many Black women mothered.

> She kept Vivian and she didn't charge me nothin either. You see, people used to look after each other, but now it's not that way. I reckon it's because we all was poor, and I guess they put theirself in the place of the person that they was helpin.[6]

Othermothers were key not only in supporting children but also in supporting bloodmothers who, for whatever reason, were ill-prepared or had little desire to care for their children. Given the pressures from the larger political economy, the emphasis placed on community-based childcare and the respect given to othermothers who assume the responsibilities of childcare have served a critical function in African-American communities. Children orphaned by sale or death of their parents under slavery, children conceived through rape, children of young mothers, children born into extreme poverty; or children, who for other reasons have been rejected by their bloodmothers, have all been supported by othermothers who, like Ella Baker's aunt, took in additional children, even when they had enough of their own.

Providing as Part of Mothering

The work done by African-American women in providing the economic resources essential to Black family well-being affects motherhood in a contradictory fashion. On the one hand, African-American women have long integrated their activities as economic providers into their mothering relationships. In contrast to the cult of true womanhood where work is defined as being in opposition to and incompatible with motherhood, work for Black women has been an important and valued dimension of Afrocentric definitions of Black motherhood. On the other hand, African-American women's experiences as mothers under oppression were such that the type and purpose of work Black women were forced to do greatly impacted on the type of mothering relationships bloodmothers and othermothers had with Black children.

While slavery both disrupted West African family patterns and exposed enslaved Africans to the gender ideologies and practices of slaveowners, it simultaneously made it impossible, had they wanted to do so, for enslaved Africans to implement slaveowner's ideologies. Thus, the separate spheres of providing as a male domain and affective nurturing as a female domain did not develop within African-American families.[7] Providing for

Black children's physical survival and attending to their affective, emotional needs continued as interdependent dimensions of an Afrocentric ideology of motherhood. However, by changing the conditions under which Black women worked and the purpose of the work itself, slavery introduced the problem of how best to continue traditional Afrocentric values under oppressive conditions. Institutions of community-based childcare, informal adoption, greater reliance on othermothers, all emerge as adaptations to the exigencies of combining exploitative work with nurturing children.

In spite of the change in political status brought on by emancipation, the majority of African-American women remained exploited agricultural workers. However, their placement in Southern political economies allowed them to combine childcare with field labor. Sara Brooks describes how strong the links between providing and caring for others were for her:

> When I was about nine I was nursin my sister Sally—I'm about seven or eight years older than Sally. And when I would put her to sleep, instead of me goin somewhere and sit down and play, I'd get my little old hoe and get out there and work right in the field around the house.[8]

Black women's shift from Southern agriculture to domestic work in Southern and Northern towns and cities represented a change in the type of work done, but not in the meaning of work to women and their families. Whether they wanted to or not, the majority of African-American women had to work and could not afford the luxury of motherhood as a noneconomically productive, female "occupation."

Community Othermothers and Social Activism

Black women's experiences as othermothers have provided a foundation for Black women's social activism. Black women's feelings of responsibility for nurturing the children in their own extended family network have stimulated a more generalized ethic of care where Black women feel accountable to all the Black community's children.

This notion of Black women as community othermothers for all Black children traditionally allowed Black women to treat biologically unrelated children as if they were members of their own families. For example, sociologist Karen Fields describes how her grandmother, Mamie Garvin Fields, draws on her power as a community othermother when dealing with unfamiliar children.

> She will say to a child on the street who looks up to no good, picking out a name at random, "Aren't you Miz Pickney's boy?" in that same reproving tone. If the reply is, "No, *ma'am*, my mother is Miz Gadsden," whatever threat there was dissipates.[9]

The use of family language in referring to members of the Black community also illustrates this dimension of Black motherhood. For example, Mamie Garvin Fields describes how she became active in surveying the poor housing conditions of Black people in Charleston.

> I was one of the volunteers they got to make a survey of the places where we were paying extortious rents for indescribable property. I said "we," although it wasn't Bob and me. We had our own home, and so did many of the Federated Women. Yet we still felt like it really was "we" living in those terrible places, and it was up to us to do something about them.[10]

To take another example, while describing her increasingly successful efforts to teach a boy who had given other teachers problems, my daughter's kindergarten teacher stated, "You know how it can be—the majority of the children in the learning disabled classes are *our children*. I know he didn't belong there, so I volunteered to take him." In these statements, both women invoke the language of family to describe the ties that bind them as Black women to their responsibilities to other members of the Black community as family.

Sociologist Cheryl Gilkes suggests that community othermother relationships are sometimes behind Black women's decisions to become community activists.[11] Gilkes notes that many of the Black women community activists in her study became involved in community organizing in response to the needs of their own children and of those in their communities. The following comment is typical of how many of the Black women in Gilkes' study relate to Black children: "There were a lot of summer programs springing up for kids, but they were exclusive . . . and I found that most of *our kids* (emphasis mine) were excluded."[12] For many women, what began as the daily expression of their obligations as community othermothers, as was the case for the kindergarten teacher, developed into fullfledged roles as community leaders.

ENDNOTES

1. The terms used in this section appear in Rosalie Riegle Troester, "Turbulence and Tenderness: Mothers, Daughters, and Othermothers" in Paule Marshall's *Brown Girl, Brownstones, SAGE; A Scholarly Journal on Black Women* 1 (Fall 1984), pp. 13–16.
2. See Tanner's discussion of matrifocality, 1974; see also Carrie Allen McCray, "The Black Woman and Family Roles," in *The Black Woman*, ed. LaFrances Rogers-Rose (Beverly Hills, CA: Sage, 1980), pp. 67–78; Elmer Martin and Joanne Mitchell Martin, *The Black Extended Family* (Chicago: University of Chicago, 1978); Joyce Aschenbrenner, *Lifelines, Black Families in Chicago* (Prospect Heights, IL: Waveland, 1975); and Carol B. Stack, *All Our Kin* (New York: Harper & Row, 1974).
3. Martin and Martin, 1978; Stack, 1974; and Virginia Young, "Family and Childhood in a Southern Negro Community," *American Anthropologist* 72 (1970), pp. 269–288.
4. Stack, 1974.
5. Ellen Cantarow, *Moving the Mountain: Women Working for Social Change* (Old Westbury, NY: Feminist Press, 1980), p. 59.
6. Thordis Simonsen, ed., *You May Plow Here, The Narrative of Sara Brooks* (New York: Touchstone, 1986), p. 181.
7. Deborah White, *Arn't I a Woman? Female Slaves in the Plantation South* (N. Y.: W Norton, 1984); Dill, 1986; Leith Mullings, "Uneven Development: Class, Race and Gender in the United States Before 1900," in *Women's Work, Development and the Division of Labor by Gender*, eds. Eleanor Leacock and Helen Safa (South Hadley, MA: Bergin & Garvey, 1986), pp. 41–57.
8. Simonsen, 1986, p. 86.
9. Mamie Garvin Fields and Karen Fields, *Lemon Swamp and Other Places: A Carolina Memoir* (New York: Free Press, 1983), p. xvii.
10. Ibid, p. 195.
11. Cheryl Gilkes, "'Holding Back the Ocean with a Broom,' Black Women and Community Work," in Rogers-Rose, 1980, pp. 217–231; "Going Up for the Oppressed: The Career Mobility of Black Women Community Workers," *Journal of Social Issues* 39 (1983), pp. 115–139.
12. Gilkes, 1980, p. 219.

QUESTION

1. How does Collins define an 'othermother'? What is the significance of the *othermother* in African-American communities?
2. How does an *othermother* approach to motherhood contribute to community development?
3. What are the advantages for children in a system of motherhood which includes *othermothers?*

- more attention
- more role models
- feeling that you can count on many people

Religion and Spirituality

The global community is characterized by an incredible array of religious and spiritual beliefs and practices. Currently, armed engagements rage in parts of the world, fueled by the conflicts over both religious tenets and the social right to express one's system of religious orientation. Historically, organized religion—in all of its manifestations—has acted as both a force of social change and a gatekeeper for the status quo. While today women are involved actively in leadership positions in numerous religious institutions and organizations, feminism asks us to consider the roles of religion and spirituality in women's oppression, and in the efforts to explore and develop women's and men's liberation.

In this section, we will consider the dynamics of religion and spirituality. How has the social status of women in the United States been defined, advanced, and limited by religion and spirituality? How are the female and the feminine constructed by religion and spirituality, both historically and in contemporary U.S. society? How do markers of social identity (e.g., race, class, ethnic origin, gender, sexuality) affect one's participation in organized religion, as well as one's "permission" to be involved? How do the forces of religion and spirituality reinforce social structures and create possibilities for human participation in the social environment?

EVE AND ADAM: GENESIS 2–3 REREAD (1973)

Phyllis Trible

In Western culture, the Biblical story of the creation of woman and man is one of the most often cited justifications for women's inherent inferiority to men. In this selection, Phyllis Trible reconsiders the creation story in Genesis 2–3. In her re-viewing of the Bible passages, Trible points to the differences between the actual construction *of the writing and the* interpretation *of it. Trible, author of* God and the Rhetoric of Sexuality, *received her Ph.D. from Union Theological Seminary and Columbia University, and teaches at Andover Newton Theological School.*

On the whole, the Women's Liberation Movement is hostile to the Bible, even as it claims that the Bible is hostile to women. The Yahwist account of creation and fall in Genesis 2–3 provides a strong proof text for that claim. Accepting centuries of (male) exegesis, many feminists interpret this story as legitimating male supremacy and female subordination.[1] They read to reject. My suggestion is that we reread to understand and to appropriate. Ambiguity characterizes the meaning of *'adham* in Genesis 2–3. On the one hand, man is the first creature formed (2:7). The Lord God puts him in the garden "to till it and keep it," a job identified with the male (cf. 3:17–19). One the other hand, *'adham* is a generic term for humankind. In commanding *'adham* not to eat of the tree of the knowledge of good and evil, the Deity is speaking to both the man and the woman (2:16–17). Until the differentiation of female and male (2:21–23), *'adham* is basically androgynous: one creature incorporating two sexes.

Concern for sexuality, specifically for the creation of woman, comes last in the story, after the making of the garden, the trees, and the animals. Some commentators allege female subordination based on this order of events.[2] They contrast it with Genesis 1:27 where God creates *'adham* as male and female in one act.[3] Thereby they infer that whereas the Priests recognized the equality of the sexes, the Yahwist made woman a second, subordinate, inferior sex.[4] But the last may be first, as both the biblical theologian and the literary critic know. Thus the Yahwist account moves to its climax, not its decline, in the creation of woman.[5] She is not an afterthought; she is the culmination. Genesis 1 itself supports this interpretation, for there male and female are indeed the last and truly the crown of all creatures. The last is also first where beginnings and endings are parallel. In Hebrew literature, the central concerns of a unit often appear at the beginning and the end as an *inclusio* device.[6] Genesis 2 evinces this structure. The creation of man first and of woman last constitutes a ring composition whereby the two creatures are parallel. In no way does the order disparage woman. Content and context augment this reading.

The context for the advent of woman is a divine judgment: "It is not good that *'adham* should be alone. I will make him a helper fit for him" (2:18). The phrase needing explication is "helper fit for him." In the Old Testament the word *helper* (*'ezer*) has many usages. It can be a proper name for a male.[7] In our story, it describes the animals and the woman. In some passages, it characterizes Deity. God is the helper of Israel. As helper Yahweh creates and saves.[8] Thus *'ezer* is a relational term; it designates a beneficial relationship; and it pertains to God, people, and animals. By itself, the word does not specify positions within relationships; more particularly, it does not imply inferiority. Position results from additional content or from context. Accordingly, what kind of relationship does *'ezer* entail in Genesis 2:18, 20? Our answer comes in two ways: (1) The word *neged*, which joins *'ezer*, connotes equality: a helper who is a counterpart.[9] (2) The animals are helpers, but they fail to fit *'adham*. There is a physical, perhaps psychic, rapport between *'adham* and the animals, for Yahweh forms (*yasar*) them both out of the ground (*'adhamah*). Yet their similarity is not equality. *'Adham* names them and thereby exercises power over them. No fit helper is among them. And thus the narrative moves to woman. . . . God is the helper superior to man; the animals are helpers inferior to man; woman is the helper equal to man.

Let us pursue the issue by examining the account of the creation of woman ([verses] 21–22). This episode concludes the story even as the creation of man commences it. . . . The ring composition suggests an interpretation of woman and man as equals. To establish this meaning, structure and content must mesh. They do. In both episodes, Yahweh alone creates. For the last creation the Lord God "caused a deep sleep (*tardemah*) to fall upon the man." Man has no part in making woman, he is out of it. He exercises no control over her existence. He is neither participant nor spectator nor consultant at her birth. Like man, woman owes her life solely to God. For both of them, the origin of life is a divine mystery. Another parallel of equality is creation out of raw materials: dust for man and a rib for woman. Yahweh chooses these fragile materials and in both cases processes them before human beings happen. As Yahweh shapes dust and then breathes into it to form man, so Yahweh takes out the rib and then builds it into woman.[10] To call woman "Adam's rib" is to misread the text, which states carefully and clearly that the extracted bone required divine labor to become female, a datum scarcely designed to bolster the male ego. Moreover, to claim that the rib means inferiority or subordination is to assign the man qualities over the woman which are not in the narrative itself. Superiority, strength, aggressiveness, dominance, and power do not characterize man in Genesis 2. By contrast, he is formed from dirt; his life hangs by a breath which he does not control; and he himself remains silent and passive while the Deity plans and interprets his existence.

The rib means solidarity and equality. 'Adham recognizes this meaning in a poem:[11]

> This at last is bone of bones
> and flesh of my flesh.
> She shall be called *'ishshah* [woman]
> because she was taken out of *'ish* [man]. (2:23)

The pun proclaims both the similarity and the differentiation of female and male. Before this episode the Yahwist has used only the generic term *'adham*. No exclusively male reference has appeared. Only with the specific creation of woman ('ishshah) occurs the first specific terms for man as male ('ish). In other words, sexuality is simultaneous for woman and man. The sexes are interrelated and interdependent. Man as male does not precede woman as female but happens concurrently with her. Hence, the first act in Genesis 2 is the creation of androgyny (2:7), and the last is the creation of sexuality (2:23).[12] Male embodies female, and female embodies male. The two are neither dichotomies nor duplicates. The birth of woman corresponds to the birth of man but does not copy it. Only in responding to the female does the man discover himself as male. No longer a passive creature, *'ish* comes alive in meeting *'ishshah*.

Some read into the poem a naming motif. The man names the woman and thereby has power and authority over her.[13] But again . . . reread. Neither the verb nor the noun *name* is in the poem. We find instead the verb *gara'*, to call: "She shall be called woman." Now, in the Yahwist primeval history this verb does not function as a synonym or parallel or substitute for *name*. The typical formula for naming is the verb *to call* plus the explicit object *name*. This formula applies to Deity, people, places, and animals. For example, in Genesis 4 we read:

> Cain built a city and *called* the *name* of the city after the *name* of his son Enoch. (v.17)
> And Adam knew his wife again, and she bore a son and *called* his *name* Seth. (v. 25)
> To Seth also a son was born and he *called* his *name* Enoch. (v. 26a)
> At that time men began to *call* upon the *name* of the Lord. (v. 26b)

Genesis 2:23 has the verb *call* but does not have the object *name*. Its absence signifies the absence of a naming motif in the poem. The presence of both the verb *call* and the noun *name* in the episode of the animals strengthens the point:

> So out of the ground the Lord God formed every beast of the field and every bird of the air, and brought them to the man to see what he would *call* them; and whatever the man *called* every living creature, that was its name. The man gave *names* to all cattle, and to the birds of the air, and to every beast of the field. (2:19–20)

In calling the animals by name, *'adham* establishes supremacy over them and fails to find a fit helper. In calling woman, *'adham* does not name her and does find in her a counterpart. Female and male are equal sexes. Neither has authority over the other.[14]

A further observation secures the argument: *Woman* itself is not a name. It is a common noun; it is not a proper noun. It designates gender; it does not specify person. *'Adham* recognizes sexuality by the words *'ishshah* and *'ish*. This recognition is not an act of naming to assert the power of male over female. Quite the contrary. But the true skeptic is already asking: What about Genesis 3:20, where "the man called his wife's name Eve"? We must wait to consider that question. Meanwhile, the words of the ancient poem as well as their context proclaim sexuality originating in the unity of *'adham*. From this one (androgynous) creature come two (female and male). The two return to their original unity as *'ish* and *'ishshah* become one flesh (2:24):[15] another instance of the ring composition.

Next the differences which spell harmony and equality yield to the differences of disobedience and disaster. The serpent speaks to the woman. Why to the woman and not to the man? The simplest answer is that we do not know. The Yahwist does not tell us anymore than he explains why the tree of knowledge of good and evil was in the garden. But the silence of the text stimulates speculations, many of which only confirm the patriarchal mentality which conceived them. Cassuto identifies serpent and woman, maintaining that the cunning of the serpent is "in reality" the cunning of the woman.[16] He impugns her further by declaring that "for the very reason that a woman's imagination surpasses a man's, it was the woman who was enticed first." Though more gentle in his assessment, von Rad avers that "in the history of Yahweh religion, it has always been the women who have shown an inclination for obscure astrological cults" (a claim which he does not document).[17] Consequently, he holds that the woman "confronts the obscure allurements and mysteries that beset our limited life more directly than the man does," and then he calls her a "temptress." Paul Ricoeur says that woman "represents the point of weakness," as the entire story "gives evidence of a very masculine resentment."[18] McKenzie links the "moral weakness" of the woman with her "sexual attraction" and holds that the latter ruined both the woman and the man.[19]

But the narrative does not say any of these things. It does not sustain the judgment that woman is weaker or more cunning or more sexual than man. Both have the same Creator, who explicitly uses the word *good* to introduce the creation of woman (2:18). Both are equal in birth. There is complete rapport, physical, psychological, sociological, and theological, between them: bone of bone and flesh of flesh. If there be moral frailty in one, it is moral frailty in two. Further, they are equal in responsibility and in judgment, in shame and in guilt, in redemption and in grace. What the narrative says about the nature of woman it also says about the nature of man.

Why does the serpent speak to the woman and not to the man? Let a female speculate. If the serpent is "more subtle" than its fellow creatures, the woman is more appealing than her husband. Throughout the myth, she is the more intelligent one, the more aggressive one, and the one with greater sensibilities.[20] Perhaps the woman elevates the animal world by conversing theologically with the serpent. At any rate, she understands the hermeneutical task. In quoting God, she interprets the prohibition ("neither shall you touch it"). The woman is both theologian and translator. She contemplates the tree, taking into account all the possibilities. The tree is good for food; it satisfies the physical drives. It pleases the eyes; it is esthetically and emotionally desirable. Above all, it is coveted as the source of wisdom *(haskîl)*. Thus the woman is fully aware when she acts, her vision encompassing the gamut of life. She takes the fruit, and she eats. The initiative and the decision are hers alone. There is no consultation with her husband. She seeks neither his advice nor his permission. She acts independently.

By contrast, the man is a silent, passive, and bland recipient: "She also gave some to her husband, and he ate." The narrator makes no attempt to depict the husband as reluctant or hesitating. The man does not theologize; he does not contemplate; he does not envision the full possibilities of the occasion. His one act is belly oriented, and it is an act of quiescence, not of initiative. The man is not dominant; he is not aggressive; he is not a decision maker. Even though the prohibition not to eat of the tree appears before the female was specifically created, she knows that it applies to her. She has interpreted it, and now she struggles with the temptation to disobey. But not the man, to whom the prohibition came directly (2:16). He follows his wife without question or comment, thereby denying his own individuality. If the woman be intelligent, sensitive, and ingenious, the man is passive, brutish, and inept. These character portrayals are truly extraordinary in a culture dominated by men. I stress their contrast not to promote female chauvinism but to undercut patriarchal interpretations alien to the text.

The contrast between woman and man fades after their acts of disobedience. They are one in the new knowledge of their nakedness (3:7). They are one in hearing and in hiding. They flee from the sound of the Lord God in the Garden (3:8). First to the man come questions of responsibility (3:9, 11), but the man fails to be responsible: "The woman whom Thou gavest to be with me, she gave me fruit of the tree, and I ate" (3:12). Here the man does not blame the woman; he does not say that the woman seduced him;[21] he blames the Deity. The verb which he uses for both the Deity and the woman is *ntn* (cf. 3:6). . . . This verb neither means nor implies seduction in this context or in the lexicon. Again, if the Yahwist intended to make woman the temptress, he missed a choice opportunity. The woman's response supports the point. "The serpent beguiled me, and I ate" (3:13). Only here occurs the strong verb *nsh'*, meaning to deceive, to seduce. God accepts this subject-verb combination when, immediately following the woman's accusation, Yahweh says to the serpent, "Because you have done this, cursed are you above all animals" (3:14).

Though the tempter (the serpent) is cursed,[22] the woman and the man are not. But they are judged, and the judgments are commentaries on the disastrous effects of their shared disobedience. They show how terrible human life has become as it stands between creation and grace. We misread if we assume that these judgments are mandates. They describe; they do not prescribe. They protest; they do not condone. Of special concern are the words telling the woman that her husband shall rule over her (3:16). This statement is not license for male supremacy, but rather it is condemnation of that very pattern.[23] Subjugation and supremacy are perversions of creation. Through disobedience, the woman has become slave. Her initiative and her freedom vanish. The man is corrupted also, for he has become master, ruling over the one who is his God-given equal. The subordination of female to male signifies their shared sin.[24] This sin vitiates all relationships: between animals and human beings (3:15); mothers and children (3:16); husbands and wifes (3:16); people and the soil

(3:17–18); humanity and its work (3:19). Whereas in creation man and woman know harmony and equality, in sin they know alienation and discord. Grace makes possible a new beginning.

A further observation about these judgments: they are culturally conditioned. Husband and work (childbearing) define the woman; wife and work (farming) define the man. A literal reading of the story limits both creatures and limits the story. To be faithful translators, we must recognize that women as well as men move beyond these culturally defined roles, even as the intentionality and function of the myth move beyond its original setting. Whatever forms stereotyping takes in our own culture, they are judgments upon our common sin and disobedience. The suffering and oppression we women and men know are the marks of our fall, not of our creation.

At this place of sin and judgment, "the man calls his wife's name Eve" (3:20), thereby asserting his rule over her. The naming itself faults the man for corrupting a relationship of mutuality and equality. And so Yahweh evicts the primeval couple from the Garden, yet with signals of grace.[25] Interestingly, the conclusion of the story does not specify the sexes in flight. Instead the narrator resumes use of the generic and androgynous term *'adham* with which the story began and thereby completes an overall ring composition (3:22–24).

Visiting the Garden of Eden in the days of the Women's Movement, we need no longer accept the traditional exegesis of Genesis 2–3. Rather than legitimating the patriarchal culture from which it comes, the myth places that culture under judgment. And thus it functions to liberate, not to enslave. This function we can recover and appropriate. The Yahwist narrative tells us who we are (creatures of equality and mutuality); it tells us who we have become (creatures of oppression); and so it opens possibilities for change, for a return to our true liberation under God. In other words, the story calls female and male to repent.

ENDNOTES

1. *See inter alia,* Kate Millett, *Sexual Politics* (New York: Doubleday, 1970), pp. 51–54; Eva Figes, *Patriarchal Attitudes* (Greenwich, Conn.: Fawcett, 1970), pp. 38f; Mary Daly, "The Courage to See," *The Christian Century,* September 22, 1971, p. 1110; Sheila D. Collins, "Toward a Feminist Theology," *The Christian Century,* August 2, 1972, p. 798; Lilly Rivlin, "Lilith: The First Woman," *Ms.,* December 1972, pp. 93, 114.

2. Cf. E. Jacob, *Theology of the Old Testament* (New York: Harper & Bros., 1958), pp. 172f; S. H. Hooke, "Genesis," *Peake's Commentary on the Bible* (London: Thomas Nelson, 1962), p. 179.

3. E.g., Elizabeth Cady Stanton observed that Genesis 1:26–28 "dignifies woman as an important factor in the creation, equal in power and glory with man," while Genesis 2 "makes her a mere afterthought" (*The Women's Bible,* Part I [New York: European Publishing Company, 1895], p. 20). See also Elsie Adams and Mary Louis Briscoe, *Up Against the Wall, Mother* . . . (Beverly Hills: Glencoe Press, 1971), p. 4.

4. Cf. Eugene H. Maly, "Genesis," *The Jerome Biblical Commentary* (Englewood Cliffs, N.J.: Prentice–Hall, 1968), p. 12: "But women's existence, psychologically and in the social order, is dependent on man."

5. See John L. McKenzie, "The Literary Characteristics of Gen. 2–3," *Theological Studies,* Vol. 15 (1954), p. 559; John A. Bailey, "Initiation and the Primal Woman in Gilgamesh and Genesis 2–3," *Journal of Biblical Literature,* June 1970, p. 143. Bailey writes emphatically of the remarkable importance and position of the woman in Genesis 2–3, "all the more extraordinary when one realizes that this is the only account of the creation of woman as such in ancient Near Eastern literature." He hedges, however, in seeing the themes of helper and naming (Genesis 2:18–23) as indicative of a "certain subordination" of woman to man. These reservations are unnecessary; see below. Cf. also Claus Westerman, *Genesis, Biblischer Kommentar* 1/4 (Neukerchener–Vluyn: Newkirchener Verlag, 1970), p. 312.

6. James Muilenburg, "Form Criticism and Beyond," *Journal of Biblical Literature,* March 1969, pp. 9f; Mitchell Dahood, "Psalm 1," *The Anchor Bible* (New York: Doubleday, 1966) *passim* and esp. p. 5.

7. See 1 Chronicles 4:4, 12:9, Nehemiah 3:19.

8. Se Psalm 121:2, 124:8; 146:5; 33:20; 115:9–11; Exodus 18:4; Deuteronomy 33:7, 26, 29.

9. L. Koehler and W. Baumgartner, *Lexicon in Veteris Testamenti Libros* (Leiden: E. J. Brill, 1958), pp. 591f.

10. The verb *bnh* (to build) suggests considerable labor. It is used of towns, towers, altars, and fortifications, as well as of the primeval woman (Koehler–Baumgartner, op. cit., p. 134). In Genesis 2:22, it may mean the fashioning of clay around the rib (Ruth Amiran, "Myths of the Creation of Man and the Jericho Statues," *BASOR*, No. 167 [October 1962], p. 24).

11. See Walter Brueggemann, "Of the Same Flesh and Bone (Gen. 2:23a)," *Catholic Biblical Quarterly*, October 1970, pp. 532–42.

12. In proposing as primary an androgynous interpretation of *'adham*, I find virtually no support from (male) biblical scholars. But my view stands as documented from the text, and I take refuge among a remnant of ancient (male) rabbis (see George Foot Moore, *Judaism* [Cambridge, Mass.: Harvard University Press, 1927]), I, 453; also Joseph Campbell, *The Hero with a Thousand Faces* (Meridian Books, The World Publishing Company, 1970), pp. 152ff., 279f.

13. See e.g., G. von Rad, *Genesis* (Philadelphia: Westminster Press, 1961), pp. 80–82, John H. Marks, "Genesis," *The Interpreter's One–Volume Commentary on the Bible* (Nashville: Abingdon Press, 1971), p. 5; Bailey, op. cit., p. 143.

14. Cf. Westermann, op. cit., pp. 316ff.

15. Verse 24 probably mirrors a matriarchal society (so Von Rad, op. cit., p. 83). If the myth were designed to support patriarchy, it is difficult to explain how this verse survived without proper alteration. Westermann contends, however, that an emphasis on matriarchy misunderstands the point of the verse, which is the total communion of woman and man (ibid., p. 317).

16. U. Cassuto, *A Commentary of the Book of Genesis*, Part I (Jerusalem: Magnes Press, n.d.), pp. 142f.

17. Von Rad, op. cit., pp. 87f.

18. Ricoeur departs from the traditional interpretation of the woman when he writes: *"Eve n'est donc pas la femme en tant que 'deuxieme sexe'; toute femme et tout homme sont Adam; tout homme et toute femme sont Eve."* But the fourth clause of his sentence obscures this complete identity of Adam and Eve: *"toute femme peche 'en Adam, tout homme est seduit 'en Eve."* By switching from an active to a passive verb, Ricoeur makes only the woman directly responsible for both sinning and seducing. (Paul Ricoeur, Finitude et Culpabilitie, II. *La Symbolique du Mal*, Aubier, Editions Montaigne [Paris: 1960]. Cf. Paul Ricoeur, *The Symbolism of Evil* [Boston: Beacon Press, 1969], p. 255).

19. McKenzie, op. cit., p. 570

20. See Bailey, op. cit., p. 148.

21. See Westermann, op. cit., p. 340.

22. For a discussion of the serpent, see Ricoeur, *The Symbolism of Evil*, op. cit., pp. 255–60.

23. Cf. Edwin M. Good., *Irony in the Old Testament* (Philadelphia: Westminster Press, 1965), p. 84, note 4: "Is it not surprising that, in a culture where the subordination of woman to man was a virtually unquestioned social principle, the etiology of the subordination should be in the context of man's primal sin? Perhaps woman's subordination was not unquestioned in Israel." Cf. also Henricus Renckens, *Israel's Concept of the Beginning* (New York: Herder & Herder, 1964), pp. 127f.

24. *Contra* Westermann, op. cit., p. 357.

25. Von Rad, op. cit., pp. 94, 148.

QUESTIONS

1. Phyllis Trible mentions a second account of creation in Genesis that seems to conflict with Genesis 2–3. How does her discussion of androgyny and ring composition allow for compatibility between these two creation accounts?

2. Many people believe that the Bible is divinely inspired. If this is the case, can we argue that interpretations of the creation story are *not* divinely inspired? Why/why not?

3. Trible urges us to be "faithful translators" and to recognize that Genesis 2–3 is not sexist. Is this as important to know as Trible argues it is, or is it still important to address the effects of the story, regardless of its original meaning? Why/why not?

Mrs. Stewart's Farewell Address to Her Friends in the City of Boston (1833)

Delivered September 21, 1833

Maria Stewart

A prolific writer and a passionate preacher, Maria Stewart is one of many powerful voices in our history. At a time when white women were discouraged from speaking the Word of God in public, Stewart, a Black woman, became well-known as a public advocate for living a religious life. Here, as she says "farewell" to the city of Boston, Stewart summarizes her understanding of religion and the religious life. She offers this understanding for herself personally and as a method for the pursuit of social justice under God's laws.

"Is this vile world a friend to grace,
To help me on to God?"

Ah, no! For it is with great tribulation that any shall enter through the gates of the holy cities [Acts 14:22].

My Respected Friends,

You have heard me observe that the shortness of time, the certainty of death, and the instability of all things here, induce me to turn my thoughts from earth to heaven. Borne down with a heavy load of sin and shame, my conscience filled with remorse; considering the throne of God forever guiltless, and my own eternal condemnation as just, I was at last brought to accept of salvation as a free gift, in and through the merits of a crucified Redeemer. Here I was brought to see,

'Tis not by works of righteousness
  That our own hands have done,
But we are saved by grace alone,
  Abounding through the Son.

After these convictions, in imagination I found myself sitting at the feet of Jesus, clothed in my right mind. For I had been like a ship tossed to and fro, in a storm at sea. Then was I glad when I realized the dangers I had escaped; and then I consecrated my soul and body, and all the powers of my mind to his service, and from that time henceforth; yea, even for evermore, amen.

I found that religion was full of benevolence; I found there was joy and peace in believing, and I felt as though I was commanded to come out from the world and be separate; to go forward and be baptized. Me thought I heard a spiritual interrogation, are you able to drink that cup that I have drank of? And to be baptized with the baptism that I have been baptized with [Matthew 20:22]? And my heart made this reply: Yea, Lord, I am able. Yet amid these bright hopes, I was filled with apprehensive fears, lest they were false. I found that sin still lurked within; it was hard for me to renounce all for Christ, when I saw my earthly prospects blasted. O, how bitter was that cup. Yet I drank it to its very dregs. It was hard for me to say, thy will be done; yet I was made to bend and kiss the rod. I was at last made willing to be anything or nothing, for my Redeemer's sake. Like many, I was anxious to retain the world in one hand, and religion in the other. "Ye cannot serve God and mammon [Matthew 6:24]," sounded in my ear, and with giant-strength, I cut off my right hand, as it were, and plucked out my right eye, and cast them from me, thinking it better to enter life halt and maimed, rather than having two hands or eyes to be cast into hell [Mark 9:43]. Thus ended these mighty conflicts, and I received this heart-cheering promise, "That neither death, nor life, nor principalities, nor powers, nor things present, nor things to come, should be able to separate me from the love of Christ Jesus, our Lord [Romans 8:38, 39]."

And truly, I can say with St. Paul that at my conversion I came to the people in the fullness of the gospel of grace [Romans 15:29]. Having spent a few months in the city of—,previous, I saw the flourishing condition of their churches, and the progress they were making in their Sabbath Schools. I visited their Bible classes, and heard of the union that existed in their Female Associations. On my arrival here, not finding scarce an individual who felt interested in these subjects, and but few of the whites, except Mr. Garrison, and his friend, Mr. Knapp; and hearing that those gentlemen had observed that female influence was powerful, my soul became fired with a holy zeal for your cause; every nerve and muscle in me was engaged in your behalf. I felt that I had a great work to perform; and was in haste to make a profession of my faith in Christ, that I might be about my Father's business [Luke 2: 49]. Soon after I made this profession, The Spirit of God came before me, and I spake before many. When going home, reflecting on what I had said, I felt ashamed, and knew not where I should hide myself. A something said within my breast, "Press forward, I will be with thee." And my heart made this reply, Lord, if thou wilt be with me, then I will speak for thee as long as I live. And thus far I have every reason to believe that it is the divine influence of the Holy Spirit operating upon my heart that could possibly induce me to make the feeble and unworthy efforts that I have.

But to begin my subject: "Ye have heard that it hath been said, whoso is angry with his brother without a cause, shall be in danger of the judgment; and whose shall say to his brother, Raca, shall be in danger of the council. But whosoever shall say, thou fool, shall be in danger of hell-fire [Matthew 5:22]." For several years my heart was in continual sorrow. And I believe that the Almighty beheld from his holy habitation, the affliction wherewith I was afflicted, and heard the false misrepresentations wherewith I was misrepresented, and there was none to help. Then I cried unto the Lord in my troubles. And thus for wise and holy purposes, best known to himself, he has raised me in the midst of my enemies, to vindicate my wrongs before this people; and to reprove them for sin, as I have reasoned to them of righteousness and judgment to come. "For as the heavens are higher than the earth, so are his ways above our ways, and his thoughts above our thoughts [Isaiah 55:9]." I believe, that for wise and holy purposes, best known to himself, he hath unloosed my tongue, and put his word into my mouth, in order to confound and put all those to shame that have rose up against me. For he hath clothed my face with steel, and lined my forehead with brass. He hath put his testimony within me, and engraven his seal on my forehead [Revelation 9:4]. And with these weapons I have indeed set the fiends of earth and hell at defiance.

What if I am a woman; is not the God of ancient times the God of these modern days? Did he not raise up Deborah, to be a mother, and judge in Israel [Judges 4:4]? Did not queen Esther save the lives of the Jews? And Mary Magdalene first declare the resurrection of Christ from the dead? Come, said the woman of Samaria, and see a man that hath told me all things that ever I did, is not this the Christ? St. Paul declared that it was a shame for a woman to speak in public, yet our great High Priest and Advocate did not condemn the woman for a more notorious offense than this; neither will he condemn this worthless worm. The bruised reed he will not break, and the smoking flax he will not quench, till he send forth judgment unto victory. Did St. Paul but know of our wrongs and deprivations, I presume he would make no objections to our pleading in public for our rights. Again; holy women ministered unto Christ and the apostles; and women of refinement in all ages, more or less, have had a voice in moral, religious and political subjects. Again; why the Almighty hath imparted unto me the power of speaking thus, I cannot tell. "And Jesus lifted up his voice and said, I thank thee, O Father, Lord of Heaven and Earth, that thou hast hid these things from the wise and prudent, and has revealed them unto babes; even so, Father, for so it seemed good in thy sight [Luke 10:21]."

But to convince you of the high opinion that was formed of the capacity and ability of woman by the ancients, I would refer you to "Sketches of the Fair Sex." Read to the 51st page, and you will find that several of the Northern nations imagined that women could look into futurity, and that they had about them, an inconceivable something, approaching to divinity. Perhaps that idea was only the effect of the sagacity common to the sex, and the advantages which their natural address gave them over rough and simple warriors. Perhaps, also, those barbarians, surprised at the influence which beauty has over force, were led to ascribe to the supernatural attraction, a charm which they could not comprehend. A belief, however, that the Deity more readily communicates himself to women, has at one time or other, prevailed in every quarter of the earth; not only among the Germans and the Britons, but all the people of Scandinavia were possessed of it. Among the Greeks, women delivered the Oracles; the respect the Romans paid to the Sibyls is well known. The Jews had their prophetesses. The prediction of the Egyptian woman obtained much credit at Rome, even under the Emperors. And in the most barbarous nations, all things that have the appearance of being supernatural, the mysteries of religion, the secrets of physic, and the rites of magic, were in the possession of women.

If such women as are here described have once existed, be no longer astonished then, my brethren and friends, that God at this eventful period should raise up your own females to strive, by their example both in public and private, to assist those who are endeavoring to stop the strong current of prejudice that flows so profusely against us at present. No longer ridicule their efforts, it will be counted for sin. For God makes use of feeble means sometimes, to bring about his most exalted purposes.

In the 15th century, the general spirit of this period is worthy of observation. We might then have seen women preaching and mixing themselves in controversies. Women occupying the chairs of Philosophy and Justice; women writing in Greek, and studying in Hebrew. Nuns were poetesses, and women of quality divines; and young girls who had studied Eloquence, would with the sweetest countenances and the most plaintive voices, pathetically exhort the Pope and the Christian Princes to declare war against the Turks. Women in those days devoted their leisure hours to contemplation and study. The religious spirit which has animated women in all ages, showed itself at this time. It has made them by turns, martyrs, apostles, warriors, and concluded in making them divines and scholars.

Why cannot a religious spirit animate us now? Why cannot we become divines and scholars? Although learning is somewhat requisite, yet recollect that those great apostles, Peter and James, were ignorant and unlearned. They were taken from the fishing boat and made fishers of men.

In the 13th century, a young lady of Bologne devoted herself to the study of the Latin language, and of the laws. At the age of twenty-three she pronounced a funeral oration in Latin, in the great church of Bologne. And to be admitted as a orator, she had neither need of indulgence on account of her youth or of her sex. At the age of twenty-six, she took the degree of Doctor of Laws, and began publicly to expound the Institutions of Justinian. At the age of thirty, her great reputation raised her to a chair, where she taught the law to a prodigious concourse of scholars from all nations. She joined the charms and accomplishments of a woman to all the knowledge of a man. And such was the power of her eloquence, that her beauty was only admired when her tongue was silent.

What if such woman as are here described should rise among our sable race? And it is not impossible. For it is not the color of the skin that makes the man or the woman, but the principle formed in the soul. Brilliant wit will shine, come from whence it will; and genius and talent will not hide the brightness of its lustre.

But, to return to my subject; the mighty work of reformation has begun among this people. The dark clouds of ignorance are dispersing. The light of science is bursting forth. Knowledge is beginning to flow, nor will its moral influence be extinguished till its refulgent rays have spread over us from East to West, and from North to South. Thus far is this mighty work begun, but not as yet accomplished. Christians must awake from their slumbers. Religion must flourish among them before the church will be built up in its purity, or immorality be suppressed.

Yet, notwithstanding your prospects are thus fair and bright, I am about to leave you, perhaps never more to return. For I find it is no use for me as an individual to try to make myself useful among my color in this city. It was contempt for my moral and religious opinions in private that drove me thus before a public. Had experience more plainly shown me that it was the nature of man to crush his fellow, I should not have thought it so hard. Wherefore, my respected friends, let us no longer talk of prejudice, till prejudice becomes extinct at home. Let us not longer talk of oppression, till we cease to oppose our own. For while these evils exist, to talk is like giving breath to the air, and labor to the wind. Though wealth is far more highly prized than humble merit, yet none of these things move me. Having God for my friend and portion, what have I to fear? Promotion cometh neither from the East or West, and as long as it is the will of God, I rejoice that I am as I am; for man in his best estate is altogether vanity. Men of eminence have mostly risen from obscurity; nor will I, although a female of a darker hue, and far more obscure than they, bend my head or hang my harp upon willows [Psalm 137:2]; for though poor, I will virtuous prove. And if it is the will of my heavenly Father to reduce me to penury and want, I am ready to say, amen, even so be it. "The foxes have holes, and the birds of the air have nests, but the Son of man hath not where to lay his head [Matthew 8:20]."

During the short period of my Christian warfare, I have indeed had to contend against the fiery darts of the devil. And was it not that the righteous are kept by the mighty power of God through faith unto salvation, long before this I should have proved to be like the seed by the way-side. For it has actually appeared to me at different periods as though the powers of earth and hell had combined against me, to prove my overthrow. Yet amidst their dire attempts, I have found the Almighty to be "a friend that sticketh closer than a brother [Proverbs 18:24]." He never will forsake the soul that leans on him; though he chastens and corrects it, it is for the soul's best interest. "And as a Father pitieth his children, so the Lord pitieth them that fear him [Psalm 103:13]."

But some of you have said, "do not talk so much about religion, the people do not wish to hear you. We know these things, tell us something we do not know." If you know these things, my dear friends, and have performed them, far happier, and more prosperous would you now have been. "He that knoweth the Lord's will and obeyeth it not, shall be beaten with many stripes [Luke 12:42]." Sensible of this, I have, regardless of the frowns and scoffs of a guilty world, plead [sic] up religion, and the pure principles of morality among you. Religion is the most glorious theme that mortals can converse upon. The older it grows, the more new beauties it displays. Earth, with its brilliant attractions, appears mean and sordid when compared to it. It is that fountain that has no end, and those that drink thereof shall never thirst; for it is, indeed, a well of water springing up in the soul unto everlasting life.

Again, those ideas of greatness which are held forth to us, are vain delusions, are airy visions which we shall never realize. All that man can say or do can never elevate us, it is a work that must be effected between God and ourselves. And how? By dropping all political discussions in our behalf, for these, in my opinion, sow the seed of discord, and strengthen the cord of prejudice. A spirit of animosity is already risen, and unless it is quenched, a fire will burst forth and devour us, and our young will be slain by the sword. It is the sovereign will of God that our condition should be thus and so. "For he hath formed one vessel for honor, and another for dishonor [Romans 9:21]." And shall the clay say to him that hath formed it, why hast thou formed me thus? It is high time to drop political discussions, and when our day of deliverance comes, God will provide a way for us to escape, and fight his own battles.

Finally, my brethren, let us follow after godliness, and the things which make for peace. Cultivate your own minds and morals; real merit will elevate you. Pure religion will burst your fetters. Turn your attention to industry. Strive to please your employers. Lay up what you can. And remember, that in the grave, distinction withers, and the high and low are alike renowned.

But I draw to a conclusion. Long will the kind sympathy of some much loved friend, be written on the tablet of my memory, especially those kind individuals who have stood by me like pitying angels, and befriended me when in the midst of difficulty; many blessings rest on them. Gratitude is all the tribute I can offer. A rich reward awaits them.

To my unconverted friends, one and all, I would say, shortly this frail tenement of mine will be dissolved and lie mouldering in ruins. O, solemn thought! Yet why should I revolt, for it is the glorious hope of a blessed immortality, beyond the grave, that has supported me thus far through this vale of tears. Who among you will strive to meet me at the right hand of Christ. For the great day of retribution is fast approaching, and who shall be able to abide his coming? You are forming characters for eternity. As you live so will you die; as death leaves you, so judgment will find you. Then shall we receive the glorious welcome, "Come ye blessed of my Father, inherit the kingdom prepared for you from before the foundation of the world [Matthew 25:34]." Or, hear the heart-rendering sentence, "Depart ye cursed into everlasting fire prepared for the devil and his angels [Matthew 25: 41]." When thrice ten thousand years have rolled away, eternity will be but just begun. Your ideas will but just begin to expand. O, eternity, who can unfathom thine end, or comprehend thy beginning.

Dearly beloved, I have made myself contemptible in the eyes of many, that I might win some. But it has been like labor in vain. "Paul may plant, and Apollos water, but God alone giveth the increase [1 Corinthians 3:6]."

To my brethren and sisters in the church, I would say, be ye clothed with the breast-plate of righteousness, having your loins girt about with truth [Ephesians 6:14], prepared to meet the Bridegroom at his coming [Matthew 25:1-13]; for blessed are those servants that are found watching.

Farewell. In a few short years from now, we shall meet in those upper regions where parting will be no more. There we shall sing and shout, and shout and sing, and make heaven's high arches ring. There we shall range in rich pastures, and partake of those living streams that never dry. O, blissful thought! Hatred and contention shall cease, and we shall join with redeemed millions in ascribing glory and honor, and riches, and power and blessing to the Lamb that was slain, and to him that sitteth upon the throne. Nor eye hath seen, nor ear heard, neither hath it entered into the heart of man to conceive of the joys that are prepared for them that love God. Thus far has my life been almost a life of complete disappointment. God has tried me as by fire. Well was I aware that if I contended boldly for his cause, I must suffer. Yet, I chose rather to suffer affliction with his people, than to enjoy the pleasures of sin for a season. And I believe that the glorious declaration was about to be made applicable to me, that was made to God's ancient covenant people by the prophet, Comfort ye, comfort ye, my people: say unto her that her warfare is accomplished, and that her iniquities are pardoned. I believe that a rich award awaits me, if not in this world, in the world to come. O, blessed reflection. The bitterness of my soul has departed from those who endeavored to discourage and hinder me in my Christian progress; and I can now forgive my enemies, bless those who have hated me, and cheerfully pray for those who have despitefully used and persecuted me.

Fare you well, farewell.
Maria S. [sic] Stewart
New York, April 14, 1834

QUESTIONS

1. Explain how Stewart relies on her faith to motivate her in her work. What does Stewart perceive her work to be?
2. What benefits does Stewart identify in religion and in a religious life?
3. Does Stewart see contradiction in her being female and Black, and preaching the Word of God? Why/why not?. What historical evidence does Stewart present to support her understanding of the role of Black women in particular, and women in general, in public preaching?
4. What conceptualization of human nature does Stewart present? How does this view of human nature structure Stewarts' perception of her engagement in "Christian warfare"?

What Became of God the Mother? Conflicting Images of God in Early Christianity (1976)

Elaine H. Pagels

In a careful examination of images and principles in early Christianity, Elaine Pagels explores the distinction between "orthodox" religious principles, and those principles defined as "heterodox." Pagels considers the question of why some religious principles are excluded from orthodoxy through the examination of the historical foundations of orthodoxy in contemporary Christianity. Pagels concludes that the power of social and cultural forces act together to make invisible both feminine symbolism and female participation in the Christian tradition. Pagels, author of The Johannine Gospel in Gnostic Exegesis *and* The Gnostic Paul, *received her Ph.D. from Harvard University and now teaches at Barnard College, Columbia University.*

Unlike many of his contemporaries among the deities of the ancient Near East, the God of Israel shares his power with no female divinity, nor is he the divine Husband or Lover of any.[1] He scarcely can be characterized in any but masculine epithets: King, Lord, Master, Judge, and Father.[2] Indeed, the absence of feminine symbolism of God marks Judaism, Christianity, and Islam in striking contrast to the world's other religious traditions, whether in Egypt, Babylonia, Greece, and Rome or Africa, Polynesia, India, and North America. Jewish, Christian, and Islamic theologians, however, are quick to point out that God is not to be considered in sexual terms at all. Yet the actual language they use daily in worship and prayer conveys a different message and gives the distinct impression that God is thought of in exclusively *masculine* terms. And while it is true that Catholics revere Mary as the mother of Jesus, she cannot be identified as divine in her own right: if she is "mother of God," she is not "God the Mother" on an equal footing with God the Father.

Christianity, of course, added the trinitarian terms to the Jewish description of God. And yet of the three divine "Persons," two—the Father and Son—are described in masculine terms, and the third—the Spirit—suggests the sexlessness of the Greek neuter term pneuma. This is not merely a subjective impression. Whoever investigates the early development of Christianity—the field called "patristics," that is, study of the "the fathers of the church"—may not be surprised by the passage that concludes the recently discovered, secret *Gospel of Thomas*: "Simon Peter said to them [the disciples}, 'Let Mary be excluded from among us, for she is a woman, and not worthy of Life.' Jesus said, 'Behold I will take Mary, and make her a male, so that she may become a living spirit, resembling you males. For I tell you truly, that every female who makes herself male will enter the Kingdom of Heaven.'"[3] Strange as it sounds, this only states explicitly what religious rhetoric often assumes: that the men form the legitimate body of the community, while women will be allowed to participate only insofar as their own identity is denied and assimilated to that of the men.

Further exploration of the texts which include this *Gospel*—written on papyrus, hidden in large clay jars nearly 1,600 years ago—has identified them as Jewish and Christian gnostic works which were attacked and condemned as "heretical" as early as A.D. 100–150. What distinguishes these "heterodox" texts from those that are called "orthodox" is at least partially clear: they abound in feminine symbolism that is applied, in particular, to God. Although one might expect, then, that they would recall the archaic pagan traditions of the Mother Goddess, their language is to the contrary specifically Christian, unmistakably related to a Jewish heritage. Thus we can see that certain gnostic Christians diverged even more radically from the Jewish tradition than the early Christians who described God as the "three persons" or the Trinity. For, instead of a monistic and masculine God, certain of these text describe God as a dyadic being who consists of *both* masculine and feminine elements. One such group of texts, for example, claims to have received a secret tradition from Jesus through James, and significantly, through Mary Magdalene.[4] Members of this group offer prayer to *both* the divine Father and Mother: "From Thee, Father, and through Thee, Mother, the two immortal names, Parents of the divine being, and thou, dweller in heaven, mankind of the mighty name."[5] Other texts indicate that their authors had pondered the nature of the beings to whom a single, masculine God proposed, "Let us make mankind in our image, after our likeness" (Gen. 1:26). Since the Genesis account goes on to say that mankind was created "male and female" (1:27), some concluded, apparently, that the God in whose image we are created likewise must be both masculine and feminine—both Father and Mother.

The characterization of the divine Mother in these sources is not simple since the texts themselves are extraordinarily diverse. Nevertheless, three primary characterizations merge. First, a certain poet and teacher, Valentinus, begins with the premise that God is essentially indescribable. And yet he suggests that the divine can be imagined as a Dyad consisting of two elements: one he calls the Ineffable, the Source, the Primal Father; the other, the Silence, the Mother of all things.[6] Although we might question Valentinus's reasoning that Silence is the appropriate complement of what is Ineffable, his equation of the former with the feminine and the latter with the masculine may be traced to the grammatical gender of the Greek words. Followers of Valentinus invoke this feminine power, whom they also call "Grace" (in Greek, the feminine term *charis*), in their own private celebration of the Christian eucharist: they call her "divine, eternal Grace, She who is before all things."[7] At other times they pray to her for protection as the Mother, "Thou enthroned with God, eternal, mystical Silence."[8] Marcus, a disciple of Valentinus, contends that "when Moses began his account of creation, he mentioned the Mother of all things at the very beginning, when he said, 'In the beginning, God created the heavens and the earth,'"[9] for the word *beginning* (in Greek, the feminine *arche*) refers to the divine Mother, the source of the cosmic elements. When they describe God in this way, different gnostic writers have different interpretations. Some maintain that the divine is to be considered masculo–feminine—the "great male–female power." Others insist that the terms are meant only as metaphors—for, in reality, the divine is neither masculine nor feminine. A third group suggests that one can describe the Source of all things in either masculine or feminine terms, depending on which aspect one intends to stress.[10] Proponents of these diverse views agree, however, that the divine is to be understood as consisting of a harmonious, dynamic relationship of opposites—a concept that may be akin to the eastern view of *yin* and *yang* but remains antithetical to orthodox Judaism and Christianity.

A second characterization of the divine Mother describes her as Holy Spirit. One source, the *Secret Book of John*, for example, relates how John, the brother of James, went out after the crucifixion with "great grief," and had a mystical vision of the Trinity: "As I was grieving . . . the heavens were opened, and the whole creation shone with an unearthly light, and the universe was shaken. I was afraid . . . and behold . . . a unity in three forms appeared to me, and I marvelled: how can a unity have three forms?" To John's question, the vision answers: "It said to me, 'John, John, why do you doubt, or why do you fear? . . . I am the One who is with you always: I am the Father; I am the Mother; I am the Son.'"[11] John's interpretation of the Trinity—as Father, Mother, and Son—may not at first seem shocking but is perhaps the more natural and spontaneous interpretation. Where the Greek terminology for the Trinity, which includes the neuter term for the spirit (*pneuma*), virtually requires that the third "Person" of the Trinity be asexual, the author of the *Secret Book* looks to the Hebrew term for spirit, *ruah*—a feminine word. He thus concludes, logically enough, that the feminine "Person" conjoined with Father and Son must be the Mother! Indeed, the text goes on to describe the Spirit as Mother: "the image of the invisible virginal perfect spirit. . . . She became the mother of the all, for she existed before them all, the mother–father [matropater]."[12] This same author, therefore, alters Genesis 1:2 ("the Spirit of God moved upon the face of the deep") to say, "the Mother then was moved."[13] The secret *Gospel to the Hebrews* likewise has Jesus speak of "my Mother, the Spirit."[14] And in the *Gospel of Thomas*, Jesus contrasts his earthly parents, Mary and Joseph, with his divine Father—the Father of Truth—and his divine Mother, the Holy Spirit. The author interprets a puzzling saying of Jesus in the New Testament ("whoever does not hate his father and mother is not worthy of me") by adding: "Whoever does not love his father and his mother in my way cannot be my disciple; for my [earthly] mother gave me death but my true Mother gave me the Life."[15] Another secret gnostic gospel, the *Gospel of Phillip*, declares that whoever becomes a Christian "gains both a father and a mother."[16] The author refers explicitly to the feminine Hebrew term to describe the Spirit as "Mother of many."[17]

If these sources suggest that the Spirit constitutes the maternal element of the Trinity, the Gospel of Phillip makes an equally radical suggestion concerning the doctrine that later developed as the virgin birth. Here again the Spirit is praised as both Mother and Virgin, the counterpart—and consort—of the Heavenly Father: "If I may utter a mystery, the Father of the all united with the Virgin who came down"[18]—that is, with the Holy Spirit. Yet because this process is to be understood symbolically, and not literally, the Spirit remains a virgin! The author explains that "for this reason, Christ was 'born of a virgin'"—that is, of the Spirit, his divine Mother. But the author ridicules those "literal-minded" Christians who mistakenly refer the virgin birth to Mary, Jesus' earthly mother, as if she conceived apart from Joseph: "Such persons do not know what they are saying; for when did a female ever impregnate a female?"[19] Instead, he argues, virgin birth refers to the mysterious union of the two divine powers, the Father of the All with the Holy Spirit.

Besides the eternal, mystical Silence, and besides the Holy Spirit, certain gnostics suggest a third characterization of the divine Mother as Wisdom. Here again the Greek feminine term for wisdom, *sophia*, like the term for spirit, *ruah*, translates a Hebrew feminine term, *hokhmah*. Early interpreters had pondered the meaning of certain biblical passages, for example, Proverbs: "God made the world in Wisdom." And they wondered if Wisdom could be the feminine power in which God's creation is "conceived"? In such passages, at any rate, Wisdom bears two connotations: first, she bestows the Spirit that makes mankind wise; second, she is a creative power. One gnostic source calls her the "first universal creator";[20] another says that God the Father was speaking to her when he proposed to "make mankind in our image."[21] The *Great Announcement*, a mystical writing, explains the Genesis account in the following terms: "One Power that is above and below, self-generating, self-discovering, its own mother; its own father; its own sister; its own son: Father, Mother, unity, Root of all things."[22] The same author explains the mystical meaning of the Garden of Eden as a symbol of the womb: "Scripture teaches us that this is what is meant when Isaiah says, 'I am he that formed thee in thy mother's womb' [Isaiah 44:2]. The Garden of Eden, then, is Moses' symbolic term for the womb, and Eden the placenta, and the river which comes out of Eden the navel, which nourishes the fetus."[23] This teacher claims that the Exodus, consequently, symbolizes the exodus from the womb, "and the crossing of the Red Sea, they say, refers to the blood." Evidence for this view, he adds, comes directly from "the cry of the newborn," a spontaneous cry of praise for "the glory of the primal being, in which all the powers above are in harmonious embrace."[24]

The introduction of such symbolism in gnostic texts clearly bears implications for the understanding of human nature. The *Great Announcement*, for example, having described the Source as a masculo-feminine being, a "bisexual Power," goes on to say that "what came into being from that Power, that is, humanity, being one, is found to be two: a male-female being that bears the female within it."[25] This refers to the story of Eve's "birth" out of Adam's side (so that Adam, being one, is "discovered to be two," an androgyne who "bears the female within him"). Yet this reference to the creation story of Genesis 2—an account which inverts the biological birth process, and so effectively denies the creative function of the female—proves to be unusual in gnostic sources. More often, such sources refer instead to the first creation account in Genesis 1:26–27. ("And God said, let us make mankind in Our image, after Our image and likeness . . . in the image of God he created him: male and female he created them"). Rabbis in Talmudic times knew a Greek version of the passage, one that suggested to Rabbi Samuel bar Nahman that "when the Holy One . . . first created mankind, he created him with two faces, two sets of genitals, four arms, and legs, back to back: Then he split Adam in two, and made two backs, one on each side."[26] Some Jewish teachers (perhaps influenced by the story in Plato's *Symposium*) had suggested that Genesis 1:26–27 narrates an androgynous creation—an idea that gnostics adopted and developed. Marcus (whose prayer to the Mother is given above) not only concludes from this account that God is dyadic ("Let *us* make mankind") but also that "mankind, which was formed according to the image and likeness of God [Father and Mother] was masculo-feminine."[27] And his contemporary, Theodotus, explains: "the saying that Adam was created 'male and female' means that the male and female elements together constitute the finest production of the Mother, Wisdom."[28] We can see, then, that the gnostic sources which describe God in both masculine and feminine terms often give a similar description of human nature as a dyadic entity, consisting of two equal male and female components.

All the texts cited above—secret "gospels," revelations, mystical teachings—are among those rejected from the select list of twenty-six that comprise the "New Testament" collection. As these and other writings were sorted and judged by various Christian communities, every one of these texts which gnostic groups revered and shared was rejected from the canonical collection as "heterodox" by those who called themselves "orthodox" (literally straight–thinking) Christians. By the time this process was concluded, probably as late as the year A.D. 200, virtually all the feminine imagery for God (along with any suggestion of an androgynous human creation) had disappeared from "orthodox" Christian tradition.

What is the reason for this wholesale rejection? The gnostics themselves asked this question of their "orthodox" attackers and pondered it among themselves. Some concluded that the God of Israel himself initiated the polemics against gnostic teaching which his followers carried out in his name. They argued that he was a derivative, merely instrumental power, whom the divine Mother had created to administer the universe, but who remained ignorant of the power of Wisdom, his own Mother: "They say that the creator believed that he created everything by himself, but that, in reality, he had made them because his Mother, Wisdom, infused him with energy, and had given him her ideas. But he was even ignorant of his own Mother."[29] Followers of Valentinus suggested that the Mother herself encouraged the God of Israel to think that he was acting autonomously in creating the world; but, as one teacher adds, "It was because he was foolish and ignorant of his Mother that he said, 'I am God; there is none beside me.'"[30] Others attribute to him the more sinister motive of jealousy, among them the *Secret Book of John:* "He said, 'I am a jealous God, and you shall have no other God before me,' already indicating that another god does exist. For if there were no other god, of whom would he be jealous? Then the Mother began to be distressed."[31] A third gnostic teacher describes the Lord's shock, terror, and anxiety "when he discovered that he was not the God of the universe." Gradually his shock and fear gave way to wonder, and finally he came to welcome the teaching of Wisdom. The gnostic teacher concluded: "This is the meaning of the saying, 'The fear of the Lord is the beginning of wisdom.'"[32]

All of these are, of course, mythical explanations. To look for the actual, historical reasons why these gnostic writings were suppressed is an extremely difficult proposition, for it raises the much larger question of how (i.e., by what means and what criteria) certain ideas, including those expressed in the texts cited above, came to be classified as heretical and others as orthodox by the beginning of the third century. Although the research is still in its early stages, and this question is far from being solved, we may find one clue if we ask whether these secret groups derived any practical, social consequences from their conception of God—and of mankind—that included the feminine element? Here again the answer is yes and can be found in the orthodox texts themselves. Irenaeus, an orthodox bishop, for example, notes with dismay that women in particular are attracted to heretical groups—especially to Marcus's circle, in which prayers are offered to the Mother in her aspects as Silence, Grace, and Wisdom; women priests serve the eucharist together with men; and women also speak as prophets, uttering to the whole community what "the Spirit" reveals to them.[33] Professing himself to be at a loss to understand the attraction that Marcus's group holds, he offers only one explanation: that Marcus himself is a diabolically successful seducer, a magician who compounds special aphrodisiacs to "deceive, victimize, and defile" these "many foolish women!" Whether his accusation has any factual basis is difficult, probably impossible, to ascertain. Nevertheless, the historian notes that accusations of sexual license are a stock-in-trade of polemical arguments.[34] The bishop refuses to admit the possibility that the group might attract Christians—especially women—for sound and comprehensible reasons. While expressing his own moral outrage, Tertullian, another "father of the church," reveals his fundamental desire to keep women out of religion: "These heretical women—how audacious they are! They have no modesty: they are bold enough to teach, to engage in argument, to enact exorcisms, to undertake cures, and, it may be, even to baptize!"[35] Tertullian directs yet another attack against "that viper"—a woman teacher who led a congregation in North Africa.[36] Marcion had, in fact, scandalized his "orthodox" contemporaries by appointing women on an equal basis with men as priests and bishops among his congregations.[37] The teacher Marcillina also traveled to Rome to represent the Carpocratian group, an esoteric circle that claimed to have received secret teaching from Mary, Salome, and Martha.[38] And among the Montanists, a radical prophetic circle, the prophet Philumene was reputed to have hired a male secretary to transcribe her inspired oracles.[39]

Other secret texts, such as the *Gospel of Mary Magdalene* and the *Wisdom of Faith,* suggest that the activity of such women leaders challenged and therefore was challenged by the orthodox communities who regard Peter as their spokesman. The Gospel of Mary relates that Mary tried to encourage the disciples after the crucifixion and to tell them what the Lord had told her privately. Peter, furious at the suggestion, asks, "Did he then talk secretly with a woman, instead of to us? Are we to go and learn from *her* now? Did he love her more than us?" Distressed at his rage, Mary then asks Peter: "What do you think? Do you think I made this up in my heart? Do you think I am lying about the Lord?" Levi breaks in at this point to mediate the dispute: "Peter, you are always irascible. You object to the woman as our enemies do. Surely the Lord knew her very well, and indeed, he loved her more than us." Then he and the others invite Mary to teach them what she knows.[40] Another argument between Peter and Mary occurs in *Wisdom of Faith.* Peter complains that Mary is dominating the conversation, even to the point of displacing the rightful priority of Peter himself and his brethren; he urges Jesus to silence her—and is quickly rebuked. Later, however, Mary admits to Jesus that she hardly dares to speak freely with him, because "Peter makes me hesitate: I am afraid of him, because he hates the female race." Jesus replies that whoever receives inspiration from the Spirit is divinely ordained to speak, whether man or woman.[41]

As these texts suggest, then, women were considered equal to men, they were revered as prophets, and they acted as teachers, traveling evangelists, healers, priests, and even bishops. In some of these groups, they played leading roles and were *excluded* from them in the orthodox churches, at least by A.D. 150–200. Is it possible, then, that the recognition of the feminine element in God and the recognition of mankind as a male and female entity bore within it the explosive social possibility of women acting on an equal basis with men in positions of authority and leadership? If this were true, it might lead to the conclusion that these gnostic groups, together with their conception of God and human nature, were suppressed only because of their positive attitude toward women. But such a conclusion would be a mistake—a hasty and simplistic reading of the evidence. In the first place, orthodox Christian doctrine is far from wholly negative in its attitude toward women. Second, many other elements of the gnostic sources diverge in fundamental ways from what came to be accepted as orthodox Christian teaching. To examine this process in detail would require a much more extensive discussion than is possible here. Nevertheless, the evidence does indicate that two very different patterns of sexual attitudes emerged in orthodox and gnostic circles. In simplest form, gnostic theologians correlate their description of God in both masculine and feminine terms with a complementary description of human nature. Most often they refer to the creation account of Genesis 1, which suggests an equal (or even androgynous) creation of mankind. This conception carries the principle of equality between men and women into the practical social and political structures of gnostic communities. The orthodox pattern is strikingly different: it describes God in exclusively masculine terms and often uses Genesis 2 to describe how Eve was created from Adam for his fulfillment. Like the gnostic view, the orthodox also translates into sociological practice: by the late second century, orthodox Christians came to accept the domination of men over women as the proper, God-given order—not only for the human race, but also for the Christian churches. This correlation between theology, anthropology, and sociology is not lost on the apostle Paul. In his letter to the disorderly Corinthian community, he reminds them of a divinely ordained chain of authority: As God has authority over Christ, so the man has authority over the woman, urges Paul, citing Genesis 2: "The man is the image and glory of God, but the woman is the glory of man. For man is not from woman, but woman from man; and besides, the man was not created for the woman's sake, but the woman for the sake of the man."[42] Here the three elements of the orthodox pattern are welded into one simple argument: the description of God corresponds to a description of human nature which authorizes the social pattern of male domination.

A striking exception to this orthodox pattern occurs in the writings of one revered "father of the church," Clement of Alexandria. Clement identifies himself as orthodox, although he knows members of gnostic groups and their writings well; some scholars suggest that he was himself a gnostic initiate. Yet his own works demonstrate how all three elements of what we have called the "gnostic pattern" could be worked into fully "orthodox" teaching. First, Clement characterizes God not only in masculine but also in feminine terms: "The Word is everything to the child, both father and mother, teacher and nurse. . . . The nutriment is the milk of the father . . . and the Word alone supplies us children with the milk of love, and only those who suck at this breast are truly happy. . . . For this reason seeking is called sucking; to those infants who seek the Word, the Father's loving breasts supply milk."[43] Second, in describing human nature, he insists that "men and women share equally in perfection, and are to receive the same instruction and discipline. For the name 'humanity' is common to both men and women; and for us 'in Christ there is neither male nor female.'"[44] Even in considering the active participation of women with men in the Christian community Clement offers a list—unique in orthodox tradition—of women whose achievements he admires. They range from ancient examples, like Judith, the assassin who destroyed Israel's enemy, to Queen Esther, who rescued her people from genocide, as well as others who took radical political stands. He speaks of Arignole the historian, of Themisto the Epicurean philosopher, and of many other women philosophers, including two who studied with Plato and one trained by Socrates. Indeed, he cannot contain his praise: "What shall I say? Did not Theano the Pythagoran make such progress in philosophy that when a man, staring at her, said, 'Your arm is beautiful,' she replied, 'Yes, but it is not on public display.'"[45] Clement concludes his list with famous women poets and painters.

If the work of Clement, who taught in Egypt before the lines of orthodoxy and heresy were rigidly drawn (ca. A.D. 160–80) demonstrates how gnostic principles could be incorporated even into orthodox Christian teaching, the majority of communities in the western empire headed by Rome did not follow his example.

By the year A.D. 200, Roman Christians endorsed as "canonical" the pseudo–Pauline letter to Timothy, which interpreted Paul's views: "Let a woman learn in silence with full submissiveness. I do not allow any woman to teach or to exercise authority over a man; she is to remain silent, *for* [note Gen. 2!] Adam was formed first, then Eve and furthermore, Adam was not deceived, but the woman was utterly seduced and came into sin."[46] How are we to account for this irreversible development? The question deserves investigation which this discussion can only initiate. For example, one would need to examine how (and for what reasons) the zealously patriarchal traditions of Israel were adopted by the Roman (and other) Christian communities. Further research might disclose how social and cultural forces converged to suppress feminine symbolism—and women's participation—from western Christian tradition. Given such research, the history of Christianity never could be told in the same way again.

ENDNOTES

1. Where the God of Israel is characterized as husband and lover in the Old Testament (OT), his spouse is described as the community of Israel (i.e., Isa. 50:1, 54:1–8; Jer. 2:2–3, 20–25, 3:1–20; Hos. 1–4, 14) or as the land of Israel (cf. Isa. 62:1–5).
2. One may note several exceptions to this rule: Deut. 32:11; Hos. 11:1, Isa. 66:12 ff; Num. 11:12.
3. *The Gospel according to Thomas* (hereafter cited as *ET*), ed. A. Guillaumount, H. Ch. Puech, G. Quispel, W. Till, Yassah 'Abd–al–Masih (London: Collins, 1959), logion 113–114.
4. Hippolytus, *Refutationis Omnium Haeresium* (hereafter cited as *Ref*), ed. L. Dunker, F. Schneidewin (Göttingen, 1859), 5.7.
5. *Ref*, 5.6
6. Irenaeus, *Adversus Haereses* (hereafter cited as *AH*), ed. W. W. Harvey (Cambridge, 1857), 1.11.1.
7. Ibid., 1.13.2.
8. Ibid., 1.13.6.
9. Ibid., 1.18.2.
10. Ibid., 1.11.5–21.1, 3; *Ref*, 6.29.

11. *Apocryphon Johannis* (hereafter cited as *AJ*), ed. S. Giversen (Copenhagen: Prostant Apud Munksgaard, 1963), 47.20–48.14.
12. *AJ*, 52.34–53.6.
13. Ibid., 61.13–14.
14. Origen, *Commentary on John*, 2.12; *Hom. On Jeremiah*, 15.4.
15. *ET, 101*. The text of this passage is badly damaged; I follow here the reconstruction of G. MacRae of the Harvard Divinity School.
16. *L'Evangile selon Phillipe* (hereafter cited as *EP*), ed. J. E. Ménard (Leiden: Brill, 1967), logion 6.
17. *EP*, logion 36.
18. Ibid., logion 82.
19. Ibid., logion 17.
20. *Extraits de Théodote* (hereafter cited as *Exc*), ed. F. Sagnard, Sources chrétiennes 23 (Paris: Sources chrétiennes, 1948).
21. *AH*, 1.30.6.
22. *Ref*, 6.17.
23. Ibid., 6.14.
24. *AH*, 1.14.7–8.
25. *Ref*, 6.18.
26. Genesis Rabba 8.1, also 17.6; cf. Levitius Rabba 14. For an excellent discussion of androgyny, see W. Meeks, "The Image of the Androgyne: Some Uses of a Symbol in Earliest Christianity," *History of Religions* 13 (1974): 165–208.
27. *AH*, 1.18.2.
28. *Exc*, 21.1.
29. *Ref*, 6.33.
30. *AH*, 1.5.4; *Ref*, 6.33.
31. *AJ*, 61.8–14.
32. *Ref*, 7.26.
33. *AH*, 1.13.7.
34. Ibid., 1.13.2–5.
35. Tertullian, *De Praescriptione Haereticorum* (hereafter cited as *DP*), ed. E. Oethler (Lipsius, 1853–54), p. 41.
36. *De Baptismo* 1. I am grateful to Cyril Richardson for calling my attention to this passage and to the three subsequent ones.
37. Epiphanes, *De Baptismo*, 42.5.

38. *AH*, 1.25.6.

39. *DP*, 6.30.

40. *The Gospel according to Mary*, Codex Berolinensis, BG, 8502, 1.7.1–1.19.5, ed., intro., and trans. G. MacRae, unpublished manuscript.

41. *Pistis Sophia*, ed. Carl Schmidt (Berlin: Academie–Verlag, 1925), 36 (57), 71 (161).

42. 1 Cor. 11:7–9. For discussion, see R. Scroggs, "Paul and the Eschatological Woman," *Journal of the American Academy of Religion* 40 (1972): 283–303; R. Scroggs, "Paul and the Eschatological Woman: Revisited," *Journal of the American Academy of Religion* 42 (1974): 532–37; and E. Pagels, "Paul and Women: A Response to Recent Discussion," *Journal of the American Academy of Religion* 42 (1972): 538–49.

43. Clement Alexandrinus, *Paidegogos*, ed. O. Stählin (Leipzig, 1905), 1.6.

44. Ibid., 1.4.

45. Ibid., 1.19.

46. 2 Tim. 2:11–14.

QUESTIONS

1. Explain why Pagels asks the question she does in the title of her article. What does Pagels identify as the central assumption of religious rhetoric?

2. What distinguishes "orthodox" religious rhetoric from "heterodox" religious rhetoric? Why is heterodox rejected by the mainstream Christian tradition?

3. Identify and describe the three characterizations of the divine Mother. What symbolism does Pagels suggest accompanies these characterizations?

4. Explain the relationship Pagels argues exists between social and cultural forces and whether religious principles are defined as "orthodox" or "heterodox."

heterodox - Egalitarian
orthodox - man / woman

Toward an Ecofeminist Ethic of Shamanism and the Sacred (1993)

Gloria Feman Orenstein

Both the feminist spirituality and the new age movements have received inspiration and guidance from Shamanism. In this essay, Gloria Feman Orenstein suggests we ought to take Shamanism seriously in our culture as a way to re-value women and nature. Additionally, Orenstein looks critically at how Shamanism is currently understood within Western feminist spirituality and new age movements. Orenstein is Professor in Comparative Literature and the Program for the Study of Women and Men in Society at the University of Southern California. She is author of The Theater of the Marvelous: Surrealism and the Contemporary Stage *and* The Reflowering of the Goddess, *and co-editor of* Reweaving the World: the Emergence of Ecofeminsm.

We have recently witnessed a growing interest in Shamanism and sacred ceremonies within the ecofeminist movement. As an ecofeminist who was the student of a woman Shaman[1] from Samiland (Lapland, northern Norway) for four and one-half years, I would like to make a number of observations based upon my experience in the field that will, hopefully, lead to some ethical considerations regarding the reclamation of Shamanism that is taking place today, both within the feminist spirituality and the new age movements.

The Place of Shamanism in Ecofeminism

The reason that ecofeminists have such a deep interest in Shamanism is that Shamanism is practiced in a wide variety of indigenous cultures that have an earth-based spirituality. Shamans from Native American and other tribal cultures have kept alive the knowledge that the earth is sacred and that not only are humans and nonhuman nature part of the interconnected web of life, but also that spirit resides in matter, as well as in other dimensions. Shamanism teaches us that everything has spirit and that via a variety of shamanic practices, humans can make contact with the spirits of the living, of the dead, of humans, plants, and animals, as well as with the deities, and can obtain knowledge from them about how to heal life on earth.

Shamanism seems to provide answers for ecofeminists about how we can live in balance on the earth and, at the same time, develop a means of communication among the many varied species inhabiting the many different realms and dimensions of the universe, both via physical and spiritual methods. Shamanism, because it functions upon the acknowledgment that spirit resides in matter, shatters the patriarchal dualism pervading the Western religions—a dualism that insists upon spirit being separate from matter. Shamanism is neither androcentric nor anthropocentric. In this sense it is ecofeminist, for it neither recognizes one gender to be superior to the other nor places humans outside of or above the cosmic cycles or the natural ecosystems. Because Shamanism was practiced since the dawn of human history and figures of Shamans are found in Paleolithic cave paintings, Shamanism also takes us outside the historical frame of reference of patriarchal history—back to prehistory and even to the civilization of the Goddess, a civilization which, at least in old Europe, according to archeologist Marija Gimbutas (1974, 1989, 1991), accorded women more prestige and equality in society than we do, was earth revering, and did not engage in war.

Many native medicine people also consider the earth to be our mother. Some indigenous religions refer to an earth mother or to a mother goddess. Thus, women involved in the feminist spirituality movement may also turn to shamanic practices in order to get in contact with the spirit of the earth mother, both for personal and communal spiritual empowerment.

Starhawk, an ecofeminist and wiccan priestess, has, through her rituals and political activism, proved once and for all that in an ecofeminist vision, there is no contradiction between spiritual and political practice. Starhawk also refers to herself as a Shaman, for she uses shamanic techniques in her spiritual work. Indeed, she has also visited the Shamans of Samiland, and was recognized by them to have shamanic powers. The Goddess rituals that Starhawk performs have a strong shamanic element. She uses her rituals to empower her activist community before undertaking protest and civil disobedience activities in order to save the earth from the many threats to our planet's survival, ranging from pollution to nuclear disaster.

Since ecofeminists are becoming more and more interested in Shamanism, it is important that we begin to examine it seriously from precisely this perspective. My comments will identify the following problems that I see surrounding Shamanism as it is practiced today by growing numbers of vision-questers.

Essentialism: Reductive, Core, and Archetypal Concepts

To speak about Shamanism as if it were a universal or generic category is to run the risk of constructing an archetype, a stereotype, or an abstraction of a Shaman, and thereby to ignore the specificity of the wide diversity of shamanic practices in a variety of indigenous cultures. It is reductive to speak of Shamanism as if it were the same all over the world. Anthropology teaches us that Shamanism differs from culture to culture. Each culture's cosmogony, cosmology, and mythology are unique, and since shamanic practices involve symbol systems, deities, and a knowledge of how the many worlds, both visible and invisible, are organized, it is an error to assume that Shamans all over the world do the same things, or that when they do so, they do them in the same way.

Reductive Views of Shamanism

In his foreword to anthropologist Ruth-Inge Heinze's recent book *Shamans of the 20th Century*, Stanley Krippner (1991) comments that "Dr. Heinze's research demonstrates that it would be erroneous to claim that shamans represent a single constellation of traits or that there is a typical shamanic personality." Further on, Ruth-Inge Heinze warns us:

> Most of all, we should apply caution when individuals claim to be shamans. "Professional" shamans never make such claims. They need not advertise, because they become known through their work. Their "miraculous" healing of sick minds and bodies, their retrieval of otherwise not accessible information, their beneficial effects on their community become known fast through word of mouth. (Heinze 1991, 6)

The rules of shamanic ethics are the same as for any other professionals, especially in the religious realm. It would be unethical for "enlightened" individuals, for example, to publicly announce their enlightenment. The degree of spiritual development is reflected in an individual's demeanor, actions, and success. The most successful shamans I met were also the most humble. They would stress that they are only the servants of the sacred and the mediators who continue to learn throughout their life (Heinze 1991, 7).

Since the word for Shaman is usually a translation from a foreign language (such as the Sami word *noidi*, which also means sorcerer), we must be conscious of whether the person in question is a Shaman, a sorcerer, a trance medium, a psychic, a channeler, or a magician. If we begin by situating the particular Shaman or Shamanism that one reclaims within its own cultural tradition, we can understand why Ruth-Inge Heinze cautions us about people who call themselves Shamans.

In the case of the Sami, my Shaman teacher was trained in her culture for thirty-five years before she could practice hearings on people outside of her extended family. When I pondered this, given the fact that she was born into a prestigious lineage of Shamans (she was the daughter of the Great Shaman of Samiland, whose father was also a Shaman), and that her talents were obvious when she was a child, I wondered *why* she had to study for so long before treating those outside of her kin group. Of course, this baffled me, since in the West we believe we can become professional at anything within four to eight years of training.

My Shaman teacher was not only a healer, but she was also a student of folklore. This is important, because she always insisted that the three principal sources of her shamanic knowledge were Sami folklore (tales, legends, and so forth); teachings from the ancestral lineage—from her father, who was her mentor, and from other ancestral spirits, who spoke to her from the spirit world; and teachings from spirit entities (what we might call "spirit guides" or "power animals"). In this category her main guide was an owl that appeared to her in her childhood.

A culture's tales and legends are of extreme importance, for through them one can learn how spirits behave. For example, if a tale speaks about what happens to someone who steals money from a sacred site, the Shaman in training learns that the karmic price of such an act might come ten years later, when that person's reindeer flock is wiped out.

A culture's tales are often cautionary. They teach strategies for dealing with all kinds of spirits, both good and evil, according to the culture's beliefs. A Westerner who goes to an indigenous culture in search of shamanic knowledge should read extensively about the culture's folklore. The serious mistake that we make is to think that folk tales and legends are not true. We have been taught not to believe in the supernatural, but one aspect of an ethical approach to forming a relationship with a shamanic culture would be understanding that the folklore of the culture is not necessarily just "lore," but that its stories are often based upon real events, and that if you visit that particular area, they might happen to you, even if you don't believe in such things.

Folk tales also show ways in which dreams are interpreted in the culture. My experience in this area was always startling. I would begin to describe a dream I had, and I would give it a sophisticated symbolic explanation. The next thing I knew, I was taken to the house of the Great Shaman and shown a photo of the very person who had appeared in my dream as my spirit guide. I had interpreted this gigantic figure, clad in a reindeer-skin tunic and large boots, to be the symbol of my Amazon self, who had just climbed a high mountain. Instead, I learned that it was not a symbol. It was the exact image of my Shaman's grandfather—

who had been given to me as a spirit guide to help me on my journey. Thus, what I had called a dream was actually a visit from a spirit in the spirit world. To have interpreted that person as a symbol of a giant or any other such figure would have missed the *very important and startling point* that this person was the spirit of the real grandfather of my Shaman.

Because these stories take place in a given geography, they also teach about the natural environment of the particular bioregion. Thus, Sami tales, which deal with winter at the North Pole, are not at all similar to tales told in the Amazon jungle. It is a mistake to assume that similar figures have similar meanings in different cultures—whether they be mothers, fathers, gods, or tricksters. To assume that there is just one universal meaning to a figure in a folktale is to negate the historic, geographic, and cultural specificity of that culture. To do this is also to deny the variability and diversity of species, both on earth and in other dimensions—be they cultures, humans, animals, plants, or spirits. Things simply are *not* the same all over the world, even though certain aspects of them may make us think they are similar.

Folk tales illustrate the workings of the laws of karma, and they are handed down over generations, because—contrary to white Western culture, which believes that all stories should end after three hundred pages or two hours in the cinema—indigenous people have not forgotten that stories continue from generation to generation. Over time, one can begin to see the shape of the agency of otherworldly spirits upon events in this world. One begins to have a feel for the agency of the spirit of a deceased ancestor or community member. This is important information for the Shaman to have in order to assess the nature of the vision she or he might have when treating a particular individual in a certain family. The Shaman must contextualize the origin of the patient's dis-ease within his or her own family and cultural history, as well as within the context of the patient's past lives. This is necessary in order to understand the kind of negativity that has taken over the patient's life (a curse, an invasion, an attack, and so forth), its origin, and its historicity.

The Concept of Core Shamanism

The concept of "core shamanism" has been the focus of Michael Hamer's shamanic workshops. His work in this field is of immeasurable value, and I fully agree with the importance of familiarizing contemporary Westerners with the possibilities provided by experiences of the "shamanic journey" or the spirit flight. However, "core shamanism" stresses the "shamanic journey" induced by drumming as the central feature of all Shamanism, and it teaches students to travel out of the body to the lower, middle, and upper spirit worlds, to meet with their power animals, their spirit guides, to learn how to perform soul retrieval, and to do shamanic hearings and counseling. One of the dangers that I see, from the ecofeminist perspective, in focusing on the spirit journey as the "core" concept of shamanism is that it both reproduces the patriarchal dualism that separates spirit from matter and prioritizes spirit over matter (that is, heaven over earth or the other world over this world).

While spirit journeys do characterize Shamanism all over the world, and while information from other realms is essential to shamanic work, to prioritize journeys to otherworldly dimensions over the social and political dimensions of the journeys made by Shamans when they are awake and conscious in this world (as opposed to being in an altered state) is to subordinate the ordinary conscious experience to the nonordinary one. Yet Shamans themselves do not necessarily prioritize experience in that way. During my training, I was always looking for these "core experiences," and instead I found that the "core" experiences of Sami Shamanism often came when spirits visited this realm, or when real animals became spirit messengers. I was "shamanized" by mosquitoes that died in my California apartment for what seemed to be no apparent reason, until I received a call from Samiland informing me of the death of my Shaman teacher's son. The mosquitoes I had encountered in the swamps during the summer had picked up the vibrations of my blood and found me via their spiritual attunement to me. This kind of event, one that illustrates the spiritual interconnectedness of all living things in the web of life, is as much a "core" concept of Shamanism as is the out-of-the-body ecstatic journey.

To prioritize information from the spirit world over information from the spirits of animals, plants, and persons in this world is to perpetuate patriarchal Christianity's privileging of spiritual beings over human beings. It is as if we believed that an out-of-body journey were more important than those journeys we make daily—and especially those pilgrimages that indigenous and tribal people often make to sacred sites in nature. By stressing the visionary journey out of the body and by omitting the sacred pilgrimage to a real site in nature from our description of so-called core Shamanism, we are deleting the crucial political dimension of the struggles of Shamans in the here and now. The land rights issues of indigenous people always remind Westerners that their land is sacred. They do not consider the earth to be less sacred than other realms.

In Samiland the Great Shaman is also the chief political leader of his people. Thus, he had to use his psychic abilities to strategize protest actions against those who wanted to take over the Sami land and rivers. Often shamanic techniques are involved in fighting these battles (returning negative energy and so forth).

Shamans that I have met use their powers in the here and now much of the time, and they do not seem to privilege the spirit-journey to other dimensions over the many other ways in which their services are performed in the body and on the earth. The shamanic worldview considers all of creation to be both spiritual and sacred. This dimension is as sacred as the spirit world. Thus, what happens to us while alive and awake, although interconnected with what is taking place in the spirit world, is also of great importance shamanically, and, of course, is also sacred. Through the spiritual journey Shamans pick up vital information from other realms, in much the same way that we get our news from abroad via satellite and TV. By the same token, one could not characterize the human experience by the "core" activity of tuning into the news from abroad, even though this is a necessary part of our daily lives. Naturally, when Shamans work in the here and now, they are calling upon forces that reconfigure our ordinary concepts of space and time. When they use their psychic powers for certain kinds of work, they are not necessarily journeying out of the body, but they are expanding our concept of what a body is and relating to the body as an energy field composed both of spirit and matter.

Naive Ecofeminism

Ruth-Inge Heinze writes:

> In the United States, we find a great number of weekend workshops announcing training in shamanism. The quality of such training is seldom put to test. It does not seem to be appropriate to attempt a revival of shamanism by combining "core elements" from different cultures. Such attempts start on the wrong foot,

> because core elements may be part of shamanic rituals, but do not constitute the essence of the ritual. They are vehicles of expression but not the message itself. . . . Shamanic techniques may be effective means for self-exploration, however, experimenters should be taught the pitfalls of psychic openings which require closing. They have to be convinced of the necessity of properly sending away the energies which they evoke during the process. (Heinze 1991, 155)

At this point I think that a personal story will provide an anecdote that illustrates her point very clearly. I was attending an ecofeminist party, and one of the women wanted to start a spirituality group. I had brought a clairvoyant with me to the party. We talked about doing Goddess rituals, and the clairvoyant asked whether any of us knew how to handle any bad effects that might occur because of what we had called up. One of the women said: "We are all coming from a pure place. We will only call upon the good. I'm sure that nothing harmful can happen."

My friend, the clairvoyant, then explained. "Look, you can be a very good person with very good intentions in ordinary life. But if, when you go to sleep, you leave the door of your house open, anyone can come in. And that has nothing to do with how good your intentions are, or how pure you are. The door happens to be open, and anyone can come in. It is the same thing when you do a ritual. You open the door to other dimensions, and other things can enter along with those that you have invited. You have to learn how to 'see' what is happening and to work with the energies, otherwise you should be very careful about getting involved in this work, and make sure to seek protection before you begin."

We have, as I have tried to show, been naive in oversimplifying Shamanism by trying to construct a "core" essence of a Shaman. By being so reductive we actually miss out on some of the important features of Shamanism, particularly ones that involve real animals and life on this planet.

There has also been a stress placed on finding one's "power animal" in neo-Shamanism. It seems to me that this emphasis also privileges spirit animals over real animals. Once again, from my own experience in Samiland, I know that I was always waiting to meet my "power animal," and my Shaman teacher was always taking me to the real reindeer, the real birds, the real mosquitoes. It wasn't until she communicated with birds, brought them to us, talked with them, and sent them away, or until she "psyched out" the problem of a lost reindeer, that I began to understand how the neoshamanic narrative from contemporary workshops had actually blinded me to the fact that real animals are also spirit and power, and, at least to my Shaman teacher, they were every bit as important, or even more so, than her owl spirit guide who had appeared to her in childhood. Sometimes I used to feel that I had a more "shamanic" perspective than she did, because I was always coming up with sophisticated symbolic interpretations of dreams and I was always looking for "power animals," while she seemed to be more interested in the real animals and she understood the figures in dreams to represent the spirits of real people. The truth is that she made less of a distinction than we do between real and spirit people or animals. To her, all was real, all was spirit and all was sacred, simultaneously. There was no contradiction in that.

Problems with the Concept of the Archetype

The concept of the archetype, which comes from Jungian psychology, although it has validity in many cases, should not be applied to Shamanism, because it renders real cultures and their histories and living inhabitants, whether human or animal, invisible, and because it prevents us from identifying the actual social and political problems of people, especially of women in indigenous cultures. Here I am referring to the glamorizing and stereotyping (that sometimes blurs into archetyping) of the images of women from "exotic" foreign cultures.

Recently I came upon a workshop to be given by Jungian psychologist Linda Leonard, entitled "The Lapp Reindeer Woman Archetype." I did not attend this workshop, so I am only referring to its title. The use of the word *Lapp* is incorrect. The Sami people were called Lapp by colonizing Westerners. In their struggle for their rights, they insist on the use of the name Sami, and they want Westerners to know that their language is the Sami language (a Finno-Ugritic language), and that their land is called Samiland, not Lapland.

When I came across the title of this workshop, I called my Shaman teacher in Norway, and I asked her if there is any reference to a reindeer woman (motif or archetype) in their folklore. She said she had never heard of it. Then I concluded that the reindeer woman image, as I have seen it depicted on Christmas and other greeting cards, is a stereotype similar to the ones we have of the Indian princess (from Native-American tribes). It is an image that glamorizes the exotic but also prevents us from seeing the real suffering in the lives of Sami women who are reindeer herders, who are losing their land, and who are losing their role in reindeer herding, as the role of reindeer herder is becoming more and more the occupation of men alone. Those who follow the archetypal approach to Shamanism also project their own personal fantasies onto a living culture, and in so doing they deauthenticate the actual lives and lore of a living people. They make it into a Disneyworld and perpetuate stereotypes that are pernicious to the culture's survival. Had I taken a workshop on the "Lapp Reindeer Woman Archetype," chances are I might have been blinded to some of the brutal realities in the lives of contemporary Sami women who herd reindeer, or who no longer do so, because they have lost this role. Sami women recently held a women's conference (Summer 1990) precisely in order to speak out about their double oppression as women in Norwegian society and as Sami, who are socialized according to the gender roles defined by Sami culture, where women now occupy the domestic role and have lost their role as reindeer herders to the men.

Trivalizing the Spirit World

When Westerners gather in a circle to perform a ceremony that they have learned either from native people or from reading about their ceremonies, do they actually believe that they are performing something as *real* as a surgical operation? Do we ever see surgeons gathering in a circle, passing out knives and scalpels to strangers, and asking those gathered with them to explore each others brains with these implements and then return to "share the experience"? Shamanism is just as *real* and as dangerous as surgery. It operates on our psyches. We may not see this operation in a literal, material way, but the results of the operation are evident in the way our vision of "reality" has been altered.

Indeed, I would question whether all people who want to study Shamanism should be permitted to do so, given the fact that Shamans learn how to enter other people's energy fields and bodies. This may explain why in traditional societies not everyone is called to this role. I have also asked myself whether a Nazi should be given shamanic training. Would such a person (or any other, for that matter) not be tempted to abuse the power contacted? Should such a person be able to sign up for a weekend shamanic workshop? Who screens the applicants, and what are the criteria for admission?

When I went to the sacred Sami site with my Shaman and her father, they both asked the spirits *if* I would be granted permission to enter their space. When I was told this, it had never occurred to me that spirits were actually present who might, indeed, have denied me entry. At the time I thought the two Shamans were describing their form of prayer. But they were not praying in the sense we conceive of prayer. They were actually speaking to *real* (but invisible to me) ancestors. These were experienced Shamans, not commercial entrepreneurs or dabblers. Now that I know about these things, I grow concerned. How do the travelers who sign up for Shaman tours know about the karma of their tour leaders or, for that matter, of the native teachers? In the West we have trivialized the reality and the power of the spirit world. In fact, we have negated it. This is the same as if we were to negate the existence of germs, just because we can't see them with the naked eye. Although we do not have instruments with which to see the spirit world, just as light waves and gravity are real, just as gamma rays and black holes are real, we should understand that things exist that we cannot necessarily see. Modern physics teaches us that when we study elementary particles, we interact with them. We also know that the stars we see might have died many years ago, but since light takes time to travel through space, we are seeing stars that no longer exist.

These lessons from modern physics should alert us to the fact that what we observe may no longer exist, that not everything that exists can be observed, and that what we study might be altered by the fact that we are interacting with it (such as elementary particles). It is arrogant of Westerners to think that if we have not identified something with our modern instruments, it does not exist. This also negates the powers and intelligence of native people. By our arrogance, by our insistence on labeling those whose wisdom was acquired without Western technology as "primitive," we open ourselves to great dangers from elements and entities of other dimensions that we have chosen to ignore. In this way we have trivialized the spirit world and attributed all agency in human affairs to humans alone.

Just as people in power in government may abuse that power, Shamans, too, may abuse their power and use it to do harm. Romanticizing and glamorizing Shamanism may, in fact, blind us to the tyranny that some Shamans may exert because of their power. This is because we continue to believe that only the visible is real. In fact, we may be under spiritual attack and not be aware of it because we choose to deny the reality and the power of the spiritual realm.

When Westerners travel to an "exotic" foreign country to visit with a local Shaman, do they know anything about the person in whose power they will place themselves, and do they have any means of protection in the event of an abuse of power? I pose these questions in the spirit of raising our consciousness about the complexity of Shamanism and how it works with energies that are invisible to us. I also bring this up in the hopes that the current commodification of packaged Shaman tours will be placed within a perspective that embraces ethics and responsibility, both toward those embarking on the journeys as well as toward the Shamans and the cultures they live in, who must be protected from being ripped off by tourists, just as the tourists must be protected from the abuses of power on the part of native Shamans, who often have political and historical reasons to view rich, white Westerners as their enemies.

I have participated in many ceremonies and rituals performed in the feminist spirituality and new age communities, and am now even more aware of the complexity of the invisible dimensions surrounding us. Most people participating in these ceremonies do not see auras, nor do they see into other dimensions. When they conjure up spirits in a ritual, how do they know what kind of energies they are bringing into the circle? It is very important to perform such rituals under the guidance of a trained spiritual leader, one who is able to witness the nature of the energy exchanges that are taking place, and one whom we have substantial reason to believe does not misuse power. For this reason alone we need to apply a code of ethics to the practice of neo-Shamanism.

Until I had first-hand experience of the *reality* of the spirit world—until I had traveled to the sacred site, heard the voices of the ancestral spirits (the dead, who called me by name); until I had seen for myself that the spirit guide who appeared to me in my dream was not a symbol but was a real spirit; until I had witnessed the spirit of the Great Shaman—as it traveled out of his body; until I had been convinced that the spirit world does exist—I had conceived of all discussions about spirituality in terms of poetry and prayer. Shamanism had been a powerful metaphor to me, connoting visionary and poetic creations. The spirit world was, before my own experience with it, something akin to the dream world. The reason I stress this is that I, too, had trivialized the spirit world. As a modern (or even postmodern) educated Westerner, I did not believe in the existence of spirits or of the spirit world.

Moreover, the Carlos Castaneda and Lynn Andrews books all have a narrative line to them, which led me to conceive of shamanic experience in terms of a kind of novel that either developed to a climax or partook of the literary genre of the "picaresque." There was a literary form to Shamanism that also did not tally with what I actually lived and led me to discredit my experience. I expected spirit guides to resemble Jimminy Cricket rather than a real cricket. I expected everything to be larger than life, something like a Disneyworld rendition of nature. Instead, what I learned was that real mosquitoes are actual spirit guides.

Our Western accounts of "reality" and our literary narratives fail to encompass a diversity of other narrative modes whose features capture the realities of shamanic experience. One example of a figure from a nonwhite Western tradition is that of the trickster. We look upon the trickster as a literary or folk figure.

However, once you become involved in shamanic practice, you begin to observe how the spirits play tricks upon you. These tricks may be humorous, or they may be dangerous. Shamans do not often tell about their experiences in the spirit world. Have we ever wondered why? The answers are sobering, to say the least! Spirits, in fact, do observe us and listen to us. If we are planning to protect ourselves, they will take note of this and plan their strategy accordingly. One must remain silent about one's interaction with the spirit world, not only because conventional Westerners will dismiss these discussions as absurd, but also because one may run risks and court dangers with the spirits if one speaks of these things. The spirit world is no more benign than the material world, and we would do well to consider this when embarking on vision quests. Moreover, it is to trivialize the spirit world, to demean and negate its authenticity, to think that if you concentrate on white light, what you get will be beneficent. This is so naive as to be sheer folly! You must have enough power to call upon enough white light to protect you. Whenever I discuss these ideas with new agers, I try to explain myself in the following way. I do not deny that white light is protective. I simply maintain that Shamans channel what I call "heavy voltage." Ordinary people may not have the power to draw upon sufficient voltage to produce the desired effect.

From an ecofeminist perspective, trivializing the spirit world also renders invalid the wisdom of women, for we can see how my communication with this powerful woman Shaman was blocked by the fact that I did not, at first, grant legitimacy to her description of reality. And *I* had been called by, as she put it, "The Great Spirit"! In my culture I was always considered to be one of the people most open to spirituality. Yet, because of my Western scientific education, I could not actually believe in the existence of the spirit world. I don't think that we in the West can ever truly communicate with people of indigenous and tribal cultures until we open ourselves up to bestowing legitimacy on their descriptions of reality. Thus, not only do national, linguistic, and cultural barriers interfere with the communication among women around the world, but beyond all this, the parameters of what we consider to be "real" separate us still further from one another.

Gender Neutralization

When we speak of Shamanism in the abstract, we also speak of it as gender neutral. However, male and female Shamans in different cultures also embody different gender roles. These roles, as they are defined in each culture, also affect the perception we may form of Shamanism. As a feminist, I have reacted to various examples of Shamanism that I have both witnessed and read about as "macho Shamanism." Indeed, it does take a lot of physical and mental (psychic/spiritual) effort to make contact with the spirit world. When I was in Samiland, I had to walk some ten or more miles to the sacred site, and I had to climb a ten-kilometer mountain in order to be able to dream of my spirit guide. In other traditions one's consciousness is altered by hallucinogens, by sensory deprivation, by drumming (the Sami's shaman drums were seized by the Christians when they were colonized, and so they no longer use them), and by other means.

When considering the strenuous physical tests from the perspective of Western gender roles, the shamanic training and tests seem to be macho. In Western cultures, most women do not trek many miles into nature to erect shelters by themselves in a "survival wilderness" mode. This is culturally constructed to be "masculine" as a gender role. However, as we know, gender roles vary from culture to culture.

In Sami culture, women are very strong. They are said to dominate. Some think the Sami may have once been a matriarchy, for in the past when a man wanted to marry a woman, he had to serve her mother for an entire year. Then the girl's mother would determine whether he was a good enough worker and whether he would serve her daughter well enough—whether he could take orders from his wife in a submissive way. The Sami are also matrilineal and matrilocal, but that doesn't preclude the existence of sexism in their culture. Whether their sexism came with the "white man," who brought liquor and colonization, or not, it currently exists, and women suffer from rape, battery, and violent crime in Samiland. Also, the gender roles are distributed so as to keep women at home. When the Great Shaman went out to do hearings, he came home to a meal cooked by his wife or his daughters. When his daughter, my Shaman, came home from her work, she had to cook and clean for the others. She developed incredible physical strength from doing the work of men plus the work of women. Yet, on some level, it was the pressure to live up to and surpass the extremes of "macho" shamanic prowess that competed with her need to rest when she was ill, in order to heal. When she went home from the hospital after her mastectomy, the first thing she did was climb a mountain. She did this in order to test the strength of her constitution and to see if she was still as capable of difficult feats of physical endurance as she had been before the operation.

Because a female Shaman may have to live up to the standards of "macho" Shamanism and learn to handle anything that crosses her path, she may choose to handle sexual assaults such as rape and battery through physical prowess or psychic means, but she may then fail to name and identify the oppression of women in her culture. She may, indeed, consider her own encounters with male violence to be part of the repertoire of shamanic tests that she has to pass. Thus her physical prowess and her spiritual powers may blind her to feminist issues that may need to be addressed on a larger scale by women who are not Shamans.

In Native-American cultures, the Berdache is a male person who assumes a feminine gender role, dresses as a female, marries a male, and is often also a highly respected Shaman. To speak of Shamanism in the abstract renders the richness of the Berdache role invisible, for it ignores the sex and gender role complexity of the Shaman, and thereby returns us to archetypal and core concepts, which have stereotypically gendered images embedded in them. In referring to such a Shaman in the abstract, we tend to overlook, and therefore to erase, the importance of the shape-shifting that the Berdache role, in fact, embodies.

Gender crossings and blendings seem to be common among Shamans cross culturally. As we previously mentioned, most Shamanism today is practiced in indigenous, nonwestern, not necessarily patriarchal cultures. When we, as Westerners from a patriarchal culture, encounter a woman Shaman, we should not expect her to behave in ways that have anything to do with the white Western cultural construction of "the feminine." Yet, if this woman has participated in Western culture, as had my Shaman teacher, she has also adopted some of the ways of the West. In relating to such women of power, we may become confused by the gender-role transitions and the shape-shiftings these women undergo in order to pass from one culture to the other. However, I would like to suggest that we not abdicate our Western feminist perspective when we observe their lives, for they themselves are often treated in ways that are extremely sexist (partially because their cultures have been colonized by Westerners), and since they are trained to handle everything and be stronger than most males and females, they may not identify with the other women of their culture or participate in feminist activities. Ellen Maret often told me that the Sami do not need feminism, because Sami women are so strong. Ultimately, Sami women held a conference to discuss their problems from the perspective of indigenous women within the framework of the issues identified by the United Nations' International Decade on Women.

Racism

The obvious points about Westerners appropriating and commodifying native practices or commercializing sacred objects do not need to be restated. Not only do we exploit indigenous people when we appropriate their shamanic knowledge, but we also tend to lump them all into one single entity, when they are, in fact, plural and diverse. Each Native American tribe or nation is an individual entity with a specific history and specific practices and languages that differ from one group to another.

When I was in Samiland, if men would harass me sexually, I would not retaliate physically, even if it were warranted in order to save myself from injury. Why? Because I reasoned that "the white man" had done enough damage to indigenous people, and I did not want to perpetuate that pattern. I did not want to bring physical harm to male members of the Sami community or family, even if, on the occasion that they were drunk and I was sober, I might have been able to. I did not defend myself, but I was fortunate in that I escaped every encounter unscathed. (Perhaps the Great Spirit was looking out for me?) When I would speak about this with my Shaman teacher, she would always say: "A Shaman has to handle all things, even drunk men." I was never satisfied by this answer. I wanted her to realize that I would not bring physical harm to any Sami people. This was respected neither by the Sami nor by her. They simply had no respect for someone who did not defend herself when attacked. On the other hand, had I done so, I am not sure whether a blow I might have dealt in self-defense might not have been misinterpreted. Indeed, now I might add, from another perspective, that what my Shaman teacher probably wanted me to learn is that a far greater harm can come to one via the spirit world. I think that now I might say that if I were to have hit a Sami man, she knew that even if he were to have been hurt by me, he could have sought to retaliate via shamanic means (he could have had energies sent to harm me). What I had to learn was that an important level of any encounter always takes place on the plane of spirit world. Today I believe that shamanically my Shaman teacher wanted me to understand that physical brutality was not exclusively "where it was at shamanically." There are spirit wars, spirit attacks, spells, curses, and so forth. There are other ways of responding besides physical violence. Perhaps this test also had to do with my learning about these other methods. But I was so focused on not doing harm that I simply ignored the many other dimensions to this problem that spoke, more specifically, to my role as a *student of Shamanism.*

In any event, I was in a quandary about all this until I spoke about it with Paula Gunn Allen, who mentioned to me that the reason I did not fight back probably had to do with my racism. At first, I did not understand what she was getting at. Then it occurred to me that if I had been sexually accosted in my own culture (pinned to the ground against my will by a drunk man), I would have fought back. Of course, I would have defended myself, even if it meant that I might have harmed an American man. But I refused to harm a Sami man. Wasn't this a sign of my white Westerner's guilt? Suddenly I realized that I was *not* treating the

Sami as equals. I was treating them as a superior racist would treat an inferior group.

The Great Shaman used to say that I represented "the white man's culture," and I always objected. I specifically objected to his not understanding that I was a woman and that I was an ecofeminist who had, in fact, given a conference about saving the earth, to which I had invited his daughter. I could *not* conceive of myself as "the white man," and I really felt that he did not understand anything at all about me as an individual until the day I made hamburger meat for the Sami children. The Sami are definitely not vegetarians. They eat a lot of reindeer meat and fish. On that day, the Great Shaman wandered into the kitchen and, smelling a foreign odor, sniffed the meat I had prepared. Then he asked me: "What animal does this come from?" I stood there perplexed. I couldn't really understand the question, and I'm sure I must have said to him: "It doesn't come from an animal. It comes from the supermarket!" It was at that moment that I realized how I was, indeed, "the white Westerner" that he took me for! It was a good fifteen minutes before I could come up with the answer "cow." I had truly forgotten about the animal whose body I was consuming.

Even in our ideological purism, we may still behave as racists, and, in fact, it is part of our white Western racism to see ourselves as ideologically "purer than thou" because we are ecofeminists or any other *ists.* We must never forget, even when we are bending over backward to make amends, that there is a haughtiness and a racially superior attitude in being "purer than thou," even when the very people we are bending over backward toward maintain that they are "purer than us" because they do not destroy the earth, and we do. Even if the others exhibit a racist attitude toward us, and even if we try not to reply in kind, the very fact that we conceive of ourselves as superior because we "know better" is, in itself, a form of racism.

Ignorance of Geo-Cosmic Realities

Through our education in the scientific worldview of the Enlightenment, we have become alienated from the earth and have forgotten that the earth is also a heavenly body. We have ceased to take into consideration the powers of the forces and the knowledge of the cycles that govern our lives. We hardly ever give a second thought to gravity, for example, without which we would all be floating off into space, and we certainly *never* think about the real magnetic force of the North and South poles. We also take for granted the amount of light and dark we experience each day. But what if all that were to change? What if we were suddenly plunged into a world in which the sun never set—or never rose? What if we were to go to live at the magnetic North Pole? Then we would begin to experience syndromes similar to jet lag, and we would take seriously the implications of the revolutions of the earth on its axis around the sun. In Samiland during most of the fall and winter, the sun sets very early in the morning. During the summer, the sun doesn't set until well after midnight.

The rituals women have begun to perform in the feminist spirituality (Goddess) movement have begun to put us back in touch with an awareness of the solstices, the equinoxes, and the lunar cycles. But how does this all relate to ecofeminist ethics and to Shamanism?

Because of our geo-cosmic ignorance and amnesia, we fail to take into consideration the fact that certain powers can only be obtained and put into practice in certain places on the earth and at certain times during the year or during the larger cosmic cycles. It is interesting that when it comes to sacred herbs, we recognize that they grow in certain places and that people who cannot obtain certain herbs cannot experience their effects. However, herbs are portable, and this suits our purposes, for we can transport the products of the Amazon jungle to California via plane. However, we can never transport the magnetism of the North Pole to California. Nor can we manifest the effects of the Arctic midnight sun in Los Angeles. When I traveled to Samiland, I became aware of the effect that the magnetic North Pole was having upon me. It was causing me to enter a deep trance state when I slept, and it was when I was in such a deep trance that I was able to hear the voices of the ancestral spirits. As I ate Sami food, I noticed that my hair and skin began to take on other characteristics. This might have been due to the purity of the air, the water, and the food, as well as to the intensity of the earth's magnetic field in which the food was grown. We have noted that people are sensitive to light deprivation and that they become depressed when they do not receive enough light. Have we thought about what an overabundance of light might do to a person or how light might affect one's consciousness? In Samiland in the summer, when the sun sets well after midnight, sometimes as late as 3:00 A.M., one enters altered states, highs, and expansive states of consciousness.

Westerners always want to bring Shamans to the United States, put them on American TV talk shows, and have them perform miracles on our turf to prove their powers. When a Shaman from Samiland insists that you must travel to the North Pole in order to study Sami Shamanism, an American may tend to balk and dismiss the Shaman as a phony. I brought my Shaman teacher to the United States to participate in a number of conferences (such as Ecofeminist Perspectives: Culture, Nature, Theory—held at U.S.C. in the Spring of 1987), but she always insisted that my real learning would not take place in the United States, but in Samiland. She was right, because my progress was intensified as soon as I came into the magnetic field of the North Pole. The results of culture shock and jet lag, when combined with the magnetism of the North Pole and the surplus of light in summer, catapulted me immediately into a shamanic state that was intensified by the presence of two powerful Shamans. It is important for us to honor the geo-cosmic realities of shamanic cultures and to realize that certain things cannot be transported elsewhere.

One of the main features of summer in Samiland is that suddenly the marshes become swamped with mosquitoes. The Sami love their mosquitoes, because they realize that "the white man" cannot stand them, and so the mosquitoes have, in some sense, kept their land from being taken by outsiders. Most people cannot bear to live with those mosquitoes. As I mentioned before, Sami Shamans communicate with their mosquitoes, and they understand that they can be messengers, guides, and protectors. Ultimately, as we come to respect the geo-cosmic specificities of particular cultures and as we realize that there are things that *cannot* be bought, sold, commercialized, and commodified, such as magnetic fields and sunsets, (whereas people have already commercialized sacred waters and herbs), we must develop an ethics and a politics that will protect the earth and the cultures that reside not only in "places of power" or in places where we can obtain special products, but everywhere on our planet, for we must remember that the specificity of each location has its own potency.

In this way, by raising our consciousness about the geo-cosmic specificities of gravity, light, magnetism, solstices, equinoxes, lunar cycles, indigenous plants, animals, climate, and so forth, we may come to value the variety of diverse cultures and regions whose multiple knowledges all serve to enhance life everywhere on our planet in an astonishing number of ways. Most of these geocosmic teachings can only be acquired in the particular region in which they originated. Finally, if we are to awaken our own shamanic abilities, then we must attune ourselves to precisely those same forces as they manifest in our own bioregions. In some cases this may require us to learn about our region from the indigenous tribes in our area; in other cases we must set about discovering the power of the places in which we live on our own. This is our challenge, if we want to save the earth. We must not run away to other "exotic" cultures, but we must begin by exploring our own backyards.

The Depoliticization of the Shamanic Vision

By universalizing and essentializing a "core" concept of Shamanism, we tend to ignore the practical and political use to which shamanic powers can also be put. When Ellen Maret Gaup-Dunfield led a contingent of women from the reindeer ranches of Samiland to stage a sit-in in the Norwegian Parliament in order to protest the hydroelectric power plant that the Norwegians were planning to erect over the Alta-Kautokeino River on the day that Prime Minister Gro Bruntland stepped into office, she used visions to create her political itinerary. When the new prime minister did not return to hear the Sami women (after twenty-four hours, as she had promised), Ellen Maret asked the women present to relate their dreams. Some had dreamed of flying to Rome, so she requested an audience with the Pope at the Vatican (in order to obtain publicity for their cause); another dreamed of flying over large cities, so she planned a strategic visit to the United Nations in New York. Ellen Maret did not make the kind of separation that we, in the West, would make between those dream-inspired journeys to Rome and New York and other dream-inspired journeys to the spirit world. Nor did she consider the dream to be an inferior means of establishing a political itinerary.

Being a political leader *was* being a spiritual leader, and vice versa. Because Shamans from indigenous peoples do not separate spirit from matter and do *not* privilege a "core" shamanic experience over a this-worldly journey, knowing that both are sacred, both are real, and both are spiritual, focusing exclusively on lower, middle, and upper world shamanic cosmology in our courses excludes the important political function that shamanic vision often serves. Furthermore, she took the visions of women to be as relevant as those of a Shaman. She did not establish a hierarchy among women as visionaries. These women from the reindeer ranches were considered to be the very people whose dreams (spirit-world contacts) would help the Sami to save their land and protect the earth. Here is ecofeminism in action.

Conclusion: New Directions

In conclusion, I would like to suggest that we begin to take the shamanic means of obtaining knowledge seriously in our culture. First we must begin to return the various shamanic practices to their specific cultures. We must not be reductive, but must see the complexities posed by the diversity of shamanic practices around the world. This will be enriching to our understanding of what Shamanism is, in the long run. Then we must set about creating a shamanic practice that is indigenous to our part of the world and our culture. However, we must revise many of our own cultural assumptions from an ecofeminist perspective.

White Westerners must cease to project their white Western fantasies of the exotic, the glamorous, and the romantic onto other cultures. We must always assume diversity, and not make assumptions about things being the same all over the world just because some aspects of them may appear similar to us.

We must also resist thinking in a dualistic manner. We must *remember* that in Shamanism, spirit resides in matter, and all that exists is sacred. We must also resist thinking in hierarchies, privileging the spirit world and its entities over the material world and its inhabitants. Nor must we engage in elitist assumptions about whose visions have the most wisdom. We must respect the folk of every culture, remembering that their experience contains wisdom, and we must seek out women teachers whenever possible, for they have generally been the guardians of earth wisdom (because of women's socially constructed roles, and not because of any inherent or "essential" characteristics).

We must also learn the folklore of the cultures we visit and remember that what we consider to be "lore" and "legend" may have actually taken place in that culture and that these stories often contain real lessons for us that we would do well to heed.

We must remember to seek spiritual protection, and we must become aware of the risks involved in shamanic practices, as well as the dangers incurred when working with people of power. They are also very human, and like non-Shamans, they may be tempted to abuse their power.

Above all, we must cease to trivialize the spirit world. We must begin to take seriously the reality of spirit—especially those of us who engage in spirituality rituals. We should practice these rituals believing that the rituals we engage in are *real* events that *do* communicate with the spirit world.

As we are taught in anthropology and folklore courses, we must *not* exploit the sacred ways or appropriate the sacred objects of other people—especially not for commercial purposes. One of the first things I was taught was that you must replace everything you take. Rather than stripping a foreign culture of its material and spiritual possessions, we should begin to contribute to its survival.

We must begin to set standards for the practice of Shamanism, in order to protect the population from charlatans and new age dilettantes who know nothing about the spirit world and less about human consciousness and psychology. New agers do not necessarily revere the earth (they pillage the earth for crystals for their new age enterprises); nor do they necessarily respect women, either. A new age neo-Shaman might easily jettison an ardent Shaman student into a state of severe mental or physical injury, simply due to the kind of ignorance, arrogance, and lack of responsibility that typifies much of the dabbling that takes place in this movement.

We must remember that Shamanism is just as serious as surgery. Would we like to have our brains operated on by someone who had not been trained in medical school? From the ecofeminist perspective on ethics, we must never lose sight of the fact that it is the misogyny and dualism at the root of white Western civilization that have caused the exploitation of both women and nature. On the other hand, we must not guilt-trip ourselves to the point of endangering our lives. Somehow we must come up with a balance in which we honor both non-Western cultures and ourselves for all that is beneficent, while constantly maintaining a critical position toward all forms of abuse of power.

If we take the lessons of Shamanism seriously, and if we revise our cosmology in time, if we practice ecofeminist ethics while honoring both the material and the spiritual realms, then, I believe, there is real hope for us to heal the earth, our homeland, now.

ENDNOTE

1. The Shaman with whom I studied was Ellen Maret Gaup-Dunfjeld, from Alta, Norway. She died of cancer at the age of 47 in May 1991. For further information, see Orenstein (1988).

QUESTIONS

1. What is the danger of thinking of Shamanism as a universal and generic category? What do these terms mean?
2. Why are ecofeminists interested in Shamanism? In what ways do Shamanism and ecofeminism overlap in terms of values and ethics?
3. What are the problems that have arisen due to Western interest in Shamanism, according to Orenstein?
4. Why is recognizing and valuing "the spirit world" important from an ecofeminist perspective?

Introduction to Native Wisdom for White Minds (1995)

Anne Wilson Schaef

A noted author, lecturer, and organizational consultant, Anne Wilson Schaef has concentrated much of her recent scholarly efforts on exploring her own Native American heritage. In this selection, an introduction to a collection of daily meditations, Schaef discusses what she calls "white minds," a concept without racial indications. Through comparison with her growing understanding of Native American cultures, Schaef critiques "white minds" as both a limitation on human potential and a threat to the unity of all living things. Like many women who have explored spirituality, Schaef offers hope for new possibilities and avenues for the creation and celebration of the human spirit.

> O Great Spirit, who made all races, look kindly upon the whole human family and take away the arrogance and hatred which separates us from our brothers.
>
> —Cherokee Prayer

A prayer for our oneness. This position of oneness is where most Native peoples begin, and it is always done with prayer. Everything is done with prayer.

For the past several years I have spent large blocks of time with Native peoples and most especially Native Elders. Intuitively, I knew this was what my mind and my soul needed.

I came to write this book as a white mind struggling to heal and find freedom.

It was many years ago that the concept of a "white mind" came into my consciousness. The first time I remember thinking of the term *white mind* was when I had the honor of getting to know Frank and Kate Fools Crow. Frank Fools Crow was a great Ceremonial Chief and Spiritual Leader of the Lakota people. Frank Fools Crow became a very important person in my life, and his influence and impact on me have continued to grow long after his death. Some of the most powerful ceremonies I have ever experienced were with him.

After one ceremony that was of particular importance to me, he sat and talked with me. He told me that in his first vision quest, he had learned that he was to bring healing to the white people and he felt that he had failed. He then said that he was giving this responsibility to me. I remember thinking, *Of course you couldn't heal the white people, regardless of how powerful you are, because it takes a white mind to understand white minds. They're quirky.*

I then promptly forgot everything he'd said to me and anything I'd thought at the time—although occasionally the term *white mind* would resurface. Lately, though, when I've been sitting with Native people, the phrase *you white folks* often comes up. I began to see that this meant something more subtle than people of the white race. *You white folks* did mean white people, of course. However, I also began to realize that "you white people" was referring to the whole perspective of Western culture and to the white minds trained in and wedded to Western civilization.

Native people know that white minds see, conceptualize the world, and think differently than Native minds. As Herb Kawainui Kane says, "Primal cultures are essentially much alike, as proved by the universality of their myths; but worldviews, beliefs, and attitudes of primal societies are so fundamentally different from those of the modern Western society that what may be perfectly logical to one group may seem bizarre and incomprehensible to the other."

I have found what Herb Kane says to be true. Still, it is so difficult for white minds to really perceive these differences and appreciate them. This is because white minds are trained to believe that there is only one right answer, one right way of perceiving the world—and that singular way can only be mastered by minds trained in the Western scientific method of thinking. Unfortunately, Western culture's way of training our minds has resulted in closed-system thinking.

For example, in a closed system, white minds set up their world in dualisms. It's either this or that. Black or white. Right or wrong. This is a very limited and limiting way of thinking. In fact, I've found that the use of the word *but* usually sets up a dualism. For myself, I try to use *and* instead of *but* to help my mind break out of the dualistic form. I've tried to do this all through this book. Test it out for yourself. See what your mind does when you read an *and* where you think a *but* should be.

Why are we so afraid of acknowledging our white-mindedness? Why is there a seeming underlying shame in identifying ourselves as having a white mind? Why do we have such difficulty admitting we don't know and understand everything? Perhaps, part of the reason is that we've been taught that Western mechanistic science gives us the key to unlock the universe, and if there are realities for which this key does not work, those realities must simply be thought out of existence. This process of thinking that which is not understood out of existence is characteristic of a closed system. White minds, seemingly, only feel secure in a closed system.

White minds are often ruled by abstract intellectual constructs that get in the way of our accessing our universal minds or spirit. A white mind has been taught to break down its world into component parts in order to try to understand how things work. White minds reduce and isolate. They don't readily move into wholes or universality. They are hierarchical and mechanistic, and see nature as a force to be tamed and used up with no regard for the future. They cannot understand that they are a part of nature. They cannot see that nature is one with all of us—a gift to be valued and sustained. White minds often have to destroy to understand or to accept what is.

Let me say here that it's not only white people who have white minds. During the civil rights movement of the 1960s blacks often spoke of "Oreos"—people who are black on the outside and white on the inside. Native Americans speak of "apples"—red on the outside and white on the inside. In the South Pacific, it's "coconuts"—brown on the outside, white on the inside. We rarely hear these terms today because Native peoples the world over are beginning to meet and share their wisdom with each other. White minds have difficulty reflecting upon themselves because they're trained to believe that the way they think is the only reality, and that they are the only reality. Yet, most of us have the capacity to transcend our white minds. We simply need help from outside ourselves to be able to move beyond our own limited views, and to reflect upon ourselves in a meaningful way.

Today, our white minds are proving destructive to ourselves and to our planet. Yet, growth, change, and healing are still possible. It means listening with open hearts and open minds to other voices, other perceptions, other cultures with which we share this earth of ours.

Warning: This Book May Be Hazardous to Your Illusions!

What is being offered to us by the Native peoples in this book is not just another form of political correctness. Being wedded to appearances is so characteristic of Western culture. So many of us want to get an intellectual idea of change and not really change the way we see and the way we live our lives every day. What we're being offered is the opportunity to move from white minds to global minds. We're being offered the possibility of moving out of the cave of white-mindedness into the waters of planetary wisdom.

So often, I've heard Elders from a wide variety of Native people say, "Our legends and myths have told us that a time would come when it would be necessary for us to share our wisdom and knowledge, and that time is now. They say, "Our legends tell us that a time will come when our wisdom and way of living will be necessary to save the planet and now we have decided to speak."

This is an impressive message—and all the more remarkable that this same message is coming from so many diverse peoples the world over. I find it incredible that these people are willing to share with anyone who will truly listen—even if the listener comes from a culture that has tried to annihilate them. Their concern is much broader than societal grudges, customs, or politics. Eddie Box, a much revered Ute Elder and medicine man, shared with me what one of his Elders had told him: "And he said when you get rid of that anger and resentment towards whites for what they have done, everything you ask with His name [the Creator] will come to you—no difficulty. Because you have built a compassion inside of you to the human race of the world. See, that is what they [the old Elders] were talking about."

So, now that we know that white minds aren't bad minds—they're just one way of trying to be human, are you ready for *Native Wisdom for White Minds*? This is a book that dares you to be uncomfortable. It offers you the opportunity to grow beyond the limitations of our most cherished illusions. It asks you to participate in conceptual blockbusting. It offers you reintegration at a soul level.

If you're ready to move from only experiencing life at a personal level to experiencing life at a universal level, this book is for you. It's a book for people who want to explore, create, and confront their isolation and loneliness of the soul. A book for people who are willing to trek in the desert of their separation so that they can move into feelings of connectedness and oneness at a level they may never have felt before.

As you sit with this book day by day, you may find your white mind expanding into unknown territory, as I did. This book can support the process of your shifting into a different way of being in the world. If offers you nothing less than a spiritual revolution—a revolution of mind, a total transformation of worldview. I have personally taken the journey I am now inviting you to begin. Over the years, I have sat with Native Elders and been welcomed into the homes and lives of Native people the world over. Just being with them has enriched my life so much. As I began to experience spiritual and emotional healing that I could never have imagined before, I realized that I needed to share this wisdom with as many other people as possible.

I want to make clear that I have had no need to delve into secrets that Native people are not willing to share. I do not need to know their secrets—their rituals, their ceremonies, or their hidden ways of healing. While I have had the honor of participating in some of their ceremonies and rituals, my experience in many of them is much too private and personal to share.

White minds tend to seek out ceremonies, rituals, or magic as a "fix." They don't seem to understand that they cannot use these "secrets" in some mechanistic way. For when this knowledge is not deeply grounded in the worldview of its own culture, it loses all meaning and power. To experience this larger, more inclusive worldview takes time, and patience, and participation. It cannot be learned as an intellectual exercise.

Like Water on Sandstone

I am aware that there is a fascination with books about indigenous peoples, especially Native Americans. Yet these books are often read and then just put away. This is not a book about the "noble savage" or the romanticizing of Native people. Most of the people with whom I have sat are just "regular" people. They have made mistakes, been warlike, left their spirituality at times, and displayed their humanness. We cannot dismiss them as being perfect or imperfect. They are simply people.

Yet they bring us a great gift. For what they have to teach us is another worldview. And they don't have to be perfect human beings to do that. Nor do we have to dismiss what they're saying because we find imperfections in their teachings—that's simply another white-mind trick!

When I thought about how to present this material, I decided to write it in the form of a meditation book. I've had some success with this form, and I like the idea of taking a bit of time each day to sit with these ideas, this healing, this worldview. Because changing worldviews takes time, I wanted the experience of this wisdom to seep in like water on sandstone—a slow process that leaves its mark.

I didn't expect this book to fit the usual concept of a meditation book—to be soothing and healing. I don't believe that being soothing and/or giving directions or answers is necessarily healing. I believe that real healing takes place at a deep level and often requires some painful cleansing along the way. This takes time and cannot be simplified.

All of the Native people quoted in this book have experienced violence and genocide from white people and Western culture, and yet their message to us is one of deep concern, peace, and healing—healing for us as individuals, healing for our societies, and healing for our planet.

This Wisdom Is for Living

Although *Native Wisdom for White Minds* is presented in the form of a meditation book, it is much more than that. It is historical, educational, political, and informational. It is confrontive, healing, provocative, expanding, loving, comforting, hopeful, and above all spiritual. Jesus said, "You shall know the truth and the truth shall set you free." There is freedom in this wisdom—freedom because it helps us return to our deep inner knowing. We may have forgotten this wisdom and I do not believe it is gone. The knowledge and wisdom of ancient ways has simply been slumbering in our souls, awaiting a time to be reawakened. The Elders believe that time is now, and I trust their wisdom. Without their help and guidance this book could not have been written. The message is theirs. I am only the messenger.

Each entry in this book presents a place for Native people to offer a voice as they want to speak. I have not tampered with their voices. Rarely do we have the opportunity to hear Native voices not modified for white ears. Then, after each person has spoken, I have shared my responses and what I have learned.

Only as we broaden our base and are willing, truly, to learn from the diversity around us can we begin to see that we have confused culture with nature. We have confused *our* culture with reality. As Helena Norberg-Hodge writes in *Ancient Futures*, "I had not realized that many of the negative trends I saw were the result of my own industrial culture rather than some natural, evolutionary force beyond our control."

I agree with her as she goes on to say, "Our static and mechanistic worldview has reached its limits, and some scientists—particularly quantum physicists—now speak of a paradigm shift away from the old 'building block' view of reality to a more organic one. In direct opposition to the trend in mainsteam culture toward greater specialization, we need to actively promote the generalists—the one who sees connection and makes links across different disciplines. In this regard, one of the most hopeful trends is the increasing respect for more feminine values and ways of thinking." And, I might add, more respect for Native values.

Over the years, part of Frank Fools Crow's ceremonies and his words have come back to me—always at the right time. As I began working on this book, I suddenly remembered his passing along to me the responsibility of bringing healing to white people. It was a powerful incentive for me to continue writing, and I felt I had his blessing.

I also remember what happened the first time I met with Australian Aboriginal Elders. They greeted me and then said, "Why are you here?"

I didn't know. I just "knew" I was supposed to be there, and they had, after all, invited me. Others tried to speak on my behalf and say the right things.

I knew better deep in my soul, so I finally said, "I'm here to see why I'm here."

They liked that and said, "Well, yes, but what took you so long? You were supposed to be here four years ago." I was! And it had not worked out.

"Then you were supposed to be here two years ago." I *was*, and instead had an emergency appendectomy!

"Well, you're here now, so let's get on with it." And they promptly started talking among themselves and ignored me, teaching me a great deal.

I've had the feeling and have been informed that Native people the world over are choosing people with whom to share their message. Most of these people are Native, and some are not. I have prayed about this responsibility, sought council from the Elders and from Native groups, and begged for guidance. It is the Native way to teach what can be taught and then to trust you. This isn't "my" book, and I *do* take responsibility for it.

With the exception of the entries about Ladakh, all of the material in this book comes from cultures with which I have had personal contact, including writings and literature. I have not been able to include all tribal cultures, and that, I feel, is my and our loss. Nor have I included information from anthropologists. In my experience, most of their material has been interpreted from a Western cultural perspective and is thus not representative of what the people themselves are saying. Also most tribal people I've met do not trust anthropologists, which is reason enough to leave their words out.

The wisdom in this book is for living . . . for living with. Native cultures have much to teach us. They know how to live in balance with themselves, with each other, with nature, and with the earth. There is an inner balance that emerges that invites us into aliveness, joy, and peace as a way of living our lives, not just as some abstract concept. I offer this wisdom to you. I only hope that, with my "white mind," I have presented this wisdom in a way that is both respectful to the Elders and their knowledge and useful to you.

Native Soul

I was born near the Cherokee Nation, and my mother was more Indian than white. I am so grateful to her for all she taught me. Many years ago a Native American medicine man said to me, "You use a lot of Indian medicine in your work. You know more than you use. And when you are ready, come to me and I will teach you what you need to know."

I have never gone to spend time with him, and yet I have been called to spend more and more time with Native peoples. I have needed to do this for my healing and for my sanity. Since I was raised among Native people and my mother was an Indian in her soul, in her way of being, and in her way of living, I came out of a philosophy of life that is community based, one with nature, and spiritual. Having been well trained in academia, I did not know the depth of my Native roots—but that old medicine man did. That was almost twenty years ago. I can now see that what I'm teaching and calling the Living Process System (living in a new paradigm) is based on a Native worldview.

I make no claim to having a real grasp of Native wisdom the way Native people do, since I was raised a white person. Yet I feel very comfortable sharing how it has affected me, what I've learned from it, and how my work emerges out of it. I know that my time with the Elders and Native people was what I needed for myself. I know that what I've discovered in myself because of this is only the tip of the iceberg. Most of all, I know that this wisdom and this worldview are important for us all now. I am no longer comfortable with Western ways of healing, especially with a psychology that is based on a mechanistic scientific worldview.

One week after I submitted my manuscript, I was at a family reunion, and my aunt casually said over her shoulder, "You knew your father was an American Indian, didn't you?"

"No," I said. "Was he?"

"I'm surprised your mother didn't tell you. He was. I'm sure of it. Cherokee, I believe."

My white mind had found its Native soul and a new journey had begun.

QUESTIONS

1. What are the characteristics of a "white mind," according to Schaef?
2. What distinctions does Schaef draw between experiencing life at the personal level and experiencing life at a universal level?
3. Try her suggestion of replacing "but" with "and"—use a reading selection with which you are familiar. Does the different language alter either the implicit or explicit meaning of the text? Why/why not?
4. Why is "white mind" not a racially-based concept? What is the basis for the concept?

Women Creating Culture

The diversity of cultures in the global community is staggering, and a bountiful source for questioning the fabric of human behavior in the social environment. One's cultural identification can be a powerful force in shaping one's sense of self, as well as one's sense of belonging—or not—to a community. While a variety of other factors influence human development, perhaps none is as pervasive and often difficult to define as culture. Embedded in any culture are the values and norms of the dominant forces within a social structure; manifestations of culture (e.g., art, literature, music, theatre) can reveal much about social conditions. In this section, we turn our attention to the dynamics of culture and explore historical and contemporary contributions of women to the creation of culture. As we have throughout this text, we will explore the impact of differences on women's participation in, and exclusion from, the creation of culture. We will look at culture as both an aspect of oppression and as a method of liberation. We will listen to women's voices; read women's words; view women's art; and experience the richness of the textures in the fabric of culture which women have contributed, and which women continue to create.

In Search of Our Mothers' Gardens (1974)

Alice Walker

With eloquent and insightful imagery, Alice Walker explores the existence of Black female heritage, as well as her connection to that heritage. By engaging in the search for "our mothers' gardens," Walker considers the historical spirituality and creativity of Black women in the United States. She perceives that heritage as both a foundation for, and a calling toward, contemporary life. In this selection, Walker looks both for and toward the heritage of Black women, in part by using perspectives which have historically either looked at the Black woman or ignored her altogether.

Alice Walker, a poet, author and teacher, has taught at Jackson State University, Tougaloo College, Wellesley College, and was a fellow at Radcliffe Institute from 1971–1973. Her books include Revolutionary Petunia, You Can't Keep a Good Woman Down, *and* The Color Purple.

> I described her own nature and temperament. Told how they needed a larger life for their expression. . . . I pointed out that in lieu of proper channels, her emotions had overflowed into paths that dissipated them. I talked, beautifully I thought, about an art that would be born, an art that would open the way for women the likes of her. I asked her to hope, and build up an inner life against the coming of that day. . . . I sang, with a strange quiver in my voice, a promise song. —*Jean Toomer, "Avey," Cane*

The poet speaking to a prostitute who falls asleep while he's talking—

When the poet Jean Toomer walked through the South in the early twenties, he discovered a curious thing: black women whose spirituality was so intense, so deep, so *unconscious*, that they were themselves unaware of the richness they held. They stumbled blindly through their lives: creatures so abused and mutilated in body, so dimmed and confused by pain, that they considered themselves unworthy even of hope. In the selfless abstractions their bodies became to the men who used them, they became more than "sexual objects," more even than mere women: they became "Saints." Instead of being perceived as whole persons, their bodies became shrines: what was thought to be their minds became temples suitable for worship. These crazy Saints stared out at the world, wildly, like lunatics—or quietly, like suicides; and the "God" that was in their gaze was as mute as a great stone.

Who were these Saints? These crazy, loony, pitiful women?

Some of them, without a doubt, were our mothers and grandmothers.

In the still heat of the post-Reconstruction South, this is how they seemed to Jean Toomer: exquisite butterflies trapped in an evil honey, toiling away their lives in an era, a century, that did not acknowledge them, except as "the *mule* of the world." They dreamed dreams that no one knew—not even themselves, in any coherent fashion—and saw visions no one could understand. They wandered or sat about the countryside crooning lullabies to ghosts, and drawing the mother of Christ in charcoal on courthouse walls.

They forced their minds to desert their bodies and their striving spirits sought to rise, like frail whirlwinds from the hard red clay. And when those frail whirlwinds fell, in scattered particles, upon the ground, no one mourned. Instead, men lit candles to celebrate the emptiness that remained, as people do who enter a beautiful but vacant space to resurrect a God.

Our mothers and grandmothers, some of them: moving to music not yet written. And they waited.

They waited for a day when the unknown thing that was in them would be made known; but guessed, somehow in their darkness, that on the day of their revelation they would be long dead. Therefore to Toomer they walked, and even ran, in slow motion. For they were going nowhere immediate, and the future was not yet within their grasp. And men took our mothers and grandmothers, "but got no pleasure from it." So complex was their passion and their calm.

To Toomer, they lay vacant and fallow as autumn fields, with harvest time never in sight: and he saw them enter loveless marriages, without joy; and become prostitutes, without resistance; and become mothers of children, without fulfillment.

For these grandmothers and mothers of ours were not Saints, but Artists; driven to a numb and bleeding madness by the springs of creativity in them for which there was no release. They were Creators, who lived lives of spiritual waste, because they were so rich in spirituality—which is the basis of Art—that the strain of enduring their unused and unwanted talent drove them insane. Throwing away this spirituality was their pathetic attempt to lighten the soul to a weight their work-worn, sexually abused bodies could bear.

What did it mean for a black woman to be an artist in our grandmothers' time? In our great-grandmothers' day? It is a question with an answer cruel enough to stop the blood.

Did you have a genius of a great-great-grandmother who died under some ignorant and depraved white overseer's lash? Or was she required to bake biscuits for a lazy backwater tramp, when she cried out in her soul to paint watercolors of sunsets, or the rain falling on the green and peaceful pasturelands? Or was her body broken and forced to bear children (who were more often than not sold away from her)—eight, ten, fifteen, twenty children—when her one joy was the thought of modeling heroic figures of rebellion, in stone or clay?

How was the creativity of the black woman kept alive, year after year and century after century, when for most of the years black people have been in America, it was a punishable crime for a black person to read or write? And the freedom to paint, to sculpt, to expand the mind with action did not exist. Consider, if you can bear to imagine it, what might have been the result if singing, too, had been forbidden by law. Listen to the voices of Bessie Smith, Billie Holiday, Nina Simone, Roberta Flack, and Aretha Franklin, among others, and imagine those voices muzzled for life. Then you may begin to comprehend the lives of our "crazy," "Sainted" mothers and grandmothers. The agony of the lives of women who might have been Poets, Novelists, Essayists, and Short-Story Writers (over a period of centuries), who died with their real gifts stifled within them.

And, if this were the end of the story, we would have cause to cry out in my paraphrase of Okot p'Bitek's great poem:

O, my clanswomen
Let us all cry together!
Come,
Let us mourn the death of our mother,
The death of a Queen
The ash that was produced
By a great fire!
O, this homestead is utterly dead
Close the gates
With *lacari* thorns,
For our mother
The creator of the Stool is lost!
And all the young women
Have perished in the wilderness!

But this is not the end of the story, for all the young women—our mothers and grandmothers, *ourselves*—have not perished in the wilderness. And if we ask ourselves why, and search for and find the answer, we will know beyond all efforts to erase it from our minds, just exactly who, and of what, we black American women are.

One example, perhaps the most pathetic, most misunderstood one, can provide a backdrop for our mothers' work: Phillis Wheatley, a slave in the 1700s.

Virginia Woolf, in her book *A Room of One's Own*, wrote that in order for a woman to write fiction she must have two things, certainly: a room of her own (with key and lock) and enough money to support herself.

What then are we to make of Phillis Wheatley, a slave, who owned not even herself? This sickly, frail black girl who required a servant of her own at times—her health was so precarious—and who, had she been white, would have been easily considered the intellectual superior of all the women and most of the men in the society of her day.

Virginia Woolf wrote further, speaking of course not of our Phillis, that "any woman born with a great gift in the sixteenth century [insert "eighteenth century," insert "black woman," insert "born or made a slave"] would certainly have gone crazed, shot herself, or ended her days in some lonely cottage outside the village, half witch, half wizard [insert "Saint"], feared and mocked at. For it needs little skill and psychology to be sure that a highly gifted girl who had tried to use her gift for poetry would have been so thwarted and hindered by contrary instincts [add "chains, guns, the lash, the ownership of one's body by someone else, submission to an alien religion"], that she must have lost her health and sanity to a certainty."

The key words, as they relate to Phillis, are "contrary instincts." For when we read the poetry of Phillis Wheatley—as when we read the novels of Nella Larsen or the oddly false-sounding autobiography of that freest of all black women writers, Zora Hurston—evidence of "contrary instincts" is everywhere. Her loyalties were completely divided, as was, without question, her mind.

But how could this be otherwise? Captured at seven, a slave of wealthy, doting whites who instilled in her the "savagery" of the Africa they "rescued" her from . . . one wonders if she was even able to remember her homeland as she had known it, or as it really was.

Yet, because she did try to use her gift for poetry in a world that made her a slave, she was "so thwarted and hindered by . . . contrary instincts, that she . . . lost her health. . . ." In the last years of her brief life, burdened not only with the need to express her gift but also with a penniless, friendless "freedom" and several small children for whom she was forced to do strenuous work to feed, she lost her health, certainly. Suffering from malnutrition and neglect and who knows what mental agonies, Phillis Wheatley died.

So torn by "contrary instincts" was black, kidnapped, enslaved Phillis that her description of "the Goddess"—as she poetically called the Liberty she did not have—is ironically, cruelly humorous. And, in fact, has held Phillis up to ridicule for more than a century. It is usually read prior to hanging Phillis's memory as that of a fool. She wrote:

> The Goddess comes, she moves divinely fair,
> Olive and laurel binds her *golden* hair.
> Wherever shines this native of the skies,
> Unnumber'd charms and recent graces rise. [My italics]

It is obvious that Phillis, the slave, combed the "Goddess's" hair every morning; prior, perhaps, to bringing in the milk, or fixing her mistress's lunch. She took her imagery from the one thing she saw elevated above all others.

With the benefit of hindsight we ask, "How could she?"

But at last, Phillis, we understand. No more snickering when your stiff, struggling, ambivalent lines are forced on us. We know now that you were not an idiot or a traitor; only a sickly little black girl, snatched from your home and country and made a slave; a woman who still struggled to sing the song that was your gift, although in a land of barbarians who praised you for your bewildered tongue. It is not so much what you sang, as that you kept alive, in so many of our ancestors, *the notion of song.*

Black women are called, in the folklore that so aptly identifies one's status in society, "the *mule* of the world," because we have been handed the burden that everyone else—*everyone* else—refused to carry. We have also been called "Matriarchs," "Superwomen," and "Mean and Evil Bitches." Not to mention "Castraters" and "Sapphire's Mama." When we have pleaded for understanding, our character has been distorted; when we have asked for simple caring, we have been handed empty inspirational appellations, then stuck in the farthest corner. When we have asked for love, we have been given children. In short, even our plainer gifts, our labors of fidelity and love, have been knocked down our throats. To be an artist and a black woman, even today, lowers our status in many respects, rather than raises it: and yet, artists we will be.

Therefore we must fearlessly pull out of ourselves and look at and identify with our lives the living creativity some of our great-grandmothers were not allowed to know. I stress *some* of them because it is well known that the majority of our great-grandmothers knew, even without "knowing" it, the reality of their spirituality, even if they didn't recognize it beyond what happened in the singing at church—and they never had any intention of giving it up.

How they did it—those millions of black women who were not Phillis Wheatly, or Lucy Terry or Frances Harper or Zora Hurston or Nella Larsen or Bessie Smith; or Elizabeth Catlett, or Katherine Dunham, either—brings me to the title of this essay, "In Search of Our Mothers' Gardens," which is a personal account that is yet shared, in its theme and its meaning, by all of us. I found, while thinking about the far-reaching world of the creative black woman, that often the truest answer to a question that really matters can be found very close.

In the late 1920s my mother ran away from home to marry my father. Marriage, if not running away, was expected of seventeen-year-old girls. By the time she was twenty, she had two children and was pregnant with a third. Five children later, I was born. And this is how I came to know my mother: she seemed a large, soft, loving-eyed woman who was rarely impatient in our home. Her quick, violent temper was on view only a few times a year, when she battled with the white landlord who had the misfortune to suggest to her that her children did not need to go to school.

She made all the clothes we wore, even my brothers' overalls. She made all the towels and sheets we used. She spent the summers canning vegetables and fruits. She spent the winter evenings making quilts enough to cover all our beds.

During the "working" day, she labored beside—not behind—my father in the fields. Her day began before sunup, and did not end until late at night. There was never a moment for her to sit down, undisturbed, to unravel her own private thoughts; never a time free from interruption—by work or the noisy inquiries of her many children. And yet, it is to my mother—and all our mothers who were not famous—that I went in search of the secret of what has fed that muzzled and often mutilated, but vibrant, creative spirit that the black woman has inherited, and that pops out in wild and unlikely places to this day.

But when, you will ask, did my overworked mother have time to know or care about feeding the creative spirit?

The answer is so simple that many of us have spent years discovering it. We have constantly looked high, when we should have looked high—and low.

For example: in the Smithsonian Institution in Washington, D.C., there hangs a quilt unlike any other in the world. In fanciful, inspired, and yet simple and identifiable figures, it portrays the story of the Crucifixion. It is considered rare, beyond price. Though it follows no known pattern of quiltmaking, and though it is made of bits and pieces of worthless rags, it is obviously the work of a person of powerful imagination and deep spiritual feeling. Below this quilt I saw a note that says it was made by "an anonymous Black woman in Alabama, a hundred years ago."

If we could locate this "anonymous" black woman from Alabama, she would turn out to be one of our grandmothers—an artist who left her mark in the only materials she could afford, and in the only medium her position in society allowed her to use.

As Virginia Woolf wrote further, in *A Room of One's Own:*

> Yet genius of a sort must have existed among women as it must have existed among the working class. [Change this to "slaves" and "the wives and daughters of sharecroppers."] Now and again an Emily Brontë or a Robert Burns [change this to "a Zora Hurston or a Richard Wright"] blazes out and proves its presence. But certainly it never got itself on to paper. When, however, one reads of a witch being ducked, of a woman possessed by devils [or "Sainthood"], of a wise woman selling herbs [our root workers], or even a very remarkable man who had a mother, then I think we are on the track of a lost novelist, a suppressed poet, of some mute and inglorious Jane Austen. . . . Indeed, I would venture to guess that Anon, who wrote so many poems without signing them, was often a woman. . . .

And so our mothers and grandmothers have, more often than not anonymously, handed on the creative spark, the seed of the flower they themselves never hoped to see: or like a sealed letter they could not plainly read.

And so it is, certainly with my own mother. Unlike "Ma" Rainey's songs, which retained their creator's name even while blasting forth from Bessie Smith's mouth, no song or poem will bear my mother's name. Yet so many of the stories that I write, that we all write, are my mother's stories. Only recently did I fully realize this: that through years of listening to my mother's stories of her life, I have absorbed not only the stories themselves, but something of the manner in which she spoke, something of the urgency that involves the knowledge that her stories—like her life—must be recorded. It is probably for this reason that so much of what I have written is about characters whose counterparts in real life are so much older than I am.

But the telling of these stories, which came from my mother's lips as naturally as breathing, was not the only way my mother showed herself as an artist. For stories, too, were subject to being distracted, to dying without conclusion. Dinners must be started, and cotton must be gathered before the big rains. The artist that was and is my mother showed itself to me only after many years. This is what I finally noticed:

Like Mem, a character in *The Third Life of Grange Copeland,* my mother adorned with flowers whatever shabby house we were forced to live in. And not just your typical straggly country stand of zinnias, either. She planted ambitious gardens—and still does—with over fifty different varieties of plants that bloom profusely from early March until late November. Before she left home for the fields, she watered her flowers, chopped up the grass, and laid out new beds. When she returned from the fields she might divide clumps of bulbs, dig a cold pit, uproot and replant roses, or prune branches from her taller bushes or trees—until night came and it was too dark to see.

Whatever she planted grew as if by magic, and her fame as a grower of flowers spread over three counties. Because of her creativity with her flowers, even my memories of poverty are seen through a screen of blooms—sunflowers, petunias, roses, dahlias, forsythia, spirea, delphiniums, verbena . . . and on and on.

And I remember people coming to my mother's yard to be given cuttings from her flowers; I hear again the praise showered on her because whatever rocky soil she landed on, she turned into a garden. A garden so brilliant with colors, so original in its design, so magnificent with life and creativity, that to this day people drive by our house in Georgia—perfect strangers and imperfect strangers—and ask to stand or walk among my mother's art.

I notice that it is only when my mother is working in her flowers that she is radiant, almost to the point of being invisible—except as Creator: hand and eye. She is involved in work her soul must have. Ordering the universe in the image of her personal conception of Beauty.

Her face, as she prepares the Art that is her gift, is a legacy of respect she leaves to me, for all that illuminates and cherishes life. She has handed down respect for the possibilities—and the will to grasp them.

For her, so hindered and intruded upon in so many ways, being an artist has still been a daily part of her life. This ability to hold on, even in very simple ways, is work black women have done for a very long time.

This poem is not enough, but it is something, for the woman who literally covered the holes in our walls with sunflowers:

> They were women then
> My mama's generation
> Husky of voice—stout of
> Step
> With fists as well as
> Hands

How they battered down
Doors
And ironed
Starched white
Shirts
How they led
Armies
Headragged Generals
Across mined
Fields
Booby-trapped
Kitchens
To discover books
Desks
A place for us
How they knew what we
Must know
Without knowing a page
Of it
Themselves.

Guided by my heritage of love of beauty and a respect for strength—in search of my mother's garden, I found my own.

And perhaps in Africa over two hundred years ago, there was just such a mother; perhaps she painted vivid and daring decorations in oranges and yellows and greens on the walls of her hut; perhaps she sang—in a voice like Roberta Flack's—sweetly over the compounds of her village; perhaps she wove the most stunning mats or told the most ingenious stories of all the village storytellers. Perhaps she was herself a poet—though only her daughter's name is signed to the poems that we know.

Perhaps Phillis Weatley's mother was also an artist.

Perhaps in more then Phillis Wheatley's biological life is her mother's signature made clear.

QUESTIONS

1. What imagery does Walker use to capture the heritage of the Black female? Explain the significance of the various images.
2. What is the "wilderness" in Okot p'Bitek's poem? How does Walker use reconsideration of Phillis Wheatley to expose elements of the wilderness in Virginia Woolf's *A Room of One's Own?*
3. How does Walker re-work the image of the Black woman as "the mule of the world"?
4. What is the significance of Walker's imagery of "our mothers' gardens"? Identify the ways Walker sees the connection of the Black woman to the creative spirit. What evidence of Black women's spirituality do you see in Walker's discussion?

Story of Shakespeare's Sister (excerpted from *A Room of One's Own*) (1929)

Virginia Woolf

Writing in the 1920s, Virginia Woolf compares women's ability to write literature in Shakespeare's time to the treatment of women writers in early twentieth century America. Woolf examines historical context to suggest that the ability to write is dependent on a variety of factors. Woolf argues that access to education, income, and "a room of one's own," are as essential to the ability to write as are talent or genius. To prove her point, Woolf mixes scholarly texts with a fictional story of what might have happened to Shakespeare's gifted sister.

Virginia Woolf, born in 1882 in London, wrote numerous essays, biographies, short stories and novels. Her novels include Jacob's Room *(1922),* Mrs. Dalloway *(1925),* To the Lighthouse *(1927),* Orlando *(1928), and* The Waves *(1931). Woolf's career ended tragically when she committed suicide in 1941.*

It was disappointing not to have brought back in the evening some important statement, some authentic fact. Women are poorer than men because—this or that. Perhaps now it would be better to give up seeking for the truth, and receiving on one's head an avalanche of opinion hot as lava, discoloured as dish-water. It would be better to draw the curtains; to shut out distractions; to light the lamp to narrow the enquiry and to ask the historian, who records not opinions but facts, to describe under what conditions women lived, not throughout the ages, but in England, say in the time of Elizabeth.

For it is a perennial puzzle why no woman wrote a word of that extraordinary literature when every other man, it seemed, was capable of song or sonnet. What were the conditions in which women lived, I asked myself; for fiction, imaginative work that is, is not dropped like a pebble upon the ground, as science may be; fiction is like a spider's web, attached ever so lightly perhaps, but still attached to life at all four corners. Often the attachment is scarcely perceptable; Shakespeare's plays, for instance, seem to hang there complete by themselves. But when the web is pulled askew, hooked up at the edge, torn in the middle, one remembers that these webs are not spun in midair by incorporeal creatures, but are the work of suffering human beings, and are attached to grossly material things, like health and money and the houses we live in.

I went, therefore, to the shelf where the stories stand and took down one of the latest, Professor Trevelyan's *History of England.* Once more I looked up Women, found "position of," and turned to the pages indicated. "Wifebeating," I read "was a recognized right of man, and was practiced without shame by high as well as low. . . . Similarly," this historian goes on, "the daughter who refused to marry the gentleman of her parents' choice was liable to be locked up, beaten and flung about the room, without any shock being inflicted on public opinion. Marriage was not an affair of personal affection, but of family avarice, particularly in the 'chivalrous' upper classes. . . . Betrothal often took place while one or both of the parties was in the cradle, and marriage when they were scarcely out of the nurses' charge." That was about 1470, soon after Chaucer's time. The next reference to the position of women is some two hundred years later, in the time of the Stuarts. "It was still the exception for women of the upper and middle class to choose their own husbands, and when the husband had been assigned, he was lord and master, so far at least as law and custom could make him. Yet even so," Professor Trevelyan concludes, "neither Shakespeare's women nor those of authentic seventeenth-century memoirs, like the Vemeys and the Hutchinsons, seem wanting in personality and character." Certainly, if we consider it, Cleopatra must have had a way with her; Lady Macbeth, one would suppose, had a will of her own; Rosalind, one might conclude, was an attractive girl. Professor Trevelyan is speaking no more than the truth when he remarks that Shakespeare's women do not seem wanting in personality and character. Not being a historian, one might go even further and say that women have burnt like beacons in all the works of all the poets from the beginning of time—Clytemnestra, Antigone, Cleopatra, Lady Macbeth, Phèdre, Cressida, Rosalind, Desdemona, the Duchess of Malfi, among the dramatists; then among the prose writers: Millamant, Clarissa, Becky Sharp, Anna Karenine, Emma Bovary, Madame de Guermantes—the names flock to mind, nor do they recall women "lacking in personality and character." Indeed, if woman had no existence save in fiction written by men, one would imagine her a person of the utmost importance, very various; heroic and mean; splendid and sordid; infinitely beautiful and hideous in the extreme; as great as a man, some think even greater.[1] But this is woman in fiction. In fact, as Professor Trevelyan points out, she was locked up, beaten and flung about the room.

A very queer, composite being thus emerges. Imaginatively she is of the highest importance; practically she is completely insignificant. She pervades poetry from cover to cover; she is all but absent from history. She dominates the lives of kings and conquerors in fiction; in fact she was the slave of any boy whose parents forced a ring upon her finger. Some of the most inspired words, some of the most profound thoughts in literature fall from her lips; in real life she could hardly read, could scarcely spell, and was the property of her husband.

It was certainly an odd monster that one made up by reading the historians first and the poets afterwards—a worm winged like an eagle; the spirit of life and beauty in a kitchen chopping up suet. But these monsters, however amusing to the imagination, have no existence in fact. What one must do to bring her to life was to think poetically and prosaically at one and the same moment, thus keeping in touch with fact—that she is Mrs. Martin, aged thirty-six, dressed in blue, wearing a black hat and brown shoes; but not losing sight of fiction either—that she is a vessel in which all sorts of spirits and forces are coursing and flashing perpetually. The moment, however, that one tries this method with the Elizabethan woman, one branch of illumination fails; one is held up by the scarcity of facts. One knows nothing detailed, nothing perfectly true and substantial about her. History scarcely mentions her. And I turn to Professor Trevelyan again to see what history meant to him. I found by looking at his chapter headings that it meant—

"The Manor Court and the Methods of Open-field Agriculture . . . The Cistercians and Sheep-farming . . . The Crusades . . . The University . . . The House of Commons . . . The Hundred Years' War . . . The War of the Roses . . . The Renaissance Scholars . . . The Dissolution of the Monasteries . . . Agrarian and Religious Strife . . . The Origin of English Sea-power . . . The Armada . . . " and so on. Occasionally an individual woman is mentioned, an Elizabeth, or a Mary; a queen or a great lady. But by no possible means could middle-class women with nothing but brains and character at their command have taken part in any one of the great movements which, brought together, constitute the historian's view of the past. Nor shall we find her in any collection of anecdotes. Aubrey hardly mentions her. She never writes her own life and scarcely keeps a diary; there are only a handful of her letters in existence. She left no plays or poems by which we can judge her. What one wants, I thought—and why does not some brilliant student at Newnham or Girton supply it?—is a mass of information; at what age did she marry; how many children had she as a rule; what was her house like; had she a room to herself; did she do the cooking; would she be likely to have a servant? All these facts lie somewhere, presumably, in parish registers and account books; the life of the average Elizabethan woman must be scattered about somewhere, could one collect it and make a book of it. It would be ambitious beyond my daring, I thought, looking about the shelves for books that were not there, to suggest to the students of these famous colleages that they should re-write history, though I own that it often seems a little queer as it is, unreal, lop-sided; but why should they not add a supplement to history? calling it, of course, by some inconspicuous name so that women might figure there without impropriety? For one often catches a glimpse of them in the lives of the great, whisking away into the background, concealing, I sometimes think, a wink, a laugh, perhaps a tear. And, after all, we have lives enough of Jane Austen; it scarcely seems necessary to consider again the influence of the tragedies of Joanna Baillie upon the poetry of Edgar Allan Poe; as for myself, I should not mind if the homes and haunts of Mary Russell Milford were closed to the public for a century at least. But what I find deplorable, I continued, looking about the bookshelves again, is that nothing is known about women before the eighteenth century. I have no model in my mind to turn about this way and that. Here am I asking why women did not write poetry in the Elizabethan age, and I am not sure how they were educated; whether they were taught to write; whether they had sitting-rooms to themselves; how many women had children before they were twenty-one; what, in short, they did from eight in the morning till eight at night. They had no money evidently; according to Professor Trevelyan they were married whether they liked it or not before they were out of the nursery, at fifteen or sixteen very likely. It would have been extremely odd, even upon this showing, had one of them suddenly written the plays of Shakespeare, I concluded, and I thought of that old gentleman, who is dead now, but was a bishop, I think, who declared that it was impossible for any woman, past, present, or to come, to have the genius of Shakespeare. He wrote to the papers about it. He also told a lady who applied to him for information that cats do not as a matter of fact go to heaven, though they have, he added, souls of a sort. How much thinking those old gentlemen used to save one! How the borders of ignorance shrank back at their approach! Cats do not go to heaven. Women cannot write the plays of Shakespeare.

Be that as it may, I could not help thinking, as I looked at the works of Shakespeare on the shelf, that the bishop was right at least in this; it would have been impossible, completely and entirely, for any woman to have written the plays of Shakespeare in the age of Shakespeare. Let me imagine, since facts are so hard to come by, what would have happened had Shakespeare had a wonderfully gifted sister, called Judith, let us say. Shakespeare himself went, very probably—his mother was an heiress—to the grammar school, where he may have learnt Latin—Ovid, Virgil and Horace—and the elements of grammar and logic. He was, it is well known, a wild boy who poached rabbits, perhaps shot a deer, and had, rather sooner than he should have done, to marry a woman in the neighbourhood, who bore him a child rather quicker than was right. That escapade sent him to seek his fortune in London. He had it seemed, a taste for the theatre; he began by holding horses at the stage door. Very soon he got work in the theatre, became a successful actor, and lived at the hub of the universe, meeting everybody, knowing everybody, practising his art on the boards, exercising his wits in the streets, and even getting access to the palace of the queen. Meanwhile his extraordinarily gifted sister, let us suppose, remained at home. She was as adventurous, as imaginative, as agog to see the world as he was. But she was not sent to school. She had no chance of learning grammar and logic, let alone of reading Horace and Virgil. She picked up a book now and then, one of her brother's perhaps, and read a few pages. But then her parents came in and told her to mend the stockings or mind the stew and not moon about with books and papers. They would have spoken sharply but kindly, for they were substantial people who knew the conditions of life for a woman and loved their daughter—indeed, more likely than not she was the apple of her father's eye. Perhaps she scribbled some pages up in an apple loft on the sly, but was careful to hide them or set fire to them. Soon, however, before she was out of her teens, she was to be betrothed to the son of a neighbouring woolstapler. She cried out that marriage was hateful to her, and for that she was severely beaten by her father. Then he ceased to scold her. He begged her instead not to hurt him, not to shame him in this matter of her marriage. He would give her a chain of beads or a fine petticoat, he said; and there were tears in his eyes. How could she disobey him? How could she break his heart? The force of her own gift alone drove her to it. She made up a small parcel of her belongings, let herself down by a rope one summer's night and took the road to London. She was not seventeen. The birds that sang in the hedge were not more musical than she was. She had the quickest fancy, a gift like her brother's, for the tune of words. Like him, she had a taste for the theatre. She stood at the stage door; she wanted to act, she said. Men laughed in her face. The manager—a fat, loose-lipped man—guffawed. He bellowed something about poodles dancing and women acting—no woman, he said, could possibly be an actress. He hinted—you can imagine what. She could get no training in her craft. Could she even seek her dinner in a tavern or roam the streets at midnight? Yet her genius was for fiction and lusted to feed abundantly upon the lives of men and women and the study of their ways. At last—

for she was very young, oddly like Shakespeare the poet in her face, with the same grey eyes and rounded brows—at last Nick Greene the actor-manager took pity on her; she found herself with child by that gentleman and so—who shall measure the heat and violence of the poet's heart when caught and tangled in a woman's body?—killed herself one winter's night and lies buried at some crossroads where the omnibuses now stop outside the Elephant and Castle.

That, more or less, is how the story would run, I think, if a woman in Shakespeare's day had had Shakespeare's genius. But for my part, I agree with the deceased bishop, if such he was—it is unthinkable that any women in Shakespeare's day should have had Shakespeare's genius. For genius like Shakespeare's is not born among labouring, uneducated, servile people. It was not born in England among the Saxons and the Britons. It is not born today among the working classes. How, then, could it have been born among women whose work began, according to Professor Trevelyan, almost before they were out of the nursery, who were forced to it by their parents and held to it by all the power of law and custom? Yet genius of a sort must have existed among women as it must have existed among the working classes. Now and again an Emily Bronte or a Robert Burns blazes out and proves its presence. But certainly it never got itself on to paper. When, however, one reads of a witch being ducked, of a woman possessed by devils, of a wise woman selling herbs, or even of a very remarkable man who had a mother, then I think we are on the track of a lost novelist, a suppressed poet, of some mute and inglorious Jane Austen, some Emily Bronte who dashed her brains out on the moor or mopped and mowed about the highways crazed with the torture that her gift had put her to. Indeed, I would venture to guess that Anon, who wrote so many poems without signing them, was often a woman. It was a woman Edward Fitzgerald, I think, suggested who made the ballads and the folk-songs, crooning them to her children, beguiling her spinning with them, or the length of the winter's night.

This may be true or it may be false—who can say?—but what is true in it, so it seemed to me, reviewing the story of Shakespeare's sister as I had made it, is that any woman born with a great gift in the sixteenth century would certainly have gone crazed, shot herself, or ended her days in some lonely cottage outside the village, half witch, half wizard, feared and mocked at. For it needs little skill in psychology to be sure that a highly gifted girl who had tried to use her gift for poetry would have been so thwarted and hindered by other people, so tortured and pulled asunder by her own contrary instincts, that she must have lost her health and sanity to a certainty. No girl could have walked to London and stood at a stage door and forced her way into the presence of actor-managers without doing herself a violence and suffering an anguish which may have been irrational—for chastity may be a fetish invented by certain societies for unknown reasons—but were none the less inevitable. Chastity had then, it has even now, a religious importance in a woman's life, and has so wrapped itself round with nerves and instincts that to cut it free and bring it to the light of day demands courage of the rarest. To have lived a free life in London in the sixteenth century would have meant for a woman who was poet and playwright a nervous stress and dilemma which might well have killed her. Had she survived, whatever she had written would have been twisted and deformed, issuing from a strained and morbid imagination. And undoubtedly, I thought, looking at the shelf where there are no plays by women, her work would have gone unsigned. That refuge she would have sought certainly. It was the relic of the sense of chastity that dictated anonymity to women even so late as the nineteenth century. Currer Bell, George Eliot, George Sand, all the victims of inner strife as their writings prove, sought ineffectively to veil themselves by using the name of a man. Thus they did homage to the convention, which if not implanted by the other sex was liberally encouraged by them (the chief glory of a woman is not to be talked of, said Pericles, himself a much-talked-of-man), that publicity in women is detestable. Anonymity runs in their blood. The desire to be veiled still possesses them. They are not even now as concerned about the health of their fame as men are, and, speaking generally, will pass a tombstone or a signpost without feeling an irresistible desire to cut their names on it, as Alf, Bert or Chas, must do in obedience to their instinct, which murmurs if it sees a fine woman go by, or even a dog, *Ce chien est à moi.* And, of course, it may not be a dog, I thought, remembering Parliament Square, the Sieges Allee and other avenues; it may be a piece of land or a man with curly black hair. It is one of the great advantages of being a woman that one can pass even a very fine negress without wishing to make an Englishwoman of her.

That woman, then, who was born with a gift of poetry in the sixteenth century, was an unhappy woman, a woman at strife against herself. All the conditions of her life, all her own instincts, were hostile to the state of mind which is needed to set free whatever is in the brain. But what is the state of mind that is most propitious to the act of creation, I asked? Can one come by any notion of the state that furthers and makes possible that strange activity? Here I opened the volume containing the Tragedies of Shakespeare. What was Shakespeare's state of mind, for instance, when he wrote *Lear* and *Antony and Cleopatra ?* It was certainly the state of mind most favourable to poetry that there has ever existed. But Shakespeare himself said nothing about it. We only know casually and by chance that he "never blotted a line." Nothing indeed was ever said by the artist himself about his state of mind until the eighteenth century perhaps. Rousseau perhaps began it. At any rate, by the nineteenth century self-consciousness had developed so far that it was the habit for men of letters to describe their minds in confessions and autobiographies. Their lives also were written, and their letters were printed after their deaths. Thus, though we do not know what Shakespeare went through when he wrote *Lear,* we do know what Carlyle went through when he wrote the *French Revolution:* what Flaubert went through when he wrote *Madame Bovary;* what Keats was going through when he tried to write poetry against the coming of death and the indifference of the world.

And one gathers from this enormous modern literature of confession and self analysis that to write a work of genius is almost always a feat of prodigious difficulty. Everything is against the likelihood that it will come from the writer's mind whole and entire. Generally material circumstances are against it. Dogs will bark; people will interrupt; money must be made; health will break down. Further, accentuating all these difficulties and making them harder to bear is the world's notorious indifference. It does not ask people to write poems and novels and histories; it does not need them. It does not care whether Flaubert finds the right word or whether Carlyle scrupulously verifies this or that fact. Naturally, it will not pay for what it does not want. And so the writer, Keats, Flaubert, Carlyle, suffers, especially in the creative years of youth, every form of distraction and discouragement. A curse, a cry of agony, rises from those books of analysis and confession. "Mighty poets in their misery dead"—that is the burden of their song. If anything comes through in spite of all this, it is a miracle, and probably no book is born entire and uncrippled as it was conceived.

But for women, I thought, looking at the empty shelves, these difficulties were infinitely more formidable. In the first place, to have a room of her own, let alone a quiet room or a sound-proof room, was out of the question, unless her parents were exceptionally rich or very noble, even up to the beginning of the nineteenth century. Since her pin money, which depended on the good will of her father, was only enough to keep her clothed, she was debarred from such alleviations as came even to Keats or Tennyson or Carlyle, all poor men, from a walking tour, a little journey to France, from the separate lodging which, even if it were miserable enough, sheltered them from the claims and tyrannies of their families. Such material difficulties were formidable; but much worse were the immaterial. The indifference of the world which Keats and Flaubert and other men of genius have found so hard to bear was in her case not indifference but hostility. The world did not say to her as it said to them, Write if you choose; it makes no difference to me. The world said with a guffaw, Write? What's the good of your writing? Here the psychologists of Newnham and Girton might come to our help, I thought, looking again at the blank spaces on the shelves. For surely it is time that the effect of discouragement upon the mind of the artist should be measured, as I have seen a dairy company measure the effect of ordinary milk and Grade A milk upon the body of the rat. They set two rats in cages side by side, and of the two one was furtive, timid and small, and the other was glossy, bold and big. Now what food do we feed women as artists upon? I asked, remembering, I suppose, that dinner of prunes and custard. To answer that question I had only to open the evening paper and to read that Lord Birkenhead is of opinion—but really I am not going to trouble to copy out Lord Birkenhead's opinion upon the writing of women. What Dean Inge says I will leave in peace. The Harley Street specialist may be allowed to rouse the echoes of Harley Street with his vociferations without raising a hair on my head. I will quote, however, Mr. Oscar Browning, because Mr. Oscar Browning was a great figure in Cambridge at one time, and used to examine the students at Girton and Newnham. Mr. Oscar Browning was wont to declare "that the impression left on his mind, after looking over any set of examination papers, was that, irrespective of the marks he might give, the best woman was intellectually the inferior of the worst man." After saying that Mr. Browning went back to his rooms—and it is this sequel that endears him and makes him a human figure of some bulk and majesty—he went back to his rooms and found a stable-boy lying on the sofa—" a mere skeleton, his cheeks were cavernous and sallow, his teeth were black, and he did not appear to have the full use of his limbs. 'That's Arthur' [said Mr. Browning]. 'He's a dear boy really and most high-minded.'" The two pictures always seem to me to complete each other. And happily in this age of biography the two pictures often do complete each other, so that we are able to interpret the opinions of great men not only by what they say, but by what they do.

But though this is possible now, such opinions coming from the lips of important people must have been formidable enough even fifty years ago. Let us suppose that a father from the highest motives did not wish his daughter to leave home and become writer, painter or scholar. "See what Mr. Oscar Browning says," he would say; and there was not only Mr. Oscar Browning; there was the *Saturday Review:* there was Mr. Greg—the "essentials of a woman's being," said Mr. Greg emphatically, "are that *they are supported by, and they minister to, men*"— there was an enormous body of masculine opinion to the effect that nothing could be expected of women intellectually. Even if her father did not read out loud these opinions, any girl could read them for herself; and the reading, even in the nineteenth century, must have lowered her vitality, and told profoundly upon her work. There would always have been that assertion—you cannot do this, you are incapable of doing that—to protest against, to overcome. Probably for a novelist this germ is no longer of much effect; for there have been women novelists of merit. But for painters it must still have some sting in it; and for musicians, I imagine, is even now active and poisonous in the extreme. The woman composer stands where the actress stood in the time of Shakespeare. Nick Greene, I thought, remembering the story I had made about Shakespeare's sister, said that a woman acting put him in mind of a dog dancing. Johnson repeated the phrase two hundred years later of women preaching. And here, I said, opening a book about music, we have the very words used again in this year of grace, 1928, of women who try to write music. "Of Mlle. Germaine Tailleferre one can only repeat Dr. Johnson's dictum concerning a woman preacher, transposed into terms of music. 'Sir, a woman's composing is like a dog's walking on his hind legs. It is not done well, but you are surprised to find it done at all.'"[2] So accurately does history repeat itself.

Thus, I concluded, shutting Mr. Oscar Browning's life and pushing away the rest, it is fairly evident that even in the nineteenth century a woman was not encouraged to be an artist. On the contrary, she was snubbed, slapped, lectured and exhorted. Her mind must have been strained and her vitality lowered by the need of opposing this, of disproving that. For here again we come within range of that very interesting and obscure masculine complex which has had so much influence upon the woman's movement; that deep-seated desire, not so much that *she* shall be inferior as that *he* shall be superior, which plants him wherever one looks, not only in front of the arts, but barring the way to politics too, even when the risk to himself seems infinitesimal and the suppliant humble and devoted. Even Lady Bessborough, I remembered, with all her passion for politics, must humbly bow herself and write to Lord Granville Leveson-Gower: ". . . notwithstanding all my violence in politics and talking so much on that subject, I perfectly agree with you that no woman has any business to meddle with that or any other serious business, farther than giving her opinion (if she is ask'd)." And so she goes on to spend her enthusiasm where it meets with no obstacle whatsoever upon that immensely important subject, Lord Granville's maiden speech in the House of Commons. The spectacle is certainly a strange one, I thought. The history of men's opposition to women's emancipation is more interesting perhaps than the story of that emancipation itself. An amusing book might be made of it if some young student at Girton or Newnham would collect examples and deduce a theory—but she would need thick gloves on her hands, and bars to protect her of solid gold.

But what is amusing now, I recollected, shutting Lady Bessborough, had to be taken in desperate earnest once. Opinions that one now pastes in a book labelled cock-a-doodle-dum and keeps for reading to select audiences on summer nights once drew tears, I can assure you. Among your grandmothers and great-grandmothers there were many that wept their eyes out. Florence Nightingale shrieked aloud in her agony.[3] Moreover, it is all very well for you, who have got yourselves to college and enjoy sitting-rooms—or is it only bed-sitting rooms?—of your own to say that genius should disregard such opinions; that genius should be above caring what is said of it. Unfortunately, it is precisely the men or women of genius who mind most what is said of them. Remember Keats. Remember the words he had cut on his tombstone. Think of Tennyson; think—but I need hardly multiply instances of the undeniable, if very unfortunate, fact that it is the nature of the artist to mind excessively what is said about him. Literature is strewn with the wreckage of men who have minded beyond reason the opinions of others.

And this susceptibility of theirs is doubly unfortunate, I thought, returning again to my original enquiry into what state of mind is most propitious for creative work, because the mind of an artist, in order to achieve the prodigious effort of freeing whole and entire the work that is in him, must be incandescent, like Shakespeare's mind, I conjectured, looking at the book which lay open at *Antony and Cleopatra.* There must be no obstacle in it, no foreign matter unconsumed.

For though we say that we know nothing about Shakespeare's state of mind, even as we say that, we are saying something about Shakespeare's state of mind. The reason perhaps why we know so little of Shakespeare—compared with Donne or Ben Jonson or Milton—is that his grudges and spites and antipathies are hidden from us. We are not held up by some "revelation" which reminds us of the writer. All desire to protest, to preach, to proclaim an injury, to pay off a score, to make the world the witness of some hardship or grievance was fired out of him and consumed. Therefore his poetry flows from him free and unimpeded. If ever a human being got his work expressed completely, it was Shakespeare. If ever a mind was incandescent, unimpeded, I thought, turning again to the bookcase, it was Shakespeare's mind.

QUESTIONS

1. Consider how the treatment given to artistically talented women has changed since Woolf's time. How has it remained the same? How do you know?

2. What conditions exist in our culture which might interfere with a woman's ability to create? What factors might encourage and support a woman's creative ability?

3. Compare Woolf's essay with Alice Walker's "In Search of Our Mothers' Gardens." Do the two pieces share similar assumptions about women's creativity? What differences in style do you see in the two pieces? How do you think Woolf might respond to Walker's critique of the need for "a room of one's own"?

Seventeen Syllables (1988)

Hisaye Yamamoto

Hisaye Yamamoto depicts the kinds of restrictions being a wife and mother has placed on many women artists' ability to produce art. In this selection, the character of Rosie tells the story of her Japanese-American mother's inability to fulfill her dreams as an artist. Through the story of Rosie's mother, Yamamoto raises the possibility that society, by virtue of its expectations, places unfair restrictions on the life and freedom of the female artist.

Hisaye Yamamoto, born in 1921, was interned in a relocation camp in Poston, Arizona during the second World War. A prize-winning author, Yamamoto was first published in 1948.

The first Rosie knew that her mother had taken to writing poems was one evening when she finished one and read it aloud for her daughter's approval. It was about cats, and Rosie pretended to understand it thoroughly and appreciate it no end, partly because she hesitated to disillusion her mother about the quantity and quality of Japanese she had learned in all the years now that she had been going to Japanese school every Saturday (and Wednesday, too, in the summer). Even so, her mother must have been skeptical about the depth of Rosie's understanding, because she explained afterwards about the kind of poem she was trying to write.

See, Rosie, she said, it was a *haiku,* a poem in which she must pack all her meaning into seventeen syllables only, which were divided into three lines of five, seven, and five syllables. In the one she had just read, she had tried to capture the charm of a kitten, as well as comment on the superstition that owning a cat of three colors meant good luck.

"Yes, yes, I understand. How utterly lovely," Rosie said, and her mother, either satisfied or seeing through the deception and resigned, went back to composing.

The truth was that Rosie was lazy; English lay ready on the tongue but Japanese had to be searched for and examined, and even then put forth tentatively (probably to meet with laughter). It was so much easier to say yes, yes, even when one meant no. no. Besides, this was what was in her mind to say: I was looking through one of your magazines from Japan last night, Mother, and towards the back I found some *haiku* in English that delighted me. There was one that made me giggle off and on until I fell asleep—

> It is morning, and lo!
> I lie awake, *comme il faut,*
> sighing for some dough.

Now, how to reach her mother, how to communicate the melancholy song? Rosie knew formal Japanese by fits and starts, her mother had even less English, no French. It was much more possible to say yes, yes.

It developed that her mother was writing the *haiku* for a daily newspaper, the *Mainichi Shimbun,* that was published in San Francisco. Los Angeles, to be sure, was closer to the farming community in which the Hayashi family lived and several Japanese vernaculars were printed there, but Rosie's parents said they preferred the tone of the northern paper. Once a week, the *Mainichi* would have a section devoted to haiku, and her mother became an extravagant contributor, taking for herself the blossoming pen name, Ume Hanazono.

So Rosie and her father lived for awhile with two women, her mother and Ume Hanazono. Her mother (Tome Hayashi by name) kept house, cooked, washed, and, along with her husband

and the Carrascos, the Mexican family hired for the harvest, did her ample share of picking tomatoes out in the sweltering fields and boxing them in tidy strata in the cool packing shed. Ume Hanazono, who came to life after the dinner dishes were done, was an earnest, muttering stranger who often neglected speaking when spoken to and stayed busy at the parlor table as late as midnight scribbling with pencil on scratch paper or carefully copying characters on good paper with her fat, pale green Parker.

The new interest had some repercussions on the household routine. Before, Rosie had been accustomed to her parents and herself taking their hot baths early and going to bed almost immediately afterwards, unless her parents challenged each other to a game of flower cards or unless company dropped in. Now if her father wanted to play cards, he had to resort to solitaire (at which he always cheated fearlessly), and if a group of friends came over, it was bound to contain someone who was also writing *haiku*, and the small assemblage would be split in two, her father entertaining the non-literary members and her mother comparing ecstatic notes with the visiting poet.

If they went out, it was more of the same thing. But Ume Hanazono's life span, even for a poet's, was very brief—perhaps three months at most.

One night they went over to see the Hayano family in the neighboring town to the west, an adventure both painful and attractive to Rosie. It was attractive because there were four Hayano girls, all lovely and each one named after a season of the year (Haru, Natsu, Aki, Fuyu), painful because something had been wrong with Mrs. Hayano ever since the birth of her first child. Rosie would sometimes watch Mrs. Hayano, reputed to have been the belle of her native village, making her way about a room, stooped, slowly shuffling, violently trembling (*always* trembling), and she would be reminded that this woman, in this same condition, had carried and given issue to three babies. She would look wonderingly at Mr. Hayano, handsome, tall, and strong, and she would look at her four pretty friends. But it was not a matter she could come to any decision about.

On this visit, however, Mrs. Hayano sat all evening in the rocker, as motionless and unobtrusive as it was possible for her to be, and Rosie found the greater part of the evening practically anaesthetic. Too, Rosie spent most of it in the girls' room, because

Haru, the garrulous one, said almost as soon as the bows and other greetings were over, "Oh, you must see my new coat!"

It was a pale plaid of grey, sand, and blue, with an enormous collar, and Rosie, seeing nothing special in it, said, "Gee, how nice."

"Nice?" said Haru, indignantly. "Is that all you can say about it? It's gorgeous! And so cheap, too. Only seventeen-ninety-eight, because it was a sale. The saleslady said it was twenty-five dollars regular."

"Gee," said Rosie. Natsu, who never said much and when she said anything said it shyly, fingered the coat covetously and Haru pulled it away.

"Mine," she said, putting it on. She minced in the aisle between the two large beds and smiled happily "Let's see how your mother likes it."

She broke into the front room and the adult conversation and went to stand in front of Rosie's mother, while the rest watched from the door. Rosie's mother was properly envious. "May I inherit it when you're through with it?"

Haru, pleased, giggled and said yes, she could, but Natsu reminded gravely from the door, "You promised me, Haru."

Everyone laughed but Natsu, who shamefacedly retreated into the bedroom. Haru came in laughing, taking off the coat. "We were only kidding, Natsu," she said. "Here, you try it on now."

After Natsu buttoned herself into the coat, inspected herself solemnly in the bureau mirror, and reluctantly shed it, Rosie, Aki, and Fuyu got their turns, and Fuyu, who was eight, drowned in it while her sisters and Rosie doubled up in amusement. They all went into the front room later, because Haru's mother quaveringly called to her to fix the tea and rice cakes and open a can of sliced peaches for everybody. Rosie noticed that her mother and Mr. Hayano were talking together at the little table—they were discussing a *haiku* that Mr. Hayano was planning to send to the *Mainichi,* while her father was sitting at one end of the sofa looking through a copy of *Life,* the new picture magazine. Occasionally, her father would comment on a photograph, holding it toward Mrs. Hayano and speaking to her as he always did—loudly, as though he thought someone such as she must surely be at least a trifle deaf also.

The five girls had their refreshments at the kitchen table, and it was while Rosie was showing the sisters her trick of swallowing peach slices without chewing (she chased each slippery crescent down with a swig of tea) that her father brought his empty teacup and untouched saucer to the sink and said, "Come on, Rosie, we're going home now."

"Already?" asked Rosie.

"Work tomorrow," he said.

He sounded irritated, and Rosie, puzzled, gulped one last yellow slice and stood up to go, while the sisters began protesting, as was their wont.

"We have to get up at five-thirty," he told them, going into the front room quickly, so that they did not have their usual chance to hang onto his hands and plead for an extension of time.

Rosie, following, saw that her mother and Mr. Hayano were sipping tea and still talking together, while Mrs. Hayano concentrated, quivering, on raising the handleless Japanese cup to her lips with both her hands and lowering it back to her lap. Her father, saying nothing, went out the door, onto the bright porch, and down the steps. Her mother looked up and asked, "Where is he going?"

"Where is he going?" Rosie said, "He said we were going home now."

"Going home?" Her mother looked with embarrassment at Mr. Hayano and his absorbed wife and then forced a smile. "He must be tired," she said.

Haru was not giving up yet. "May Rosie stay overnight?" she asked, and Natsu, Aki, and Fuyu came to reinforce their sister's plea by helping her make a circle around Rosie's mother. Rosie, for once having no desire to stay, was relieved when her mother, apologizing to the perturbed Mr. and Mrs. Hayano for her father's abruptness at the same time, managed to shake her head no at the quartet, kindly but adamant, so that they broke their circle and let her go.

Rosie's father looked ahead into the windshield as the two joined him. "I'm sorry," her mother said. "You must be tired." Her father, stepping on the starter, said nothing. "You know how I get when it's *haiku*," she continued, "I forget what time it is." He only grunted.

As they rode homeward silently, Rosie, sitting between, felt a rush of hate for both—for her mother for begging, for her father for denying her mother. I wish this old Ford would crash, right now, she thought, then immediately, no, no, I wish my father would laugh, but it was too late: already the vision had passed through her mind of the green pick-up crumpled in the dark against one of the mighty eucalyptus trees they were just riding past, of the three contorted, bleeding bodies, one of them hers.

Rosie ran between two patches of tomatoes, her heart working more rambunctiously than she had ever known it to. How lucky it was that Aunt Taka and Uncle Gimpachi had come tonight, though, how very lucky. Otherwise she might not have really kept her half-promise to meet Jesus Carrasco. Jesus was going to be a senior in September at the same school she went to, and his parents were the ones helping with the tomatoes this year. She and Jesus, who hardly remembered seeing each other at Cleveland High where there were so many other people and two whole grades between them, had become great friends this summer—he always had a joke for her when he periodically drove the loaded pick-up up from the fields to the shed where she was usually sorting while her mother and father did the packing, and they laughed a great deal together over infinitesimal repartee during the afternoon break for chilled watermelon or ice cream in the shade of the shed.

What she enjoyed most was racing him to see which could finish picking a double row first. He, who could work faster, would tease her by slowing down until she thought she would surely pass him this time, then speeding up furiously to leave her several sprawling vines behind. Once he had made her screech hideously by crossing over, while her back was turned, to place atop the tomatoes in her green-stained bucket a truly monstrous, pale green worm (it had looked more like an infant snake). And it was when they had finished a contest this morning, after she had pantingly pointed a green finger at the immature tomatoes evident in the lugs at the end of his row and he had returned the accusation (with justice), that he had startlingly brought up the matter of their possibly meeting outside the range of both their parents' dubious eyes.

"What for?" she had asked.

"I've got a secret I want to tell you," he said.

"Tell me now," she demanded.

"It won't be ready till tonight," he said.

She laughed. "Tell me tomorrow then."

"It'll be gone tomorrow," he threatened.

"Well, for seven hakes, what is it?" she asked, more than twice, and when he had suggested that the packing shed would be an appropriate place to find out, she had cautiously answered maybe. She had not been certain she was going to keep the appointment until the arrival of her mother's sister and her husband. Their coming seemed a sort of signal of permission, of grace, and she had definitely made up her mind to lie and leave as she was bowing them welcome.

So as soon as everyone appeared settled back for the evening, she announced loudly that she was going to the privy outside, "I'm going to the *benjo!*" and slipped out the door. And now that she was actually on her way, her heart pumped in such an undisciplined way that she could hear it with her ears. It's because I'm running, she told herself, slowing to a walk. The shed was up ahead, one more patch away, in the middle of the fields. Its bulk, looming in the dimness, took on a sinisterness that was funny when Rosie reminded herself that it was only a wooden frame with a canvas roof and three canvas walls that made a slapping noise on breezy days.

Jesus was sitting on the narrow plank that was the sorting platform and she went around to the other side and jumped backwards to seat herself on the rim of a packing stand. "Well, tell me," she said without greeting, thinking her voice sounded reassuringly familiar.

"I saw you coming out the door," Jesus said. "I heard you running part of the way, too."

"Uh-huh," Rosie said. "Now tell me the secret."

"I was afraid you wouldn't come," he said.

Rosie delved around on the chicken-wire bottom of the stall for number two tomatoes, ripe, which she was sitting beside, and came up with a leftover that felt edible. She bit into it and began sucking out the Pulp and seeds. "I'm here," she pointed out.

"Rosie, are you sorry you came?"

"Sorry? What for?" she said. "You said you were going to tell me something."

"I will, I will," Jesus said, but his voice contained disappointment, and Rosie fleetingly felt the older of the two, realizing a brand-new power which vanished without category under her recognition.

"I have to go back in a minute," she said. "My aunt and uncle are here from Wintersburg. I told them I was going to the privy."

Jesus laughed. "You funny thing," he said. "You slay me!"

"Just because you have a bathroom *inside,*" Rosie said, "Come on, tell me."

Chuckling, Jesus came around to lean on the stand facing her. They still could not see each other very clearly, but Rosie noticed that Jesus became very sober again as he took the hollow tomato from her hand and dropped it back into the stall. When he took hold of her empty hand, she could find no words to protest; her vocabulary had become distressingly constricted and she thought desperately that all that remained intact now was yes and no and oh, and even these few sounds would not easily come out. Thus, kissed by Jesus, Rosie fell for the first time entirely victim to a helplessness delectable beyond speech. But the terrible, beautiful sensation lasted no more than a second, and the reality of Jesus' lips and tongue and teeth and hands made her pull away with such strength that she nearly tumbled.

Rosie stopped running as she approached the lights from the windows of home. How long since she had left? She could not guess, but gasping yet, she went to the Privy in back and locked herself in. Her own breathing deafened her in the dark, close space, and she sat and waited until she could hear at last the nightly calling of the frogs and crickets. Even then, all she could think to say was oh, my, and the pressure of Jesus' face against her face would not leave.

No one had missed her in the parlor, however, and Rosie walked in and through quickly, announcing that she was next going to take a bath. "Your father's in the bathhouse," her mother said, and Rosie, in her room, recalled that she had not seen him when she entered. There had been only Aunt Taka and Uncle Gimpachi with her mother at the table, drinking tea. She got her robe and straw sandals and crossed the parlor again to go outside. Her mother was telling them about the *haiku* competition in the *Mainichi* and the poem she had entered.

Rosie met her father coming out of the bathhouse. "Are you through, Father?" she asked. "I was going to ask you to scrub my back."

"Scrub your own back," he said shortly, going toward the main house.

"What have I done now?" she yelled after him. She suddenly felt like doing a lot of yelling. But he did not answer, and she went into the bathhouse. Turning on the dangling light, she removed her denims and T-shirt and threw them in the big carton for dirty clothes standing next to the washing machine. Her other things she took with her into the bath compartment to wash after her bath. After she had scooped a basin of hot water from the square wooden tub, she sat on the grey cement of the floor and soaped herself at exaggerated leisure, singing "Red Sails in the Sunset" at the top of her voice and using da-da-da where she suspected her words. Then, standing up, still singing, for she was possessed by the notion that any attempt now to analyze would result in spoilage and she believed that the larger her volume the less she would be able to hear herself think, she obtained more hot water and poured it on until she was free of lather. Only then did she allow herself to step into the steaming vat, one leg first, then the remainder of her body inch by inch until the water no longer stung and she could move around at will.

She took a long time soaking, afterwards remembering to go around outside to stoke the embers of the tin-lined fireplace beneath the tub and to throw on a few more sticks so that the water might keep its heat for her mother, and when she finally returned to the parlor, she found her mother still talking *haiku* with her aunt and uncle, the three of them on another round of tea. Her father was nowhere in sight.

At Japanese school the next day (Wednesday, it was), Rosie was grave and giddy by turns. Preoccupied at her desk in the row for students on Book Eight, she made up for it at recess by performing wild mimicry for the benefit of her friend Chizuko. She held her nose and whined a witticism or two in what she considered was the manner of Fred Allen; she assumed intoxication and a British accent to go over the climax of the Rudy Vallee recording of the pub conversation about William Ewart Gladstone; she was the child Shirley Temple piping, "On the Good Ship Lollipop"; she was the gentleman soprano of the Four Inkspots trilling, "If I Didn't Care." And she felt reasonably satisfied when Chizuko wept and gasped, "Oh, Rosie, you ought to be in the movies!"

Her father came after her at noon, bringing her sandwiches of minced ham and two nectarines to eat while she rode, so that she could pitch right into the sorting when they got home. The lugs were piling up, he said, and the ripe tomatoes in them would probably have to be taken to the cannery tomorrow if they were not ready for the produce haulers tonight. "This heat's not doing them any good. And we've got no time for a break today."

It *was* hot, probably the hottest day of the year, and Rosie's blouse stuck damply to her back even under the protection of the canvas. But she worked as efficiently as a flawless machine and kept the stalls heaped, with one part of her mind listening in to the parental murmuring about the heat and the tomatoes and with another part planning the exact words she would say to Jesus when he drove up with the first load of the afternoon. But when at last she saw that the pick-up was coming, her hands went berserk and the tomatoes started failing in the wrong stalls, and her father said, "Hey, hey! Rosie, watch what you're doing!"

"Well, I have to go to the *benjo,*" she said, hiding in panic.

"Go in the weeds over there," he said, only half-joking.

"Oh, Father!" she protested.

"Oh, go on home," her mother said. "We'll make out for awhile."

In the privy Rosie peered through a knothole toward the fields, watching as much as she could of Jesus. Happily she thought she saw him look in the direction of the house from time to time before he finished unloading and went back toward the patch where his mother and father worked. As she was heading for the shed, a very presentable black car purred up the dirt driveway to the house and its driver motioned to her. Was this the Hayashi home, he wanted to know. She nodded. Was she a Hayashi? Yes, she said, thinking that he was a good-looking man. He got out of the car with a huge, flat package and she saw that he warmly wore a business suit. "I have something here for your mother then," he said, in a more elegant Japanese than she was used to.

She told him where her mother was and he came along with her, patting his face with an immaculate white handkerchief and saying something about the coolness of San Francisco. To her surprised mother and father, he bowed and introduced himself as, among other things, the *haiku* editor of the *Mainichi Shimbun,* saying that since he had been coming as far as Los Angeles anyway, he had decided to bring her the first prize she had won in the recent contest.

"First prize?" her mother echoed, believing and not believing, pleased and overwhelmed. Handed the package with a bow, she bobbed her head up and down numerous times to express her utter gratitude. "It is nothing much," he added, "but I hope it will serve as a token of our great appreciation for your contributions and our great admiration of your considerable talent."

"I am not worthy," she said, falling easily into his style. "It is I who should make some sign of my humble thanks for being permitted to contribute."

"No, no, to the contrary," he said, bowing again.

But Rosie's mother insisted, and then saying that she knew she was being unorthodox, she asked if she might open the package because her curiosity was so great. Certainly she might. In fact, he would like her reaction to it, for personally, it was one of his favorite Hiroshiges.

Rosie thought it was a pleasant picture, which looked to have been sketched with delicate quickness. There were pink clouds, containing some graceful calligraphy, and a sea that was a pale blue except at the edges, containing four sampans with indications of people in them. Pines edged the water and on the far-off beach there was a cluster of thatched huts towered over by pine-dotted mountains of grey and blue. The frame was scalloped and gilt.

After Rosie's mother pronounced it without peer and somewhat prodded her father into nodding agreement, she said Mr. Kuroda must at least have a cup of tea after coming all this way, and although Mr. Kuroda did not want to impose, he soon agreed that a cup of tea would be refreshing and went along with her to the house, carrying the picture for her.

"Ha, your mother's crazy!" Rosie's father said and Rosie laughed uneasily as she resumed judgment on the tomatoes. She had emptied six lugs when he broke into an imaginary conversation with Jesus to tell her to go and remind her mother of the tomatoes, and she went slowly.

Mr. Kuroda was in his shirtsleeves expounding some *haiku* theory as he munched a rice cake, and her mother was rapt. Abashed in the great man's presence, Rosie stood next to her mother's chair until her mother looked up inquiringly, and then she started to whisper the message, but her mother pushed her gently away and reproached, "You are not being very polite to our guest."

"Father says the tomatoes. . . . Rosie said aloud, smiling foolishly.

"Tell him I shall only be a minute," her mother said, speaking the language of Mr. Kuroda.

When Rosie carried the reply to her father, he did not seem to hear and she said again, "Mother says she'll be back in a minute."

"All right, all right," he nodded, and they worked again in silence. But suddenly, her father uttered an incredible noise, exactly like the cork of a bottle popping, and the next Rosie knew, he was stalking angrily toward the house, almost running in fact, and she chased after him crying, "Father! Father! What are you going to do?"

He stopped long enough to order her back to the shed. "Never mind!" he shouted. "Get on with the sorting!"

And from the place in the fields where she stood, frightened and vacillating, Rosie saw her father enter the house. Soon Mr. Kuroda came out alone, putting on his coat. Mr. Kuroda got into his car and backed out down the driveway onto the highway. Next her father emerged, also alone, something in his arms (it was the picture, she realized), and, going over to the bathhouse woodpile, he threw the picture on the ground and picked up the axe. Smashing the picture, glass and all (she heard the explosion faintly), he reached over for the kerosene that was used to encourage the bath fire and poured it over the wreckage. I am dreaming, Rosie said to herself, I am dreaming, but her father, having made sure that his act of cremation was irrevocable, was even then returning to the fields.

Rosie ran past him and toward the house. What had become of her mother? She burst into the parlor and found her mother at the back window watching the dying fire. They watched together until there remained only a feeble smoke under the blazing sun. Her mother was very calm.

"Do you know why I married your father?" she said without turning.

"No," said Rosie. It was the most frightening question she had ever been called upon to answer. Don't tell me now, she wanted to say, tell me tomorrow, tell me next week, don't tell me today. But she knew she would be told now, that the telling would combine with the other violence of the hot afternoon to level her life, her world to the very ground.

It was like a story out of the magazines illustrated in sepia, which she had consumed so greedily for a period until the information had somehow reached her that those wretchedly unhappy autobiographies, offered to her as the testimonials of living men and women, were largely inventions: Her mother, at nineteen, had come to America and married her father as an alternative to suicide.

At eighteen she had been in love with the first son of one of the well-to-do families in her village. The two had met whenever and wherever they could, secretly, because it would not have done for his family to see him favor her—her father had no money; he was a drunkard and a gambler besides. She had learned she was with child; an excellent match had already been arranged for her lover. Despised by her family, she had given premature birth to a stillborn son, who would be seventeen now. Her family did not turn her out, but she could no longer project herself in any direction without refreshing in them the memory of her indiscretion. She wrote to Aunt Taka, her favorite sister in America, threatening to kill herself if Aunt Taka would not send for her. Aunt Taka hastily arranged a marriage with a young man of whom she knew, but lately arrived from Japan, a young man of simple mind, it was said, but of kindly heart. The young man was never told why his unseen betrothed was so eager to hasten the day of meeting.

The story was told perfectly, with neither groping for words nor untoward passion. It was as though her mother had memorized it by heart, reciting it to herself so many times over that its nagging vileness had long since gone.

"I had a brother then?" Rosie asked, for this was what seemed to matter now; she would think about the other later, she assured herself, pushing back the illumination which threatened all that darkness that had hitherto been merely mysterious or even glamorous. "A half-brother?"

"Yes."

"I would have liked a brother," she said.

Suddenly, her mother knelt on the floor and took her by the wrists. "Rosie," she said urgently, "Promise me you will never marry!" Shocked more by the request than the revelation, Rosie stared at her mother's face. Jesus, Jesus, she called silently, not certain whether she was invoking the help of the son of the Carrascos or of God, until there returned sweetly the memory of

Jesus' hand, how it had touched her and where. Still her mother waited for an answer, holding her wrists so tightly that her hands were going numb. She tried to pull free. Promise, her mother whispered fiercely, promise. Yes, yes, I promise, Rosie said. But for an instant she turned away, and her mother, hearing the familiar glib agreement, released her. Oh, you, you, you, her eyes and twisted mouth said, you fool. Rosie, covering her face, began at last to cry, and the embrace and consoling hand came much later than she expected.

QUESTIONS

1. What is the conflict between Rosie's parents? Why is it significant in a consideration of whether and how women are able to create culture?
2. Why doesn't Rosie want her mother to write haiku? Do you think her reasons are symbolic of cultural attitudes? Why/why not?
3. Why do you suppose Rosie's mother asks for the promise that Rosie will never marry?
4. What is the significance of Yamamoto's title?